PENGUIN BOOKS

Opus Dei

John L. Allen is the Vatican correspondent for the *National Catholic Reporter* and a Vatican analyst for CNN and National Public Radio. He has also reported for the BBC and will appear in a BBC documentary on Opus Dei later this year. Considered by many as the single best source of insights on Vatican affairs in the English language, (particularly through his internet column 'The Word from Rome'), he is the author of four books on the Catholic Church, including *The Rise of Benedict XVI* and *Conclave: The Politics, Personalities, and Process of the Next Papal Election* (1992). His work has appeared in *The New York Times*, *The Boston Globe*, and many other publications.

OPUS DEI

The truth about its
rituals, secrets and
power

JOHN L. ALLEN, JR.

PENGUIN BOOKS

PENGUIN BOOKS

Published by the Penguin Group
Penguin Books Ltd, 80 Strand, London WC2R ORL, England
Penguin Group (USA) Inc., 375 Hudson Street, New York, New York 10014, USA
Penguin Group (Canada), 90 Eglinton Avenue East, Suite 700, Toronto, Ontario, Canada M4P 2Y3
(a division of Pearson Penguin Canada Inc.)
Penguin Ireland, 25 St Stephen's Green, Dublin 2, Ireland
(a division of Penguin Books Ltd)
Penguin Group (Australia), 250 Camberwell Road,
Camberwell, Victoria 3124, Australia (a division of Pearson Australia Group Pty Ltd)
Penguin Books India Pvt Ltd, 11 Community Centre,
Panchsheel Park, New Delhi – 110 017, India
Penguin Group (NZ), cnr Airborne and Rosedale Roads, Albany,
Auckland 1310, New Zealand (a division of Pearson New Zealand Ltd)
Penguin Books (South Africa) (Pty) Ltd, 24 Sturdee Avenue,
Rosebank, Johannesburg 2196, South Africa

Penguin Books Ltd, Registered Offices: 80 Strand, London WC2R ORL, England

www.penguin.com

First published in the United States of America by Doubleday 2005
First published in Great Britain by Allen Lane 2005
Published in Penguin Books 2006
1

Printed in England by Clays Ltd, St Ives plc

ISBN-13: 978-0-141-02465-3
ISBN-10: 0-141-02465-8

To my grandfather, Raymond Leo Frazier, who died at ninety-two during the preparation of this book. He was the primary role model in my life, a great man, and, I believe, a saint. He taught me much of what I know about integrity, good cheer, and enjoying the simple things in life. He was also a first-class storyteller, some of which I hope has rubbed off. And to my wife, Shannon, for her patience and understanding, which at times during this project were tested to the limits of human endurance.

CONTENTS

OPUS DEI

INTRODUCTION

If you want a guiding metaphor for Opus Dei, the spiritual organization founded in Spain in 1928 by Saint Josemaría Escrivá that has become the most controversial force in Roman Catholicism, think of it as the Guinness Extra Stout of the Catholic Church. It's a strong brew, definitely an acquired taste, and clearly not for everyone.

Putting things this way immediately runs the risk of being superficial, not to mention giving offense, since Opus Dei is not a commercial product but a spiritual path that aims at the sanctification of the secular world, a path followed with great fidelity and moral seriousness by some eighty-five thousand people worldwide and admired by millions of others. It is also bitterly opposed by a substantial sector of opinion inside and outside the Catholic Church. To compare Opus Dei to a beer could seem like a way of trivializing it. Yet the "Guinness Extra Stout" image captures something important about the role Opus Dei occupies on the Catholic stage, and it's worth taking a moment to tease it out.

In an era when the beer market is crowded with "diet" this and "lite" that, Guinness Extra Stout cuts the other way. It makes no apologies for either its many calories or its high alcohol content. It packs a frothy, bitter taste that has been compared by some wags to drinking motor oil with a head. Precisely because it resists faddishness, it enjoys a cult following among purists who respect it because it never wavers. Of course, if you think it tastes awful, its consistency may not be its greatest selling point. Yet while Extra Stout may never dominate the market, it will always have a loyal constituency.

To apply this image to the Catholic Church, the four decades since the Second Vatican Council (1962–1965) have also to some extent been marked by a "less is more" spirit. Broadly speaking, the thrust of Vatican II was to throw open the windows of the Church, updating and rejuvenating it by returning to the gospel basics, offering a greater openness to the world, and promoting greater unity among the divided Christian family and with all of humanity. In the rites and rituals of the Church, there was a strong push for simplification, most notably the dropping of Latin as the principal language of worship and adopting the vernacular. Many traditional devotions and practices fell into disuse while spiritual disciplines such as the Friday fast were relaxed. Ecumenical and interreligious dialogue replaced apologetics as the primary way of interacting with people in other confessions and religious traditions. Priests and nuns often stopped wearing distinctive religious garb, fearing that it came across as a sign of privilege or a way of distancing themselves from the people they wanted to serve. In many sectors of opinion, the Church's mission came to be understood in terms of promoting human and social development in the here and now, with too much talk about prayer and the sacraments seen as pie-in-the-sky spiritualizing. Memorization of doctrine gave way in much Catholic education to a more analytical and critical approach, and charitable activity was supplemented by attention to the structural dimension of global injustices and what has come to be known as "social sin." All of these statements are caricatures of complex theological and ecclesial trends, but they indicate broad lines of development.

In this era of new ecclesiastical brews, Opus Dei offers a robustly classical alternative. Like Guinness, the "market share" of Opus Dei in global Catholicism is, given its outsize public image, remarkably small. According to the 2004 *Annuario Pontificio,* the official Vatican yearbook, Opus Dei numbers 1,850 priests in the world, along with 83,641 laity, for a total of 85,491 members, representing .008 percent of the global Catholic population of 1.1 billion (55 percent of Opus Dei members, by the way, are women). For a sense of scale, the archdiocese of Hobart on the Australian island of Tasmania contains 87,691 members, meaning that all by itself it's bigger than Opus Dei worldwide.

Opus Dei, which in Latin means "the Work of God," is formally classified as the only "personal prelature" in the Catholic Church, which means that the head of the group in Rome, currently Bishop Javier

Echevarría Rodríguez, has jurisdiction over members for matters that regard the internal life of Opus Dei. For matters concerning all Catholics, members of Opus Dei remain under the jurisdiction of the local bishop. Usually, however, Opus Dei is seen as part of a flowering of lay-led movements and groups in the twentieth century, and it found international fame in the period after the Second Vatican Council.

The core idea of Opus Dei, as presented by Escrivá, is the sanctification of ordinary work, meaning that one can find God through the practice of law, engineering, or medicine, by picking up the garbage or by delivering the mail, if one brings to that work the proper Christian spirit. In order to cultivate such a spirit, Opus Dei members undergo extensive doctrinal and spiritual formation, and generally don't cut corners in the pursuit of holiness. Most Catholics don't visit the Blessed Sacrament anymore? Opus Dei members are required to do so every day. Most Catholics don't pray the rosary? Again, Opus Dei members do it every day. In Kenya, Archbishop Raphael S. Ndingi of Nairobi jokingly told me that in the old days, if you wanted to identify Opus Dei members in Africa, the thing to do was to give them a ride. If they asked to be let off a mile from their destination so they could say the rosary, they were Opus Dei. Many Catholics today take at least some aspects of Church teaching with a grain of salt, but Opus Dei members are encouraged to "think with the Church," meaning to accept the entirety of Church teaching on faith and morals. There is a strong emphasis within the clergy of Opus Dei on old-school priestly discipline. They wear clerical dress, pray the breviary, and spend lots of time in the confessional. One sign of their earnestness is that to date, not a single priest of Opus Dei in the United States has been accused of sexual abuse or removed from ministry under the special rules approved in 2002 for the American Church by the Vatican.

It's not quite right to call this a "traditional" alternative to a more "liberal" postconciliar Catholicism, since from a historical point of view Opus Dei is not traditional at all. Its vision of laity and priests, women and men, sharing the same vocation and being part of the same body, all free to pursue that vocation within their professional sphere as they see fit, was so innovative that Escrivá was accused of heresy in 1940s Spain. Inside Opus Dei, most priests have lay spiritual directors, which is a break with traditional clerical culture, and the laity of Opus Dei, both men and women, cast votes for their prelate (meaning the cleric in charge), which is as close to the democratic election of a bishop as one comes in today's Catholic Church. Opus Dei was the first institution in the Catholic Church to request, and to receive in 1950, Vatican permission to enroll non-Catholics and even non-Christians among its "cooperators," meaning nonmember supporters.

More broadly, Escrivá's insistence that the real work of bringing the gospel to the world is to be carried out by laypeople through their secular occupations marks something of a Copernican shift for Catholicism, which has tended to see the laity as a supporting cast in the spiritual drama, with priests and nuns as the lead actors. In a sense, the culture wars of the post–Vatican II period, marked by perennial antagonism between "left" and "right," have obscured the original spiritual insights of Opus Dei. What people see is the uncompromising orthodoxy and papal loyalty in which Opus Dei's message is wrapped, but rarely the message itself.

Despite this, the spirituality and doctrinal convictions of most Opus Dei members do frequently seem "traditional" by contemporary standards, if only in the sense that they have clung to older prayers, practices, and disciplines in a time when many of those traditions were being understood in new ways or abandoned. In that sense, Opus Dei is a jolt to a certain kind of Catholic sensibility, to say nothing of a secular outlook that often doesn't understand institutional religion.

Perhaps because of its "Stout Catholicism" ethos, Opus Dei has become a marker for the broader culture wars in the Church and in the culture. Self-described Catholic "liberals" typically dislike and oppose Opus Dei. "Conservatives" generally find themselves drawn to its defense, if only because they dislike its critics so intensely. In the broader secular world, Opus Dei has become a shorthand reference for a secretive, closed society with an elitist flavor, a bit like Skull and Bones or the Masons. Thanks to the runaway commercial success of Dan Brown's novel *The Da Vinci Code,* these perceptions of Opus Dei have gone mass-market.

Because Opus Dei sets the bar high for its members, the landing can be especially rough when things go wrong. Many ex-members, enough to suggest this is something more than innuendo, report having been hurt by their experiences—they say they were brought to the brink of physical and emotional exhaustion, their contacts with the outside world attenuated, and their approach to both Opus Dei and authority in general steered in the direction of unthinking obedience. As a result, Opus Dei is criticized by a certain percentage of its ex-members with a startling ferocity, some of whom talk about "spiritual abuse" or even violations of their human rights. They claim that the internal climate in Opus Dei—which they describe as defensive, insular, and at times quasi-apocalyptic—can be very different from the image Opus Dei would like to project. In English, the Opus Dei Awareness Network gives voice to these perspectives, as does the www.opuslibros.org Web site in Spanish. These descriptions are contested by tens of thousands of satisfied members as well as ex-members who are still on good terms with Opus Dei. It may be that both groups are describing more or less the same reality, but as seen through different prisms—one convinced that Opus Dei is indeed a "work of God," the other equally sure that Opus Dei is, to a significant extent, a human instrument of control and power.

Two Distinctions

The mystique and controversy surrounding Opus Dei make careful analysis a complicated task. In sorting through the issues, two distinctions may be helpful. The first is between the *message* of Opus Dei and the *institution* of Opus Dei. Whatever one makes of the fact that a minority of Opus Dei members wear a barbed chain called a "cilice" around their thigh for two hours a day, for example, or that Opus Dei will not publicize the names of its members, these are institutional practices derived from, and therefore secondary to, what Opus Dei is supposed to be all about. Given the attention those practices sometimes draw in the press and on the gossip mill, one can spend a lot of time reading and talking about Opus Dei without ever really touching upon its stated goals and mission.

At its core, the message of Opus Dei is that the redemption of the world will come in large part through laywomen and men sanctifying their daily work, transforming secularity from within. "Spirituality" and "prayer," according to this way of seeing things, are not things reserved primarily for church, a set of pious practices marked off from the rest of life; the real focus of the spiritual life is one's ordinary work and relationships, the stuff of daily living that, seen from the point of view of eternity, takes on transcendent significance. It is an explosive concept, with the potential for unleashing creative Christian energy in many areas of endeavor. The ambition is nothing less than reaching across centuries of Church history to revitalize the approach of the earliest Christians—ordinary laywomen and men, indistinguishable from their colleagues and neighbors, going about their normal occupations, who nevertheless "catch fire" with the gospel and change the world.

As legitimate as public curiosity is about the hot-button issues surrounding Opus Dei, such as secrecy, money, and power, phrasing the conversation exclusively in these terms risks approaching Opus Dei through a back door, never quite seeing it as it sees itself. For that reason, after two chapters that offer a basic overview of Opus Dei and its founder, section 2 of this book (comprising chapters 3 through 6) is devoted to four cornerstones of the spirit of "the Work," as members refer to the core ideas of Opus Dei: the sanctification of work; being contemplatives in the middle of the world; Christian freedom; and "divine filiation," meaning a lively appreciation of one's identity as a son or daughter of God. Section 3 then takes up the most frequent questions about Opus Dei, from the status of women to methods of soliciting new members. Section 2 is therefore primarily about the message of Opus Dei, section 3 about the institution, though these distinctions are not airtight. As in any organization, Opus Dei's aims and aspirations help shape the institutional culture, just as the exigencies of the institution sometimes influence the way those aims are understood and applied.

As another way of expressing this distinction, several former members who remain on friendly terms with Opus Dei say their experience taught them that being drawn to the ideals of the group, especially that one's daily work can be a pathway to holiness, is not the same thing as being called to membership. One ex-member, who left Opus Dei after more than twenty-five years, put it this way: "It took me a long time to see that understanding and 'buying into' Opus Dei's message does not necessarily constitute a vocation to Opus Dei. . . . I am in complete agreement with Opus Dei's message of the universal call to holiness, and of Saint Josemaría's spirituality of the sanctification of one's ordinary work and life. That is what attracted me to Opus Dei, and what still does. Yet, while I most definitely feel called to spread this universal call to holiness, I have never felt called to do it specifically 'according to the spirit and practice of Opus Dei.'"

The second distinction is between the *sociology* of Opus Dei members and the *philosophy* of Opus Dei. That philosophy can be summed up in the word "secularity," which means, in part, that Opus Dei doesn't wish to act as an interest group with its own agenda, but to form motivated laity who will draw their own conclusions in the realms of politics, law, finance, the arts, and so on. There is no Opus Dei "line" on tax policy, or the war on terrorism, or on how health care ought to be delivered, and in fact one will find that the Opus Dei membership holds a wide variety of views on these questions. One sees this in an especially concentrated form in Spain, where it's not uncommon for politicians who are members of Opus Dei to be subjected to withering attacks in the press by pundits who are also members of Opus Dei.

Today, however, the deepest political fault lines in the West tend to run along cultural issues such as abortion and homosexuality, and the emphasis within Opus Dei on "thinking with the Church" places its members solidly on the right on those questions—not as members of Opus Dei, but as Catholics who favor a traditional reading of Church doctrine. Inevitably, this means that the kinds of people drawn to Opus Dei, at least in some parts of the world, are more likely to come from conservative circles, so that many Opus Dei members bring with them conservative attitudes on a host of other issues, both on secular politics and on debates inside the Catholic Church. Thus the political and theological tilt inside Opus Dei is clearly to the right, though with exceptions. This has little to do with the philosophy of Opus Dei, however, but rather with the sociology of where its "market" is these days.

These sociological tendencies are to some extent the accidents of a particular historical moment, and could change. Opus Dei had a different profile in Spain in the 1930s, '40s, and '50s, when it was regarded as a "liberalizing" force in both secular politics and the Church. As the terms of debate within Catholicism and the broader culture evolve, it's possible to imagine a future in which Opus Dei's membership would once again appear less "traditional," less compactly "conservative." One of the challenges of this book, therefore, will be to sort out what's essential about Opus Dei from some of the secondary features that reflect the baggage of a given epoch, either inside the Catholic Church or in the world at large.

Conspiracy Theories

Opus Dei seems to stimulate the most fevered centers of conspiratorial imagination in many people's brains. Think I'm kidding? As part of the research for this book, I once had a telephone conversation with a critical former member of Opus Dei who was willing to talk about her experiences. She opened the conversation, however, by saying she had one question before we began: Was my wife a member of Opus Dei? I laughed out loud, given that my wife is, first of all, Jewish, and a bit ambivalent about Roman Catholicism in general; and second, a convinced leftist hostile to Opus Dei on general principles. Throughout my work on this book she repeatedly struggled with a tension between liking many of the Opus Dei members she met on a personal basis, and yet feeling obligated to oppose them. Where in the world, I wanted to know, could someone have gotten the impression that Shannon was a member of "the Work"?

It turns out that my wife had sent out an e-mail some weeks before to a limited group of friends describing some of her recent activities in Rome. One item on the list was that she had attended a small party thrown by a member of Opus Dei for a friend who was returning to the United States. Shannon went because she wanted to say good-bye, not to sign up for the Opus experience. Yet this throwaway reference, which obviously made the rounds in cyberspace, became the basis of a theory that Shannon was in Opus Dei, which by itself would have been enough in some people's minds to taint the project.

Therefore, let's get this out of the way: I am not now, nor have I ever been, a member of Opus Dei. No one in my family belongs to Opus Dei. I don't work for Opus Dei and am not financially or professionally dependent on it. Research for this book, including travel in eight countries (Spain, Italy, Peru, Kenya, Uganda, Russia, the United Kingdom, and the United States), was paid for out of my own pocket. I'm not an enamored member, nor an embittered ex-member. I am a journalist who specializes in the Catholic Church, fascinated with the reports surrounding Opus Dei, and curious to know how much reality stands behind them. In pursuit of that aim, I have logged more than three hundred hours of interviews, flown tens of thousands of miles, spoken with friends and foes of Opus Dei such as cardinals, archbishops, and bishops along with ordinary faithful, and scoured the literature about Opus Dei in several languages.

I believe I have come as close to understanding Opus Dei as an outsider can, and I hope I can begin to separate fact from fiction with respect to the most common public perceptions.

Though this is not an "authorized" study, the organization granted me privileged insider's access that no journalist has previously enjoyed. When Doubleday first spoke with me about this project, I approached the people at the Rome headquarters of Opus Dei with some trepidation, given their legendary reputation for secrecy. I told them that I was considering writing a book on Opus Dei and wanted to know if they would cooperate. Their immediate response was "yes," and so I signed the contract and began to work. In the interests of fairness, I have to say that they never faltered in their commitment to full disclosure. I have moved in and out of Opus Dei facilities all over the world, in both men's and women's branches. I have been given access to *Noticias* and *Crónica,* Spanish-language journals normally reserved only for members. I have been shown private correspondence from the Opus Dei archives that I requested. I lived for five days in an Opus Dei residence in Barcelona, the Colegio Mayor Pedralbes, with the idea of following the official "plan of life" over that time. (Among other things, the experience strengthened my conviction that I am utterly unsuitable for membership in Opus Dei.) All the high-ranking members of Opus Dei inside the Catholic Church gave me interviews, including Cardinals Juan Luis Cipriani and Julián Herranz, Vatican spokesperson Joaquín Navarro-Valls, and the prelate, Bishop Javier Echevarría Rodríguez. The cooperation from Opus Dei was so total, in fact, that at one point a senior officer in Rome told me that the organization was performing a "global striptease" on my behalf.

Why would Opus Dei do this? First, my impression is that they are simply much less secretive than is commonly believed. They didn't have to be convinced of the virtues of cooperation; on the contrary, I found them anxious to tell their story. Second, I believe their calculation was that even an objective book that gives voice to criticisms of the group would be preferable to the mythology and prejudice that so often clouds public discussion. They were prepared to take their blows, in other words, as long as they're not below the belt. Whether they'll still feel that way after reading what follows, of course, remains to be seen.

Several notes of thanks are in order here. First, chapter 10 of this book is heavily dependent upon the work of Joseph Harris, one of the best

numbers crunchers in the Catholic Church. I hired Joe to help develop a
financial profile of Opus Dei, and he succeeded beyond my wildest
dreams. This book for the first time offers a detailed financial profile of
Opus Dei in the United States, and a "best guess" estimate of its financial profile worldwide, largely due to Joe's efforts. Second, I wish to thank
Marc Carroggio of the Opus Dei Information Office in Rome, whose assistance in arranging contacts with members of Opus Dei in various parts
of the world was invaluable. I also wish to thank Sharon Clasen, an
ex–numerary member and a critical voice, who helped me with my research on other ex-members and observers. Dianne and Tammy DiNicola
of the Opus Dei Awareness Network were also helpful. Thanks are also
due to Tom Roberts, my editor at the *National Catholic Reporter,* who tolerated my frequent absences from Rome and episodic ups-and-downs in
my availability to the newspaper in order to allow this project to proceed.
All my colleagues at *NCR* have been helpful in ways beyond my capacity
to describe. I also want to extend a word of thanks to the readers of The
Word from Rome column, who, knowing of my work on this book, have
sent hundreds of e-mails in the last twelve months sharing their own experiences and perspectives on Opus Dei. While not all of them have
found an echo in these pages, they all helped shape my approach, suggested questions, opened new horizons, and were helpful in all manner of
unpredictable ways. I want to thank the hundreds of members of Opus
Dei around the world, as well as critics and neutral observers, who
opened their homes and their lives to me. Talking about one's spiritual life
is never easy in the best of circumstances, and doing so in front of a journalist holding a mini-disc recorder is perhaps the most trying circumstance of all. Yet, realizing the importance of the subject, these people
opened up for me and let me in, from a professor of business ethics in
Barcelona, Spain, to a Japanese immigrant running a laundry in Lima, to
an expert in Pennsylvania on extricating people from cults. I am thankful
beyond words for their graciousness, honesty, and courage, regardless of
their perspective. Finally, a word of thanks to my long-suffering wife,
Shannon, who never really wanted me to do this book and who suffered
mightily during its gestation. I know how trying all the travel, extra hours,
and endless conversation about Opus Dei was, and somehow I will find a
way to make it up to her.

This book is an attempt to tell the truth on a subject where ideology and fantasy often have the upper hand. Ideology, in my view, is the corruption of reason and is morally akin to lying. Rather than taking an ideological approach here, I try to come at the subject from an experiential and firsthand point of view. All I can ask is that readers set aside whatever biases they may have with regard to Opus Dei and try to absorb what follows on its own terms. In the end, it is not the aim of this book to produce an apologia for Opus Dei, nor a polemic against it. It is not up to me to say whether Opus Dei is right or wrong, good or bad, or whether it should enjoy its present prominence in Roman Catholicism or not. What I hope to do is provide the tools for readers to reach their own judgments. Despite the polarizing nature of discussion about Opus Dei, I hope we can all agree that a discussion rooted in reality is more likely to be productive.

> December 8, 2004
> Feast of the Immaculate Conception

ESSENTIALS

Chapter One

A QUICK OVERVIEW OF OPUS DEI

*The Tablet of London, a well-known English Catholic pub-*lication, recently published a series of jokes about various groups within the Catholic Church, and here's how the one on Opus Dei goes: How many members of Opus Dei does it take to screw in a lightbulb? The answer is, one hundred . . . one to screw in the bulb, and ninety-nine to chant, "We are not a movement, we are not a movement."

Though perhaps a bit catty, the joke makes a good point, which is that Opus Dei has sometimes been better at explaining what it is *not* rather than what it *is*. Escrivá strongly insisted that Opus Dei is not a religious order, thus it is not comparable to the Franciscans or the Dominicans. Its members remain fully immersed in the world and do not retreat to monasteries or cloisters. They find God through the mundane details of daily secular life. In later years Opus Dei has fought similar battles to insist that it is not a "lay movement," because it includes clergy. This is precisely what gives Opus Dei its unique character: It is an institution of laypeople and priests together, men and women, sharing the same vocation but playing different roles. Over the years Opus Dei has been classified within Church structures in a variety of different ways: as a pious union, a priestly society of common life without vows, a secular institute, and finally, since 1982, as a "personal prelature." At each stage before the final one, Opus Dei's leading thinkers insisted that the existing structures within the 1917 Code of Canon Law, the official body of law for the Catholic Church prior to 1983, were inadequate to reflect the group's true nature. In effect, members argued, an entirely new concept, something like the personal prelature, had to be carved out in order to give Opus Dei the juridical configuration that corresponded to its original spiritual impulse and vision.

So what was that impulse?

Members of Opus Dei date the group's foundation to October 2, 1928, when Josemaría Escrivá, then a young Spanish priest making a retreat at a Vincentian monastery in Madrid, experienced a vision, revealing to him "whole and entire" God's wish for what would later become Opus Dei. Obviously the vision was not "entire" in the sense that it answered every question, since it required subsequent inspirations to demonstrate to Escrivá that there should be a women's branch to Opus Dei (that came in 1930) and that Opus Dei should also include a body of priests, the Priestly Society of the Holy Cross (1943). Yet in some sense, Escrivá insisted, the blueprint for Opus Dei was contained in that original experience on the Feast of the Guardian Angels in 1928. Here's how he once described it: "On October 2, 1928, the feast of the Holy Guardian Angels—by now nearly forty years have gone by—the Lord willed that Opus Dei might come to be, a mobilization of Christians disposed to sacrifice themselves with joy for others, to render divine all the ways of man on earth, sanctifying every upright work, every honest labor, every earthly occupation."

Escrivá and the members of Opus Dei are thus convinced that their organization is rooted in God's will. As Escrivá himself once put it, "I was not the founder of Opus Dei. Opus Dei was founded in spite of me." Originally Escrivá did not even give this new reality a name; "Opus Dei," which is Latin for "work of God," came from an offhand comment from Escrivá's confessor, who once asked him, "How's that Work of God going?" This is why members usually refer to Opus Dei as "the Work."

The core idea revealed to Escrivá in that 1928 vision, and unfolded in subsequent stages of Opus Dei's development, was the sanctification of ordinary life by laypeople living the gospel and Church teaching in their fullness. This is why one of the leading symbols for Opus Dei is a simple cross within a circle—the symbolism betokens the sanctification of the world from within. The idea is that holiness, "being a saint," is not just the province of a few spiritual athletes, but is the universal destiny of every Christian. Holiness is not exclusively, or even principally, for priests and nuns. Further, holiness is not something to be achieved in the first place through prayer and spiritual discipline, but rather through the mundane details of everyday work. Holiness thus doesn't require a change in external circumstances, but a change in attitude, seeing everything anew in the light of one's supernatural destiny.

In that sense, admirers of Escrivá, who included Pope John Paul II, believe the Spanish saint anticipated the "universal call to holiness" that would be announced by the Second Vatican Council. The late cardinal of Florence and right-hand man of Pope Paul VI, Giovanni Benelli—who crossed swords with Escrivá over the years—nevertheless once said that what Saint Ignatius of Loyola, the founder of the Jesuits, was to the sixteenth-century Council of Trent, Escrivá was to the Second Vatican Council. That is, he was the saint who translated the council into the life of the Church.

In a December 2004 interview, the number-two official of Opus Dei, Monsignor Fernando Ocáriz, a Spanish theologian who has served since 1986 as a consultor to the Congregation for the Doctrine of the Faith, the Vatican's doctrinal agency, explained that Escrivá's understanding of the "universal call to holiness" had two dimensions, subjective and objective. The subjective is the invitation to individual persons to sanctification, meaning that all people, regardless of their station in life, are called to become saints. The objective is the realization that all of creation, and every situation in human experience, is a means to this end.

"All human realities, all the circumstances of human life, all the professions, every family and social situation, are means of sanctification," Ocáriz said. "It's not just that everyone is supposed to be a saint despite the fact of not being priests or monks, but precisely that all the realities of life are places that can lead one to the Lord."

Commenting on The Song of Songs from the Old Testament, Escrivá once put this idea in lyrical form. "I will seek the one my soul loves in the streets and public squares," he wrote. "I will run from one part of the world to the other . . . seeking the peace of my soul. And I find it in the things that come from outside, which for me are not an obstacle; on the contrary, they are a path and a stairway to draw closer and closer, to unite myself more and more with God." That instinct to find God "in the things that come from outside," the normal hustle and bustle of the workaday world, is the Opus Dei impulse.

Escrivá once described Opus Dei as "an intravenous injection in the bloodstream of society." Members would be doctors and lawyers and university professors and barbers and bus drivers, and from the outside they would appear to be exactly the same as everyone else. There's a famous story about the first three priests ordained for Opus Dei—Alvaro del Portillo, José María Hernández de Garnica, and José Luis Múzquiz—that illustrates this point. Escrivá noticed that not one of them smoked, which was rather odd in Spain in 1944. He told them that one of them was going to have to take up smoking, lest people get the impression there was something unwordly about these Opus Dei guys. The choice fell on Portillo, who would eventually succeed Escrivá. Opus Dei's lay members would not wear special religious habits, they would not be cloistered, and they would not claim to possess a special state of life. The idea was to redeem the world, not by retreating from it, but by "Christianizing it," carrying out all the tasks of daily living with a new spirit. Escrivá's shorthand formula was, "Sanctify your work. Sanctify yourself in your work. Sanctify others through your work."

It's worth underlining the revolutionary character of this vision in Spain in the 1930s and 1940s. As Escrivá described it, Opus Dei is not supposed to be a clergy-driven enterprise. Laypeople are supposed to share the same vocation with the clergy, in a situation of full equality. The clergy, in his understanding, are more akin to support staff, experts in the spiritual life who offer the sacraments and means of doctrinal and spiritual formation, but the real "action" is out in the world. Only a layperson can decide how a particular lawsuit, or surgery, or newspaper article, can be made an offering to God, carrying others toward sanctification. The idea was to form people and then "turn them loose," trusting them to exercise their freedom. This includes, in principle, a commitment to male/female equality. In Opus Dei, women receive the same doctrinal and theological formation as men, including those men who will eventually be ordained priests. All this was a break from a traditional clericalist mentality, and Escrivá was denounced in some circles in Spain as an anticlericalist, even a heretic. There was talk of reporting him to the Vatican.

Everything about Opus Dei, at least from the official point of view, exists to promote this aim: forming ordinary laymen and women in Christian doctrine and spirituality, so that they may sanctify the world from within, using their own judgment about the best means to do so in their particular profession or walk of life. Officially speaking, Opus Dei is unlike virtually any other organization with which most people come into contact. It is not a lobby or an interest group, has no collective financial or political interests, and has no agenda. Escrivá called it "a disorganized organization," in the sense that the home office does not issue memos at 8:00 A.M. with marching orders for the day. Opus Dei is responsible for formation, and its members do the rest. "Opus Dei does not act, its members do" is a frequent mantra.

Critics, it should be noted, generally insist that this is a smoke screen, that the "real" aims of the organization—the acquisition of political power, or financial gain, or new recruits—are hidden. For now, however, it's worth stepping through the way Opus Dei organizes its life and describes itself, in part so we can compare that with the criticisms later on.

Becoming a Member

As Opus Dei has become more prominent, it sometimes happens that a person walks in off the street and announces, "I want to be a member of Opus Dei." In such cases, these people are advised to learn a little something about Opus Dei first. Generally, however, it doesn't work this way. Membership usually arises out of getting to know Opus Dei, either through family who are members, or by exposure to one of Opus Dei's "corporate works" such as a school or youth center, or through some other activity that may be run by members even though it's not formally sponsored by Opus Dei, such as a TV news agency or a clinic—anyplace it's possible to form a personal friendship. However it happens, a prospective member usually has been attending evenings of recollection, retreats, and other Opus Dei events well ahead of the decision to "whistle," the insider's lingo for the moment of joining. It is treated as a very serious choice, because belonging to Opus Dei is not seen as being a pastime or a hobby. It is a *vocation,* thus akin in life-changing significance to the decision to get married or to enter the priesthood.

What's the draw? At a supernatural level, the answer is always that God has given someone a vocation to Opus Dei. At the human level, however, various factors can be the points of initial attraction. For some, it may be reading the works of Escrivá; in that department, most members say the first thing to catch their attention was the idea that study or work could be their path to holiness. For others, it may be that Opus Dei offers an environment in which a serious, prayerful Catholic can feel supported. For many, it's the example set by the numeraries, who often come across as smart, dedicated, devout, and happy people, living coherent lives based on their faith. In other words, they "walk the walk." Opus Dei centers can also be a lot of fun. When I visited the Windmoor Center at Notre Dame in September 2004, for example, I arrived for their weekly Friday night fried chicken dinner, which was preceded by a meditation and followed by beers and chat. The atmosphere can be infectious, combining prayer and Catholic orthodoxy with a lighthearted, collegial, and intellectually stimulating group of people.

Since Opus Dei is not a religious order, members do not take "vows," nor does their status under Church law change when they join. Laypeople remain laity. Instead, they affliate themselves by means of that quintessential secular instrument, a contract. Essentially, members strike a deal with Opus Dei: They agree to live in the spirit of Opus Dei and to support its apostolic activities, and in return Opus Dei agrees to provide doctrinal and spiritual formation.

The formula of the contract is as follows:

Member

I, in the full use of my freedom, declare that with firm resolve I dedicate myself to pursue sanctity and to practice apostolate with all my energy according to the spirit and praxis of Opus Dei. From this moment until next March 19th, I assume the obligation:

> *First, to remain under the jurisdiction of the Prelate and the other competent authorities of the Prelature, in order to dedicate myself faithfully to everything that has to do with the special purposes of the Prelature;*
> *Second, to fulfill all the duties of a Numerary/Associate/Supernumerary member of Opus Dei, and to observe the norms by which the Prelature is governed, as well as the legitimate rulings of the Prelate and the other competent authorities of the Prelature regarding its government, spirit and apostolate.*

Representative of the Prelate

I, representing the Prelate, declare that from the moment of your incorporation into the Prelature, and for as long as that incorporation continues in force, Opus Dei assumes the obligation:

First, to devote constant care and attention to your doctrinal, spiritual, ascetical and apostolic formation, and to provide you with the special pastoral attention of the priests of the Prelature;

Second, to fulfill its other obligations with respect to its faithful, as determined in the norms by which the Prelature is governed.

Members remain free outside the terms of this contract, as does Opus Dei. At least in theory, members have no right to "represent" Opus Dei in their professional work, or to act on its behalf, and Opus Dei does not seek to influence them beyond their spiritual growth. To take a concrete example, Luis Valls, a seventy-eight-year-old Spanish member of Opus Dei, recently stepped down as executive chairman of Banco Popular, Spain's third-largest commercial bank with $47.9 billion in assets. Valls, who lives in an Opus Dei center in Madrid, has always insisted that nobody in Opus Dei dictated banking strategy to him, and that at no time were any resources from the bank diverted for Opus Dei purposes. He was not an "Opus Dei banker," but a banker who happened to be in Opus Dei. The impact of Opus on his business career and on his life, he insists, has been of a different order: "Without religious convictions, I would have been a rascal."

Exactly how Opus Dei finds new members is a subject of some controversy, since critics have suggested that the organization engages in ruthless and manipulative "recruiting" that resembles the tactics of religious cults. We'll examine those charges in chapter 14. Here, we'll simply outline the various stages of Opus Dei membership.

Whistling

"Whistling" means writing a letter asking to join Opus Dei. This is known more formally as "requesting admission." Escrivá used the term "whistling" with reference to the sound a teapot makes when it's ready to boil. The idea is that it's been heating up for a long time, just as a prospective member has been "heating up" through exposure to the life and activities of Opus Dei. Someone can whistle at the age of sixteen and one-half, though one has to be eighteen to be formally incorporated into Opus Dei. One can become an "aspirant," meaning someone thinking about joining Opus Dei, at fourteen and one-half. It should be noted that a prospective member needs the permission of the director of their local

Opus Dei center before writing the letter. It's not infrequent, members say, for someone to ask several times before receiving permission.

Admission

This term refers to a short ceremony with two other members of Opus Dei, usually an Opus Dei priest and an Opus Dei lay director, in which the new member verbally agrees to "live in the spirit of Opus Dei," and Opus Dei promises to provide means of formation. It is considered the first stage of membership, and usually comes six months after one writes the letter—though often prospects have been treated informally as members, and have thought of themselves that way, since the moment they "whistled." The period between the admission and the oblation, marking formal incorporation into Opus Dei, is generally considered a time of discernment in which the new member can experience "the life" without having made a definitive commitment to it.

Oblation

The oblation usually occurs a year and a half after whistling, and this is the stage at which the formal contract is executed between the member and Opus Dei. Oblation marks formal juridical incorporation into Opus Dei, and a prospective member must have reached eighteen years of age. The commitment has to be renewed each year on March 19, which is the Feast of Saint Joseph, the patron saint of workers and a major patron saint for Opus Dei. Though the commitment made in the oblation is not permanent, it is understood that one has given over his or her life to the vocation in Opus Dei in such a serious fashion that to leave afterward would be a "grave matter." On March 19 each year, the member is expected to renew the contract in the privacy of his or her own prayer, and then inform Opus Dei that it has been done. If one fails to do this, one is automatically no longer a member.

Fidelity

The "fidelity," five years after the oblation, is a lifetime commitment to Opus Dei, without need of annual renewal. One is now a permanent member of the "supernatural family" of Opus Dei, and in order to leave after this stage, one should write a letter to the prelate informing him of one's intentions. (In practice, however, those who leave often do so without observing these formalities.) The "fidelity" is reached only six and a half years after someone first "whistles," and since that can't be done before sixteen and a half, this means that one has to be at least twenty-three years old in order to make this kind of commitment to Opus Dei. There is no upper age limit for members, and people as old as eighty have made their "fidelity."

Categories of Members

Opus Dei, according to official Vatican figures, has 85,491 members in the world, of which 1,850 are priests, and the rest, 83,641, are laity. While there are different categories of membership, Opus Dei regards these as distinctions only in terms of how available members are for Opus Dei activities. There are no distinctions in vocation, no "grades of holiness." The categories are: supernumeraries, numeraries (along with a subset of numerary assistants), and associates, and a set of nonmember supporters called "cooperators." While this terminology today has the vague flavor of a secret society, it's based on the traditional Spanish nomenclature for the various categories of university professors. An argot that today seems exotic was therefore originally intended to show how ordinary Opus Dei really is.

Supernumeraries
The majority of members of Opus Dei, some 70 percent, fall into this category. The supernumeraries are the least available to the activities of Opus Dei, generally because they're married or have other family or personal commitments. (There is, however, no obligation to be married.) They live in their homes, as opposed to a center of Opus Dei. A husband and wife can both be supernumeraries, but they don't have to be, and there are plenty of cases where one partner is a supernumerary of Opus Dei and the other is not. Supernumeraries receive spiritual direction from a numerary of Opus Dei, often the director of the center nearest their home, and generally go to a priest of Opus Dei for confession. While much of the public fascination with Opus Dei concerns the numeraries, members say the real "action" is with the supernumeraries, since the point of Opus Dei is not to found a series of schools and charitable works, but to transform ordinary life. One member put it to me this way: "Until

you get a picture in your mind of a mom in a beat-up station wagon trying to get the kids to soccer practice, you won't understand Opus Dei."
Supernumeraries are expected to contribute financially to support the
works of Opus Dei, based on their means. American supernumerary
Russell Shaw, a noted Catholic author who once worked for the U.S.
bishops, told me that he contributes two hundred dollars a month. Some
supernumeraries will give more, many will give less. Although supernumeraries are members of Opus Dei, they do not stop being members of
their local diocese and parish. Many Opus Dei supernumeraries are active as parish council members, Eucharistic ministers, lectors, youth
group leaders, and so on.

Numeraries

Numeraries, about 20 percent of the total, are members who make Opus
Dei their immediate family. They make commitments of celibacy and live
in Opus Dei centers. Some numeraries work full-time for Opus Dei,
though most hold an outside job in their area of professional competence.
There are numeraries who are surgeons, lawyers, writers, and TV personalities. Whatever money isn't needed for personal living expenses goes to
support the activities of Opus Dei. (Numeraries in the United States who
make healthy salaries often run afoul of the Internal Revenue Service,
since it's hard for the IRS to swallow that somebody making $200,000
gives $150,000 of it to charity. Numeraries are audited at a rate above the
national average.) Because numeraries undergo a more extensive program
of theological and spiritual formation, they are entrusted with the key
leadership roles within Opus Dei. Only a numerary can be director of an
Opus Dei center, for example. Some numeraries go to Rome to study theology at the University of the Holy Cross. A subset of numeraries has responsibility for offering spiritual and doctrinal formation to other
members of Opus Dei, and they are called the *inscripti*. Numeraries are
the key to the geographical expansion of Opus Dei, since opening a center in a new country requires the presence of at least a couple of numeraries who can find jobs, support the center financially, learn the language
if necessary, and get operations off the ground. It is also the numeraries
who practice the spiritual disciplines that tend to excite certain minds.
They wear the cilice, a small spiked chain strapped around the upper
thigh, for a couple of hours most days, except for feast days and Sundays.

Numeraries also use the "discipline," a small cordlike whip, applied to the back once a week while reciting a prayer, often the Our Father. Because the demands on numeraries are high, it tends to be the category that experiences the greatest challenges. Much of the public criticism of Opus Dei comes from ex-numeraries.

Numerary Assistants

A special subset of numeraries is composed of approximately four thousand women who devote themselves full-time to the domestic care of Opus Dei centers and other facilities. Concretely, this means being involved in the cooking, cleaning, and financial administration of the household. It is analogous to being a full-time mother, and is usually understood that way by the numerary assistants. The idea, which Opus Dei members say came out of Escrivá's own family life, was that Opus Dei residences should feel like homes, not bureaucratic institutions, which requires a "woman's touch." Within Opus Dei, the domestic care of centers is also regarded as full-time professional work, for which the numerary assistants are paid. In some cases, especially in larger facilities, the assistants hire other women to do the manual labor, while in smaller centers the assistants often perform the tasks themselves. It's customary for the assistants and the other women who perform domestic work in Opus Dei facilities to wear a uniform while carrying out certain tasks, such as cleaning or serving meals. Critics have charged that Opus Dei promotes a submissive and traditionalist view of femininity, in part because the "numerary assistant category" is restricted to women. Members of Opus Dei respond that it is not discrimination to observe that women often have an aptitude for homemaking that men lack. Further, they say, this was the vision of Escrivá, and it's not up to them to change it.

Associates

The associates are celibate members, like numeraries, but family responsibilities or personal circumstances mean that they normally live with their own families, or wherever is most suited to their work and other circumstances. The distinction between a numerary and an associate is the residence; beyond that, the expectations and commitment are the same. For example, Moses Muthaka, twenty-eight, is an associate of Opus Dei in Nairobi who is the assistant director of the Informal Sector Business

Institute, an Opus Dei–run center that teaches basic business skills to poor Kenyans involved in the vast off-the-books "informal economy," selling sweets, secondhand clothing, or basic furnishings. Muthaka has four brothers and five sisters, and only one is "settled," with a stable means of income. His father died in 1996 and his mother is "up-country," meaning back in the family's village. The younger brothers and sisters are dependent on Muthaka to provide food, shelter, and to keep them in school. Ron Hathaway, on the other hand, is an American surgeon with expertise in cranial and facial reconstruction for children, whose career took him to Indianapolis, Indiana, where there is no center of Opus Dei. He was originally a supernumerary, but decided that being an associate was a better fit, in part because it liberates him to be "completely available" to his five-hundred-plus patients. It also frees him, he said, to confront superiors and HMOs who don't have the best interests of his patients at heart. Without the pressures of supporting a family, he can take more professional risks.

Priests

The prelature of Opus Dei has 1,850 priests "incardinated" into it, meaning under the direct authority of the prelate in Rome, Bishop Javier Echevarría. The primary work of these priests is the pastoral care of Opus Dei members, though a few have other commitments, such as running parishes, teaching at universities and seminaries, or running Opus Dei activities. The priests of the prelature come from the ranks of the male numeraries. There are also roughly two thousand other diocesan priests who belong to the Priestly Society of the Holy Cross, discussed below. They are also considered full members, but their full-time work is not for Opus Dei, but for the diocese where they are located.

Cooperators

Though not members of Opus Dei, the "cooperators" are friends of the organization who offer support through prayers, involvement in its activities, and, sometimes, financial contributions. Opus Dei counts among its cooperators not only Catholics, but also other Christians, Jews, Muslims, and Buddhists as well as people with no religious affiliation. Opus Dei was the first Catholic institution that, as a matter of law, approved by the

Vatican in 1950, had the right to enroll non-Catholics. On the far Catholic right, this fact has sometimes fueled criticism of Opus Dei as being "indifferentist," that is, treating Catholicism as just one among many religions. There are 164,000 cooperators of Opus Dei in the world, 57 percent of whom are women. There is also an even wider network of some 900,000 people around the world who take part in Opus Dei meetings and means of formation, some of whom may eventually become co-operators.

It's not just individuals who fall into this category. There are some five hundred religious communities of both men and women who are also, institutionally, "cooperators." I visited a community of Carmelite sisters in San Vicente de Cañete, Peru, for example, whose prioress, Sister María de Jesús, told me that they decided to become cooperators in part because local Opus Dei members were helpful when the convent needed work, including providing them with free lumber. She also said the priests from the territorial prelature of Yauyos, under the direction of an Opus Dei bishop since 1957, have been extremely faithful in coming to say Mass. "In twenty-seven years, never have they missed a Mass," she told me. "I know that other communities struggle with this."

Geographic Distribution

Spain is far and away the country in which Opus Dei is most numerically prominent. There are some 35,000 members of Opus Dei in Spain, more than 40 percent of the global total. Madrid is the city with the single greatest number of Opus Dei members. Plans for international expansion were laid in the 1930s, but had to be delayed by the onset of the Spanish civil war. A list of the sixty-two countries in which Opus Dei operates at least one center, and the years in which they arrived, follows.

1946: Portugal, Italy, and Great Britain
1947: France and Ireland
1949: Mexico and the United States
1950: Chile and Argentina
1951: Colombia and Venezuela
1952: Germany
1953: Guatemala and Peru

1954: Ecuador
1956: Uruguay and Switzerland
1957: Brazil, Austria, and Canada
1958: Japan, Kenya, and El Salvador
1959: Coast Rica and Holland
1962: Paraguay
1963: Australia
1964: The Philippines
1965: Belgium and Nigeria
1969: Puerto Rico
1978: Bolivia
1980: Congo, Ivory Coast, and Honduras
1981: Hong Kong
1982: Singapore and Trinidad-Tobago
1984: Sweden
1985: Taiwan
1987: Finland
1988: Cameroon and the Dominican Republic
1989: Macao, New Zealand, and Poland
1990: Hungary and the Czech Republic
1992: Nicaragua
1993: India and Israel
1994: Lithuania
1996: Estonia, Slovakia, Lebanon, Panama, and Uganda
1997: Kazakhstan
1998: South Africa
2003: Slovenia and Croatia
2004: Lithuania

The seven countries with the highest number of Opus Dei members, in descending order, are: Spain, Mexico, Argentina, Italy, the United States, the Philippines, and Colombia.

The development of Opus Dei in a given country depends on local circumstances. Great Britain, for example, was one of the first three countries outside Spain in which Opus Dei set up shop, and Escrivá spent more time in London than in any other city except Madrid and

Rome. He spent five summers in England, from 1958 to 1962, calling it a "crossroads of the world." He developed a liking for the Victoria and Albert Museum, and because of his devotion to Saint Thomas More, he twice went to the Anglican Church of St. Dunstan to pray at the tomb of the Roper family, where More's head is kept. In January 2005 a London parish named for Saint Thomas More was entrusted to the priests of Opus Dei. Yet Opus Dei has had little expansion in England. After almost sixty years in the country, Opus Dei counts scarcely more than five hundred members, meaning an average of fewer than ten new members each year. In part, this may have been influenced by the caution about Opus Dei expressed by the late Cardinal Basil Hume of Westminster, which filtered down to other English bishops.

In Peru, on the other hand, the diffusion of Opus Dei, and of popular devotion to Escrivá, has been striking. There are 1,630 Opus Dei members in Peru, almost 2 percent of the global total, which includes 400 numeraries and another 180 associates. The figure also includes 200 priests and an astounding 11 active bishops, plus two bishops emeriti, representing almost one-third of the total number of Opus Dei bishops in the world. In this case the growth is due in part to a decision of Pius XII to entrust a territorial prelature to Opus Dei, called Yauyos, in 1957, which gave it a strong geographic base and infrastructure. In this zone of Peru, popular devotion to Escrivá rivals the following that Padre Pio enjoys in southern Italy. One can walk into the main outdoor market in Cañete and find an Escrivá holy card in every stall, with merchants bragging that they've got one from the canonization, while the guy in the next stall only has the beatification edition. There is even a cab company named for Escrivá ("cab" in this sense meaning a kind of rough-and-tumble motorcart); there's also one named after the Virgin Mary, and one for the Holy Family, but locals say that the fleet named after Escrivá gets more business. I met one local, Francisco Matías Guapaya Quispe, who is so devoted to Escrivá and Opus Dei that his three oldest sons are named Josemaría, Alvaro, and Javier, for the three prelates, and two of his daughters are named Dolores, for Escrivá's mother, and Carmen, for his sister. For an added splash of Catholicity, the baby of the family is named John Paul.

What Do Members Do?

Opus Dei members say that what they "do," in the first place, is perform the ordinary tasks of their daily lives—going to work, raising their kids, paying their taxes, and spending time with their friends. The real point of Opus Dei, they say, is not to engage in specifically religious activities, but to transform those ordinary tasks into pathways to holiness.

In support of that aim, members utilize the means of formation provided by Opus Dei. These means are personal before they are collective, designed to give the member a grasp of the doctrinal and moral teaching of the Church, and to promote his or her personal sanctity. Each member of Opus Dei undertakes to follow a daily "plan of life," known in English as "the norms." The norms include:

- Offering the day to God first thing in the morning, symbolized by saying *serviam,* "I will serve."
- Daily Mass, including receiving Communion.
- Daily praying of the rosary.
- Mental prayer, usually one half hour in the morning and another half hour in the evening.
- The noontime Angelus prayer or the Regina Coeli, depending on the liturgical season.
- A daily examination of conscience.
- Meditation on spiritual readings, about ten minutes.
- Daily reading of the New Testament, around five minutes.
- A daily visit to the Blessed Sacrament, often immediately after supper and including the saying of three Our Fathers, three Hail Marys, three Glory Be prayers, and making a "spiritual communion," meaning an act of union with Christ that doesn't involve physically receiving Communion during Mass.
- A daily set of prayers in Latin called the Preces, which include invocations to the Holy Spirit, Jesus Christ, the Blessed Virgin Mary, Saint Joseph, the Guardian Angels, and Saint Josemaría, then prayers for the Holy Father, the bishop of the diocese, unity among all those working to spread the gospel, the prelate of Opus Dei and the other members of the Work, and invoca-

tions to Saints Michael, Gabriel, Raphael, Peter, Paul, and John (the patrons of Opus Dei).

Other characteristic practices of Opus Dei members include:

- Saying short prayers throughout the day called "aspirations," such as "Jesus, Mary and Joseph, I give you my heart and my soul," or "Jesus, I love you with all my heart"; for 2005 the prelate of Opus Dei suggested to members: "Everything with Peter to Jesus through Mary."
- Saying three Hail Marys as an intention for holy purity and blessing oneself with holy water before going to bed.
- Practices of corporal mortification (discussed in chapter 8).

Beyond this individual program, every week there's a "circle," which is a class given by a member (usually a layperson, but occasionally a priest) on some points of the spirit and practice of Opus Dei, plus an examination of conscience. Every month there's an evening or day of recollection, usually comprised of two to three meditations given by a priest, and a talk like the ones in the circle, plus times of silence for personal prayer. Every year the supernumeraries attend a workshop for several days, and the numeraries attend an annual course, which normally lasts three weeks. In addition, every year there are retreats in the classic sense, meaning several days, in silence, with lots of meditations. Also, every member of Opus Dei receives spiritual direction from a numerary or associate.

On May 23, 2004, I attended a recollection for men held at the Roman parish of Sant'Eugenio, which is entrusted to the clergy of Opus Dei. The custom on these occasions is to go into the chapel, where the lights are darkened, while the priest leads opening prayers. He then sits at a table with a lamp, to see his notes, and delivers a meditation. Afterward, participants assemble in a living room for a talk on a spiritual subject given by one of the lay members, then they return to the chapel for another meditation. The event ends with an examination of conscience. On this particular morning the meditations were given by Father Michele Díaz, a Spaniard who has lived in Rome for more than thirty years. The focus of the first talk was on the Eucharist, and Díaz challenged his audience to understand that "you don't come to the Eucharist to receive, but to give," meaning that Catholics should be prepared to give themselves to God. "In Rome, the restaurants are always full, but the churches are often empty," Díaz lamented. "There are tabernacles without even one person to adore Christ." The talk in the living room was given by a supernumerary who spoke about May as the month of the Virgin Mary, recommending that participants use a rosary to conduct "mini-pilgrimages" during the month. During the second meditation, Díaz dealt with the subject of purity. He quoted Escrivá to the effect that "the battles are won on the periphery, not in the center." That means, Díaz said, that one must struggle to control even "the most minimally impure thoughts."

In September 2004, I sat in on a workshop at the Shellbourne Conference Center in Valparaiso, Indiana, about an hour outside of Chicago. This particular morning the group was working from the seventh edition of the *Catechism of Opus Dei,* published in Rome in 2003 and translated into English in London in 2004. This 133-page document, divided into four parts and organized in a question-and-answer format, is not distributed to the public, as it is for the internal use of members. (The edition I saw had a note to the effect that Escrivá had been forced to withdraw the fourth edition of the document due to "intense and hidden opposition to the Work," and all the copies are numbered.) In fact, the document seemed little more than a structured overview of Opus Dei's history and self-understanding.

This morning's session was devoted to the opening question of chapter 1, "What Is Opus Dei?" The answer provided was: "Opus Dei is a personal prelature with its own statutes, which serves the entire Church and forms part of its pastoral and hierarchical structure." Additional explanation in smaller print followed. The priest leading the discussion had the supernumeraries read out portions of the *Catechism,* stopping and developing ideas every so often and taking questions as they arose. He told an oft-cited story about Escrivá to illustrate the equality between priests and laity in Opus Dei: One time Escrivá walked into a get-together and saw that all the priests were sitting in chairs while the laity were on the floor. He took a seat on the floor, and when someone tried to give him a chair, he said that he did not found a society where priests were higher than the rest, and then left the room. When he came back, naturally, the priests were seated on the floor.

Numeraries, who live in the centers of Opus Dei, are expected to attend a get-together (known as a *tertulia*) every day, which is the equivalent of family time. They receive a program of theological formation equivalent to seminary studies for a candidate for the priesthood. They also take longer retreats each year, usually three weeks, which are doctrinal courses that are sometimes combined with language study or other activities typical of a vacation period. In general, numeraries are also expected to be "available" in a variety of informal ways, such as helping out in the youth center after returning home from work, running a catechetical program for kids on Sundays, or simply lending a hand for the unforeseen tasks that arise, such as getting visitors back and forth to the airport or helping plan special events. These are seen as "family responsibilities."

All members of Opus Dei are expected to have jobs. In the case of supernumerary mothers, the job may be homemaking, especially since Opus Dei families tend to be large. For some numeraries, the job may involve full-time or part-time work for Opus Dei itself, running a center or other apostolic work, or serving in the regional, national, or world headquarters. The expectation of all members is that they will apply a serious professional ethic to their work and strive to meet the highest secular standards.

Beyond this, at least as far as official Opus Dei explanations go, members are free to do what they want. That is to say, it is up to individual members to decide how to translate the doctrinal and spiritual teachings they receive into their professional careers, their friendships, their political choices, their consumer preferences, and so on. No one in Opus Dei attempts to tell members how to vote. No Opus Dei priest instructs a supernumerary on which vice presidency to apply for in his banking career, or which newspaper to write for in her journalistic career. To the extent that Opus Dei members tend to cluster in certain careers, partisan options, or cultural circles, they say that's by personal preference rather than administrative diktat.

Corporate Works and Independent Initiatives

Beyond what they do strictly on an individual basis, members also sometimes come together to take part in projects, such as schools, youth centers, or agricultural institutes. In some cases Opus Dei provides doctrinal and spiritual guidance for one of these projects, in which case it becomes a "corporate work" of Opus Dei. This doesn't mean that Opus Dei owns it, but rather that Opus Dei stands behind the means of formation it provides. In many cases, nonmembers of Opus Dei are involved in the foundation and administration of these activities.

Opus Dei corporate works include:

- Fifteen universities, with roughly 80,000 students. The largest is the University of Navarra in Pamplona, Spain, which has faculties of law, medicine, philosophy and letters, pharmacology, natural sciences, canon law, theology, communications, and economics. The most recent Opus Dei universities are the Biomedical Campus in Rome and the University of the Isthmus in Guatemala.

- Seven hospitals, with more than 1,000 doctors and 1,500 nurses who care for some 300,000 patients. They include two hospitals in Africa: the Monkole Hospital in the Democratic Republic of Congo, and the Niger Foundation Hospital in Nigeria.

- Eleven business schools with a student population of 10,000, including the Instituto de Estudios Superiores de la Empresa (IESE) in Barcelona, a branch of the University of Navarra. Others include the Instituto Panamericano de Alta Dirección de Empresa (IPADE) in Mexico City, and the Instituto de Altos Estudios Empresariales (IAE) in Buenos Aires, Argentina.

- Thirty-six primary and secondary schools, with roughly 25,000 students. There are five in the United States: the Heights (boys) and Oakcrest (girls) Schools in the Washington, D.C., area; the Montrose School (girls) in Boston; and Northridge Prep (boys) and the Willows School (girls) in Chicago. Others include the Nagasaki Seido School in Japan and the Kianda School in Kenya.

- Ninety-seven vocational-technical schools, enrolling 13,000 students. Most are schools that teach basic professional and life skills to young men and women, and most are located in poor neighborhoods. They include: ELIS for boys and SAFI

for girls, in Rome; Junkabal, in Guatemala; Condoray and
Valle Grande in Peru; Punlaan in Manila, the Philippines;
Kinal in Guatemala; and Pedreira in São Paulo, Brazil.

- One hundred and sixty-six university residences that house
6,000 students, the vast majority of whom are not members of
Opus Dei. The residences offer living quarters, libraries, study
areas, and academic support, and make religious services
available for those who choose to participate. The residences
include Netherhall in London, Pedralbes in Barcelona, Spain,
and He Shan in Taipei, Taiwan.

In addition, there are other institutions that are not considered
corporate works, but where Opus Dei offers spiritual assistance. Some
of these institutions may evolve into corporate works. They include:

- Two universities, with roughly 4,000 students.
- One business school, with 300 students.
- Two hundred and thirteen secondary and primary schools,
with roughly 100,000 students.
- Fifty-nine vocational-technical schools, with approximately
16,000 students.
- An undetermined number of medical clinics, most of them
small-scale. Among the most recent is Aq'on Jay, a dispensary
in the zone of Tecpán in Chimaltenango, Guatemala, a day
hospital founded on the occasion of the canonization of
Escrivá in 2002. The clinic has twenty doctors and twenty-
seven nurses. Twenty-seven pharmacies have also been
opened in isolated zones of the region.

One note about the corporate works: Sometimes Opus Dei is seen as
an "elitist" organization, in part because some of their best-known corporate works, such as the IESE business school in Barcelona, or Strathmore
University in Nairobi, or the Heights School in Washington, D.C., tend
to cater to the best and brightest. To be fair, Opus Dei also operates many
corporate works targeted at low-income and at-risk populations, such as
the Midtown Center in Chicago, which runs summer programs for black

and Hispanic youth in order to equip them for academic success; the Besana School on the outskirts of Madrid, where the student body is composed largely of recent immigrants from Latin America and North Africa; or the Valle Grande Rural Institute in Peru, where poor farmers are taught how to diversify their crops and get them to market, so they can feed their families and give their children a future. One could also consider the Gatina Nursery School on a tea plantation outside Nairobi, which is not a corporate work of Opus Dei, but is supported by the nearby Opus Dei–run Kimlea School for girls. Kimlea provides a couple of part-time teachers along with milk and cookies each day for the approximately one hundred young children on the plantation, and these meager resources sometimes make the difference between life and death.

In other cases, a few Opus Dei members, often in tandem with non-members, will come together to launch a project with which Opus Dei has no official relationship. For example, two Opus Dei supernumeraries in London, John and Jane Phillips, recently combined forces with a handful of other concerned Catholic parents and launched their own school, called Oakwood. It may or may not one day become a corporate work, but for now it is simply a private initiative with no official connection to Opus Dei. Another example is the Rome Reports television news agency specializing in the Catholic Church, launched by an Opus Dei numerary, Santiago de la Cierva, based in Rome. In this case it is highly unlikely that Opus Dei would ever assume it as a corporate work, because Opus Dei resists doing anything as an organization outside of providing educational and social services. Escrivá once said it would be absurd to think that Opus Dei as such could ever manage banks, or mines, or any other commercial enterprises.

To the outside world this distinction between "corporate works," which are officially related to Opus Dei, and projects of individual members, which are not, can seem like hairsplitting. If a given institution is staffed largely by Opus Dei people and it seems to reflect the "spirit of the Work," why bother denying that it's Opus Dei? Aside from the tax and liability issues involved, there are three considerations in terms of Opus Dei's self-understanding. First, some of the people involved in these initiatives may not even be Catholic, let alone members of Opus Dei. In the case of Northridge Prep in Chicago, for example, one of the founders was Jewish, another Episcopalian. Second, Opus Dei does not want to stifle creativity and initiative by suggesting that one needs to wait for orders from headquarters before proceeding. That would contradict Escrivá's emphasis on the freedom of members to act as they see fit in temporal affairs. Third, it would compromise the concept of "secularity," meaning that members of Opus Dei out in the world are not acting as agents of the Catholic Church, but as citizens just like everybody else. They are not supposed to claim any special privileges by virtue of being Catholic; in fact, Escrivá once said that he "despised" people who attempted to trade off the Catholic label for advantages in business or politics.

Personal Prelature

Controversy over Opus Dei first burst into public view in the Anglo-Saxon world in 1982, when Pope John Paul II granted Opus Dei the canonical status of a "personal prelature." One way to think of a prelature is as a limited kind of diocese, only in this case one whose borders are defined by contract rather than by geography. A prelature is led by a "prelate," usually a bishop. Membership in the prelature does not exempt a Catholic from the authority of the local diocesan bishop, whether it's New York or New Delhi. For things that pertain to all Catholics, Opus Dei members are subject to the local bishop. For example, if a member of Opus Dei wants an annulment, meaning a Church declaration that his marriage is invalid, he has to go to the local bishop, not the prelate of Opus Dei. In principle, the jurisdiction of the prelature concerns only the internal business of Opus Dei. Members of Opus Dei agree to be subject to the prelature in areas where Catholics are otherwise free to make their own choices.

Though the Second Vatican Council anticipated the creation of personal prelatures in 1965, and the new Code of Canon Law issued in 1983 contained law for these prelatures in canons 294–296, to date Opus Dei remains the only "personal prelature" in the Catholic Church.

Escrivá was a lawyer by training, and his graduate thesis was titled *La Abadesa de las Huelgas* (*The Abbess of Las Huelgas*), an extraordinary case of quasi-episcopal jurisdiction exercised by the abbess of a famous medieval convent in Burgos, Spain. Escrivá was almost unique among the founders in the Catholic Church in his attention to the canonical and juridical fine print. The evolution of Opus Dei's legal status is an epic story, and it fills some 655 pages in the *The Canonical Path of Opus Dei: The History and Defense of a Charism,* published in the United States by the Opus Dei–affiliated Midwest Theological Forum. Opus Dei was approved as a pious union in 1941, then it was folded into the Priestly Society of the Holy Cross in 1943, then it became a secular institute in 1947, and finally a personal prelature in 1982.

Opus Dei argues that this evolution was not a matter of seeking special privilege, but of finding a canonical form that would protect Escrivá's vision. To take but one example of the problems created by the lack of an appropriate structure, indicative of dozens that arose over the years: Under canon 500 of the 1917 Code of Canon Law, a secular institute could not be composed of both men and women, so in theory Opus Dei should have been split into two separate bodies. The new 1983 Code does not apply any such requirement to personal prelatures.

It is difficult to overestimate the importance of the question of canonical status for Opus Dei, historically and psychologically. There's a great deal that cannot be understood about Opus Dei—its insistence on its own singularity, its standoffish attitude with respect to religious orders and lay movements, its fussiness about canonical vocabulary and categories, and its seemingly insatiable appetite for signs of approval from Church authorities—until one understands that, seen from inside, Opus Dei's identity is terribly fragile. The constant fear is of being sucked into one of two models in canon law: a religious order, to which laity could be attached only in a derivative way; or a lay association, in which there is really no room for priests. The idea of priests and laity, men and women, all part of one organic whole, sharing the same vocation and carrying out the same apostolic works, has not been part of Catholic tradition, at least not since the early centuries. The push for a personal prelature, seen from within, was not about the exercise of raw power politics, but rather protecting this fledgling form of life.

The Priestly Society of the Holy Cross

The Priestly Society of the Holy Cross is an association for the priests of Opus Dei as well as diocesan priests who wish to share in their spirituality and doctrinal formation. Canon 278 of the Code of Canon Law gives diocesan priests the right to join spiritual associations of their choosing.

Escrivá was so concerned about the formation of priests that he once contemplated leaving Opus Dei to create a separate initiative for them, but decided the same end could be achieved by means of a "society" that would unite the priests of Opus Dei with diocesan priests from around the world. Both are considered members of Opus Dei, but only the priests of Opus Dei are under the jurisdiction of the prelate. The technical term for this jurisdiction is "incardination," meaning that these priests are under the direct canonical authority of Opus Dei. Priests who are incardinated into the prelature of Opus Dei are considered numeraries, while the priests who remain incardinated in their dioceses are supernumeraries or associates. As with the lay members of Opus Dei, these are distinctions in how available the priests can be for the activities of Opus Dei, but all are considered to have the same vocation and all are fully members.

For diocesan priests to sanctify their work, according to Escrivá, they must have a strong relationship with the bishop. The Priestly Society of the Holy Cross thus does not see itself replacing the local bishop as the primary point of reference for his priests. In fact, there are also bishops who belong to the Priestly Society; Archbishop John Myers of Newark, New Jersey, is one example. The official aim of the society is "promoting holiness in its members through the fulfillment of their priestly duties," offering them the spiritual teachings and practices of Opus Dei as a means to this end. The means of formation the diocesan priests of the society receive are similar to those offered to supernumeraries, such as doctrinal or ascetical classes and monthly days of recollection.

The society was created in 1943 by Escrivá, in part to ensure a supply of priests devoted to the pastoral care of members in a time before Opus Dei had the canonical capacity to incardinate clergy. The first ordinations for Opus Dei occurred in 1944, and these three priests became the first members of the Priestly Society of the Holy Cross. There are today 1,850 priests incardinated into the prelature and an additional 2,000 diocesan priests who are members of the priestly society.

Priests ordained for Opus Dei come from the ranks of numeraries and associates, a requirement that has the practical value of ensuring that no one suspects Opus Dei of "poaching" someone else's vocations. These priests automatically become members of the priestly society upon ordination. The prelate is the "president general" of the society. By law, however, there are no superiors, and diocesan priests in the society remain fully subject to their diocesan bishop.

Governance

The internal government of Opus Dei is determined by the organization's statutes. The ultimate authority is the prelate, the successor of Escrivá as "Father." So far, Opus Dei has had two prelates: Alvaro del Portillo, who was elected upon Escrivá's death in 1975 and made a bishop in 1991 by Pope John Paul II; and the current prelate, Bishop Javier Echevarría, seventy-three. He was elected in 1994 following the death of Portillo and made a bishop in 1995. The office of prelate is, according to the statutes, the only one held for life. There was a natural progression from Escrivá to Portillo to Echevarría, since Portillo was Escrivá's closest collaborator and Echevarría was Escrivá's personal secretary.

For the priests of Opus Dei, the prelate is their bishop, and they have the same relationship to him that a diocesan priest would have to the local bishop. Every priest of Opus Dei who ministers to anyone outside the prelature, however, has to have faculties to do so from the bishop of the diocese in which he is operating.

The prelate is aided by two central councils, both of which have headquarters in Rome. The General Council is the chief body for the men's branch, while the Central Advisory Council administers the women's branch. Both advise the prelate on matters of common concern. At present a German numerary named Marlies Kücking is head of the Central Advisory Council, while the prelate, Echevarría, heads the General Council. The theory is that the two bodies are separate but equal. It's not just that they have different structures, but there is a kind of taboo against them even communicating with each other in a direct way. I once asked Sarah Cassidy, an English numerary and member of the Central Advisory Council, if it would be normal for her to call her male counterparts to talk things out, such as whether or not Opus Dei ought to expand in a given country. Her response was no, that if they felt the need to contact the men, they would do so in writing.

As far as equality goes, Kücking says the women have the same weight in deliberations as the men, a practice that she said goes back to the days of Escrivá. "It would often be the case that he would come to us and say, 'The General Council has said x, what do you think?' If we said something contrary, he often deferred to us," she said in an interview in November 2004 at Villa Sacchetti, the headquarters of the women's branch. It's in the same building as Villa Tevere, but with its own entrance and separate quarters. Kücking said that when the Central Advisory Council proposes something, "The prelate will listen and ask questions, but generally he approves whatever we propose, saying you know the issues better, even if he knows the reality perfectly well."

The composition of the two councils is more or less the same. They are made up of members of Opus Dei who have responsibility for over-seeing various areas of apostolic work (youth, supernumeraries, and numeraries), plus offering study plans in philosophy and theology, or administration. Besides the prelate, there are two other figures common to the two branches: the vicar-general, Ocáriz, and the secretary-vicar, currently Father Manuel Dacal Vidal. Both are required by statute to be priests. Each council also nominates the regional delegates, meaning officials for each of the "regions" of Opus Dei, a term that is more or less synonymous with "country," so that France is a region, Kenya a region, and so on. Members of the two councils serve eight-year terms.

The regional level reflects the same basic structure. Each has a regional vicar, or counselor, who is the top authority, assisted by two councils, one for the men and another for the women. In the United States the vicar is Father Thomas Bohlin, whose office is in the new seventeen-story Opus Dei headquarters in Manhattan at Thirty-fourth and Lexington. In large regions such as the United States, the territory is further subdivided into "delegations," and with the same basic structure, that is, a vicar and two councils, one for men and another for women. Regions (or, if there are any in a given country, delegations) are further divided into "centers." According to the 2004 Vatican *Annuario,* there are 1,751 centers of Opus Dei in the world. Every center is governed by a director, who is a layperson, assisted by a local council. Every center must consist at least of a director and two other Opus Dei members. Since the centers are strictly segregated by gender, there is no need for two councils.

The center is the basic building block of Opus Dei. A center does not have to be a physical place, though usually it is a residence or corporate work. In theory, however, the center is a unit for organizing the means of formation and pastoral care of the members of Opus Dei in a particular area. Before a new center can be opened, Opus Dei has to secure the permission of the bishop in whose diocese it would be located, and under canon law, the local bishop has the right to visit the center periodically and to inspect its oratory and tabernacle and its place for confessions. If Opus Dei is to take over the administration of a parish in the diocese, as it has, for example, at Saint Mary of the Angels Parish in Chicago, or Sant'Eugenio Parish in Rome, or Saint Thomas More Parish in London, the bishop and Opus Dei have to enter into an agreement.

General Congress

"General congresses" of Opus Dei are usually held every eight years, attended by delegates representing the countries in which Opus Dei is present. At these congresses the work of the prelature is studied and proposed directions are presented to the prelate. During the congress, the prelate appoints new councils. When it is necessary to choose a new prelate, a general elective congress is convened. Following the statutes, the prelate is chosen from among those priests of the prelature who have the right age, length of time in Opus Dei, priestly experience, and so on. His election must be confirmed by the pope, who thereby confers the office on the person elected. It's worth noting that the female delegates propose the candidates and the men vote, which means that the election of the head of Opus Dei is fairly close to the democratic election of a bishop.

Chapter Two

ESCRIVÁ

Josemaría Escrivá de Balaguer is a riveting historical figure, one of the most scrutinized and talked-about Catholic saints of all time. Born into a prosperous middle-class family in the Spanish province of Aragon in 1902, the infant Escrivá was once left for dead due to a runaway case of what is believed to have been meningitis, only to stage a miraculous recovery after his mother took him to the nearby Marian sanctuary of Torreciudad. As a young cleric, Escrivá witnessed the horrors of the Spanish civil war. At one point he escaped death only by pretending to be mad and hiding in an insane asylum, and later he and a small band of followers made a harrowing trek across the Pyrenees Mountains to reach safety in the Nationalist zone. Escrivá moved to Rome in 1946, where he guided the expansion of the new reality he believed God had called him to found. He lived the drama of the Second Vatican Council and the liberalizing trend that took hold of the Catholic Church afterward, which did not always sit well with Escrivá—obedience to the pope was a core value for him, and "dissent" was not part of his vocabulary. After he died in 1975, letters supporting his beatification reached the Vatican from 69 cardinals, 241 archbishops, 987 bishops, and 41 superior generals of religious congregations. Even in death, however, Escrivá made waves. Few beatifications in modern times have generated more public debate, but he was beatified in 1992, followed swiftly by canonization in 2002. Today Escrivá is reviled by some, and venerated by millions more. At his canonization, some 350,000 people filled St. Peter's Square and the surrounding area.

Although the aim of this book is to understand Opus Dei today, we cannot avoid at least a brief treatment of Escrivá, because so much of the controversy surrounding Opus Dei is inextricably linked to debates over its founding father. Was he, as Opus Dei members believe, one of the great saints of Church history, a spiritual teacher akin to Thomas à Kempis or Thérèse of Lisieux, and a founder comparable to Saint Dominic and Saint Ignatius of Loyola? Or was he, as critics insist, a petty dictator full of vainglory and barely suppressed rage? Is it possible that somehow he was all of these things? Other controversies beckon: Did Escrivá have a soft spot in his heart for the fascist regime of Gen. Francisco Franco? Did he once seek to minimize the Holocaust and express admiration for Hitler? Was he disillusioned by the Second Vatican Council and dismissive of the popes who presided over it? Is there a cult of personality around Escrivá that suppresses dissent of the glowing image provided in official hagiographical materials?

Picking through these debates is often a frustrating and distasteful exercise for people convinced that Escrivá is a saint, who feel as if they've been through all this a thousand times over the course of several decades. Yet these points continue to be widely recycled, both in the popular press and in watercooler gossip within the Catholic Church, especially in the Anglo-Saxon world where Escrivá is a less familiar figure. Until the public feels it has been given complete and convincing answers, doubts about Escrivá, and the work he founded, will linger.

The Escrivá Story

Josemaría Escrivá, baptized José María Julián Mariano, was born on January 9, 1902, in the provincial town of Barbastro, located in the Spanish region of Aragon. Throughout his life he would use slightly different versions of his name, eventually settling on Josemaría Escrivá de Balaguer, combining the first two names to indicate the closeness of Joseph and Mary.

Aragonites are legendarily hardheaded, a quality captured in the famous story of the Madonna of the Pilar, located in Saragossa, the regional capital. The tradition goes that when Saint James, the brother of Jesus, came to evangelize Spain, he had success everywhere except Aragon, where the people were too stubborn to change their ways. The Madonna came to comfort and encourage James, appearing atop a pillar. It is the only place where, according to tradition, Mary appeared miraculously while she was still alive. Both admirers and detractors of Escrivá say that one can see traces of this Aragonite penchant for plain talk and obstinacy in his character. There's a famous Spanish proverb that holds, "Give a man from Aragon a nail and he'll hammer it in with his own head."

Today, the house at 11 Plaza Mercado in Barbastro, where Escrivá was born and spent his early years, has been converted and is a women's center of Opus Dei. One iron railing on the top floor, preserved inside the building, is all that remains of the original structure. Poking around inside, one can see that it would have been a comfortable middle-class home for the family of a reasonably prosperous textiles merchant, which was the occupation of Escrivá's father, José. As it was one hundred years ago, the Escrivá home is still located on the edge of the central plaza in Barbastro, thus right in the middle of the ebb and flow of life in a midsized city in Aragon. The night I visited in June 2004, there was a free concert in the square, and, as was undoubtedly the case in Escrivá's time, men and women sat on their balconies in the apartments ringing the square to take in the action. Ironically, next to the Escrivá home today sits a grocery store called San Pedro, or "Saint Peter," as if the connection between the founder of Opus Dei and the papacy had been there from the beginning.

José and Dolores Escrivá were married in 1898, and their first child, a daughter named Carmen, arrived one year later. Josemaría followed, then three more girls: María Asunción, María Dolores, and María del Rosario. The three younger girls all died in the years 1910–1913.

At one stage in infancy, Josemaría also became extremely ill. His mother took him to the ancient shrine of Our Lady of Torreciudad, begging her intercession, and the boy survived. Later, partly in gratitude, Escrivá would direct the construction of a major complex at the Torreciudad shrine, making it the lone pilgrimage center in the world administered by Opus Dei. (Controversy followed even here. On June 25, 1979, the Basque separatist group ETA set off a bomb in the Chapel of the Madonna of Guadalupe at Torreciudad, linking Opus Dei with the antiterrorism policies of the Spanish government.)

Between 1913 and 1914, the textiles business operated by José Escrivá and two other Spanish businessmen failed, leaving the Escrivás in significantly reduced financial circumstances. Although Spanish law would have allowed him to declare bankruptcy, José insisted on paying off debts to creditors and workers, a step that left his family in even more dire straits. They had to dismiss their servants and resolved to make a new start somewhere else. In 1915 they moved to Logroño, in the center of the Rioja wine-growing region of Spain. The father took a job with another textile firm and relocated the family in a more modest apartment that was hot in the summer and cold in the winter. The Escrivás, who had been accustomed to living a bourgeois life in Barbastro, now found themselves expert in "keeping up appearances." Opus Dei members sometimes attribute the group's capacity to create the appearance of elegance even with inexpensive, cast-off materials to instincts forged in the Escrivás' experience of financial hardship.

Josemaría was a pious child, having made his First Communion in Barbastro. The family took advantage of new rules implemented by Pope Pius X that lowered the minimum age requirement, a move intended to foster wide reception of the sacrament. Sometime between Christmas 1917 and Epiphany 1918, Escrivá had the first of a lifetime of mystical insights. He noticed, he would later say, the outlines of a Carmelite monk's bare feet in the snow, and the experience filled his heart with a desire to serve God. He began going to daily Mass, made a confession regularly, and embarked on a program of daily prayer. He considered a vocation as a Carmelite priest, but in the end felt that God was calling him in another direction. He wanted to be a diocesan priest but was nagged with guilt, since, as the only son in the family, he knew his parents would depend on him for financial support. When his younger brother Santiago was born in 1919, however, it resolved any doubt.

In 1920 he transferred to the pontifical university in Saragossa. Escrivá did well, both academically and personally, and in September 1922 he was appointed a seminarian-superior at Saragossa. He came to know Cardinal Juan Soldevila y Romero of Saragossa, so that when the elderly cardinal was struck down by anarchists on June 4, 1923, it hit Escrivá hard. Escrivá was ordained to the priesthood on March 28, 1925, and two days later celebrated his first public Mass in the Chapel of the Madonna at the Cathedral of Our Lady of Pilar, where as a seminarian he once passed an entire night in prayer. He next took a degree in canon and civil law. Eventually he settled in Madrid, both to pursue a doctorate in civil law and to begin his priestly career. He arrived in 1927 and would live in Madrid continuously, except for disruptions caused by the Spanish civil war, until 1946, when he moved to Rome. In Madrid, Escrivá was an indefatigable priest, becoming the chaplain to a group of religious women called the Damas Apostólicas and spending countless hours visiting the poor and the sick in Madrid's hospitals and slums. In those days he lived on very limited means, surviving largely on stipends that, in today's money, work out to approximately .03 cents per Mass.

The turning point in Escrivá's life came on October 2, 1928, during a retreat at the residence of the Vincentian Fathers in Madrid, when he heard the ringing of the bells for the Feast of the Guardian Angels and experienced a vision in which, according to Portillo, his confessor for more than twenty years, "He saw Opus Dei, as the Lord wanted it and as it would be, down through the centuries."

From 1928 forward, Escrivá dedicated himself to building the new reality that he believed God had revealed to him—even though, as he would later insist, "I did not want to be the founder of anything." He began writing letters outlining the "spirit" of this new reality, well before there was more than a handful of members. The first lay member of Opus Dei, Isidoro Zorzano, joined in August 1930, and today Opus Dei is pursuing a cause for his beatification. In 1933, Escrivá established the first center of Opus Dei, a residence for university students he called DYA, for the Spanish initials for "law and architecture," or Derecho y Arquitectura. Members joked, however, that it also stood for Dios y Audacia, meaning "God and daring."

When the civil war erupted in Spain, Escrivá attempted to remain in hiding in Madrid after the city fell to the anticlerical Republican forces. For five months he feigned insanity in a mental asylum run by a friend; later he took refuge in the Honduran consulate. Eventually he and a band of early Opus Dei members fled to the Nationalist zone, which involved making a perilous trek over the Pyrenees into Andorra, and then back into Spain. They arrived in Burgos, the Nationalist capital in northeastern Castille. After Franco's forces triumphed, Escrivá returned to Madrid. In 1939 he published the first edition of *Camino,* or *The Way,* a collection of 999 bits of spiritual wisdom that would become his classic. The book has gone through 125 editions in 25 languages. Later, several other works by Escrivá would be published, including *Furrow, The Forge,* and *Christ Is Passing By.*

In 1946, Escrivá relocated to Rome, a sign, as he would later explain it, that Opus Dei's horizons were bigger than postwar Spain. The primary motive for the move was to allow Escrivá to oversee efforts to find a juridical status for Opus Dei that would protect its identity. It was also smart church politics, as it allowed Escrivá and his aides close proximity to decision-makers in the Vatican. Escrivá's top lieutenant, Father Alvaro del Portillo, began a career in the Roman Curia that would span decades before he took over as head of Opus Dei after Escrivá's death in 1975.

From Rome, Escrivá would direct the worldwide expansion of Opus Dei. During the 1940s he traveled extensively in Europe preparing the basis for new Opus Dei outposts. In 1948 he launched the Roman College of the Holy Cross, which in time would also spawn a pontifical university. In 1952 he founded the University of Navarra in Pamplona, Spain, which would grow to become the cornerstone of Opus Dei's "corporate works." For much of this time Escrivá prepared the materials leading up to a 1969 congress that first proposed the idea of transforming Opus Dei into a personal prelature. During the later years of his life he traveled extensively, offering catecheses and promoting Opus Dei. Escrivá died on June 26, 1975, the date that would eventually be assigned as his feast day. He was beatified on May 17, 1992, and canonized on October 6, 2002.

Controversies

Escrivá is a polarizing figure, and over the years the interpretation of his life has become one of the primary battlegrounds on which debates over Opus Dei have been fought. In this section we will review the most prominent controversies over Escrivá, attempting to provide a summary of the arguments on both sides.

Escrivá's Personality

Some critics suggest that Escrivá lacked the virtues of a saint. He was vain, they say, often controlling, and somewhat paranoid, with an explosive temper. In some cases, such claims come not from revisionist historians but from firsthand witnesses and former Opus Dei members who knew Escrivá in his lifetime. These critical accounts, however, are contradicted by other witnesses—early members of Opus Dei; high-ranking churchmen who were familiar with Escrivá; and politicians, businesspeople, and journalists with whom he had dealings.

Miguel Fisac and María Angustias Moreno

Miguel Fisac was one of that small band who made the trek with Escrivá across the Pyrenees. Fisac, a member of Opus Dei from 1936 to 1955, has described Escrivá as a "very complicated and disconcerting" figure who issued "harsh judgments" and "never spoke well of anyone, inside or outside the Work," including his closest collaborator, Portillo. (Defenders note that there is film footage of Escrivá praising Portillo.) Escrivá felt defensive about his control over the spirit of Opus Dei, Fisac charged, so much so that he resented the success of a book written by an Opus Dei priest, Father Jesús Urteaga, explaining the group's spirituality. Fisac said that Escrivá was especially scathing toward men and women in religious orders. He said he personally witnessed cases in which people had been "humiliated" by Escrivá. An architect, Fisac also criticized Escrivá for spending "millions of dollars" on Villa Tevere, the Roman headquarters, for things of "little taste" that were nevertheless "very important" to him.

María Angustias Moreno was a numerary from 1959 to 1973 who held senior posts within the women's branch of Opus Dei. Moreno wrote a 1976 book about her experiences inside Opus Dei, *El Opus Dei: Anexo a una historia*. In it, she said that if Escrivá is indeed a saint, that designation cannot be based on his "simplicity and humility." She contends, for example, that inside Opus Dei in her day, many priests, such as Alvaro del Portillo and Salvador Canals, had achieved sufficient distinction to merit the ecclesiastical title "monsignor." But as long as Escrivá was alive, only *he* was called "monsignor" inside the Work. Further, Moreno alleged, Escrivá never attended the funeral of a cardinal or other dignitary. He would receive VIPs only at Villa Tevere, as if they had to come to him. Moreno called Escrivá a "dictatorial and arrogant" personality. In fact, when Escrivá died in 1975, she wrote that her conditioning as a member of Opus Dei led her to be dumbfounded that something as human as death could happen to "the Father."

María del Carmen Tapia

One of the most important set of observations on Escrivá comes from a former Venezuelan numerary, María del Carmen Tapia, in her book *Beyond the Threshold: A Life in Opus Dei*, published in 1992. Tapia was a numerary from 1948 to 1966, and for five of those years she lived and served at the Rome headquarters of the women's branch of Opus Dei. She arrived in Rome in 1952 with another numerary, María-Luisa Moreno de Vega, to assist Escrivá in establishing the first connections between the headquarters in Rome and the incipient new foundations of Opus Dei women in England, Ireland, the United States, Germany, and some countries in South America, until the women's central government was established a few months later. She held two important positions in the central government, and she also headed the Opus Dei Printing Press. During those years, she had almost daily contact with Escrivá. Tapia writes that Escrivá had a rather intense and forceful character, and she noticed a tendency in Escrivá to berate anyone who did not accomplish tasks to perfection. She says she suppressed any negative reaction because she had been conditioned to regard "the will of the Father" as tantamount to "the will of God."

For ten years Tapia was the directress, or top official, of the women's branch in Venezuela, until she was called to return to Rome. In her last year in Venezuela, she said, serious "slanders" against her might have begun to reach Rome. Shortly after her arrival at Villa Sacchetti, the headquarters of the women's branch in Rome, she was placed in what she describes as "virtual arrest," "deprived of the most basic freedom," for several months, until she eventually left Opus Dei. Tapia says that Opus Dei even kept her personal documents; except for the passport that was given to her a few hours before she left Rome, they were never returned. The last day of her stay, she said, she was confronted by Escrivá, who raved at her, hurling a series of slurs, accusing her of being full of "bad spirit" and "worthless." She also claims that he warned her that if she ever spoke about what she had experienced during those months in Rome, she would be dishonored. This was the last time she met Escrivá.

During the process leading to Escrivá's 1992 beatification, Tapia volunteered to offer her memories as testimony. The church tribunal in charge of the process, however, did not permit her to testify, a decision she attributes to "regrettable and slanderous information" about her that she says some authorities in Opus Dei provided to the tribunal. That account is supported by *El Pais,* the most read Spanish newspaper, which obtained confidential records from the Madrid tribunal, including the testimony of Bishop Javier Echevarría, the current prelate of Opus Dei and Escrivá's former secretary. In that testimony, sworn before a panel of judges and intended to be confidential, Echevarría was asked to explain the circumstances under which Tapia left Opus Dei, and he referred to behaviors that had been "perverse," without adding detail.

Today, Tapia says that the hardest part is that these "false assessments" still exist as a document and remain to this day in the Holy See. She hopes that Opus Dei will formally retract the negative statements made about her during the beatification process. She has put this request to Opus Dei, asking that "the slanderous document be withdrawn, removed and rectified once and for all for the sake and for the love of truth and justice." Tapia said she sees this as a smear on her and her family's good name, and believes that Opus Dei has a moral responsibility to correct the record.

On the occasion of the canonization of Escrivá in 2002, Tapia said in response to inquiries from reporters that the "slanderous misinformation" given to Escrivá by advisers he trusted made Escrivá an involuntary victim, causing him to react in a very unfortunate way. In an interview with the Catholic News Service, she said, "Faith was, in my opinion, the most relevant feature in the life of Monsignor Escrivá: his unshakeable confidence in God." Tapia said that people who expected her to provide damning testimony in the beatification process would have been "surprised and disappointed" by what she planned to say. In the last Spanish edition of Tapia's book *Tras el Umbral: Una vida en el Opus Dei* (Ediciones B, Barcelona, 2004), her dialogues with several international press agencies in relation to the canonization of Escrivá are included. She states clearly her position on Opus Dei, expressing forgiveness and understanding toward the human condition of those who hurt her so badly and placing herself under God's judgment as the only One able to judge.

Julián Herranz

The negative memories are balanced by friends and coworkers who insist on noting Escrivá's good humor, compassion, and spiritual depth.

Cardinal Julián Herranz, a Spaniard and member of Opus Dei since

1950, told me about the first time he met Escrivá, back in Madrid. A young man and a new member of Opus Dei had just died, and Escrivá arrived at the center where Herranz lived to lead the mourning:

> *Clearly he was feeling a very strong human anguish, like a father for his son. He asked, "Where, where?" We had carried [the deceased] into the chapel, and placed him in front of the Tabernacle. Escrivá entered, went to the front, knelt in front of the Tabernacle for a little while, then got up and led us in the responsorial for the repose of the soul. . . . When we entered the sitting room, he was another person. He was smiling very affectionately, almost beaming. This bothered me, because I had just seen him suffering, and now he seemed so different. We started to talk, and he said, "This is a sad day, but a happy one at the same time." The young man who died had suffered very much, because his parents were opposed to his vocation. Saint Josemaría said, "He won the last battle, he was faithful to the last breath to the will of God. This makes for a great life, always doing the will of God, never saying no to the Lord. . . . I'm happy, because I had a son like him. You should be happy that you had a brother like him."*
>
> *In that moment, I understood that this man was a saint. He knew how to live the double dimension, human and supernatural, of Christ. He was a very human man, very much a father, who suffered and struggled. At the same time, he was a great priest. He was a Christian completely configured to Christ.*

Javier Echevarría

Echevarría, Portillo's successor as head of Opus Dei, met Escrivá for the first time when Echevarría was sixteen and Escrivá was a mature man of forty-six. He said he was struck by Escrivá's "incredible sense of good humor" as well as the way Escrivá "took everyone seriously," including himself. Once, Echevarría said, when he was getting ready to finish high school, Escrivá said he'd like to talk with him. He invited Echevarría to join him for a drive to an Opus Dei center where Escrivá was to give some talks. Echevarría said he really didn't want to go, because whenever he took an extended drive he tended to get carsick. Nevertheless, he accepted. Sure enough, he said, as they were driving, he vomited all over himself and the car. In the pre–Vatican II heyday of clericalist Spain, to soil the car of a monsignor was a serious matter, and Echevarría said he was terrified. Escrivá, however, did not give any sign of disgust or annoyance. Instead, he stopped the car, picked up some paper towels and helped him clean off, and then went on as if nothing had happened. "This helped me understand the man," Echevarría said. "Not just the priest, but the man."

"He was a man with great patience," Echevarría said. "This doesn't mean that he couldn't get angry. Sometimes, he was upset, and he would show it. He could say things very, very clearly. But always after he spoke that way, he would say, 'If I spoke with the wrong tone, forgive me. The things I said to you, I saw them as true before God, and that's why I said them. I have to be sincere with you. But if the tone was too strong, forgive me, because I only wanted to give you this warning so that you would understand, so that you can be holy.' "

Observers of Opus Dei say this is one line of demarcation between the ex-members who have gone on to become critics and those such as Echevarría who have persevered. The critics tend to perceive Escrivá's stern reprimands as evidence of rage, or even of a personality disorder, while others took them as evidence of his fatherly love and concern.

Other Recollections

The late Cardinal Franz König of Vienna, one of the liberal champions of the Second Vatican Council and generally not regarded as a fan of conservative movements in the Church, nevertheless was impressed by Escrivá. In a 2001 interview, König said: "It was during the days of the Council that I met Blessed Escrivá de Balaguer. I'd been told that he fostered the role of the laity in everyday life, in the world of work. He was out to make the Church, without Roman collars or episcopal regalia, active through its lay members. In my opinion he was a man energized by a magnanimous spirit. We spoke a lot about what was happening in the world; I soon realized that in him I saw the Church alive. . . . I'd say that in his case the Holy Spirit found very receptive human ground."

Praise has come from other surprising ecclesiastical sources. Cardinal Carlo Maria Martini, former archbishop of Milan and long considered the "great white hope" of the liberal wing of the Church to succeed John Paul II as pope, said, "The spiritual fecundity of Monsignor Escrivá has something of the incredible in it. . . . Someone who speaks and writes as he does manifests to himself and others a sincere, genuine sanctity."

Escrivá was also a personal acquaintance of Archbishop Oscar Romero of El Salvador, today revered as a martyr and a champion of the liberation theology movement. On July 12, 1975, after Escrivá died, Romero wrote to Paul VI to ask, "in the name of the greater glory of God and the welfare of souls," that a cause be opened for Escrivá's beatification. Romero expressed "profound gratitude to the priests of Opus Dei, to whom I have confided, with much fruitfulness and satisfaction, the spiritual direction of my own life and that of my priests. . . . Monsignor Escrivá, whom I knew personally, could enter into a continuous dialogue with the Lord, with great humanity. It became immediately clear that he was a man of God, his behavior was full of delicacy, affection, and good humor." Historians note, however, that this letter was written before the 1977 murder in El Salvador of Father Rutilio Grande, an event that "radicalized" Romero and led him to distance himself from some earlier conservative views.

Even outside Catholic circles, Escrivá drew positive reactions. The Viennese psychiatrist Viktor Frankl, a Holocaust survivor and author of *Man's Search for Meaning,* once traveled to Rome with his wife and spoke with Escrivá. Afterward, Frankl summarized his impressions: "If I am to say what fascinated me particularly about his personality, it is, above all, the refreshing serenity which emanated from him and warmed the whole conversation. Next, the unbelievable rhythm with which his thought flows, and, finally, his amazing capacity for getting into immediate contact with those he is speaking to. . . . Msgr. Escrivá evidently lived totally in the present instant, he opened out to it completely, and gave himself entirely to it."

What is one to make of these contradictory impressions? When I visited Barbastro, the town of his birth, I asked locals about their famous native son. Many said with pride that Escrivá was a typical son of Aragon: blunt, fiery, salty-tongued, hardheaded, and proud, yet also warm, compassionate, full of good humor, with no trace of self-pity or self-doubt. If that was the man, perhaps the qualities described above could indeed coexist in the same soul. As Catholic author Robert Royal put it in a 1998 review of Tapia's book, some of the criticism of Escrivá "seems to assume that truly holy people must be without flaws, this despite the history of the saints from Peter and Paul down to the present."

Escrivá's Name

A particular form of the vanity charge surrounds two mutations in Escrivá's name. First, Escrivá frequently emphasized "de Balaguer," denoting the town in Catalonia from which his family originated. Fisac charged that Escrivá suffered from an inferiority complex with respect to the Spanish nobility, and that this was an attempt to artificially elevate his social standing. In 1934, Escrivá had been appointed rector of the Real Patronato de Santa Isabel, a royal foundation that included a school taught by the Sisters of the Assumption of Mary and a convent of Augustinian nuns. He held this position, except for the interruption of the civil war, until he moved to Rome in 1946; among other things, it gave him a canonical reason to remain in Madrid despite being ordained for the diocese of Saragossa. Fisac wrote that once the nuns of Saint Isabel introduced Escrivá to a group of nobles, who asked if he was part of the Escrivá de Romaní, a well-known aristocratic family. When he said no, Fisac said, the nobles reacted in a negative way that left a deep impression. Fisac said that Escrivá explained this to him, suggesting that this was why he wanted to emphasize "de Balaguer."

Another twist came in 1968, when Escrivá petitioned the Spanish Ministry of Justice to restore a minor noble title once granted to his family by the archduke of Austria in 1718: the Marquis of Peralta. A relative in Escrivá's maternal line, according to genealogical research, had served as minister for war and justice under the archduke. On July 24, 1968, the Ministry of Justice granted his request. Some critics of Escrivá have suggested that he had political motives for seeking out the title. In 1968, Franco was preparing to name Prince Juan Carlos as his successor, and some believe that Escrivá aspired to a key government position, thinking that his public stature, along with noble standing, would make him an ideal pick. Or perhaps, others suggested, Opus Dei was planning to take over the Knights of Malta, a prestigious Catholic organization dating back to the Middle Ages, whose constitutions require that the grand master be a celibate of noble birth. In fact, neither hypothesis was realized.

That Escrivá had a certain romantic affection for the Spanish nobility and the royal family, no one doubts. His official biographer, Opus Dei member Andrés Vázquez de Prada, writes that Escrivá's father, José, always felt a deep loyalty to the crown. Yet Escrivá's defenders say that in 1965, when aides first learned that he actually had the right to two noble titles (the Marquis de Peralta and Baron of Saint Philip), he declined to request either. Portillo, his close aide, pointed out to Escrivá that, as the eldest son in his family, under Spanish law only he could petition for the title. He could then transfer it to his younger brother, Santiago, in case it might prove of some benefit. Escrivá, according to Vázquez de Prada, consulted widely among the Spanish hierarchy before making the request, as well as in the Roman Curia, including Cardinals Angelo Dell'Acqua, an auxiliary bishop of Rome; Giacomo Antoniutti, prefect of the Congregation for Religious; Arcadio Larraona Saralegui, prefect of the Congregation for Rites; and Paolo Marella, president of the Secretariat for Non-Christians. Larraona, according to Vázquez de Prada, was especially strongly in favor of the idea, insisting that Escrivá had not just the right but the duty to claim the title. Larraona argued that Escrivá had always taught members of Opus Dei that they should exercise their rights as citizens. Escrivá never used the title and transferred it to his brother in a judicial act of June 22, 1972.

Escrivá and Franco

Because Opus Dei had its most notable growth in the period from the end of the Spanish civil war in 1939 to the death of Escrivá in 1975, a period of time that overlaps with the reign of Gen. Francisco Franco, Escrivá's attitude toward Franco has long been a subject of controversy. Some have suggested that Escrivá was pro-Franco and a close associate of the general, and that, as a consequence, a fascistic spirit has permeated Opus Dei. This presumed affinity for Franco has become a standard trope in the media: The *Village Voice,* for example, in 2004 characterized Escrivá as "the follower of Franco." *U.S. News & World Report* in 2003 noted, "Over objections to Escrivá's ties to Gen. Francisco Franco's authoritarian regime, Pope John Paul II canonized the priest last year." The *Chicago Tribune* in 2003 wrote, "When Gen. Francisco Franco won the war, Escrivá allied his movement with Franco's authoritarian regime, with several Opus Dei members occupying key positions in his government. Opus Dei officials, however, currently downplay Escrivá's actively supporting Franco."

This is not just the judgment of the popular press. Mary Vincent, a lecturer in history at the University of Sheffield in England, in a 1996 essay on political Catholicism in Spain in the twentieth century, wrote: "Of all Catholic institutions, the Opus Dei was most closely associated with the Franco regime . . . the Opus remained faithful to a regime its members clearly found congenial."

Before coming to Escrivá, it's worth noting that in the context of the Spanish civil war, in which anticlerical Republican forces killed 13 bishops, 4,000 diocesan priests, 2,000 male religious, and 300 nuns, virtually every group and layer of life in the Catholic Church in Spain was "pro-Franco." Criticism of Franco came from Catholic circles outside Spain—the neo-Thomist Jacques Maritain, for instance, insisted that Aquinas's "just war" theory could not be used to justify the indiscriminate bombing of civilians by Franco's Condor Legion. French Catholic writers François Mauriac and Georges Bernanos were also critical. Yet inside Spain, Catholic support was virtually uniform. As John Hooper notes in his book *The New Spaniards,* "Spanish prelates blessed Franco's troops before they went into battle, and were even pictured giving the Fascist salute." On the day of his victory, Franco received a telegram of congratulations from Pope Pius XII. Franco was anointed as caudillo, or leader, by Cardinal Isidro Gomá y Tomás, and laid his sword at the feet of the Christ of Lepanto.

In that milieu, the fact that Escrivá met Franco and did not challenge his authority is not terribly surprising. In Escrivá's public utterances, however, there is no instance in which he either praised or criticized the regime.

That silence applies as well to the later stages of Franco's regime, by which time Spanish Catholic opinion had passed from support to opposition. By the 1960s and 1970s, as Hooper notes, the era of the *curas rojos,* or "red priests," had arrived. Opposition priests exploited the legal privileges granted to the Catholic Church in order to allow strikes and sit-ins on Church property, aligning the Church with the pro-democracy movement. For the Basque country, where Franco's Spanish nationalism had always collided with Basque separatism, a special priests' prison had to be constructed in Zamora. In 1972, Pope Paul VI appointed a "red bishop" as auxiliary of a working-class suburb of Madrid, Bishop Alberto Iniesta Jiménez, a sign that the pope supported this more confrontational spirit.

When Cardinal Vincente Enrique Tarancón, a friend of Paul VI, was elected president of the bishops' conference in 1971, that too was an indication that the wheels were turning. A more moderate figure than Iniesta, Tarancón was nevertheless supportive of a democratic, pluralistic transition. During this ferment, Escrivá insisted that Opus Dei remain nonaligned.

In the 1930s and 1940s, when the overwhelming sentiment in Catholic Spain was pro-Franco, Escrivá's silence was therefore often read to betoken a hidden liberalism; by the 1960s and 1970s, when Catholic opinion had shifted, that same silence was interpreted as masking a pro-Franco conservatism.

In terms of the personal relationship between Escrivá and Franco, the record indicates that the two men knew each other but could not be described as "friends." Only three in-person meetings are documented: one in 1946, when Escrivá was assigned by the Spanish bishops' conference to preach at an annual retreat for Franco and his wife (each year a Spanish priest was selected to lead a retreat for the couple); a second in 1953, when an anti-Franco member of Opus Dei, Rafael Calvo Serer, had been defamed in the Spanish press, and Escrivá demanded an audience with Franco to defend him; and a third, in 1962, during negotiations with the Spanish government for the civil recognition of degrees granted by the Opus Dei–run University of Navarra in Pamplona. The spiritual exercises took place in the Pardo Palace from April 7 to April 12, 1946, and were arranged by Monsignor Leopoldo Eijo y Garay, bishop of Madrid.

Beyond this, after Escrivá moved to Rome in 1946, he would write Franco each time he returned to Spain, largely to make him aware of his presence on Spanish soil. These notes, some of which are reproduced in the Vázquez de Prada biography, are courteous but formal.

The presumption of a pro-Franco stance on the part of Escrivá and Opus Dei is usually anchored in the fact that in 1957, three members of Opus Dei became ministers in Franco's government. Alberto Ullastres Calvo, a professor of economic history at the University of Madrid, became minister of trade; Laureano López Rodó, a scientist, became technological secretary of the State Department (later he became minister without portfolio and commissioner for the economic development plan); and Mariano Navarro Rubio, managing director of Banco Popular, took over the Treasury Department. In 1962 another member of Opus Dei,

Gregorio López Bravo Castro, became minister of industry. In *Spain: Dictatorship to Democracy,* Raymond Carr and Juan Pablo Fusi described these Opus Dei ministers as "proponents of rapid—capitalist—growth and of the 'neutralization' of politics through prosperity."

Opus Dei was not the only Catholic organization in Spain that had members who served the Franco regime. The president of Catholic Action in Spain, Alberto Martín Artajo, was appointed minister of foreign affairs in July 1945, and before accepting the post, he received the official blessing of the Spanish bishops. Yet out of 116 ministers appointed by Franco in eleven governments between 1939 and 1975, only eight were members of Opus Dei. One of the eight died three months after being appointed, and four others held office during only one government. The Opus Dei ministers were considered part of the "technocratic" wing of the Franco regime, and some historians credit them with ushering in economic reforms that brought the Spanish economy into the modern world.

There were also numerous members of Opus Dei active in the anti-Franco opposition. Rafael Calvo Serer, a numerary of Opus Dei, was a liberal monarchist and influential literary figure. In 1953 he was expelled from the Consejo Superior de Investigaciones Científicas, or Superior Council for Scientific Research, for having published an essay in Paris critical of the Franco government. From 1966 he was publisher of the newspaper *Madrid,* until it was closed down under government censorship. Facing a series of judicial processes from Franco's courts, he went into exile in Paris. Upon his return he joined forces with the secretary of the Spanish Communist Party to found the Junta Democrática, designed to prepare the way for a democratic transition after Franco. Antonio Fontán, another member of Opus Dei, was a collaborator with Calvo Serer on *Madrid.* The offices of the newspaper were eventually blown up by pro-Franco forces. Manuel Fernández Areal, a numerary of Opus Dei, was jailed under Franco for critical pieces he published in the *Diario Regional de Valladolid.*

Father Pere Pascual, a priest of Opus Dei, was a lay numerary in the 1960s when he founded a clandestine union for journalists who were trying to push the Franco regime toward reform. Pascual was involved in one of the first serious protests against Franco's regime in Barcelona, which is recalled as the *caputxinada.* It took place in a friary of the Capuchin fathers in Sarrià, a neighborhood of Barcelona, between March 9 and 11, 1966. It began with a clandestine meeting of a new students' union, set up to rival the official students' association linked to the Falange. The union brought together people from a variety of political views, including the center-left and the clandestine Communist Party. One hour into the meeting on March 9, Franco's police arrived and demanded that everyone leave the friary and produce their documents. About two hundred of those taking part decided to remain, carrying on with their lectures, roundtables, and debates. For more than forty-eight hours they were guests of the Capuchins. When the meeting finally broke up, Pascual, who was among the organizers, was charged in a Spanish court and barred from publishing. In addition to Pascual, two other lay members of Opus Dei, Robert Espí and Francesco Brosa, took part in the *caputxinada*. The event had a strong symbolic value across Spain, in part because it embodied a nonviolent, cultural form of protest.

As a footnote to the above, the only cardinal, archbishop, or bishop in Spain ever jailed under Franco was Herranz, at the time a young Opus Dei numerary and university student. He had taken part in a small-scale act of civil disobedience that involved painting the slogan "We want an agrarian revolution in Andalusia" on a wall in Madrid. (Herranz's father had been a doctor in Andalusia, and Herranz said he was sensitive to issues of land reform and agrarian justice there.) Franco's police arrested the youths, thinking they were communists. They were held overnight in prison, but released after a search of Herranz's pockets turned up a rosary. That, according to police logic, was proof positive that he wasn't a communist. Of the episode, Herranz said: "I liked this [protest], especially before a society that was a little too flat, a little too much to the right."

This activity was happening with the knowledge of Escrivá, who, according to the principals involved, never intervened, either with members who served in the Franco government or with members who protested against it. Escrivá insisted that members of Opus Dei should be free to do as they please in secular politics, as long as they uphold the teachings of the Catholic Church.

Escrivá's private attitude toward Franco can perhaps best be glimpsed from a letter he wrote to Pope Paul VI in 1964, published by the Italian magazine *Famiglia Cristiana* in 1992. In it, Escrivá says he warned the Spanish bishops that, "If the revolution [that is, a violent anti-Franco uprising] were to break out, stopping it would be very difficult: and there-fore—using words of Sacred Scripture—'don't think that a single scape-goat [that is, Opus Dei] will be sufficient; all of you will be scapegoats.' One could gather ample collections of public and excessive eulogies which the bishops have addressed to the regime, which is something that no one can do with me, although I recognize that Franco is a good Christian."

Escrivá goes on to say he thinks it's important to prepare an evolution in the Spanish regime in order to avoid the threat of anarchy and commu-nism, which would harm the Church. He advises against creating a sin-gle Catholic political party in Spain, "because it could begin by being useful to the Church and end up using the Church, which would then be unable to free herself from it, and might instead have to suffer a kind of moral blackmail." Escrivá says the Church must be "above all group and all party commitments."

The overall impression one gets is that Escrivá strove to maintain neutrality with respect to the Franco regime, even if privately he felt some sympathy for a leader trying by his lights to be an upright Christian. A charge of being "pro-Franco" cannot be sustained, except in the generic sense that most Spanish Catholics were initially supportive of Franco. For one thing, as we have seen above, there was widespread participation by Opus Dei members in anti-Franco activity. The most one can say is that Escrivá was not "anti-Franco" either. His main concern seemed to be the stability of Spanish society, in order to hold radical movements at bay that might renew the horrors of the civil war. Escrivá did not attempt to dic-tate particular political solutions, either to his members or to the Spanish authorities.

Escrivá and the Second Vatican Council

Several critics of Opus Dei have charged that Escrivá was disillusioned by the Second Vatican Council, because of the liberalization it unleashed within Roman Catholicism, and was angry with the two popes of the council, John XXIII (1958–1963) and Paul VI (1963–1978). John Roche, an Opus Dei member from 1959 to 1973, has written that he heard Escrivá comment that he "no longer believes in popes or bishops, only in the Lord Jesus Christ," and that "the Devil was very high up in the Church." Former Opus Dei member Father Vladimir Felzmann, a British national of Czech origin, has said that Escrivá was so disgusted with the liturgical reforms of Vatican II that he once toyed with the idea of taking Opus Dei into the Orthodox Church, until he discovered that "their churches and congregations are too small for us."

For many members of Opus Dei, this is among the most difficult charges against Escrivá to comprehend, given their insistence that Escrivá anticipated Vatican II's "universal call to holiness." That is, Escrivá said that sanctity was not the exclusive province of a religious elite several decades before Vatican II formalized it as the teaching of the Church. Pope John Paul II, in an address to a meeting of university students connected to Opus Dei at Castel Gandolfo, the pope's summer residence, on August 19, 1979, said that Escrivá's vision "anticipated that theology of the laity that characterized the Church of the Council and the post-conciliar period."

At least in a formal sense, Escrivá did not oppose Vatican II as it was unfolding. Two Opus Dei priests, Portillo and Herranz, worked on one of the conciliar commissions that prepared the documents adopted at Vatican II. They staffed the commission on the Discipline of the Clergy, which prepared the decree *Presbyterorum Ordinis* on priestly life and ministry. Portillo also served as secretary for the Ante-Preparatory Commission on the Laity, and was a consultor to several other commissions during the four years that the council was in session. His books *Faithful and Laity in the Church* (1969) and *On the Priesthood* (1970) are largely the fruit of that experience. Portillo and Herranz carried out this work with Escrivá's knowledge and support.

Further, whatever Escrivá may have said in moments of frustration, it seems highly unlikely that he ever contemplated a formal break with the pope. Fidelity to the papacy, in fact, is an Opus Dei hallmark. In a recent biography of Escrivá, Italian journalist Andrea Tornielli quotes Cardinal Giovanni Cheli, former head of the Pontifical Council for the Pastoral Care of Migrants and Refugees, who said he spoke with Escrivá shortly after Pope John XXIII died. Cheli said he started to speculate about who the new pope might be, and Escrivá cut him short. "Even if the man elected pope were to come from a tribe of savages with rings in his nose and ears, I would immediately throw myself at his feet and tell him that the entire Work is at his unconditional service," Escrivá said. On another occasion, in 1969, Pope Paul VI's secretary of state, French cardinal Jean

Villot, informed Escrivá that something he had written about secular institutes was displeasing to the pope. Escrivá's response was unconditional: "Your Eminence, tell the Holy Father that for my part I am neither Luther nor Savonarola; that I accept with all my heart the decisions of the Holy Father, and that I will write him a letter to confirm my complete readiness to place myself, in the hands of the Roman Pontiff, at the service of the Church."

In the latter stages of Paul VI's pontificate, there was a falling out between Escrivá and the pope's key advisers, especially Monsignor Giovanni Benelli, who would go on to become the cardinal-archbishop of Florence and a major contender to be pope himself. This rupture, however, had little to do with doctrinal questions. Instead, part of the problem was that Benelli wished to fashion a Catholic political party in Spain along the lines of Italy's Christian Democrats. Escrivá refused to enlist Opus Dei, invoking the logic quoted above that a single Catholic party might not be a good idea for the Church, and further, that he could not dictate the political choices of his members. Benelli took this as an indication of disloyalty, and for some time relations between the Vatican and Opus Dei were cool. Repeated requests by Escrivá for an audience with Paul VI went unanswered, and there was no progress toward changing Opus Dei's canonical status.

No doubt Escrivá was troubled by much in the postconciliar period, which was marked by declining vocations, widespread resistance to certain aspects of papal teaching, and an avant-garde spirit in ritual and practice. In 1974, Escrivá told a Chilean journalist: "The Mother of God cries and suffers; Jesus has all of his wounds open another time. You know— and, disgracefully, this is not a secret—that the Church is very disturbed, there's much heretical propaganda within the Church of God. There are many persons who are creating scandal; people who should be light and certainty, who should promote faith but instead sow doubt, who should give strength and instead prompt weakness, who should inspire value but instead create fear."

As his defenders point out, Escrivá was not alone in drawing these conclusions. Pope Paul VI himself once said of the postconciliar unrest, "Satan's smoke has made its way into the temple of God through some crack." Pope Benedict XVI, when he was John Paul II's top doctrinal official, described an "avalanche" of decline after Vatican II: "I am convinced that the damage we have incurred in these twenty years is due, not to the 'true' council, but to the unleashing *within* the Church of latent polemical and centrifugal forces; and *outside* the Church it is due to the confrontation with a cultural revolution in the West: the success of the upper middle class, the new 'tertiary bourgeoisie,' with its liberal-radical ideology of individualistic, rationalistic and hedonistic stamp."

Liberal Catholics often see such sentiments as indicating a failure of nerve. Whatever the merits of that diagnosis, it does not seem to apply to Escrivá any more than to a broad swath of conservative Catholic opinion.

The Quality of Escrivá's Thought

Some critics have charged that Escrivá's spiritual teaching is banal and unoriginal, that its merits have been exaggerated through a "cult of personality" formed in Opus Dei around "the Father." Such criticism tends to focus especially on Escrivá's best-known work, *The Way*.

This is not just a sentiment of embittered ex-members, or liberal critics. Hans Urs von Balthasar, the Swiss theologian who inspired the Communio movement in Catholic theology and who has become a favored source for the Church's conservative wing, wrote in 1963 that he felt *The Way* provided an "insufficient spirituality" to support a worldwide religious organization. In 1979, von Balthasar wrote to a Swiss newspaper that had cited him in a negative article about Opus Dei, stipulating that he had indeed expressed reservations about *The Way,* but this did not justify an attack on Opus Dei *tout court*. Still, he did not soften his critique of *The Way*. In 1984 the Swiss TV service for the German language interviewed von Balthasar at his home in Basel. A journalist reminded von Balthasar that he had once defined *The Way* as a "little manual for Boy Scouts at the upper level." Von Balthasar responded, "I would still hold to that position today."

Von Balthasar is not alone in his judgment. Kenneth Woodward, for many years the chief religion writer for *Newsweek,* wrote in his book *Making Saints,* "Escrivá was an unexceptional spirit, derivative and often banal in his thoughts, personally inspiring perhaps but devoid of original insights." One French literary critic denounced *The Way* as "a vulgar, egotistical, and mediocre vision."

Yet *The Way* has not sold four and a half million copies worldwide without having its fans. The Cistercian monk and popular spiritual writer

Thomas Merton once said of the *The Way,* "It will certainly do a great deal of good by its simplicity, which is a true medium for the Gospel message." Then-cardinal Albino Luciani of Venice, who would later become Pope John Paul I, praised the author of *The Way* on July 25, 1978, as "this revolutionary priest who was vaulting over traditional barriers, pointing out mystical goals even to married people."

Sympathetic readers of Escrivá say that *The Way* was a collection of notes and insights jotted down in haste to provide spiritual guidance to young Spaniards at the time of the civil war, and thus does not represent the most mature form of his thought. For that, they say, one should turn to his last book, *Christ Is Passing By,* and to a homily entitled "Passionately Loving the World" delivered at the University of Navarra on October 8, 1967, and published in a 1974 collection, *Conversations with Msgr. Escrivá,* which also contains transcripts of interviews Escrivá gave to various press outlets around the world.

Consider these extracts from "Passionately Loving the World":

You must realize now, more clearly than ever, that God is calling you to serve him in and from the ordinary, secular and civil activities of human life. He waits for us every day, in the laboratory, in the operating theater, in the army barracks, in the university chair, in the factory, in the workshop, in the fields, in the home and in all the immense panorama of work. Understand this well: there is something holy, something divine hidden in the most ordinary situations, and it is up to each one of you to discover it.

I often said to the university students and workers who were with me in the thirties that they had to know how to materialize their spiritual lives. I wanted to warn them of the temptation, so common then and now, to lead a kind of double life: on the one hand, an inner life, a life related to God; and on the other, as something separate and distinct, their professional, social and family lives, made up of small earthly realities.

No, my children! We cannot lead a double life. We cannot be like schizophrenics, if we want to be Christians. There is only one life, made of flesh and spirit. And it is that life which has to become, in both body and soul, holy and filled with God: we discover the invisible God in the most visible and material things.

> *The genuine Christian approach—which professes the resur-*
> *rection of all flesh—has always quite logically opposed "dis-*
> *incarnation," without fear of being judged materialistic. We can,*
> *therefore, rightly speak of a Christian materialism, which is boldly*
> *opposed to those materialisms which are blind to the spirit.*

Reading such passages, it becomes easier to understand why dynamic young intellectuals such as Raimundo Panikkar found Escrivá's teaching attractive. Panikkar was part of the Opus Dei brain trust in the early years and has gone on to become part of Catholicism's theological avant-garde, especially on issues of religious pluralism.

Ocáriz, the vicar-general of Opus Dei and probably the group's most accomplished theologian, said in response to a question that he believes Escrivá could one day be declared a doctor of the Church, meaning a saint particularly known for having an unusual depth of understanding and orthodoxy. "I think his was an original contribution comparable to other Doctors of the Church, but the question of such a distinction also depends on many others factors, like whether it's opportune," Ocáriz said. "It's unpredictable." There are currently thirty-three recognized doctors of the Church, the most recent addition to the list being Saint Thérèse of Lisieux, who died in 1897.

Jutta Burggraf, an Opus Dei numerary who teaches theology at the University of Navarra, conceded that theology was not Escrivá's most distinctive gift. She said he was a "founder first, then a theologian," contrasting him with von Balthasar, who founded the Community of Saint John in Basel, but was "a theologian first, then a founder."

Escrivá and Hitler

Father Vladimir Felzmann, an ex–Opus Dei member, in a January 13, 1992, interview in *Newsweek* magazine, alleged that Escrivá had once said to him that Hitler had been "badly treated" by world opinion because "he could never have killed six million Jews. It could only have been four million at the most." Felzmann said Escrivá made the comment to him, alone, outside the Aula Magna of the Roman College of Opus Dei, during the interval of a film on the war. Opus Dei spokespersons have said they find it implausible that Escrivá made such a remark.

In a statement released January 11, 1992, Felzmann clarified that he was not suggesting that Escrivá was anti-Semitic, but that because of his antipathy to communism, Escrivá was "pro-Hitler and pro-Germany." Another phrase widely attributed to Escrivá, though never verified as authentic, has the same flavor: "Hitler against the Jews, Hitler against the Slavs, means Hitler against Communism."

In some circles, despite Felzmann's disclaimer, these rumors have tainted Escrivá with the charge of being anti-Semitic. The *Jerusalem Post* of October 20, 2003, for example, in an editorial about the pending beatification of Anne Catherine Emmerich, a nineteenth-century German nun whose visions were the basis of Mel Gibson's movie *The Passion of the Christ*, said she was merely the latest in a series of anti-Semitic saints. The *Post* listed "Opus Dei founder Josemaría Escrivá de Balaguer, Pope Pius IX, the Polish priest Maximilian Kolbe and Alojzije Stepinac, archbishop of Zagreb in the 1940s who supported the pro-Nazi regime in Croatia" in this category.

One documentary source for Escrivá's attitude toward the Jewish people, frequently cited by spokespersons for Opus Dei, is a video clip from February 14, 1975, during a meeting in Venezuela. A member of the audience rose to ask Escrivá a question, and the exchange runs like this:

> **Speaker:** "Father, I'm Jewish . . ."
>
> **Escrivá:** "I love the Jews very much because I love Jesus Christ madly, and he is Jewish. I don't say he was, but he is. *Iesus Christus eri et hodie ipse et in saecula*. Jesus Christ continues to live and he is Jewish like you. And the second love of my life is also Jewish—the Blessed Virgin Mary, Mother of Jesus Christ. So I look on you with affection. . . .
>
> **Speaker:** I think you have answered my question, Father.

Several Jewish sources have witnessed to what they consider Escrivá's affinity for Judaism. For example, Rabbi Angel Kreiman, former chief rabbi of Chile and vice president of the World Council of Synagogues, spoke at a congress on Escrivá in Rome in 2002: "Many of Josemaría Escrivá's concepts call to mind the Talmudic tradition and reveal his profound love for the Jewish world. . . . That which most likens his teaching to Judaism is the vocation of man to serve God through creative work, perfecting creation every day, through perfection of work." Kreiman, who lost his wife in 1994 in the bombing of a Jewish social service agency in Argentina, added, "Opus Dei members helped me, right from the beginning of my seminary studies, to persevere in my vocation, and I have also seen them do it with other rabbis, for which I am deeply grateful." Spanish Rabbi Simón Hassan Benasayag wrote, "The invention of a Nazism or of an anti-Semitism on the part of the Founder is fantasy at its most extreme."

As far as Opus Dei today is concerned, there is little indication of any residual anti-Semitism. The Israeli ambassador to the Holy See, Oded Ben-Hur, told me in a December 2004 interview that his personal experiences with Opus Dei "have always been positive," and that he has "never detected any traces" of anti-Semitism. Ben-Hur has a good working relationship with Opus Dei in Rome; in fact, my first meeting with Bishop Javier Echevarría, the current prelate of Opus Dei, was at a luncheon at Ben-Hur's Rome residence.

Felzmann has made a related charge, originally voiced in 1992 and repeated in 2001, that all the male members of Opus Dei in 1941 (at the time about fifty) volunteered for Spain's "Blue Division" to fight on the Eastern Front with the German army against Russia. Spanish historian Alfredo Méndiz, a member of Opus Dei, responded to Felzmann, arguing that many idealistic young Spanish Catholics, not just Opus Dei members, volunteered to fight the Bolsheviks. Some members of Opus Dei, though not all, volunteered, but none actually went. In any event, Méndiz said, what drove Spaniards to side with the Blue Division was not anti-Semitism or affection for Hitler, but a desire to fight against Stalin, seen as the enemy of religion.

Finally, there is an irony worth noting, which is that opposition to Opus Dei from the far right has sometimes criticized Escrivá and Opus Dei for being "crypto-Jewish." In 1942 a professor of law in Spain associated with the Falange noted that some members of Opus Dei had founded a society called Socoin, an acronym for Sociedad de Colaboración Intelectual. This professor argued that the actual meaning of the term comes from rabbinical Hebrew, where the term *socoim* referred to a sect of murderers. He suggested that Opus Dei was a "Jewish sect of Freemasons," or at least "a Jewish sect connected to Freemasonry." In 1994 a publishing house in Colombia called Orion Publications put out a book called *Opus Judei,* devoted to exposing "the Hidden Judaism of Opus Dei." The book alleges that secret Jewish currents in Spain in the twentieth century infiltrated Opus Dei, and that much of Opus Dei's symbolism and vocabulary comes out of the Jewish mystical tradition of the Kabbalah. It further suggests links between the financial operations of Opus Dei and "international Judaism."

Escrivá in Person

Whatever one makes of Escrivá's positions on Spanish politics or Vatican II, these were not the qualities that packed halls around the world when he traveled, or that sold tens of millions of copies of *The Way,* or that caused devotion to him to spread after his death. To some extent, one could attribute these phenomena to a well-oiled Opus Dei marketing machine, though that may be giving Opus Dei too much credit. As with any sales force, ultimately they're only as good as the product they're pitching. Something about the man had to stir people's souls, otherwise the vast crowds for his beatification and canonization, in numbers that far outstripped the total worldwide membership of Opus Dei, would be inexplicable. One does not have to regard Escrivá as a saint to realize that there had to be something charismatic about him.

Fortunately, one isn't left entirely to guess what those qualities might have been, because Escrivá was captured on film often enough to provide one way of gaining a basic sense of his personality. He wasn't the media sensation that Mother Teresa was, but unlike Francis or Ignatius of Loyola, one can at least see Escrivá preaching and teaching in a variety of settings over a period of years. The films are available in a series called *Meetings with St. Josemaría Escrivá.*

The first impression one gets from watching Escrivá "live" is his effervescence, his keen sense of humor. He cracks jokes, makes faces, roams the stage, and generally leaves his audience in stitches in off-the-cuff responses to questions from people in the crowd. It's an impression that stands in stark contrast to the foreboding public image that Escrivá and Opus Dei usually carry; he comes off in these sessions as a smiling, warm figure. There's nothing Sturm und Drang about him. Second, Escrivá is implacably positive. Anytime he's offered an opportunity to polemicize, or to criticize a current in the culture or the Church, he changes the subject, often praising the questioner: "I know you are a good mother," or "I'm sure your newspaper kiosk is well run and a worthy offering to God."

Finally, his preference for the personal rather than for the structural is clear. If asked about social concerns, Escrivá spends most of his time talking about individual spirituality, the need for personal conversion, and sanctity. Perhaps because of that instinct, he had a capacity to seem to speak directly to specific persons, even in very crowded settings.

On June 26, 1974, for example, Escrivá spoke in Buenos Aires, Argentina. He took a question from a recent convert from Islam, who jokingly assured Escrivá that the three women standing near him were his wife and two daughters, not a "harem." Escrivá complimented the man on his sincerity, but added that he has "great affection for the Muslims." Among other things, he laughed, "There are now two editions of *The Way* in Arabic, so they have me in their pocket." The questioner then wanted to know what Opus Dei should do about the "filth" that was coursing through the culture, in the form of sexual promiscuity, pornography, and so on. Escrivá's advice? "First, be a good husband to your wife, and a good father to your daughters," he said. "Take care of your interior life. Do that first, and think of these other things later."

Another man asked Escrivá's advice on a practical matter. He coached a little league soccer team, but his wife complained that it took him away from home too much. Should he quit? Escrivá smiled, then quipped: "No, keep coaching. Just let your wife be the referee sometimes." More seriously, he said, "I believe that if your wife could speak right now, she would say she wants you to continue, because you're not just taking care of these boys' bodies, but their souls. But be a good husband as well." A woman in a wheelchair asked what the handicapped can do for Opus Dei. Escrivá said, "First, I want to tell you that I envy you. You are not paralyzed, not at all. You have an incredibly active interior life." He then encouraged her to offer her suffering to God so that priests may be good, may celebrate the sacraments well, and may purify their hearts.

On February 11, 1975, Escrivá spoke to an open-air crowd in Caracas, Venezuela. A woman rose to say that she had a seriously disabled child at home and was in contact with other parents who had children in similar conditions. What could Escrivá say to her? "Congratulations," Escrivá began. The woman appeared puzzled. "Congratulations," he repeated, "because this child is a great honor for you. God sends these children to families that have an enormous capacity to love." He encouraged the woman to be in contact with associations who work with disabled children and to get the help she needs, but never to stop feeling proud of the privilege God had given her.

A man rose to say that while he was Catholic, his mother was Presbyterian. What could he do to bring her to the truth of the Catholic faith? "Do your work well," Escrivá responded. "Be a good son, a faithful husband, and for the rest, be patient." Escrivá said he would pray for the man's mother. "Would it offend her if you asked her to pray for me?" he asked. The questioner indicated not, and Escrivá replied, "Then ask her, will you?" Another man said he had been waiting weeks to ask Escrivá a question, but now that the time had come, all he really wanted to do was give him a hug. Escrivá waved him onstage, where the two men embraced, and the questioner obviously did not want to let go. Escrivá managed to extricate himself, and then joked: "I feel like I've just hugged every man in Venezuela."

These situations did not call for deep theological reflection, but rather pastoral care at the retail level, and Escrivá delivered. He was capable of being firm, and made no effort to hide an uncompromising Catholic moral stance; at one point in Venezuela, a woman asked him about purity and he did not mince words. "People should abstain from sex outside of marriage and should remain faithful within it, staying with their spouse until death . . . period." But even in these moments, they were not the maledictions of a Bible-thumper, nor the hand-wringing of someone who believes that the world is doomed. Critics say that this was Escrivá's public face, and that he could be a darker figure in private. But at least as far as the public person goes, Escrivá came across as animated, passionate, and optimistic, a combination that goes a long way to explaining his appeal.

Summary

Perhaps the single greatest problem in evaluating Escrivá is that reactions to him tend to pass through one or more filters. Observers interpret his life in terms of their judgments on Opus Dei, or the Catholic Church and its vicissitudes after the Second Vatican Council, or the political history of Europe in the twentieth century. None of this is very helpful in coming to an honest assessment of the man. Sometimes, too, the positions surrounding Escrivá are so extreme, on all sides, that it's hard to glimpse the real person.

His defenders can do more harm than good. In their passion, some Opus Dei members can make it sound like Escrivá was always the smartest, the greatest, and the most holy, someone who always saw farther than others. I have heard a number of Catholic theologians in Rome, for example, grind their teeth at the suggestion that it never occurred to anyone before Escrivá in the twentieth century that laypeople might have a vocation to holiness. What about Saint Francis de Sales or Saint Alphonsus Liguori, these theologians ask? For that matter, what about Saint Francis of Assisi, who originally conceived of the Franciscans as a lay movement, was never a priest, and accepted ordination as a deacon only because the Vatican said he couldn't lead his community without it? What about Saint Angela Merici in Italy, who in the sixteenth century envisioned a group of women who were consecrated to God but who lived and exercised their apostolate in the world, without habit or life in common? What about the Jesuit, Père Pierre-Joseph Picot de Clorivière, who during the French Revolution founded new societies of laymen and women who would be "religious before God but not before men"? Granted that Opus Dei has a different structure and vision, isn't there some precedent?

To their credit, other members of Opus Dei recognize the need for a more mature approach to "the Father." One priest in the United States told me that Opus Dei has to get over the notion that everything must remain forever as Escrivá decreed it, because not everything he ever thought or said came directly from God. A numerary in England told me that he hopes someone will write a new biography of Escrivá with a more "warts and all" approach, because reading the existing literature, one is dogged by a sense that this is just "too good to be true."

On the other hand, there is also little doubt that in their opposition to Opus Dei, some observers are driven to demonize even seemingly innocuous episodes of Escrivá's life, such as the dusting off of a minor noble title in 1968 in order to pass it on to his brother in 1972.

Trying to sift through the varying presentations of Escrivá, the charges and countercharges, one is left with the impression of a complex, singular personality. At his best Escrivá could be warm, compassionate, full of life and laughter, and deeply thoughtful on spiritual questions, not to mention a dedicated and tireless priest. At his worst he could be prone to anger and sometimes derisive about those with whom he disagreed, up to and including top authorities in the Church. Yet nowhere is it written that saints have to be perfect people, and there is testimony that, even as a flawed human being, Escrivá changed people's lives for the better, giving them a sense of being loved by God and called to help build God's reign.

As Escrivá himself wrote in *Christ Is Passing By*, "Let's not deceive ourselves: in our life we will find vigor and victory *and* depression and defeat. This has always been true of the earthly pilgrimage of Christians, even of those we venerate on the altars. Don't you remember Peter, Augustine, and Francis? I have never liked biographies of saints which naively—but also with a lack of sound doctrine—present their deeds as if they had been confirmed in grace from birth. No. The true life stories of Christian heroes resemble our own experience: they fought and won; they fought and lost. And then, repentant, they returned to the fray."

OPUS DEI·FROM THE INSIDE

❋

Chapter Three

SANCTIFICATION OF WORK

*Walter and Norma Nakasone are the children of Japanese im-*migrants to Peru, and both grew up in families that converted to Catholicism upon their arrival in Latin America. Walter, thirty-eight, is in the third generation of his family to settle in Peru, while Norma, thirty-nine, is in the second of hers. They have three children: Naoki, eleven; Naohiko, eight; and Naoyuki, four.

In 2000, both Walter and Norma became supernumeraries of Opus Dei, which they encountered for the first time as university students in Lima. Norma was the first to attend Opus Dei events while Walter was more skeptical, saying he "didn't want to lose my identity." Both eventually decided, however, that Opus Dei offered a valuable path of spiritual formation. Walter today runs a small laundry that his father founded, called the Real (Royal) Laundry, in the working-class Rimac neighborhood of Lima. During an interview in June 2004, in their apartment one floor above the laundry, I asked Walter to explain what the "sanctification of work," perhaps the most important core principle of Opus Dei, means to him.

"Before I joined Opus Dei, when I was cleaning shirts in my dad's laundry, I would often let little stains slide by, especially if they were under the collar or someplace else hard to reach," he said. "It was too much hard work, and I would tell myself that if anybody ever complained, I could always say that I hadn't seen the stain. But after joining Opus Dei, I take this much more seriously. I try to get out all the stains, however tiny or hard to see," Nakasone said. "I realize now that I'm not just cleaning the shirt for the client, but for God."

Quite an advertisement, among other things, for laundries staffed by Opus Dei members.

Nakasone thereby expressed a central idea of Escrivá, which is that all work, even the most menial or hidden, is ultimately for God. Opus Dei members tell the story of Escrivá taking his early followers up to the top of the cathedral in Burgos, capital of the Nationalist zone during the Spanish civil war. He asked them to look at the ornate stone carvings at the pinnacle of the cathedral and noted that these exquisitely crafted pieces were completely invisible from the ground level. The vast majority of visitors to Burgos would never see them. Escrivá said that the craftsmen who fashioned the carvings would have understood the spirit of Opus Dei. These works of art, he said, were made for God's eyes.

The concept of sanctification of work was at the heart of Escrivá's message, and it is as close to a "prime directive" as there is in Opus Dei. Escrivá compared the office desk and store counter, or for that matter the steam room at Nakasone's laundry, to the altar of the Mass; they are all places where Christ is made present, Escrivá said, albeit in different ways, and they are all places where the drama of human redemption is played out. Extending the image, Escrivá taught that through the sacrament of baptism, Christians are made "the priests of our own existence," which means that just as a priest offers bread and wine to God at the Mass, so each Christian is to lift up and offer to God his or her daily work.

Genesis 2:5 says that the human person is made to work, and thus, according to Escrivá, work is the right environment in which to find God. In this sense, Escrivá rejected the medieval theological notion that work is a consequence of original sin and a form of punishment. Instead, he said, only the tedious side of work is a result of sin; work itself is noble, and it is precisely through work that the human person is fulfilled and participates in God's act of creation. As Escrivá once put it, "Anyone who thought that our supernatural life is built up by turning our back on work would not understand our vocation. For us, in fact, work is a specific means to sanctity . . . External work should not cause any interruption in prayer, just as the beating of our heart does not interrupt the attention we give to our activities, whatever they may be."

This is the reason that Saint Joseph is a key figure for Opus Dei. Saint

Joseph, the carpenter, is the patron saint of workers, the one who taught Christ how to work as he grew up in Nazareth. Each year, members must renew their contract with Opus Dei on March 19, in honor of Saint Joseph. According to Escrivá, Jesus did not start redeeming the world with the Sermon on the Mount, or with his entrance into Jerusalem. He spent thirty years in hard and hidden work in Joseph's workshop, and in that period he was already transforming and redeeming reality. Disciples of Christ are called to appreciate and sanctify the ordinary work of the world, Escrivá said, just as Christ did. Thus Escrivá's famous exhortation: One must "sanctify work, sanctify oneself in work, and sanctify others through work."

Escrivá's approach appeals to people who take their work seriously, even in the most surprising contexts. For example, the former coach of Italy's national soccer team, Giovanni Trappatoni, said in January 1999, "Josemaría Escrivá has taught many athletes that their efforts in training and in competition, their companionship with teammates, their esteem for their opponents, their humility in victory and good spirit in defeat, are a specific path for reaching God and for serving others." Trappatoni is a cooperator of Opus Dei.

Monsignor Fernando Ocáriz, vicar-general of Opus Dei and an accomplished theologian, said that sanctifying work as Escrivá understood it means "making one's work a real offering to God," which he said implies two things: 1) "seeking to do work well, because if I truly believe this act is an offering to God, it would be absurd not to try to do it well"; and 2) "having the correct intention to seek to serve God and others through this particular work." This, Ocáriz said, is "a battlefield, because there's always egoism, pride, and so on" that accompanies any human endeavor, but that's the nature of Opus Dei's spiritual path.

This emphasis on ordinary secular work as the setting for the drama of salvation also helps explain why Escrivá so ferociously resisted any comparison or assimilation of Opus Dei to a religious order. Though members of orders themselves often work—indeed, the famous motto of the Benedictines is *ora et labora,* "pray and work"—the religious life nevertheless involves some degree of retreat from the ordinary secular world. Escrivá believed instead that Opus Dei members should be fully immersed in the world.

Escrivá made a special point of noting that part of the "Spirit of the

Work" is excellence, not just from a spiritual point of view, but according to the highest standards of professional evaluation. The Opus Dei approach consists in "doing work well," as Escrivá put it, "with human perfection also, and fulfilling all professional and social obligations well." The idea is that you cannot offer work to God if it's badly done. This accent on doing a good job according to objective standards, and not just spiritualizing about it, was once expressed in pithy form by the French Catholic writer Etienne Gilson, who wrote in 1949: "They tell us that it was faith that built the Medieval cathedrals. Agreed . . . but geometry also played its part."

Based on this vision, one finds most members of Opus Dei to have a strong work ethic, and a great respect for professional competence wherever they find it. Again, from Escrivá: "What use is it telling me that so-and-so is a good son of mine—a good Christian—but a bad shoemaker? If he doesn't try to learn his trade well, or doesn't give his full attention to it, he won't be able to sanctify it or offer it to our Lord. The sanctification of ordinary work is, as it were, the hinge of true spirituality."

For many members, it was the idea of finding God and achieving holiness in and through their professional activity that was the original appeal of Opus Dei. For example, Russell Shaw, a well-known Catholic writer in the United States who once served as the secretary for public affairs for the U.S. bishops, and who is an Opus Dei supernumerary, said this was what first intrigued him: "There was something about this notion of a group of committed Catholic laymen, skilled in their professions, who were doing serious professional work and working seriously along spiritual lines. Somehow that caught my fancy," he said.

Applications

María José Font, fifty, is a Spanish lawyer and one of six partners at a major downtown law firm in Barcelona as well as a trained architect. Her specialty is commercial law for builders, and she handles deals for some of the biggest firms in Spain, routinely working ten-to-twelve-hour days in a high-pressure context. She studied at Harvard for three months while a young student, before making the decision to commit to life as a numerary. During a spring 2004 interview in her office, I asked what "sanctification of work" means in her work as an attorney.

"When a person is in a state of grace, living in the presence of God, offering God their work, it multiplies its effects," she said. "I don't just work for the sake of clearing my desk. I also offer whatever I'm doing for peace in Iraq, for example, or for the situation in the Congo, or hoping that the president of the United States will make the right decision about abortion, or whatever he has to deal with that day." In other words, Font explained, her work becomes prayer, and in that sense it has value at the spiritual level beyond its immediate professional consequences.

Obviously, she said, the sanctification of work also means that she strives to meet the highest secular standards in the legal profession, which among other things gives her a certain comfort level in dealing with the other partners in the firm, who are all male. "I have no problem with them, even though in many ways this is still a man's world. They listen to me," she said, "and part of the reason is because they know I'm good at what I do."

For Diane Lechner, a supernumerary in the Chicago area who is married with seven children, the primary setting in which the "sanctification of work" becomes practical is as a mother and homemaker. Though she has a bachelor's degree in speech and a master's in audiology, she said, "I knew I wanted to stay home when we had kids." At first, she said, this was a difficult adjustment, because like many young stay-at-home mothers, she struggled with nagging doubts about putting her career on hold. Around this time she met Opus Dei, and, she said, "I liked the fact that I could offer my work as a mother to God as a prayer.

"Opus Dei values motherhood and values marriage," Lechner said. "I found a lot of support, a lot of exchanges among mothers. To me, being a mother is the most challenging, rewarding job I could have here on earth. No one else can be a good mother to my children. Saint Josemaría said that all women's work is important, in the home and in the office, and I definitely believe that." The concept of sanctification of work, Lechner said, helped her see the most mundane tasks in a new light. "Clean that bathroom at home for your family," she said. "Work is never wasted. Nothing can undo work done as prayer, because you've gained eternal merit."

Later, she said, after her children were grown, she went to work as a sales associate at a high-end department store. There, she tried to apply the concept of sanctification of work not just in terms of doing her job well and attempting to be a positive influence on colleagues, but also by sanctifying her work environment in small ways. One trick, she said, was to make a small cross out of paper clips and leave it on the cash register. Then when she would look at it throughout the day, she would make small acts of mental prayer, thereby consecrating even the simple tasks of ringing up a sale or restocking a shelf.

Jim Burbidge, a supernumerary, is a London bus driver who works route 213, from Sutton to Kingston, taking in all of the southwest part of the city. The late November night in 2004 that I dropped by his home, I met his wife, Theresa, and two of their five children—Anne Marie, now attending university, and Dominic, who's still in high school. Jim and Theresa are both Opus Dei members, and have obviously tried to raise their children to be serious Catholics. Dominic, who greeted me in the coat and tie of an English comprehensive school, came off as an earnest young man full of certitudes about theology and the spiritual life. Jim, however, had a much simpler approach to understanding what "sanctification of work" means in his career. "I try to give people a good ride," he said. "I try to make sure the bus is clean, that things are orderly and calm. I try to greet people with a smile," he said, knowing that commuting to and from work can often be a stressful experience. Burbidge said he also prays for his passengers as he drives, offering up to God the intentions of every person who comes onto the bus.

Burbidge said he also tries to influence his colleagues by being a good friend, and, as the opportunity allows, sharing with them something of his faith life. He said he has occasionally invited colleagues to attend events of Opus Dei, though none so far have joined Opus Dei as a result. Burbidge said, however, that he doesn't see that as the point—he's trying to help them be better people and, as the circumstances warrant, be better Christians.

Fidelis Katonga, librarian at the University of Strathmore in Nairobi, Kenya, and a supernumerary, frames his reading of the sanctification of work in terms of human relations. "It gives me a positive attitude," he said. "At the end of the day, I have to give my best. I'm not doing it just for myself. Sometimes the students drive me up a wall, but I know I have to take it cool, not let it get to me. You keep your head on your shoulders, take things in stride, because this is a service to God. All those annoying students are actually opportunities God has given you to sanctify yourself and others. I don't just offer my own intentions, but of all the students I'm in charge of."

Ellen Royals, in her first year as a teacher at the Opus Dei–affiliated Oakcrest School for girls in suburban Washington, D.C., is not a member of Opus Dei, though both her father and mother are supernumeraries. She said she has heard about the idea of "sanctification of work" since she was a baby, and had a very simple answer when asked what it means to her. "I hate teaching Latin," she told me over a November 2004 interview at Oakcrest. As a first-year teacher, however, she got stuck with it. "I'd much rather be teaching history, literature, almost anything else. But if I came off that way in the classroom, the kids would know it. I have a job to do, and for those forty to fifty minutes every day the girls need to see me smiling, taking the task at hand, and doing it the best I can. What the idea of sanctification of work helps me to see is that I can get to heaven by doing this job. I want to cut corners sometimes, but remembering that helps me put 150 percent into everything I do."

John Hunt, a former community banker in the Chicago area, is today an Opus Dei supernumerary and executive director of a nonprofit foundation called the Alliance for Character Education that attempts to promote values-based instruction, a sort of "moral literacy," in schools. Hunt said that he first encountered Opus Dei over a buffet supper at the Northview Study Center in Chicago, largely because his boss had asked him to go. Hunt said he was attracted by the idea of sanctifying his work as a banker. For him, that meant above all taking a personal interest in his business associates.

"Opus Dei fosters this whole idea of friendship with people, that you can have an impact on someone's life if they're open and disposed to living their faith to a greater degree," Hunt said. "I was really attracted by the idea of taking business relationships to a deeper level. What Opus Dei has helped me do is to get together with someone in business, talking initially about surface things, but then pushing on by expressing interest in their family life and so on, until eventually we're talking about matters of the spirit and of faith. I've met a lot of folks over the years in business and civic circles, and for sure my friendships are deeper and stronger because of what I've learned in Opus Dei about sanctifying work."

Challenges

While the concept of sanctification of work is considered by members of Opus Dei to be a precious resource in their professional activity, often helping them to achieve levels of success they otherwise would have regarded as impossible, their affiliation with Opus Dei can also create practical difficulties. For one thing, given the climate of intrigue and suspicion that surrounds Opus Dei, especially in the wake of public episodes such as the Robert Hanssen spy case in the United States and publication of *The Da Vinci Code,* the very fact of being a member can sometimes create friction.

Bringing this up can elicit exasperated sighs from members of Opus Dei, since they tend to regard affiliation with Opus Dei as a private matter of their spiritual lives that is, or at least should be, irrelevant in terms of their capacity to do a job. For example, Vatican spokesperson and Spanish numerary Joaquín Navarro-Valls is a trained psychiatrist in addition to being a veteran correspondent for *ABC,* a major secular daily in Spain. As the main spokesperson for Pope John Paul II and now for Pope Benedict XVI, Navarro is legendary for his capacity to remain unflustered even by the most aggressive questions about the Catholic Church and the pope. Yet when it comes to his membership in Opus Dei, he sometimes runs out of patience.

In an interview for this book, I asked Navarro-Valls if being in Opus Dei had ever created problems in his work, and his rather testy response was, "What has that got to do with anything?" Later in the day he called me and said, "Look, John, it's as if somebody were to ask what difficulties in your reporting from the Vatican are created by the fact that your wife is Jewish. I mean, what difference does that make? What has it got to do with how well you do your job? Who cares?

"I was a foreign correspondent in Egypt, in Israel, and in Greece," Navarro said. "Inevitably I had to write on Islam, on Judaism, and on Orthodoxy. Nobody, neither public officials nor religious leaders, was the least concerned, or even curious, about my personal beliefs. They were concerned only with the accuracy and fairness of my reporting. Very much the same happened when I worked as a medical doctor in a hospital for fourteen years. They were interested in good medical attention, and that was what I tried to give them."

One understands the point, which is that members of Opus Dei want to be evaluated in the workplace not as members of Opus Dei, but as professionals held to the same standards as everyone else. Still, the practical reality is that life doesn't always work like that, especially when we're talking about membership in a group with the mystique of Opus Dei. For one thing, because members generally do not broadcast their connection to Opus Dei, sometimes they find themselves the object of whispering campaigns in the workplace, as coworkers speculate, "Are they or aren't they?" Then the member has to negotiate when it's appropriate to tell people and under what circumstances, and whether doing so in a generalized way would simply invite more anxieties than it might resolve. One especially delicate issue for numeraries is their commitment to celibacy, since offices and university campuses often have a very active social life. Knowing when to "play the celibacy card" can be a tough question to resolve.

For those members who work in or around the Catholic Church, the ecclesiastical controversies surrounding Opus Dei can create special complications. Russell Shaw's case may be emblematic. He joined Opus Dei in 1979 while still on the staff of the U.S. bishops' conference. He tells the story of how his colleagues reacted:

"At that time the general secretary of the bishops' conference was Bishop Thomas Kelly, a good friend of mine. We were close and got along very well. Kelly had the custom of opening the mail every day with senior staff. He and the associate general secretaries and his secretary, and I and maybe one or two other people, depending on the circumstances, would get together first thing in the morning and sit down with the day's mail, to determine what are the issues we've got to deal with today.

"After one of these sessions, Kelly gave me a high sign, as if to say, 'Will you please stay behind after the others have left?' So I stayed in the office with him, and I still remember he came to me, obviously embarrassed. He said something like, 'I hate to say this to you, but people are saying that you're a member of Opus Dei.' I'm sure he wanted me to say, 'In a pig's eye!' But I said, 'Well, actually I'm not technically a member yet, but I hope one of these days fairly soon I will be.' Then I explained my current status vis-à-vis Opus Dei, and he accepted it quite well. Once it was out on the table he was very gracious and gentlemanly about it.

"I don't recall having heard anything more about the subject from Kelly or anyone else around the bishops' conference. But I couldn't help but be aware that other people in the organization knew I was a member,

and that they were not all wildly enthusiastic about the idea. I still wonder, by the way, how I had been fingered as being a member of Opus Dei.
I wasn't doing anything strange as far as I know, talking oddly or levitat-
ing. I had started going to daily Mass in the chapel there, but a lot of other
people did that who weren't members. I don't know to this day what I did
that caused somebody to come to Kelly and say, 'Shaw is a member of
Opus Dei.' Maybe in the next world I'll find out."

The point is not that joining Opus Dei ruined Shaw's career, because
it has not. After finishing his service for the bishops, he went on to become spokesperson for the Knights of Columbus and now is a popular author and lecturer. Yet the connection to Opus Dei did generate an extra
source of tension; among other things, press criticism of Opus Dei would
sometimes bring Shaw into the picture. An article by the late Vatican
writer Peter Hebblethwaite in the *National Catholic Reporter* once suggested that Shaw was involved in a behind-the-scenes effort with a
Roman cardinal and the head of the Knights of Columbus to have the ban
on birth control in Paul VI's encyclical *Humanae Vitae* declared infallible,
something that Shaw laughingly denies. This may fall into the category of
"irritant" more than anything truly debilitating, but it does indicate that
the pursuit of secular excellence can have special complications for members of Opus Dei.

A further difficulty related to the Opus Dei work ethic is that, according to some ex-members, the standards for excellence may sometimes be
set too high. Especially for numeraries, the expectations for commitment
and accomplishment have been among the factors that they say helped
trigger their decision to leave. Sharon Clasen, for example, moved into the
Bayridge Center in Boston in 1981 as a freshman at Boston College, and
by May 1982, at the age of eighteen, she was a supernumerary in Opus
Dei. She had been counseled to become a supernumerary first, because
she was a convert to Catholicism. Three years later, in 1985, she became
a numerary. She then moved to an Opus Dei center of studies for women
called Brimfield, in Newton, Massachusetts. There, she was expected to
keep up her full-time academic work at Boston College, attend Opus Dei
formation classes in the evening, and be "available" to the center both for
helping out around the center and also for numerous social occasions.

"No matter if you have like this huge exam the next day they'll say,
'Well, your family is more important, and God will give you the grace to

pass your exam,' " Clasen said in a May 2004 interview. "Then people pray to the Holy Spirit. They do these novenas to the Holy Spirit, so they'll be inspired in their sleep to pass their exams, and so they'll put like a prayer card to the Holy Spirit under their pillow. But it never worked for me," Clasen said. In the end, she said, she felt "exhausted and drained," unable to meet what she considered "inhuman" expectations. Clasen has other concerns about Opus Dei, but said that the physical and psychological demands were among the key factors leading to her break with Opus Dei.

In the course of research for this book, I lived for five days in an Opus Dei residence for college students in Barcelona, Spain, called Colegio Mayor Pedralbes. Because of the different rhythms of Spanish culture, in which it is not at all unusual to have dinner at 10:00 P.M. and a social get-together at midnight, I was perhaps predisposed to find the experience wearying. Nevertheless, I was struck by the multiple demands placed on the numerary members: keeping up a full-time job, helping out in activities sponsored by the residence, and simply being "available" for get-togethers and other social activities. Moreover, there was an obvious expectation that numeraries would not only find a way to juggle these commitments, but do them all well. The numeraries with whom I spoke seemed fulfilled and content, but I could also see how a young person attracted to the idealism and challenge could, after a period of trying to live up to these demands, feel drained and damaged. As one Opus Dei numerary in the States put it, "This is not for the faint of heart."

A Catholic Form of Calvinism?

Despite the headaches that membership in Opus Dei may produce in terms of relations with colleagues, or the burnout that trying to live up to high expectations may cause, the real difficulty created by the concept of the sanctification of work probably lies on the spiritual level. The danger is that "sanctification of work," with its attendant emphasis on always doing one's work well, will translate into a cult of success, a kind of mania of accomplishment intended to show that one has the "correct intention" of which Ocáriz and others in Opus Dei speak.

The emphasis on excellence in secular work is part of the reason that Opus Dei has been accused of "elitism" over the years, since it is a spirituality with a certain white-collar appeal. It is no accident that Opus Dei runs one of the elite business schools in Europe, the Instituto de Estudios Superiores de la Empresa (IESE), located in Barcelona. There is something entrepreneurial and results-oriented about Opus Dei. Indeed, some critics have accused Opus Dei of being a sort of Catholic version of Calvinism, the idea being that one demonstrates one's election by God through worldly achievement and prosperity.

Even sympathetic observers of Opus Dei sometimes have this impression. Monsignor Joseph Obunga, for example, is secretary-general of the Uganda Episcopal Conference. Opus Dei arrived in Uganda just in 1996, and the first impression it has made on observers such as Obunga, who is not a member of Opus Dei, is that of an "elitist" organization.

"Opus Dei is committed, but it is committed only to the high class," Obunga told me in a September 11, 2004, interview in his office in Kampala. "That is my observation. If you ask an ordinary person on the street, 'What is Opus Dei?'—he is not going to answer you. He may not even know. When Opus Dei came, they first settled near Makerere University, with the professors. Now they are working among the members of parliament, among the government ministers maybe, among people of the high class. But an ordinary Christian or Catholic today in Uganda, you ask them about Opus Dei and they won't know." Obunga said he welcomed Opus Dei's work with that slice of life. "Opus Dei fits in among the people of that class, the high class. If Opus Dei can have their communities, that's where their impact will come. They're doing good work for that class," he said.

Such impressions rankle most Opus Dei members. Spokespersons are careful to point out that barbers, bus drivers, taxi drivers, and mechanics are also members of Opus Dei, to say nothing of Japanese immigrants who run laundries in Peru. As a Spanish supernumerary in Barcelona named Nuria Chinchilla said to me, "I know one numerary whose mother cleaned houses for a living, and his father worked in a factory. But these people are never in the news, so we're stuck with a reputation for elitism."

Ocáriz argues that the comparison with Calvinism is wrong on principle.

"In Calvinistic thinking, perfection in work, human success in work, is sought as a sign and guarantee of predestination," he said. "In the Work, it's not like this at all. Many times, Escrivá said we have to be convinced that if we seek to do our work well, offering it to God for serving others, even when objectively this work doesn't turn out well, before God it's just as valid as if it had. In other words, we should seek the objective outcome of work well done, but that's not the ultimate end. . . . We seek success not as a personal triumph, but as a mode of serving others." Ocáriz said this approach also implies "the equal importance of all work," whether one is a street-sweeper or president of the United States, an attitude which he said is "also very far removed from a Calvinistic spirit."

Bishop Javier Echevarría, the prelate of Opus Dei, said in a December 2004 interview that right now, given the global economic situation, a number of members are out of work. "From an external point of view, this could be considered a failure. But if they are giving their best to God, they are living in the spirit of Opus Dei," he said.

At the same time, it would be disingenuous to pretend that there is not strong pressure within Opus Dei to succeed externally wherever possible, in part since professional excellence is seen as a good evangelizing tool. Win the respect of one's colleagues on professional grounds, the theory runs, and they will be more likely to listen to you about matters of faith. Here is how Dominique le Torneau, an Opus Dei member, puts it in the 1984 book *What Is Opus Dei?*: "To win over others, a person must take to heart his need to carry out his duties as well as the best of his companions, and if possible better than the best."

One Italian numerary put the spiritual risk for Opus Dei members of striving to be "better than the best" this way: "The real danger is not that we end up worshiping worldly success, as the Calvinists do, or thinking that we have to prove our election by God. The real danger is that we can mistake a means for an end. You can get so caught up in trying to do your job well, because that's what the Father expects of us, that you think about work morning, noon and night. It becomes what occupies your heart and your mind, and you forget the real reason that you're supposed to be doing all of this. Being busy and doing things well is important in the Work, but all of that is supposed to be about sanctifying the world. The challenge is to remember that."

Chapter Four

CONTEMPLATIVES IN THE MIDDLE OF THE WORLD

Several times in the past year, I have found myself in a car for an extended period with members of Opus Dei. On July 9, 2004, for example, I headed up into the Andes Mountains with Father Clemente Ortega, pastor of Saint John the Baptist of Matucana-Huarochiri Parish in the town of Matucana, in the diocese of Chosica-Huayacan, maybe two hours outside of Lima. Ortega, fifty-two, also covers twenty-four smaller parishes in outlying, isolated mountain villages. Some of them are no more than seventy kilometers from Lima as the crow flies, but it takes him four or five hours in a jeep to reach them by narrow dirt paths. His communities are lucky to see him once every three weeks, and Ortega, a central-casting version of a no-nonsense priest, gets up to the mountains more often than most; some Andean communities see a priest once every two months, or less.

Ortega is a member of the Priestly Society of the Holy Cross, but his rectory in Matucana belies images of Opus Dei elitism. For one thing, there is no running water, so if you want to use the toilet at night, you have to haul buckets of water upstairs to the guest room. For another, the contract for his telephone does not permit international calls, and there's no cell phone coverage this far out from Lima, so one morning I found myself in a scene from the 1980s Michael Douglas movie *Romancing the Stone,* desperately trying to scrape together enough change to use the one local phone that could make international calls in order to phone in corrections to that week's Word from Rome column.

As I drove with Ortega up the mountain, and as we wound our way on the narrow dirt paths that pass for roads in this part of the world, I noticed a number of roadside shrines with small monuments and flowers. Thinking this was some unique Peruvian devotion, I asked Ortega about it. "Oh, no," he said. "Those are spots where someone died in a car accident." It was not the most reassuring comment as we whistled around blind corners at what suddenly seemed breakneck speed. (In reality, it took us all morning to cover what amounted to ninety miles.)

In the midst of all this, Ortega at one point pulled a rosary out of his pocket and announced that it was time to pray. The other couple of Opus Dei numeraries in the truck whipped out their rosaries as well, and, shouting to be heard over the rumbling of our four-wheel-drive jeep, Ortega led us through the joyful mysteries of the rosary.

In any number of other circumstances—driving from Barcelona to Barbastro in Spain, for example, or from Lima to Cañete in Peru, or from downtown Nairobi to the airport for a flight to Kampala, Uganda—I have had a similar experience, though none quite so hair-raising. One minute we're talking local politics or sports, and the next minute we're reading a passage from Escrivá and then spending time in quiet meditation. This is one dimension of what Opus Dei members mean by being "contemplatives in the middle of the world." They don't have to retreat into specifically "religious" enclaves in order to pray, but they can do so from within their ordinary daily settings, where they work and play and live. Prayer, in this sense, is a natural extension of daily life.

The concept of contemplation in the middle of the world, however, cuts deeper than simply praying in the car rather than in the chapel. The idea is that all of one's life is a prayer, that there are no separate compartments of existence marked off as "religious" and "secular." Worship and praise of God do not, in this sense, require doing anything specifically "religious," though Opus Dei members, as we have seen, follow an ambitious program of daily religious observance. Those are means to an end, which is to infuse everything one does, the most ordinary tasks in the middle of a busy day, with a contemplative dimension.

Maria Olga Gallo Riofrio, a twenty-two-year-old Peruvian who lives at an Opus Dei university residence in Peru but who is not a member, summed up this spirit in a conversation outside a school for mentally disabled kids in Lima, the Ricardo Bentin School, where she is a volunteer teacher along with several members of Opus Dei. "These kids have problems, and Opus Dei is trying to help them," she told me. "To them, teaching these kids is just as important as being in Church. In fact," she stressed, "it's no different than being in Church. This is prayer, too."

Susan Kimani, fifteen, is a student at the Opus Dei–affiliated Kianda School in Nairobi, Kenya, and she's one of those "fifteen going on forty-five" teenagers, a strikingly poised and articulate young woman who seems ready to walk into a courtroom or a corporate boardroom and hold her own this afternoon. Kimani is not an Opus Dei member, but she described their idea of a seamless integration of life as she's experienced it at Kianda. "At other schools, what happens in class and what happens in life are two very different things," she said. "Here, life is life. You can talk to teachers about your problems at home, with your friends. In a lot of other places, people can be suffering in class and the teacher would never know. Here, they know you inside and out, and there's a natural interest in you as a person as well as a student."

Among other implications, if lived properly, this spirit should make the transition from specifically "religious" contexts back out into the secular world virtually seamless. An Opus Dei member is not supposed to be one person in church, or in a center, and another person in the stock market or the operating room or the barbershop. The transition from one to the other setting should be effortless—or to use the word most commonly invoked inside Opus Dei, "natural." One should approach all the aspects of one's life with the same spirit of reverence and contemplation, avoiding a kind of spiritual or moral schizophrenia. This idea, in Opus Dei argot, goes under the heading of the "unity of life."

Unity of life, as Opus Dei sees it, is about discovering a lens through which all of one's life can be seen as a single, whole thing. This, members say, is what transforms a series of random or isolated movements, the endless string of hours, days, and years that make up a life, into a meaningful unity—a work of art. The spirit of Opus Dei is supposed to transform a multitude of different steps and contrasting movements into a single dance, so that at any given moment one realizes that one is always one and the same person. Sometimes, in religious contexts, people speak of their "spiritual life," referring to their prayers and practices of piety. But for Opus Dei, the "spiritual life" must include work, friendships, social life, family—everything. Naturally, this is supposed to have an impact on *how* Opus Dei members do whatever they do. Ultimately, the "spiritual life" is nothing more or less than human life. Nothing falls outside that. There are no compartments that aren't labeled "God's business."

One of the consequences of being "contemplatives in the middle of the world," as Opus Dei understands it, is that it tends to evaporate the "religious" as a distinct category of experience. One's most "religious" experiences may be in the office, on the playing field, in the kitchen, on the street, in the bedroom, or in the hospital. Escrivá once said that his monastic cell was the street, meaning that an Opus Dei member is supposed to walk out of church for the same reason they walk in—to be in union with God.

Finally, "unity of life" also leads to an attitude of taking everything one does seriously, whether it's a corporate deal involving billions of dollars, a piece of legislation that could have enormous social consequences, or taking the garbage out at night. Just as one should not compartmentalize one's moral instincts or doctrinal beliefs, likewise one should not "shut off" the sense of service to God just because a given task is, from a certain point of view, less important. The idea is that one should not pursue excellence in some areas of life and tolerate mediocrity in others simply because, from an external point of view, they may seem less important. This reaches down into the very basic aspects of daily life; one will rarely find an Opus Dei member, for example, who is sloppy in dress or personal appearance. Within Opus Dei there is an enormous attention paid to what are usually called "the little things," meaning the small tasks of daily living that, from the point of view of eternity, take on an enormous significance. The old bit of wisdom rings true in a special way for Opus Dei members: "If something's worth doing, it's worth doing well."

If lived properly, being a contemplative in the middle of the world means that one never knows where prayer ends and the rest of life begins. To return to Father Clemente, it's not that, from his point of view, our drive into the Andes included a few moments of prayer. It's rather that the entire experience was a prayer, and a few moments of it were explicitly phrased as such through saying the rosary.

Applications

Katie Doyle, seventeen, is a senior at Oakcrest, the Opus Dei–affiliated girls' school in McLean, Virginia, in suburban Washington, D.C. Oakcrest bought the facility from the McLean Bible Church, a bustling evangelical denomination, so it still has something of the sprawling feel of a megachurch. Today the school has a student body of 230 girls in grades six through twelve, some 70 percent of whom are Catholic, and it's likely that none is more perky and outgoing than Doyle. She's a beautiful, articulate young woman who will be a freshman at the University of Virginia next year and who comes across in many ways as a quintessential high school kid. She acts in plays, laughs about her "buddy" the school janitor, and chats a mile a minute with her friends, including Lily Nelson, seventeen, and Meghan Hadley, sixteen. Doyle jokes about asking the numeraries who teach at Oakcrest questions about Opus Dei because "it's a great way to get them off the subject," and she also made it clear that she was in no hurry to finish our interview, because otherwise she'd have to go back to class. Yet when we got onto what difference coming to Oakcrest has made in her life, she becomes more deliberate, choosing her words carefully.

"As seniors we take philosophy, and we've been reading Aristotle," she said. "He talks about how man is a rational animal. To deliberately take away your reason is a serious thing, it almost makes you less than human. This really struck me, because I always had a sense that getting drunk was wrong, but I was never really able to explain it to my friends, who would just say, 'Why not?' I think that's part of what you get out of Oakcrest. You understand better why your whole life, even the ordinary decisions on a Saturday night, is important."

Doyle, who is not a member of Opus Dei and doesn't have any plans to join, said she's not worried about losing her faith at a major secular university next year, because "I'm comfortable with being Catholic. I know what the Church teaches, and I agree with it. I know that it doesn't make any difference whether I go to a Catholic school or not, because I can be just as 'religious' at UVA. The challenge to try to live my faith is the same."

The idea embedded in Doyle's story is that all of one's life should be of a piece, and that whether one is in an explicitly "Catholic" environment such as Oakcrest or a sprawling secular context such as the University of Virginia, one is always and everywhere the same person.

Alexandre Havard, an Opus Dei numerary, is director of the European Training Center, an Opus Dei–affiliated institution in Helsinki, Finland. He described what being a "contemplative in the middle of the world" means in Finnish culture.

"Maybe it's that when you go to the sauna with a friend, you don't let him get out before you've asked him a few questions about his life and his faith," he said. "Don't let him center the conversation just on questions like the quality of the snow." Havard said this approach actually cuts against the Finnish grain. "There's a rule for the sauna—they say religion in the sauna is bad for one's health," he joked.

More seriously, Havard said, the idea of contemplation in the midst of daily work is a tonic for most Finns. "Finnish people are serious workers, so they always, or almost always, walk the talk," he said. "This is a good beginning for contemplation, because contemplation in the world means, in the first place, doing your job well. But this is just a beginning, and many Finns stop here. They confuse a 'work ethic' based on external things with goodness, which is always transformational. Finns love to speak about their work ethic and they are proud of it, but they need contemplation. And when they discover it, they love it."

In that sense, Havard said, the concept of unity of life, integrating contemplation and work, overcomes a serious ethical gap for many Finns. "The problem with a 'work ethic' is the very concept. It suggests that outside work there is another ethics, other norms with different content. Actually you may find Finns who will insist on the 'work ethic,' but at the same time will get drunk every Friday, divorce their wife, and abandon their children, and all this with the absolute security of being ethical people just because they pay their bills and keep their professional promises.

"Contemplation is that which makes unity of life," Havard said. "A contemplative man or woman does not fulfill different 'roles' during the day: the role of a professional, of a husband or wife, of a father, of a friend. The contemplative soul looks for God always and everywhere: in his work, in his family, in his friendships and hobbies, and even when he is alone. A 'work ethic' may lead to a double life and hypocrisy, whereas contemplation leads to unity of life and sincerity.

"To be contemplative in the Finnish context, therefore, means to go beyond the rules and discover that God may transform you through the exercise of your profession. This is an idea Luther would have resisted, but many modern Finns, even deeply religious people, are far from being Lutherans. Their personal experience is that God does not act from outside, but from inside. I know a Protestant pastor in Tornio, about a thousand kilometers north of Helsinki at the frontier with Sweden and Lapland, who buys fifty books of Josemaría Escrivá every month for his parishioners. They love what Escrivá says. Every month some thirty Lutherans meet with this pastor to discuss the teaching of Saint Josemaría. The 'contemplation thing' is something that makes them crazy, in the good sense of the word."

Pablo Cardona, a forty-year-old Spanish numerary with an undergraduate degree in physics and a graduate degree in management, runs a program on business ethics at the Instituto de Estudios Superiores de la Empresa (IESE), Opus Dei's elite business school in Barcelona. He works with giant international companies such as Deutsche Bank, Microsoft, and Motorola, trying to help them reflect on how basic principles of morality can be translated into business practice.

"My way of understanding work is embedded in my way of understanding of the human person," Cardona told me in May 2004 during an interview in his seminar room. "What's the value of a person, how should you treat people, and what is the mission of companies in society? I cannot separate my way of living my Christian faith from my way of looking at companies. That's why I've been working with these big companies for many years now, on trying to help them live up to their mission, their commitment with different stakeholders, and not just with stockholders.

"Maximization of profit tends to get all the attention" in the business world, Cardona said. "So for the last three or four years I've been trying to show leaders in the corporate world what a more holistic approach would look like. Because of my way of looking at the world, and the meaning of people and organizations in society, I've been trying to find what is wrong with the basic incoherence" between human values and the dominant approach to running companies. "When you ask general managers, it's not that they aren't trying, it's that they don't know what to do. So, what I have been developing is a managerial system that starts with mission all the way down. . . . I don't explain just how to use the notebook or a palm pilot, I talk about priorities in life. When you have a deeper view, an anthropological view, then you can go further in these issues.

"It's all about aligning who you are as a human being with how you do business," he said. "It's about what the Founder called unity of life. . . . Opus Dei will never act as a structure. Opus Dei will go to their heart and say, 'Okay, in your position in your profession, how can you affect the people around you with Christian faith? What does it mean that Christ was resurrected and you are a son of God? What does that mean for you and for the people around you?' This is the same if you're a professor here in a top business school, or if you are whatever."

Matthew Odada is a professor of East African studies at Makerere University in Kampala, Uganda, who has been attending Opus Dei recollections and courses of formation since the center opened in Kampala in 1996, near the university. Though he is not a member of Opus Dei, he told me in September 2004 that he is part of a circle of some forty cooperators in Kampala. He is a soft-spoken man who takes long pauses and thinks carefully before responding to questions. He told me that he believes Escrivá's emphasis on unity of life may be the distinctive contribution of Opus Dei to civil society in today's Africa.

"The central obstacle to the construction of a decent political and civil order in Africa is corruption," he said. "Too many Africans believe that paying bribes and siphoning off resources for the benefit of oneself, or one's kin groups or tribe, is acceptable. In fact, Africans are generally very moral people, with a strong emphasis on community and family, but too many of us make a sharp distinction between private morality and public conduct. People don't have any sense of what it means to bring ethics into politics, or business, or whatever. In that context, I think Opus Dei has a strong contribution to make. They could help shape a generation of African leaders who know what it means to bring their personal integrity into their public roles." Odada said he welcomes Opus Dei to Uganda and hopes it expands in Africa, with the desire that it will spread this message—that one can't "compartmentalize" being religious as something distinct from the way he or she runs a business or an office in the civil government. The idea is not to turn every businessman or politician in Uganda into a "contemplative" in the specifically religious sense of the term, but to help them see the importance of "unity of life," whatever their moral system may be.

It was noted above that part of "unity of life," as Opus Dei sees it, means treating even seemingly insignificant tasks with seriousness. As an illustration of this attention to the "little things," consider the Shellbourne Conference Center, located about an hour outside of Chicago in Valparaiso, Indiana. Five Opus Dei numeraries and eight numerary assistants make up the staff, along with roughly thirteen high school girls who work at the center part-time in the summers. The center, originally built in the 1960s, with a new wing added in 1986, hosts retreats given by priests or lay members of Opus Dei. The clientele is generally, though not exclusively, made up of Opus Dei members. Some seven hundred people move through the facility over the course of a year, and its annual operating budget is around $1 million. Daily Mass is offered in at least one of the center's four chapels, all of which have the Blessed Sacrament reserved for prayer and adoration throughout the day. Confession is also regularly available, following a posted schedule.

When I visited Shellbourne in September 2004, I was shown around by a female numerary, Lali Sánchez Aldana, the director. As we walked through the kitchens and laundry rooms, Sánchez Aldana made a point of mentioning that when it comes to preparing materials for the Mass, there are special facilities. There is a small kitchen set aside exclusively for the baking of altar breads, some of which are packaged and shipped out to parishes and other Catholic facilities that request them. There is also a special laundry room dedicated exclusively to washing and ironing the linens used in the four chapels. "When priests celebrate Mass here, they always comment on how crisp and fresh the altar cloths are," Sánchez Aldana said with obvious pride. "The chapels are always clean and orderly, the flowers are fresh, and everything is in its place."

Some might find such attention to detail fussy, if not what Catholic moral theology used to call "scrupulous," meaning an insistence on following rules that risks becoming excessive, driven by doubts about being in a "state of grace." Yet seen from the point of view of the unity of life, this is all of a piece. If one truly believes that Christ is present in the Mass, then one is obligated to do it right, infusing even the most minor details, such as the condition of the altar cloth, with a transcendental significance.

By the same token, this is why Opus Dei facilities typically look so immaculate. Indeed, one of the first things people usually comment on is how clean these places look. When I toured the diocesan seminary in Cañete, Peru, for example, in the territorial prelature of Yauyos, my attention was immediately drawn to how the floors in every hallway sparkled. When I was at Torreciudad, the Opus Dei–operated Marian shrine in Spain, I met Manolo Fernández Gómez, an Opus Dei associate and former communist, who told me that when he visited the University of Navarra in Pamplona for the first time, the thing that immediately struck him was, "You could eat out of their ashtrays, they were so clean." Further, Opus Dei facilities usually come off as being well appointed, creating the appearance (and, to be honest, sometimes the reality) of wealth. In fairness, however, sometimes this is a matter of Opus Dei people knowing how to make the very most of limited means.

To take another example of unity of life, Xavi Casajuana is a thirty-one-year-old supernumerary of Opus Dei who lives in Sabadell, an industrial city about thirty minutes outside of Barcelona. He works as a computer technician at a factory that makes electric motors. He describes his approach to work: "I am always happy. The people in my company don't understand why on Monday morning at seven o'clock, I'm always laughing. But to me, it doesn't matter if it's Monday or Friday. . . . There's a radio station here that has a disc jockey who always says, 'Finally it's Friday.' I don't like that. Why not say 'Finally it's Monday,' or 'Finally it's Thursday'? I strive to be as happy as I can every day of the week, not just on Friday. After all, I'm supposed to be the same person every day of the week." That's one way of explaining unity of life—one should have the same spirit every day, because every day brings another opportunity to offer up one's life as an act of praise.

Finally, an American priest of Opus Dei, Father John Wauck, who teaches in the faculty of communications at Opus Dei's Santa Croce University in Rome, explains one of the consequences of "unity of life" as he sees it: "I think it is characteristic of Opus Dei that its members, priests and laypersons, do not have a particular 'religious tone' for talking about 'spiritual things,' " he said. "There's not much change in pitch when the conversation gets 'religious.' At the crudest level, you could say that there tends to be little 'unction.' We have only one voice—a normal everyday human voice—for talking with God and man. It's the same person, same voice, same heart."

Challenges

At one level, a danger associated with the concept of "unity of life" is that it can mean that Opus Dei members never let their guard down. It can translate into an obsessive-compulsive approach to even the smallest details of daily living, a relentless insistence that everything be "just so." To be honest, this may be a greater danger in Anglo-Saxon cultures than in the Mediterranean environment, where Opus Dei has had its widest diffusion. Certainly Opus Dei centers in Italy, for example, practice the *bella figura*, or keeping up appearances, but most Italian members I know also have the capacity for the well-known Italian shrug, the instinct for knowing when rules and systems have to give way to the realities of human subjectivity. Their insistence on the "unity of life" is real but, in typically Italian fashion, nonfanatical. Escrivá once captured this idea by saying that the Christian should not be a "neurotic collector of good-behavior reports."

Perhaps a deeper challenge is maintaining the spirit of being "contemplatives in the world" as Opus Dei grows and develops institutionally, and, albeit inadvertently, offers members an increasing range of ways to be involved in Opus Dei activities rather than being "in the middle of the world." I spoke with a supernumerary in Pamplona who teaches at the University of Navarra, for example, who said that while he enjoys his work and likes his colleagues, paradoxically he regards the environment as being contradictory to Escrivá's original intent. "You live in an Opus Dei bubble here," he said. "You work in an Opus Dei institution, you socialize with Opus Dei friends, you go to Mass at Opus Dei centers, and you send your kids to Opus Dei schools. Where is 'the world' in all of that?"

Granted, Pamplona is a unique case; there's no other location on earth where one could move in quite so self-contained an Opus Dei environment. Granted, too, that there is no necessary opposition between being in a corporate work of Opus Dei and being in "the world," given the commitment of Opus Dei to secularity. A corporate work that is open and engaged with the culture is no place of refuge. Yet it is increasingly possible for Opus Dei families to send their children to Opus Dei schools from kindergarten through graduate school, to spend their spare time taking part in Opus Dei activities, and to make friends largely through Opus Dei's extended informal network. They can read books by Opus Dei authors, or published by Opus Dei publishing houses. The risk is retreating into a "virtual ghetto."

Critics have long charged that this is one of the greatest areas of inconsistency in Opus Dei—that it talks about secularity and lay spirituality, but at least some members live in near isolation resembling preconciliar forms of religious life. In fact, such charges make no sense when leveled against people such as Greg Burke, an American numerary who's the Rome correspondent for Fox News, or Ana Royo, a supernumerary I met in Barbastro, Spain, who works as a flight attendant for a Spanish airline. Their professional activity carries them out into the wider world every day. Yet there's equally no denying that Opus Dei members are expected to be *in* but not *of* the world; this is partly the reason, for example, that numeraries generally do not attend movies or sporting events. Hence the challenge is to maintain enough distance to remain critical while not lifting people out of the warp and woof of normal social experience.

A related charge is that Opus Dei sometimes tries to impose styles of life on facilities it administers, such as university residences, that don't seem especially "secular." For example, ex-numerary Dennis Dubro, an American, was sent by Opus Dei to help run a university residence— Warrane College in Sydney, Australia, a men-only facility where even male visitors were not allowed beyond the ground floor. "My directors had spent four years telling me, and I had spent those years telling others, that we had a lay spirituality; and here they were trying to turn this university residence into a cloister," Dubro said.

Most Opus Dei members respond that there is no real risk of their disengagement from secularity; nobody in Opus Dei is walled off in a monastery or living in a hermitage. Still, at a psychological level, there is a sense in which some people are attracted to Opus Dei precisely because it offers an alternative to the prevailing ethos—both in the broader culture and, to some extent, within the Catholic Church. There can be a temptation to treat Opus Dei as a refuge, a safe harbor, and to put down anchor rather than "setting out into the deep" as Pope John Paul II often said.

Becket Gremmels, for example, is a twenty-one-year-old student at the University of Notre Dame who said he was made fun of in high school because of his earnest piety; the other kids called him "churchy." In college, he said, he wanted an environment where he wouldn't have to worry about becoming "less orthodox, getting watered down." He tried the Franciscan University of Steubenville, in Ohio, which enjoys a reputation as a fairly conservative Catholic environment, but found that for his tastes, "too many people were going through the motions." He said he discovered what he was looking for at Windmoor, the Opus Dei center near the Notre Dame campus. When he gets to graduate school, he plans to consider a vocation to Opus Dei. In itself, there's nothing wrong with the fact that Opus Dei can provide a safe, supportive atmosphere for Catholics such as Gremmels. The inherent risk, however, is that such Catholics may come to see Opus Dei as a place to hide from a world that doesn't understand them rather than as a means to see that world in a new light in order to transform it.

The challenge is to remember that being contemplative—being prayerful, intentional about one's spirituality—is only half the battle, and not the specifically Opus Dei half. The Opus Dei spirit is to live those qualities in the workaday world, not to construct a series of enclaves, either real or virtual. The touchstone has to be the gospel story of the Transfiguration, when Peter, James, and John went onto the mountaintop with Jesus and witnessed him in his glory. Peter wanted to pitch tents to stay with Jesus, but that was not their destiny. Their call was to follow Christ in the street, in all its brokenness and squalor, and all its potential for redemption. That, too, is where members of Opus Dei are supposed to be found.

Chapter Five

CHRISTIAN FREEDOM

Lluís Foix is a prominent Spanish journalist who lives and works in Barcelona. He's a regular "talking head" on three television programs and three radio programs, a columnist for the secular left-of-center *Vanguardia* newspaper in Barcelona, and a regular contributor to both its news and sports pages. He's held just about every job there is in Spanish journalism, from being an editor and deputy editor to, for four years, serving as a foreign correspondent in Washington, D.C. He has also been an associate of Opus Dei since 1961. He lives at home to take care of his mother, who is blind and has Alzheimer's disease.

In other words, Foix is a prototypically driven, successful, and morally serious member of Opus Dei, someone very much involved in public life in Spain, and a person who embodies the spirit of the "sanctification of work." One might assume that, given Foix's influence and prominence, the leadership of Opus Dei would be in close contact with him in order to coordinate efforts toward common aims, and to assure maximum efficiency in terms of being "on message."

In fact, Foix says, after forty-one years as a member of Opus Dei, he's still waiting for someone in the Work to tell him what they think of a single article he's ever written or a single comment he's ever made on television.

"It just doesn't come up," he told me in a reluctant June 2004 interview over coffee in Barcelona. I say "reluctant" because it was obvious that, despite being a very public person, Foix doesn't enjoy talking about what he considers his private life. In fact, he said, no one in Opus Dei has ever brought up his journalism, or, for that matter, his politics. He smiles and says it's just as well, since for at least the last six years, he's voted for the left rather than the conservative People's Party of former prime minister José María Aznar. (In the Spanish press, Aznar is widely assumed to be the darling of Opus Dei.) Foix made it clear that this is not because he's in love with the left, but because he's even more disappointed in the right. He emphasizes that no one in Opus Dei has ever attempted to influence his choices in this regard, either.

"People tend to think that Opus Dei is a political, a social, an economic movement, blah blah blah," Foix said. "It's not, at least as far as I know. They tend to look at others as persons, to try to help them in their spiritual lives, to understand them as human beings. That's it, so far as I can see. I've never had a director of Opus Dei ask me about anything else, like what I think about this issue or that politician. As a member of Opus Dei, I am left completely free."

Foix also wanted to make another point: "We are not robots, you know? We're normal people. Sometimes I don't feel like working. When I see a beautiful woman walking down the street, I have the same feelings you do. On Saturday, well, the thing is that I will go to my hometown and take care of the olive trees, of the vineyards that my father handed over to me when he died. It's normal living, not under anybody's thumb."

In a sense it's a great irony that Opus Dei has attracted a reputation for having a cultlike control of its members, because at least at the notional level, there is perhaps no other group in the Catholic Church that emphasizes freedom and liberty more than Opus Dei, along with the personal responsibility that this freedom implies.

The basic idea is that outside the spiritual guidance and doctrinal formation offered by Opus Dei, the organization has no "agenda," and its members are completely free to act as they see fit, taking full responsibility for their choices. This is not just a matter of Opus Dei's own self-understanding, but of Vatican policy, since the 1982 decree from the Congregation for Bishops erecting Opus Dei as a personal prelature read: "The lay faithful belonging to the prelature, within the limits of Catholic faith and morals and Church discipline, enjoy the same freedom as other Catholics and their fellow citizens; as a result, the prelature is not responsible for the professional, social, political or economic activities of any of its members."

Opus Dei members, in their capacities as professors, or lawyers, or street sweepers, are, at least in theory, responsible to their superiors at work, but never to the directors or clergy of Opus Dei. Moreover, Opus Dei is never supposed to exploit the positions that any of its members may have obtained, either in the Church or in the secular realm, to obtain preferential treatment. "Opus Dei is an apostolic undertaking," Escrivá wrote. "It is interested only in souls. Our morality does not permit us to behave like a self-help or mutual support society." That, too, is what Opus Dei means by the "freedom" of its members—freedom from any attempt on the part of the organization to take advantage of them.

Escrivá treated no single topic touching the internal life of Opus Dei more than the freedom of its members. He repeated the theme literally dozens of times throughout his writings, emphasizing it with a ferocity that one finds about few other matters.

For example, Escrivá once wrote: "With our blessed freedom Opus Dei can never be, in the political life of a country, a kind of political party: there is and always will be room within Opus Dei for all outlooks and approaches allowed by a Christian conscience, and it is impossible for the directors to bring any influence to bear." Escrivá derided what he called the "pseudo-spiritual one-party mentality." Another citation: "God wants us to serve him freely—*ubi autem Spiritus Domini, ibi libertas*—'Where the Lord's spirit is, there is freedom'—and therefore an apostolate which did not respect freedom of consciences would certainly be wrong."

Perhaps the most famous remark along these lines came in an instruction Escrivá drew up for the directors of centers in Opus Dei, urging them to encourage members to be aware of their own freedom: "If directors were to impose a specific criterion in temporal affairs, the other members who thought differently would immediately rebel, and rightly so. I would see myself having the sad duty of blessing and praising those who firmly refused to obey, and of correcting with holy indignation directors who wished to exercise an authority they can never have." The bottom line, according to Escrivá, was this: "Personal freedom and responsibility are the best guarantees of the supernatural purpose of the Work of God."

Bishop Alvaro del Portillo, Escrivá's successor, once told biographer Peter Berglar that part of the reason Escrivá never made public comments on political issues is that he wanted to respect the freedom of the members of Opus Dei, since if "the Father" were to take a position, there would be strong moral pressure for everyone else to fall in line. His determination to transcend political divisions ran deep; during the run-up to the Spanish civil war, for example, he encouraged the young people with whom he was in contact to play soccer on politically mixed teams, so it never became the "blacks" versus the "reds." The same point could be made not just for politics, but for business, cultural affairs, and any other area in which people organize to advance common interests. Opus Dei as such, Escrivá insisted, must not take sides.

Inside Opus Dei, it is widely understood that the role of the priests and lay directors is to assist members with their spiritual lives, to impart knowledge of the doctrine of the Catholic Church, and that's all. Priests are discouraged from making political comments that might alienate people who need to confide in them. The leadership is not supposed to inquire about the personal choices of members or their professional activities. A young university student involved in Opus Dei once expressed surprise to Escrivá that no one had asked him about his political opinions, and Escrivá responded: "Instead you will be asked other 'uncomfortable' questions. They will ask you if you pray, if you use your time well, if you please your parents, if you study, because for a student to study is a serious obligation."

To a great extent, members told me, it actually works this way. Members of Opus Dei around the world repeatedly said that no one inside the organization has ever asked how they voted, or what approach they take to their job, or how they manage their finances.

Applications

Rafael Rey is a leading conservative politician and member of Congress in Peru. He's widely seen as an opponent of that country's center-left president, Alejandro Toledo, and a onetime ally of former president Alberto Fujimori, remembered as something of an autocrat. Rey is also a numerary of Opus Dei. Rey's political declarations are often explosive, and many Peruvians assume that they're hatched in close coordination with the cardinal of Lima, Juan Luis Cipriani, who is also a member of Opus Dei. But in a June interview in his Lima office, Rey told me, "No one from Opus Dei has ever spoken to me about politics. They speak solely about the spiritual formation of the person, about God, and about religious and doctrinal formation. They push me to try to behave morally, in accord with Christian teaching. That's it.

"No official of Opus Dei," Rey said, "has ever asked me for an intervention on a political matter. Inside the centers of Opus Dei we don't talk politics," at least in a disputatious sense, he said. "I know lots of people in Opus Dei who think differently than I do." As an example, Rey mentioned another Peruvian politician, Rodrigo Franco Montes, who before his death in 1987 at the hands of the Shining Path terrorist movement was a member of the center-left party of former president Alan García. Montes was also a numerary from the mid-1970s to the early 1980s, then left to get married, but remained on good terms with Opus Dei. Rey was strongly opposed to the García government, and he and Montes clashed on many issues. Rey and Montes lived together in the same Opus Dei center, Rey said, and never discussed politics inside the house. "The Founder said we must respect the liberty of others, and we take that seriously," Rey told me.

Rey said that what he gets from Opus Dei is of an entirely different order. "I have a strong character," he said, "and I am hated by the powers that be. I need help in working at being patient, at understanding others, being forgiving. I need help in seeing my errors, my defects, and seeking forgiveness. That's the kind of thing I would discuss with someone from Opus Dei, not my political choices."

The same point, members say, applies to the world of business. Rafael López Aliaga is a senior executive with Perurail in Lima, Peru, and president of a society called Peruval Corp. S.A. He is also an associate in Opus Dei, living at home so that he can care for his parents and his brother, who has a form of mental illness that requires expensive medical care.

López grew up in Chiclayo, a provincial town in Peru, and first met Opus Dei when he was in high school and finished in first place in the local examinations for university admissions. The results were published in a local newspaper. Out of the blue, a seventeen-year-old Opus Dei numerary came looking for him at his father's factory to invite him to an event in Piura, some five hours away. Although López said he was favorably impressed by the kid's moxie, he didn't go, even though he was curious about Opus Dei because he had read a critical article that referred to

Opus Dei as an "octopus." Eventually, however, he attended the Opus Dei university in Piura, largely because the local university was closed due to a strike. Eventually he began reading the works of Escrivá, and after a year in Piura, he "whistled."

López said that no one from Opus Dei has ever attempted to influence his business career or asked him to give preferential treatment to other members of Opus Dei. In fact, he said, being an associate has actually been a business liability, since he has given up four hours every evening for twenty years to help out at the Sama Center in downtown Lima, an Opus Dei center that offers courses and other programming for boys. He leads conversations on moral issues, runs "circles," or weekly meetings, for Opus Dei supernumeraries and cooperators, organizes sporting events for the boys who come to the center, and teaches free courses pitched at the postgraduate level for undergraduate students. This includes a nine-day annual program for the best business students from all over Peru, infusing the strictly business instruction with some elements of the Opus Dei "plan of life"—Mass is offered every day, meditations are organized, and so on.

"The striking thing about Opus Dei is the exclusively spiritual focus," López said. "Its impact on my professional career has been in pushing me to be a more moral, honest executive, treating my employees and colleagues as human beings rather than just cogs in a machine. I have been left free to decide what path my career should take, what investment decisions to make, whom to hire, and that sort of thing. It is almost unthinkable to me that anyone in Opus Dei would attempt to influence my choices at that level."

To take an American example, Doug Hinderer is senior vice president of human resources for the National Association of Realtors in Chicago, and an Opus Dei supernumerary. He and his wife, Shirley, have nine children, consistent with a tendency inside Opus Dei toward having large families. The boys go to Northridge Prep, the Opus Dei boys' school in Chicago, and the girls to the Willows, the Opus Dei girls' school. Hinderer said they'd actually like to have more kids but so far haven't had any luck, so they got a dog, named Hunter.

Hinderer said that no one in Opus Dei has ever asked him about his career moves, though in theory when he transferred from the for-profit corporate world to a nonprofit organization, it could have had an impact on his ability to contribute financially to Opus Dei. Instead, he said, the conversations with Opus Dei clergy and lay directors are entirely focused on spiritual matters.

"They don't let me off the hook in confession, and I really respect that," Hinderer said. "One priest actually said to me once, 'You're feeding me a line of shit.' I was pretty surprised to hear a priest talk like that, but the thing was, he was absolutely right. That's the kind of thing that Opus Dei does."

This is not to say that on occasion, some members of Opus Dei have not attempted to use the organization as a kind of extended political or business network in order to advance their own careers or achieve other ends. People who know Opus Dei, however, say that generally this sort of activity runs afoul of the emphasis on "freedom" fairly quickly. For example, Andrew Reed, head of the middle school at the Heights, the Opus Dei boys' school in suburban Washington, D.C., and not a member of Opus Dei, told me in a December 2004 conversation that once a supernumerary had pulled him aside to tell him that he should join Opus Dei because "it would be good for my career." Reed said that person eventually left Opus Dei on less than good terms. "I don't think he really understood what it was all about," Reed said.

Limits to Freedom

From the outside, this talk about freedom can be difficult to understand, since it so often seems that Opus Dei does act as a unified force, both in ecclesiastical matters and in secular politics. In Church affairs, for example, Monsignor Fernando Ocáriz, the vicar-general of Opus Dei who also serves as a consultor for the Congregation for the Doctrine of the Faith, was one of the primary authors of the 2001 document *Dominus Iesus,* which reasserted the superiority of Roman Catholicism over other religions. No member of Opus Dei, at least publicly, took a leading role in widespread criticism of the document. Prominent Opus Dei members in the United States, such as Russell Shaw and Father C. John McCloskey, are identified with the Catholic right (without suggesting that Shaw and McCloskey, or any two Opus Dei members, agree on every issue). It would be difficult to name a single Opus Dei member who figures prominently on the Catholic left, at least in intra-Church debates. The two

Opus Dei cardinals in the world, Cardinal Juan Luis Cipriani of Lima, Peru, and Cardinal Julián Herranz of the Pontifical Council for the Interpretation of Legislative Texts, while very different personalities, would both be located on the conservative wing of the College of Cardinals. In terms of secular politics, while there are a few Opus Dei members involved in leftist parties around the world, the membership's center of gravity is clearly on the right.

How is this possible, if Opus Dei means what it says about freedom? The primary challenge facing Opus Dei, at least on this front, is to give a credible answer to that question.

Part of the answer is sociological. Opus Dei tends to attract a certain kind of person, and generally, though certainly not exclusively, that person tends to be "conservative" on both ecclesiastical matters and questions of secular politics. There is no need for a central organizing committee or orders from on high. There is already a rough consensus about what issues are important, what causes matter, and which vehicles are best adapted for advancing them. When members are "set free" to work at the transformation of the secular world, those who choose to be involved in politics or public commentary are generally going to end up pulling in the same direction, without Opus Dei dictating those choices or attempting to influence them.

Second, there is a clear limit to freedom of thought and action inside Opus Dei, which is the teaching of the Catholic Church. In a homily entitled "Freedom: A Gift from God," Escrivá put the point this way: "Reject the deception of those who appease themselves with the pathetic cry of 'Freedom! Freedom!' Their cry often masks a tragic enslavement, because choices that prefer error do not liberate. Christ alone sets us free, for He alone is the Way, the Truth and the Life." Opus Dei members do not consider themselves "free" to espouse positions that run contrary to the faith or morals of the Church. You will not find an Opus Dei member opposing the Church's teaching on birth control, for example, or upholding the morality of abortion, or suggesting that there is no God or that Christ was simply an itinerant preacher. This is not because members of Opus Dei are forced into taking these positions, or because there is the threat of an inquisitorial process if they speak or publish unorthodox thoughts. It is rather because people who decide to join Opus Dei are by and large already "on the team" in terms of Church teaching and are attracted to

Opus Dei because it is a place where they will not encounter the same skeptical approach that one often finds in the secular world, or, for that matter, in some Catholic circles.

Perhaps the best way of putting this point I encountered came from Katie Doyle at the Oakcrest School. I asked her if she thought an Opus Dei member would be "free" to question the Church on birth control. Her answer? "If you are going to be in Opus Dei, you're not the kind of person who agrees with only half of what the Church teaches," she said. "You're already a pretty strict, conservative Catholic."

A Factory of Fundamentalism?

As an aside, Doyle's comment hints at something that is probably not adequately appreciated about Opus Dei, and it goes to the question of "freedom." Looked at from the outside, Opus Dei often presents a fairly compact image of papal loyalty and adherence to a conservative reading of Catholic doctrine. The tendency in some quarters, therefore, is to assume that Opus Dei is a "factory of fundamentalism," taking impressionable minds and molding them in a narrow outlook.

No doubt there are cases of people who come to Opus Dei with no particular intellectual inclinations, and exposure to the formal instruction and informal chat inside Opus Dei nudges them in a conservative direction. On the other hand, it is probably more often the case that prospective members are drawn to Opus Dei because they already have a rather conservative perspective. In those cases, prolonged exposure to Opus Dei, according to most observers, generally has a broadening effect. The constant emphasis on "freedom" tends to make them a bit more generous when dealing with contrary views, and while they may not relax their own stands, they tend at least to become less judgmental and more charitable. Further, within the limits marked out by the *Catechism of the Catholic Church,* there is a striking plurality of schools and intellectual approaches within Opus Dei.

Pia de Solenni, an American laywoman who works at the Family Research Council in Washington, D.C., and who is not a member of Opus Dei, wrote her doctoral dissertation at the Opus Dei–run University of Santa Croce in Rome after studying at a couple of other pontifical universities. Here is her observation: "At Santa Croce, okay, you can say it's conservative. But you get in there and you have Thomists, and you have phenomenologists, and you have neo-Platonists. It's really interesting that so many trains of thought exist within that one university. That's remarkable, I think, because I've never seen that in any other place. They go after each other at conferences and in journals, but that's what you're supposed to be doing if you're interested in the intellectual life."

To take one example, in late 2004 and early 2005 the Catholic world was once again locked in a debate over AIDS and condoms, this time because a spokesperson for the Spanish bishops' conference suggested that condoms could be a legitimate part of an anti-AIDS strategy. Ironically, the two most dazzled sectors of opinion were far-right Catholics and the secular media, both of which, albeit for different reasons, associate the Church with an outright and absolute ban on condoms. Many Catholic moralists and even some Vatican officials, on the other hand, tend to believe that in a situation in which immoral sexual conduct is going to happen in any event, the use of a condom to prevent the transmission of AIDS could be considered a "lesser evil."

One voice suggesting this position belonged to Monsignor Angel Rodríguez Luño, an Opus Dei priest, a professor at Santa Croce University in Rome, and a consultor for the Congregation for the Doctrine of the Faith. "The problem is, anytime we try to give a nuanced response, we see headlines that say, 'Vatican approves condoms,' " Rodríguez Luño told the *Washington Post* on January 23, 2005. "The issue is more complicated than that. From a moral point of view, we cannot condone contraception. We cannot tell a classroom of sixteen-year-olds they should use condoms. But if we are dealing with someone or a situation in which persons are clearly going to act in harmful ways, a prostitute who is going to continue her activities, then one might say, 'Stop. But if you are not going to, at least do this.' " Sex outside marriage already breaks the sixth commandment, Luño said; unprotected sex outside marriage risks breaking the fifth commandment, too, "Thou shalt not kill." In effect, Rodríguez Luño was distinguishing between principle and casuistry, meaning the application of principles to specific cases. Rodríguez Luño also knew full well that neither the pope nor any Vatican agency has ever spoken on the specific question of whether condom use can be justified as a lesser evil in the context of AIDS. It was a subtle argument that surprised, and dismayed, some conservatives.

Over a period of time, witnessing the kind of pluralism that de Solenni describes, and that Rodríguez Luño illustrates, generally has the effect of "rounding out" people whose points of departure are somewhat more rigid. Rather than creating fundamentalists, in other words, one can make the argument that just as often, Opus Dei ends up converting them. If it indeed works this way, it would be in keeping with the vision of Escrivá, who in a 1965 letter said he wanted Opus Dei members to be broad-minded, "always acknowledging whatever is good in others, never falling into the narrowness of a closed, cliquish outlook, but being men and women with an open and universal heart."

Different Models

At an even deeper level, the reason the outside world struggles to take seriously what Opus Dei says about freedom is that there are often two different models of freedom operating in the conversation. For most strains of secular thought, freedom is understood in what philosophers call "voluntaristic" terms, meaning in terms of the individual will. One is "free" when there are no external constraints on one's freedom of action—when, in effect, one can do whatever one wants. In this sense, if one can't take a position in favor of birth control inside Opus Dei, one is not fully "free."

The understanding of freedom current inside Opus Dei, however, is different. It harkens back to a more classic Aristotelian/Thomistic approach, in which freedom is not an ultimate good in itself. Rather, freedom is ordered to the truth, so the truly free person is not simply doing whatever he wants, but is acting in accord with God's design for authentic human flourishing. To use a rather tired example, the alcoholic is not "free" simply because he takes a drink when he wants it. He won't be free until he stops drinking, even though that may not be what he "wants" at this moment.

In a homily on freedom, Escrivá put it this way:

> Don't you see? Freedom finds its true meaning when it is put to the service of the truth which redeems, when it is spent in seeking God's infinite Love which liberates us from all forms of slavery. Each passing day increases my yearning to proclaim to the four winds this inexhaustible treasure that belongs to Christianity: "the glorious

freedom of the children of God!" This is essentially what is meant by a "good will," which teaches us to pursue good, after having distinguished it from evil. . . . But there are people who do not understand. They rebel against the Creator, in a sad, petty, impotent rebellion, and they blindly repeat the futile complaint recorded in the Psalms, "let us break away from their bondage, rid ourselves of their toils." They shrink from the hardship of fulfilling their daily task with heroic silence and naturalness, without show or complaint. They have not realized that even when God's Will seems painful and its demands wounding, it coincides perfectly with our freedom, which is only to be found in God and in his plans.

To put the point as one Italian Opus Dei numerary said to me: *"Abbiamo libertà, sì, ma libertà dentro un impegno"* [We have freedom, yes, but freedom within a commitment.]

If there is incomprehension about "freedom" inside Opus Dei, the cause is often not so much that the critics are lying and Opus Dei is telling the truth, or vice versa; it's that the two sides are using the same term, "freedom," but they mean different things by it. Of course, the Aristotelian/Thomistic model is not just Opus Dei's concept of freedom, but one at the heart of much traditional Catholic reflection. Still, because Opus Dei tends to be the leading case in point for people outside that tradition who struggle to understand it, the burden will fall disproportionately on Opus Dei to find ways of explaining its understanding of freedom to a culture that has very different starting points.

Chapter Six

DIVINE FILIATION

One of the foundational stories about Escrivá concerns a train ride he took in Madrid in 1931, just three years after his original vision on the Feast of the Guardian Angels that marked the beginning of Opus Dei. On this particular weekday, Escrivá was on his way across town, on a tram, in the middle of reading the Madrid daily newspaper *ABC,* when all of a sudden he was gripped by a divine illumination, one so overwhelming that he couldn't contain himself. He started shouting at the top of his voice: *"Abba,* Father, Father!" *Abba* is a word from Aramaic, the language spoken by Jesus, and it translates roughly as "Dad." It's one of the few words left untranslated by the authors of the New Testament, who generally wrote in Greek.

Needless to say, the other passengers were startled by the outburst, but that didn't stop him. What Escrivá said he experienced in that moment was an overwhelming, direct awareness of being a son of God, what in technical language he would come to call *divine filiation.* The idea is that by creating us, God made us his creatures; but by redeeming us, in the person of Jesus Christ and his sacrifice on the Cross, God made us his adopted sons and daughters, so in a very direct sense we are "children of God," with all of the love and tenderness that relationship implies.

Naturally, within Opus Dei it is seen as significant that this revelation took place, not in a monastery or cathedral, but in a streetcar, jammed with ordinary people going about their daily business in the world. It was, in this sense, a case of form reinforcing function—the revelation took place *in* the world, in order to underscore a truth *about* the world. As

Escrivá later put it himself, "The street does not prevent us from having a contemplative dialogue with God. For us, the hustle and bustle of the world is precisely the place of prayer."

This sensation of being a beloved child of God was a key concept for Escrivá. This is so much so that once, during a "meditation" (a reflection on a gospel reading), when he heard a young priest say that the foundation of the spiritual life of a member of Opus Dei is humility, Escrivá cried out, "No, my son, it is divine filiation!" Later he would arrive at this formula: If secularity and the sanctification of work is the framework of Opus Dei, divine filiation is its foundation. In his biography of Escrivá, Peter Berglar writes that Escrivá spent long hours before the statue of the Christ Child at the Saint Isabela Convent in Madrid, where he was chaplain, meditating on what it meant to be a child of God, like Christ himself.

At one level the concept of divine filiation should give those who take it seriously a remarkable serenity, confidence, and even pride. After all, if we truly are children of God (as we are all children of Adam), then in the end everything is destined to work out for the best. Escrivá wrote, "Seek comfort in divine filiation: God is your most loving father. This is your refuge, a sheltered harbor where you can drop anchor no matter what disturbs the surface of the sea of life." One Opus Dei numerary from the States told me, if he were to translate Escrivá's concept of divine filiation into the language of a younger generation raised on *Survivor* and *OC,* it would come out something like this: "Dude, what could go wrong? Don't you know who my Dad is?"

Monsignor Fernando Ocáriz, vicar-general of Opus Dei, explained his understanding of the concept of divine filiation in a December 2004 interview.

"This idea should hold true for every Christian, so it's nothing specific to Opus Dei," Ocáriz said. "It's only specific to us in the sense that Saint Josemaría pushed us, asked us, to put this concept at the center of our Christian awareness. So, what does it imply? Fundamentally, it suggests a life of continual prayer, so to speak, and not just in special moments. It favors a kind of supernatural instinct of addressing ourselves to God, asking for help, giving thanks for things, and asking forgiveness for our sins and weaknesses with serenity and trust. The spirit of filiation implies confidence and trust in the Lord, meaning that we don't see the Lord with 'fear,' in the negative sense of that term, not the solid Biblical concept of 'fear of the Lord,' which means respect and affection, a 'fear' of offending this Lord whom we love. It gives us a climate in the spiritual life of quiet, of calm, of trust."

Ocáriz said the concept of divine filiation also has consequences for the way in which work is carried out. "It pushes us to regard our work as our own, no matter the circumstances. This is what the Founder said. Even an employee who works in a large company where his tasks are assigned by someone else, and in that sense they can be very anonymous, at bottom this is still his work, because he's doing the things of God. From a human point of view, he's nobody's boss, and he doesn't decide himself what to do. Still, this is *his* work, because ultimately it's God's work."

Ocáriz teased out one final implication. "The concept of divine filiation also implies conversion, in light of our own limits and our own failures. Divine filiation creates a climate of returning to the Lord with trust, with spontaneity. From a dogmatic point of view, these are not original insights. But putting them into practice, into the heart of Christianity, is the hard part."

Escrivá himself, in his writing and preaching, seemed to draw five primary consequences from the concept of divine filiation.

- First, if being a son or daughter of God means that every Christian is, in a sense, *ipse Christus*, or "Christ himself," then everything a Christian does is part of the redemption of the world. As we have seen, for Escrivá this refers not just to the drama of Holy Week, but also to those long years of quiet work in Joseph's workshop. When Christ was working on a table, that act too was part of the redemption of all created reality. Among other things, this suggests that what he came up with was likely to be a terrific table. It implies a real attention to craft and to detail. Even the most ordinary and mundane tasks, seen from the perspective of divine filiation, take on a transcendent significance.
- Second, being a child of God also has consequences on the moral plane. If a Christian is another Christ, that implies an obligation to act with upright moral conduct. John Paul II called this "Christian anthropology." Once you realize what human life

really is, that is, being a son or daughter of God, this imparts a dignity to that life that, among other things, sets limits to what can be done with it. It makes abortion, for example, or cloning, or euthanasia morally unacceptable—not merely because the Church says so or because they may have socially negative consequences, but because they imply a lack of awareness about the intrinsic dignity of that life. Even more fundamentally, it means that every interaction with another person is an encounter with a child of God, therefore other people have to be treated with respect and compassion.

- Third, divine filiation flows out into what Opus Dei calls *apostolate,* what in a less politically correct age was known as "proselytism." The idea is that if every human being is a child of God and another Christ, the more they know about what that entails, and the more fully they live their identity, the better off they'll be. "Winning souls" for Christ, for the Church, and, if possible, for Opus Dei, is seen as a high priority.

- Fourth, an awareness of divine filiation should produce happiness, a genuine contentment with life, which is based on a realistic assessment of the human condition rather than momentary euphoria. "Our way is one of joy, of loving fidelity to the service of God," Escrivá wrote. "Our joy is not the warm glow of a foolish smile, a sort of physical well-being. It has deep roots. . . . Joy is an inevitable consequence of divine filiation, of knowing ourselves loved by our father God, who holds us close, helps us, and always forgives us." For this reason, visitors to Opus Dei centers will normally be struck by the cheerfulness and mirth of the place, which appears to many people as impressive and contagious, though critics charge that it can be forced and artificial.

- Fifth, Escrivá linked the concept of divine filiation to a more sobering reality: the Cross. He reflected on the "illumination" of 1931 in these terms: "You worked in such a way, Lord, that I might understand that to have the Cross meant to encounter happiness, joy. And the reason, I see with greater clarity than ever, is this: to have the Cross means to identify oneself with Christ, to be Christ and to be a Son of God." This linkage between the idea of divine filiation and the Cross of Christ was, for Escrivá, fundamental. If we are in some mysterious sense other Christs, other sons and daughters of God, then we too are destined for Calvary. Escrivá said on this point:

Purify your intentions, carrying out all your occupations for love of God, embracing with joy the cross of every day. I have repeated it a thousand times, because I hold that these ideas have to remain engraved in the heart of Christians. When we don't limit ourselves to tolerating, and, instead, love adversity, physical and moral suffering, and we offer it to God in reparation for our personal sins and the sins of all human beings, I assure you the pain will not crush you. In this case one is not carrying just any cross, but discovers the Cross of Christ, with the consolation of knowing that it is the Redeemer who offers himself to bear the weight of it.

In this sense Escrivá even suggested that every Christian is in a sense a "coredeemer," meaning that every Christian cooperates with and participates in Christ's work of redemption of the world. A final way Escrivá once put the point, from *The Way of the Cross:* "God is my father, even though he sends me suffering. He loves me tenderly, though he wounds me. Jesus suffers to fulfill the most holy will of God. . . . And I, who also want to follow God's will by following in the footsteps of the Master, can I complain if I meet suffering along the way? It is a clear sign of my divine filiation, for he is treating me like his divine Son."

Applications

I met Manuel Jesus Saavedra, fifty-four, at his barbershop, called Cesar's, in downtown Lima, Peru. Saavedra, who comes from the northern highlands in the Andes Mountains, was a barber in the Peruvian navy for sixteen years, and now, so to speak, he's in "private practice." He's not a member of Opus Dei, but since 2002 he has been a very enthusiastic cooperator. He also has a son who's a member of Opus Dei. Above the mirror in front of his barber's chair is a picture of Escrivá, so clients generally look at it while he's cutting their hair, and he said that's created the occasion for some very interesting conversations about matters of faith and spirituality.

I asked Saavedra what divine filiation means to him.

"It teaches me to love persons, because they're children of God," he said. "So a client doesn't just get twenty minutes of my time and a good haircut. I also try to give fifteen to twenty minutes just to talk, to find out a little something about them, to share a little something of myself," he said. "When I started this, I thought that people didn't want to talk about God, but I've learned that they really do. I'm not trying to convert anybody," he said, "but I do hope that they'll think about things more seriously."

Saavedra said that when clients see his picture of Escrivá, some become critical. Opus Dei in Peru has long been a subject of fierce controversy, in large part because it's linked in the public mind with Cardinal Juan Luis Cipriani of Lima and the politician Rafael Rey. Both are high-profile conservatives and divisive figures. "I'm happy they say these things to me, so I can respond," Saavedra said. Since his shop is in a working-class neighborhood populated by Peru's indigenous Quechua-speaking peoples, one criticism Saavedra said he often hears is that Opus Dei is "for white people, for rich people, with yellow hair." He said he tells them, "I have a son like me, dark-skinned, and he lives in a bad neighborhood, but he's in the Work." Bringing the point back to divine filiation, Saavedra said, "We are all children of God, and so we have to love everyone."

Saavedra said that the concept of seeing his work as a means to redeeming the world has become very important to him and his family, since his sons are also barbers. "I want to die with my scissors in my hands," he said.

Marlies Kücking is the head of the Central Advisory Council, the governing body for Opus Dei's women's branch, and so one could call her the "top woman" in the group's power structure. She's been in Rome since 1964 and has seen a great deal of water flow under the bridge. Kücking was the prefect of studies in 1965, for example, to whom María del Carmen Tapia, who worked at Villa Sacchetti and later served as regional director for women in Venezuela, made her "confidence," meaning the regular weekly spiritual direction that members receive from their directors, after she had been recalled to Rome. The episode began the falling out that led to Tapia's exit from Opus Dei in May 1966, after eight months of what she called virtual "house arrest." Tapia later recalled that Kücking accused her of having "intense pride."

I sat down with Kücking on November 25, 2004—Thanksgiving Day, though in Rome it was just another Thursday. Kücking, a German, told me she met Opus Dei for the first time during a college trip to Rome in 1954. She said a young member of the women's branch who lived at Villa Sacchetti, headquarters for the women of Opus Dei where Kücking today has her office, explained the concept of finding God in the middle of the world. Raised in a fairly traditional German Catholic family, Kücking said she was thunderstruck by the idea. "To pray, I thought one had to go into the church, or take part in a procession," Kücking said. "But just in the street? This idea never left me." Kücking "whistled" as a numerary at the age of eighteen. At first, she said, she didn't tell her mother, but she said it soon became obvious that "something had changed" when she began going to Mass every day and no longer went to the cinema or to parties. Her parents were concerned, and at that time in Germany children weren't considered adults until twenty-one, so in theory they could have made her wait three years before taking up her new life. Instead, however, they went to talk to a charming Opus Dei priest in October 1956, and, Kücking said, came back with just one question: "What do you need?"

Before long, headquarters in Rome asked Kücking and the other couple of female numeraries in Germany to open a center. They found a run-down apartment building in Cologne that had been ruined during the war. Four or five families lived there, Kücking said, and never cleaned it, so it was "horrible." These are the images she recalls, she said, when people talk about the "wealth" of Opus Dei. Initially there were two numeraries living in the center, Kücking said, a Mexican and herself, and the economic problems were very serious. One Saturday, she said, she literally didn't know how they were going to buy food for the next day, but through an odd series of circumstances, things worked out. That experience, she said, taught her what divine filiation really means, in the sense of having a complete abandonment to and trust in God.

Kücking said that for her, divine filiation is "the foundation of everything" inside Opus Dei and of her own personal spirituality.

"We are sons and daughters of God, not only when we pray, but when we joke around, when we have fun, when we eat, in every instant of our lives. Obviously, this gives you strength, a dimension of life, an attitude, to accept whatever God sends us. In that sense, the 'Spirit of the Work' is to take every difficulty with joy. Also, to live as a daughter of God, I also have to work in this world, I have to bring the world closer to God. This idea therefore not only impels me to work, but to do my very best, because every task has this huge, eternal aim behind it."

Diane Lechner is a Chicago-area supernumerary introduced briefly in chapter 3. She is a mother of seven children, four boys and three girls, and until the children were old enough to move around on their own, she was a stay-at-home mom. She explained that with seven very rambunctious children crashing around the house at all hours of the day and night, she initially struggled to find time for her spiritual life. But reflecting on what Escrivá had said about divine filiation, she said, "helped me to keep God first and foremost in my life." Concretely, she said, it gave her the resolve to make sure that she carved out time for prayer and meditation, for "the norms" that are part of the daily routine of an Opus Dei member. She found that when she did so, the other priorities in a mom's life sorted themselves out.

"If I put the diapers first, the norms would never get done," Lechner said. "But if I did my reading and prayer, everything else fell into place."

Edna Kavanagh offers a window into how Opus Dei members apply the concept of "divine filiation" in terms of outreach to others, what's known as *apostolate*. Kavanagh is a classic citizen of the world. Her grandfather on one side was English, on the other side Spanish, and her parents met in Buenos Aires, Argentina, where she was born. She emigrated to Europe in 1959 after being sent to Amsterdam as part of Argentina's ladies field hockey team, which played in that year's world championship. (Kavanagh said her team won only one match, but they had a blast.) She went on to become a successful businesswoman with a Dutch import-export firm, becoming a Dutch citizen in 1967.

She learned about Opus Dei in Holland when one of its members asked her to give some talks to groups of female professionals, after she was named the country's Businesswoman of the Year in 1984. She said that Opus Dei's emphasis on sanctification of work appealed to her immediately, since she was both a practicing Catholic and a very serious professional. She eventually became a supernumerary. I met her in May 2004 at the Opus Dei shrine of Torreciudad, in Spain, where she was participating in an annual workshop for supernumerary women.

Given what was going on in Dutch Catholicism at the time Kavanagh got to know Opus Dei—Holland was considered the most liberal Catholic community in the world in the 1970s and 1980s—Kavanagh said she learned right away that Opus Dei was a source of controversy. "I noticed that people would be less open with me, or would wait to have an opportunity either to say something or to put a question, which in a way was almost always nasty," she said. Since Kavanagh studied law, she said she has a "keen sense of justice," and felt that many of the attacks on Opus Dei were unfair. Once, she said, somebody asked her why, if she wanted to pray every day, she didn't "become a Carmelite." That, she said, would have been more acceptable to many of her Dutch Catholic friends. Still, she persevered with Opus Dei, attracted by the notion that she could blend her professional work with her spiritual life.

The idea of "apostolate," on the other hand—trying to bring others to the practice of the faith—was much more difficult. Kavanagh said she stuck with it based on her understanding of divine filiation.

"I thought that was going to be very difficult if you have to do that individually, with individual people. It's one thing to stand up and give a very nice talk about any subject of faith, but it's something completely different to talk with people, to give yourself to them, to open your inner life to other people so that they can recognize, hopefully, that they are children of God," Kavanagh said. This, according to many Opus Dei members, is the heart of what "apostolate" means. It's linked to personal friendship and sincerity. If one is trying to live as a child of God, as Opus Dei understands it, then as friendships develop, the opportunity will naturally arise for sharing what that identity entails.

"Suddenly you realize that if you're open for what God wants for you, he makes it easy," Kavanagh said. "He puts people in your way. I thought I had to go knock at a door and say, 'Here I am,' or something like that. In fact, opportunities simply present themselves in the course of your professional encounters and your personal friendships, to help people see who they really are in light of God's love. That was quite new. And that has grown tremendously. My retired life now is doing that sort of thing in groups, in families, in places all over the country."

Finally, Father Soichiro Nitta, regional vicar for Opus Dei in Japan, told me over lunch in a Roman trattoria that he thinks the concept of divine filiation may prove to be Opus Dei's most important contribution to Japanese culture.

"After World War II, the figure of the father disappeared from the Japanese family," he said. "The father used to be a great authority figure in addition to being a parent who would love you no matter what. These two concepts, authority and unconditional love, were rolled into one. After the war, however, there was a tremendous reaction against authoritarianism and anything that reminded people of the old social system. Everything had to be equal.

"As a result, today the concept of a loving Father who also sets rules and expects obedience—in other words, the Christian concept of the paternity of God—is very difficult for Japanese people to understand. So Opus Dei has something to offer here, because this idea was so central to Saint Josemaría. Maybe we can make a contribution not just to the spirituality of the Japanese people, but also to the health of the family, which is not in very good shape in Japan."

Nitta, by the way, is one of only nine native Opus Dei priests in Japan. He said that while there really isn't a "Japanese" version of Opus Dei, since the spirit is the same everywhere, there is at least one Western custom that isn't followed in Japanese centers—wearing shoes indoors. "That's hard for me in Rome," he said. "Every time I get back to my room at Villa Tevere, the first thing I do is take them off."

Challenges

Escrivá drew two consequences from divine filiation that, in a certain sense, stand in tension with one another: 1) respect for all human beings, regardless of who they are or how they think, because of their dignity as children of God; and 2) an apostolic desire to help people respond more intentionally to what that dignity entails, from the point of view of the Roman Catholic faith. This creates a difficult balancing act between accepting people as they are and guiding them toward what they can become. In itself, this tension is not unique to Opus Dei. In many ways it's the dynamic of all friendship—the oscillation between loving one's friends unconditionally and yet prodding them to realize the best versions of themselves. True friendship embraces both poles of this tension between loving someone "as is" and as they "could be."

Maintaining the proper balance is, however, perhaps a special challenge for members of Opus Dei, especially directors and others responsible for spiritual guidance, because of the deep passions stirred by a religious vocation. If the right combination of acceptance and challenge is offered, a person's heart can be set aflame and new horizons for love and service opened; if handled badly, however, a person's psyche can be bruised and hard feelings can result. Much of the criticism that ex-members level against Opus Dei comes down to this, that in pushing them toward the "could be" dimension of themselves, directors sometimes ran roughshod over the "as is." Again, this is not a problem unique to Opus Dei—any parent, any lover, any friend struggles with the same tension. In Opus Dei, however, because the religious commitment involved is so profound, the sensitivity called for is even greater. The trick is to maintain a balance between seeing human beings in light of their supernatural destiny, wanting them to grow spiritually and morally, and seeing them as human beings all the same, with all the tolerance, patience, and respect for the freedom of others that human nature requires.

Carlo De Marchi, an Italian who is the top official in Opus Dei for work with youth, said it this way: "One of the obligations in this area . . . is to find a balance between the human and supernatural enthusiasm of someone who already knows God's plan for himself or herself, and respect for the 'long term' of humanity. Every person has his or her pace, and Jesus walks at everyone's own rhythm, as he did with the disciples of Emmaus. Beyond this, in a certain sense, all one can do is give a good example, encourage people, and not try to speed things along."

On another level, perhaps the most serious challenge posed by divine filiation is how members interpret the ready identification with the Cross. As Escrivá frequently stressed, for a Christian to realize his or her identity as *ipse Christus*, "Christ himself," in the sense of being a child of God, means embracing the destiny of Christ to be persecuted, misunderstood, and to suffer. Certainly that idea has deep historical roots in Christian spirituality, and so far as it goes it's unassailable. Pushed to an extreme, however, it can turn into a lust for suffering, a kind of celebration of pain for its own sake. Critics of Opus Dei have long insisted that Escrivá himself went too far in this direction, especially in his spiritual practices. Whether that charge has merit remains to be seen, but even at a conceptual level, one can understand how the identification with the Cross of Christ carries that potential.

A related risk is that by accepting suffering as the inevitable fate of Christians, one can actually suffer injustice a bit too gladly. On a personal level, this does not seem to be a terribly serious problem for most Opus Dei members. Because of the strong emphasis within Opus Dei on being citizens just like everyone else, most members are quite willing to invoke their rights when they feel unjustly treated. Yet when it comes to Opus Dei itself, historically the organization sometimes has been hesitant or unwilling to engage its critics in the public debate, and this silence has been justified internally in terms of accepting the Cross. After all, Jesus said in Matthew's Gospel, "Blessed are you when people revile you and persecute you and utter all kinds of evil against you falsely on my account. Rejoice and be glad, for your reward is great in heaven, for in the same way they persecuted the prophets who were before you."

The risk is that this spiritual reading of criticism can actually become a rationalization for indifference toward public opinion, a kind of blasé attitude of "they'll never understand us" that reinforces instinctive reactions of defensiveness and unwillingness to engage the broader conversation. I'll develop the point later, but Opus Dei members will sometimes congratulate themselves for not responding aggressively to public curiosity, often quoting the Founder, as if this were the more spiritually noble path. In fact, however, it can sometimes simply be an excuse for inertia, or a lack of imagination, or even an unwillingness to explain themselves to the outside world. Moreover, as its spokespersons constantly stress, Opus Dei is not a self-standing reality, but an integral part of the Catholic Church. By allowing misunderstanding and opposition to fester, therefore, damage is done not just to Opus Dei, but to the entire Church, which has embraced and approved Opus Dei. Of course, many members inside Opus Dei understand this perfectly well, and the organization's capacity, not to mention its desire, to answer criticisms and explain itself publicly has grown tremendously in recent decades. Still, the inherent risk in its understanding of divine filiation is that it will "spiritualize" questions and doubts from the outside world as part of what is meant by the Cross, providing a ready excuse for ignoring even potentially valid criticisms.

Finally, this same identification with the Cross can produce a kind of hesitance about opposing injustice. If suffering plays a positive role in the spiritual life, what's the point of working for reforms that might eliminate it? In the real world, most people in Opus Dei do not seem captive to such quiescence. Opus Dei members are engaged in fighting poverty, disease, and racism, and working for justice all across the world. The Opus Dei–run Strathmore University in Kenya, for example, was the first racially integrated institution of higher learning in East Africa. The Midtown Center in Chicago provides black and Hispanic youth with tools to help them succeed academically, and I met a number of graduates of that program who say they owe much of their professional and personal success to it. Such examples could be multiplied. Even so, however, the question of what "accepting the Cross" means should be a perennial topic for reflection. Striking a balance between accepting suffering when it comes and resisting it when one can is a perpetual challenge—not just for members of Opus Dei, but for everyone.

QUESTION MARKS
ABOUT OPUS DEI

Preface

This section deals with the most common public concerns about Opus Dei, and no doubt some admirers of Opus Dei will object that the attention is excessive. The controversies treated in the chapters that follow—about secrecy, women, money, power, recruiting, demands for obedience and corporal mortification—have been around for a long time, in some cases dating back to the 1940s, and members of Opus Dei have responded to them on myriad occasions over that span of time. Many sympathetic observers regard these questions as already asked and answered, and will be puzzled at the lengthy treatment here. Others contend that giving so much space to controversial matters risks obscuring the core spiritual message of Opus Dei, by focusing on things that are at best secondary to the spirit of the Work and, in some cases, completely extraneous to it.

I understand such wearied sighs. Yet the reality is that in the court of public opinion, these questions are still very much alive. Ordinary men and women, Catholics and non-Catholics alike, when given the opportunity, often put precisely these questions about Opus Dei: Is it true that men and women are segregated, and if so, why? Did Opus Dei bail out the Vatican Bank? Do members whip themselves, and if so, why? Is Opus Dei a secret society? Is Opus Dei a right-wing political force? Does Opus Dei intentionally target young and impressionable recruits? Perhaps it is the case, as Opus Dei members often contend, that these fires are fanned by a sensationalistic press and by critics with axes to grind. But however we got here, the reality is that until fair-minded observers believe they have been given the full truth on these points, it will be difficult to focus their attention on the spiritual message that Opus Dei wants to present. Moreover, this is not just a matter of ill will or prurient curiosity; at the bottom of these controversies are legitimate questions about how Opus Dei does business, and they deserve a serious response. The problem with existing discussion about Opus Dei is not that these questions are raised but that the responses given are so often based on rumor, myth, and misinformation, from all sides.

The burden of these chapters, therefore, is to painstakingly step through each of the most common public controversies about Opus Dei, providing as much information and context as possible to think clearly about them. The aim is not principally to resolve the disputes—that's work for the reader to do—but to provide the best set of tools possible for doing that work.

While there are many streams that feed these concerns, the strongest current has always come from the testimony of ex-members—some from the earliest years in Spain, some from the 1960s and 1970s, a few from as recently as 2004—scattered across various parts of the world. In many cases in the chapters that follow, the testimony of critics such as Alberto Moncada, María del Carmen Tapia, John Roche, Tammy DiNicola, Sharon Clasen, and Dennis Dubro will be compared to the practices, policies, and experiences of the present. Opus Dei points out, rightly, that the criticism made by these individuals is not the whole story, that many ex-members remain on good terms with the organization and recount very different versions of their experiences. In at least some cases, they say, the horror stories told by critics such as Moncada and DiNicola reflect bad choices made by individuals, and not the overall tenor of Opus Dei.

Be that as it may, it's important to point out that, where the testimony of the critics is hard to reconcile with the present reality as it's described by those inside Opus Dei, this doesn't necessarily mean that the critics are wrong, or dishonest. It may be that they are accurately describing their experiences from the times and places they were in Opus Dei, and in the meantime, Opus Dei has changed. In a number of cases Opus Dei readily concedes this sort of evolution—as, for example, in the case of "screening" the mail of numeraries, which was once standard practice in

Opus Dei centers but has fallen into disuse in the age of cellular phones, SMS, and e-mail.

One could argue that, in at least some cases, the critical accounts of some former members played a positive role in the evolution of Opus Dei, helping to flag problematic areas that needed attention. A spokesperson for Opus Dei in England, Andrew Soane, has acknowledged the point, saying in December 2004 with respect to the Opus Dei Awareness Network, the anti–Opus Dei group founded by DiNicola and her mother: "I've been on the ODAN Web site, and it's helped raise my antenna and point out things that could be addressed." In that sense, the critics may sometimes have functioned, as a friend and colleague of mine puts it, as "canaries in the mine," alerting Opus Dei to potential hazards in its thought and practice. None of this suggests that every bit of criticism from ex-members is valid, merely that organizations, like the human be-ings who make them up, tend to learn more from what goes wrong than from success, more from criticism than from praise, and no doubt that has been true of Opus Dei over the seventy-seven years of its existence. Fairness means recognizing that there are places where Opus Dei today does not seem as the critics describe it, but this does not in itself make the critics untrustworthy. It may be that on some particulars, they helped Opus Dei more than anyone yet realizes.

Chapter Seven

SECRECY

LexisNexis is the most comprehensive database of newspapers, magazines, and news agencies in the English language. A search combining the terms "Opus Dei" and "secret" from 2000 to 2004 generates a total of 575 entries, which works out to one article every two and a half days that, in some fashion, played on the widespread public impression that Opus Dei is "secretive." That's just in English. If one were to factor in French, Spanish, German, and Italian, to say nothing of Dutch or Flemish or Portuguese, languages for which LexisNexis is much less complete, no doubt not a single day went by over that four-year period that, somewhere in the world, Opus Dei was not tagged as a "secret" organization. No other proof seems necessary that Opus Dei has an image problem.

Nor is this a recent phenomenon. The first substantive article about Opus Dei in a major English language news outlet came in *Time* magazine on March 18, 1957, after three members of Opus Dei became ministers in the Spanish government of Gen. Francisco Franco. That piece referred to Opus Dei as the "White Masons," a reference to their reputation for secrecy. (Ironically, in an indication of how times have changed on other matters, the 1957 *Time* piece also reported that in the Spanish politics of the day, Opus Dei was seen as having "liberal leanings.")

It isn't just journalists and pundits who think of Opus Dei as a secret society. Their characterizations might be written off as ill will, or typical media sensationalism. These impressions, however, have come solidly from within the Catholic Church. The earliest controversies over Opus Dei date from intra-Church rivalries in Spain in the 1930s and early

1940s, and included charges of secrecy and cultlike behaviors that today seem downright bizarre. These events are documented in volume 2 of the Vázquez de Prada biography of Escrivá.

The "White Masons"

In the late 1930s, Opus Dei members in Madrid noted that young people who had seemed enthusiastic about Escrivá's message were suddenly resistant to attending circles or get-togethers. Seeking to understand why, they discovered that rumors were circulating that chapels in Opus Dei centers were decorated with Masonic and cabalistic symbols, that Opus Dei's Communion hosts had a strange perfume, that while kneeling Opus Dei members would put their hands behind their backs in a strange ritual, that Opus Dei members would crucify themselves in bloody fashion upon a large wooden cross, and that strange lights would appear in the Opus Dei chapel while Escrivá would simulate levitation by hypnotizing his audience. At around the same time, a well-known and charismatic Spanish Jesuit, Father Ángel Carrillo de Albornoz, publicly accused Opus Dei of being a "secretive, heretical society of a Masonic stamp."

These rumors reached the highest levels of Spanish society. In July 1941 a civil court erected under Franco, the Tribunal for the Repression of Masonry, opened a formal inquest of Opus Dei based on charges that it was a "Masonic branch connected to Jewish sects." In the end the process was archived without action. In 1942, however, the information services of the Falange published a "Confidential Report on the Secret Organization Opus Dei," charging that its clandestine nature was "opposed to the ends of the Spanish state." Around the same time, the civil governor of Barcelona, Antonio Correa Veglison, opened an investigation. Correa called in Opus Dei member Alfonso Balcells and demanded that he explain what was going on behind the group's closed doors. Correa, according to a later recollection from Balcells, said he knew that Opus Dei was "a sect of illuminati or something similar." In Valencia, the local police sent a young woman, María Teresa Llopis, into a set of spiritual exercises led by Escrivá. Llopis later said that the police asked her to discover if there were "secret passages" underneath the Opus Dei center as well as Masonic symbols. In some cities in Spain there were public burnings of Escrivá's book *The Way*.

The rumors about Opus Dei ricocheted from the Spanish Catholic Church into the civil courts and all the way to Rome. On July 3, 1942, the general of the Jesuits, at the time a Pole, Father Vladimir Ledochowski, sent a report on Opus Dei to the Vatican in which he charged that although *The Way* presented "healthy Christian doctrine," Escrivá's book was intended for "non-initiates" and that inside Opus Dei there were "traces of a secret tendency to dominate the world with a sort of Christian Masonry." Historians note the irony that similar charges were once circulated against the Jesuits as well as other prominent groups within the Catholic Church, such as the Knights Templar (which, like Opus Dei, developed in the Pyrenees Mountains, in Spanish Aragon, and in southern France).

Later, in 1948, the vicar-general of the Madrid diocese informed Escrivá that he had been denounced to the Holy Office, today the Congregation for the Doctrine of the Faith, in the Vatican. (In his diary, Escrivá recorded his response: "I'm happy about it! Because from Rome, from the pope, nothing can come to me but light and good.") Even the Vatican itself sometimes felt in the dark about the occult power of Opus Dei. In January 1971, Pope Paul VI's secretary of state, French cardinal Jean Villot, wrote to Escrivá to ask for a list of all the Opus Dei members who worked in the Vatican. Though Villot did not give a reason for the request, it suggested concern that an "infiltration" was under way. Escrivá responded promptly with the information.

From this intra-ecclesiastical debate, accusations against Opus Dei leapt back into the secular sphere. In 1986 the Italian parliament conducted an investigation of Opus Dei, part of a broader national debate over the behind-the-scenes influence of secret societies such as the infamous Masonic lodge P2. The investigation was led by Oscar Luigi Scalfaro, a staunch Catholic, later to become president of Italy. After eight months, Scalfaro's report cleared Opus Dei. "Opus Dei is secret neither in law nor in fact," Scalfaro concluded. In support of that statement, Scalfaro noted: "The vicariate of Opus Dei for Italy has its headquarters in Milan, at Via Alberto di Giussano 6, while in Rome it operates an information office, which can be identified through that normal instrument of daily work that is the telephone book."

Yet just two years later things ended differently in a case before Switzerland's Federal Court in Lausanne. It involved a dispute between an Opus Dei–affiliated educational organization and a Swiss newspaper, and the court found that Opus Dei was a "secret organization" that operates "covertly." In a related Swiss case, however, a different court sided with the Opus Dei–affiliated group. In January 1996 a French parliamentary commission compiled a list of 172 "sects," or dangerous religious movements in France, and Opus Dei made the list. The result drew protest from the French and Italian bishops. As far as a Vatican response, there was nothing official, but two months later John Paul II named a parish church in Rome after Escrivá.

The debate over alleged secrecy is not just part of Opus Dei's past, but is very much alive today. When I was in Washington, D.C., some months ago to give a public lecture, I bumped into an American archbishop who came to hear the talk. In the course of conversation beforehand, I mentioned that I was writing a book about Opus Dei. He replied that the "main thing" that troubles him about Opus Dei is its reputation for secrecy. "Would Russell Shaw, for example, admit to being a member?" he asked. In fact, as noted in chapter 3, Shaw, a supernumerary, is quite open about his membership, even down to volunteering how much money he donates to Opus Dei every month. (In an interview at the Catholic Information Center in Washington, D.C., Shaw gave me the figure before I even had the chance to ask.) The point, however, is that the archbishop's question testifies to the widespread impression.

The late Cardinal Basil Hume of Westminster in England, a Benedictine who was considered one of the more progressive cardinals of his day, had much the same set of concerns. In 1981 he issued a set of guidelines for the activity of Opus Dei in his diocese. They required that members be eighteen, that parents be notified when young people join, that members be free to leave and to choose spiritual directors outside Opus Dei, and that Opus Dei activities carry clear indications of their sponsorship. This last point responded to complaints that Opus Dei facilities often have generic-sounding names such as Baytree or Netherhall, and it may not be clear that they're linked to Opus Dei.

Even though Hume wrote that his guidelines "must not be seen as a criticism of the integrity of the members of Opus Dei or of their zeal in promoting their apostolate," his concerns did not go away. In a previously unpublished exchange of correspondence, on September 7, 1983, then-bishop John Gran of Oslo, Norway, wrote to Hume: "The situation is this—Opus Dei is endeavoring to spread northwards and to establish cells in the Scandinavian dioceses. At our upcoming plenary, we shall try to work out a common policy concerning Opus Dei, the idea being that we'll either accept or reject the 'onslaught.' I would very much appreciate your view (which will be kept confidential) on this prelature, its mode of operation and its finality. Any advice you might have will also be accepted with gratitude." On September 12, 1983, Hume wrote back suggesting that Gran keep in mind the guidelines laid down for Opus Dei in Westminster, which "reflect some of the experience we have had." He also suggested that Gran obtain a copy of the Opus Dei "Statutes." In the event, Opus Dei arrived in Sweden in 1984, but to date has not opened centers in either Norway or Denmark.

In another previously unpublished letter, dated January 29, 1987, Hume responded to a private inquiry from then-cardinal Stephen Kim Sou-hwan of Seoul, South Korea. Kim had contacted Hume for advice about whether he should allow Opus Dei to enter his diocese. Hume responded: "I know that Opus Dei contains many good people and does good work, but—strictly between ourselves—I would always be cautious in their regard. I do not like the secretiveness that seems to surround their activities, and I have suspicions about pressure that can at times be put on youths. So my advice to you would be that if you were to accept them in your diocese, that you make it clear what you expect of them."

Kim retired in April 1998. To date, Opus Dei has not opened a center in South Korea. There are cooperators of Opus Dei in South Korea, and members make visits from Hong Kong.

Even bishops sympathetic to Opus Dei sometimes share these worries. Auxiliary Bishop Joseph Perry, one of a handful of African-American bishops in the U.S. conference, went to the Jesuit-run Marquette University in Milwaukee, Wisconsin, and was a regular visitor to an Opus Dei center on the west side of the city. He told me in a September 2004 interview that he is not a member of Opus Dei, but that in college he would meet with an Opus Dei priest once a month and attended get-togethers. Before he got to know Opus Dei, he shared the widespread impression that it was "elitist," but said his personal contacts have been "entirely positive." Since arriving in Chicago, Perry said, he has attended evenings of recollection and celebrated liturgies at Saint Mary of the Angels Parish, entrusted to Opus Dei. He prays regularly with Father

Peter Armenio, the vicar of Opus Dei in Chicago who, among other things, serves as a chaplain to the Chicago Bears. "Opus Dei helps laity and priests bridge the connection between ordinary life and our salvation," Perry said. "I like to think that I'm the kind of bishop who would not be locked in on one option. As far as Opus Dei goes, I say put it out there and see who's interested. It won't be everyone's taste."

Yet even Perry said that it would be good for Opus Dei to collaborate more with the local clergy and thereby diminish its reputation for elitism and secrecy. "They need to give an answer to that," he said.

Chapter 5 noted the irony that Opus Dei should have a reputation for internal repression, since Escrivá repeatedly stressed the importance of freedom. Similarly, outsiders are often startled to find that, despite charges of secrecy, Escrivá was emphatic in his insistence that there should not be, and is not, anything "secretive" about Opus Dei. In an interview contained in the book *Conversations with Monsignor Escrivá*, for example, he was asked about rumors that Opus Dei is a secret society, and here is how he responded:

> *The members of the Work detest secrecy because they are ordinary faithful, the same as anyone else. They do not change their status when they join Opus Dei. It would be repulsive for them to carry a sign on their back that said, "Let it be known that I am dedicated to the service of God." That would be neither lay nor secular. But those who associate with members of Opus Dei and are acquainted with them realize that they belong to the Work, for, even if they do not publicize their membership, neither do they hide it. . . . Any reasonably well informed person knows that there is nothing secret about Opus Dei.*

Membership

John Hooper in *The New Spaniards* expresses the basic reason many people believe Opus Dei is secretive:

> *The Jesuits, to take the example of their most implacable enemies, are no doubt capable of exercising immense behind-the-scenes influence. But you are not likely to discover one day that the editor of,*

say, a financial journal for which you have been writing, or the chairman of an engineering company with which you have been negotiating, is also a member of the Society of Jesus. . . . You do not expect, but you may well find, especially if you live in Spain, that someone you work alongside, or over, or under, does not go home at night to a family, or a partner, or flatmates, but to a community in which there are lengthy periods of silence; that for two hours each day he or she is wearing a cilicio, *a chain with pointed links turned inwards, on the upper thigh (so that neither it nor the wounds it inflicts can be seen); and that, once a week, your colleague whips his or her buttocks with a* disciplina, *a five-thonged lash, for as long as it takes to say the prayer* Salve Regina.

Setting aside the salacious details (which apply only to Opus Dei celibates, approximately 30 percent of the organization's membership), the broad impression Hooper provides is correct. What is disconcerting about Opus Dei for many people isn't so much what members believe or what they do as the fact that one never quite knows who's in and who's out. Most Opus Dei members are laypeople in the midst of the secular world, and from an external point of view there is nothing distinguishing about them. They do not wear religious habits, they do not shave their heads or walk about barefoot soliciting alms. They don't wear special pins in their lapels or put bumper stickers on their cars. Further, Opus Dei members generally do not list their affiliation on their curriculum vitae, considering it part of their private spiritual life. While their friends know that they're part of the Work, colleagues and casual acquaintances may indeed be in the dark. Officially, Opus Dei takes the position that because numeraries live in Opus Dei centers and make Opus Dei their immediate family, their membership is almost definitionally "public" and hence they will usually confirm it if asked. Supernumeraries, on the other hand, who are generally married and live in private homes, are free to decide whether or not they wish to make their membership public; as an institution, Opus Dei will neither confirm nor deny someone's status.

This reality has led to intricate theories as to how to spot an Opus Dei member. These theories tend to be especially popular in Spain, about the only country on earth where there's a statistically significant possibility that a random person may actually be a member of Opus Dei. One popular hypothesis is that Opus Dei members wear Atkinson's cologne, in imitation of Escrivá. Another rumor, laughingly relayed to me in Madrid by Robert Duncan, a supernumerary who is a spokesperson for the Spanish gas company, is that Opus Dei businessmen can be spotted if a button on the sleeve of their suit jacket is missing. Yet another is that Opus Dei members smoke strong Ducados cigarettes, to project a "one of the boys" bearing. For the record, members deny that any of these things are true (without denying that some members may smoke, wear cologne, or have a button missing).

Closer to the mark, it's said that you can spot an Opus Dei member if he or she has a small statue of a donkey, a common symbol in Opus Dei centers, representing the donkey that carried Christ into Jerusalem. Escrivá compared himself to that donkey, saying his job was to carry Christ so that people could see him, then slip away. There is also an Opus Dei shibboleth; when two members meet, one may say to the other, *Pax,* to which the proper response is, *in aeternum.* This too, however, is not foolproof, since it presumes that the two members know that both are in Opus Dei, which isn't always the case. Moreover, they tend to be discreet, exchanging the greeting only when nonmembers aren't around. I had to wait six months before I actually witnessed it, at a restaurant along the highway between Barbastro and Torreciudad in Spain, when an Opus Dei member happened to overhear the conversation at our table and wandered over to say hello to the Opus Dei guy sitting with us.

Discretion

Given the frequent ridiculousness of the "Is he or isn't he?" guessing game, one might ask why Opus Dei members are not more open about their affiliation, in the sense of wearing some insignia or putting it on their business cards. Why not?

For one thing, there is a history of what is known inside Opus Dei as "discretion," meaning not advertising one's membership too brazenly. In part this is a matter of maintaining the secular, lay character of Opus Dei. If members were to broadcast an exterior sign of their vocation, they say, it would violate this spirit of "secularity" by making them seem different. Opus Dei members are not supposed to be like members of religious orders.

An additional reason, at least in the workplace, is that "bragging" about being in Opus Dei could be interpreted as trying to take advantage of membership to gain some personal or professional edge, and that was anathema to Escrivá, who said that no one has the right to claim to represent Opus Dei in a secular matter. All members have to stand on their own two feet, not hiding behind the Opus Dei "label."

Escrivá also insisted that Opus Dei practice what is known as "collective humility," meaning that it should not seek self-aggrandizement. The point was written into the 1950 "Constitutions" of Opus Dei: "Opus Dei professes collective humility, and consequently . . . its members will not use any distinctive insignia, and will be prudent when speaking of the Work to people not belonging to it, since their way of acting should be simple and not call attention to itself. Neither will Opus Dei participate, ordinarily, in social acts or be represented in them." All of this was designed to ensure that Opus Dei did not become a special interest group, so that members were left free in social affairs.

Finally, a historical reason for discretion had to do with the canonical status of Opus Dei. From 1947 to 1982, Opus Dei was classified in canon law as a "secular institute," which meant that it was treated as a development out of religious life. Among other complications, the Vatican ruled in 1950 that members of secular institutes could not be involved in business, which meant that supernumeraries who had business careers were, technically, in violation of Church law. Until that sort of thing could be straightened out, Escrivá and others in Opus Dei felt, "discretion" was in order.

Today, spokespersons invoke this tendency to confuse Opus Dei with religious orders as a primary reason for what, according to them, is an undeserved reputation for secrecy. Father Tom Bohlin, the regional vicar (and top Opus Dei official) in the United States, put it this way in a October 2004 interview, when I asked him if there was any merit to the view that Opus Dei is secretive: "No, there's no merit to that at all. I think it's a question of coming to understand who we are, what we're about, what we do. People approach us with certain preconceived ideas, which are very understandable, from a clerical milieu, of hundreds of years of history of religious orders."

According to spokespersons for Opus Dei, however, Escrivá revised his views on "discretion" as Opus Dei became better established. At one point in the 1960s, Escrivá said that he had "erased the word 'discretion' from my dictionary." In a letter to all the members of Opus Dei dated

November 21, 1966, Escrivá wrote: "I was amused for a while with the erroneous idea of discretion that some people have. Some, who have not grasped that we are the same as other citizens—we are not *like* them, we are their equals—think that we are living a fiction . . . because we do not carry a placard on our shoulders or a Christ on a banner. Others reason the same as they did forty years ago when discretion—which could not be more indiscreet—led us to bear the weight of the gestation of the Work as a mother guards in her womb the new creature: Where is the secret, if that was a secret shouted out loud? And now? I do not want to hear people speak of discretion: It is better to say and do things with naturalness."

Evolution

One can see evidence of this evolution by comparing the 1950 "Constitutions" of Opus Dei, the Vatican-approved Church law regulating its internal life, with the 1982 "Statutes," the law currently in force. The 1950 document cites an obligation to "speak cautiously with outsiders" and, in the case of both numeraries and supernumeraries, "to maintain a discreet silence with respect to the names of other members." The document specifies that this caution applies especially to new members, and to those who have left. In perhaps the most controversial provision, it states that before revealing their membership in Opus Dei, members should receive authorization from their director. Yet the "Constitutions" also state that Opus Dei and many of its members must be well known publicly, since its activities must always unfold under the civil law, and that members are always to avoid "secrecy and clandestine activity." The motives for discretion, it says, are "humility and apostolic effectiveness."

The 1982 "Statutes," which took the place of the 1950 "Constitutions," prohibit "secrecy or clandestine activity" and say that members are to act with naturalness, but "without hiding that they belong to the prelature." Priests of Opus Dei are "to behave always and everywhere with the greatest naturalness among their brother priests, without in any way appearing secretive, since nothing should be found in them that would need so to be hidden." In keeping with Escrivá's desire to "erase" the term, the word "discretion" does not appear. The requirement from 1950 that members should have a director's authorization before revealing their membership has likewise been removed.

From my experience, I've asked hundreds of people over the last year whether they were members of Opus Dei, and I've never found anyone unwilling to answer, though occasionally members outside the Anglo-Saxon world are bit surprised by the directness of the question. This book itself is one piece of evidence for their openness, since I quote more than one hundred members of Opus Dei, almost always by name, and identify what kind of member they are (numerary, supernumerary, and so on). Compare this to the fact in February 2004, when American TV journalist Tim Russert asked President George W. Bush about his alleged membership in Yale's famous Skull and Bones society, Bush said he couldn't answer. When a journalist put the same question to a spokesperson for Sen. John Kerry, also allegedly a Skull and Bones member, the answer was: "John Kerry has absolutely nothing to say on that subject. Sorry."

Why Not Publish the List?

The reasons reviewed above may explain why individual members have been reluctant to broadcast their connections to Opus Dei. But what about corporate practice? Why doesn't Opus Dei publish a directory of its members, so that whoever wants to can see who's in and who's out?

David Gallagher, a numerary and officer for Opus Dei in the United States, explains: "People who join Opus Dei do so for strictly spiritual purposes and do not expect their membership to become a news item. They naturally tell their family and friends of their membership. Opus Dei officials respect the privacy of members and their right to inform whomever they wish about their membership. They do not identify them publicly to the press or otherwise. In order for a policy of declining to confirm when someone is a member to be meaningful, it is also necessary to decline to deny it when someone is not a member."

So much for the official answer. Another element to the story, as difficult as this may be to believe, is that Opus Dei does not have a master list of all its members in the world. Under the process for becoming a member outlined in chapter 1, a candidate to be a numerary writes a letter to the prelate in Rome, so those letters are preserved in the archieves in Villa Tevere. Letters requesting admission as a supernumerary, on the other hand, are addressed to the regional vicar. Each year Opus Dei furnishes the Vatican basic data about its membership, so Villa Tevere asks each region to give it a number of supernumeraries, but the names are not forwarded. A "master list" of members of Opus Dei thus doesn't exist and, on the basis of the different ways that regions handle records, one probably couldn't be compiled without some difficulty. One could argue that Opus Dei *should* do a better job of keeping track of its members, but the point is that it's not that they have a list and refuse to divulge it; such a list does not exist.

To be fair, too, things have changed in the way the officials of Opus Dei handle membership questions. While Opus Dei spokespersons will not comment on the record about whether a given individual is a member, they often are willing to do so off the record, especially when it's a high-profile person. For example, I had no trouble establishing that, media reports to the contrary, neither former FBI director Louis Freeh nor U.S. Supreme Court justice Antonin Scalia is a member of Opus Dei. (Freeh's brother John was a numerary member of Opus Dei, though he later left, and his sons attended the Heights, the Opus Dei–run boys' school in suburban Washington, D.C.) Neither, for that matter, is Clarence Thomas or Mel Gibson, other names often linked to Opus Dei in the American press, and neither is TV pundit Robert Novak. Similarly, in Peru there is a rumor that the founder of one of the country's largest supermarket chains, E. Wong, is a member of Opus Dei, apparently because at the 1999 installation Mass of Cardinal Juan Luis Cipriani, who is a member of Opus Dei, some of the security workers wore E. Wong vests. I had no difficulty ascertaining that Wong is not a member.

Moreover, it is difficult to make the argument that in a democratic society, which recognizes the right of free association, Opus Dei ought to be obliged to divulge a listing of members. Scalfaro, who conducted the 1986 Italian parliamentary investigation, was emphatic that not publishing a list of members does not make Opus Dei a "secret society." He noted that after the fascist period under Mussolini, Italian law was changed so that the state no longer had the power to compel organizations to divulge their membership lists, and this was seen as a step forward for democracy and human rights. "Neither according to the [Italian] constitution, nor to the law now in force, can it be demanded that an association, in order to be licit and non-secret, should be compelled to publicize externally the identity of its own members," Scalfaro said. "The prohibition of secrecy does not signify an obligation to make everything public."

Penetration in Tough Markets

The indistinguishability of Opus Dei members can create problems in Western societies that have high expectations for transparency, but it can also be an asset in cultures where traditional religious operatives have a hard time getting a foothold. As laypeople and ordinary citizens, Opus Dei members can set up shop in places such as China, North Korea, or Saudi Arabia, where Christian proselytism is either forbidden or heavily discouraged. They have the capacity to "penetrate tough markets" for the Catholic Church.

This point was made in an April 23, 1979, letter from then-father Alvaro del Portillo and Father Javier Echevarría of Opus Dei to Cardinal Sebastiano Baggio, at the time the prefect of the Congregation for Bishops, summarizing the arguments for transforming Opus Dei into a personal prelature. After reviewing some of the canonical fine points, Portillo and Echevarría wrote: "This is all without taking account of the apostolate of penetration which, through occasions created by normal professional activity (specialized courses and cultural exchanges, international meetings and congresses, invitations for economic experts, technicians, teachers, etc.), can be developed in nations under totalitarian regimes of an anti-Christian or atheist character, or in any event marked by a strong nationalism, that renders difficult and often impossible, *de jure* or *de facto,* the activity of religious and missionaries, and even the organized presence of the Church as an institution."

This capacity of Opus Dei to penetrate places where traditional religious personnel aren't welcome has applications also in the secularized West. "The transformation of Opus Dei from a secular institute into a personal prelature . . . would offer the Holy See the possibility of utilizing with greater efficiency a mobile corps of priests and laity (accurately prepared) who could be present anyplace, with a spiritual and apostolic ferment for Christian living, above all in social contexts and professional activities where it's often not easy for the normal means the Church has at its disposal to be effective," Portillo and Echevarría wrote in April 1979.

Carl Schmidt, a longtime Opus Dei numerary in the United States, said he was invited to speak at a Jesuit residence in the early 1960s, and one Jesuit there recognized this potential.

"I can remember giving that talk, and there were two reactions in the question period afterward. One was from an older Jesuit who said something like, 'I've worked for thirty-five in Jesuit sodalities, and our constant question is, what is a lay spirituality? It seems to me here's the answer. . . .' The other was a younger Jesuit who said, 'Let's face it, fellows. What we don't like about Opus Dei is that these guys are out there where we can't go. For four hundred years we've been on the forefront, but now these guys have opened up a front where we can't go.' "

Schmidt, knowing the long history of tensions between the Jesuits and Opus Dei, smiled as he recounted his response. "I answered, 'Well, you said it, Father, not me,' " he laughed.

A Point of Comparison

Opus Dei is not the only group within the Catholic Church that sometimes practices "discretion" about membership. As a point of comparison, consider the Istituto Secolare Missionarie della Regalità, or Missionaries of the Kingship of Christ, a secular institute composed of some three thousand women present in fifty-three countries. The community was founded in 1919 in Assisi, Italy, by Father Agostino Gemelli and Armida Barelli, an Italian laywoman involved in the Catholic Action movement.

Members of the Missionaries of the Kingship of Christ take a vow of celibate chastity and gather periodically for formation in the Franciscan tradition, but do not live as a community. They remain laywomen working in various professional and social environments, who seek to promote the ideal of following Christ from within the secular world. The community was approved by the Vatican in 1948. Members are autonomous in their professional and political choices. They are responsible for their own finances, although they are expected to draw up an annual budget and allocate as much of their resources as possible to "gospel priorities," usually meaning charity.

Members do not wear distinctive dress or religious symbols. According to a description of their norms provided by the Italian branch, they are to "maintain a reserve about their vocational choice and their membership in the institute." In other words, they don't tell people that they are members. The idea is to protect the secularity of their way of life, and not to distinguish themselves from other laypeople in the everyday world. Historically, the "reserve" has also allowed members of secular institutes to live and work unnoticed in environments hostile to the Church.

The similarities with Opus Dei are obvious, even though the Missionaries of the Kingship of Christ more closely resemble a religious community. Both Opus Dei and the Missionaries of the Kingship of Christ were part of an early-twentieth-century movement to overcome the estrangement of the Catholic Church from the secular world. In order to do that, many groups made a decision to be low-key about who they were and what they did, in order to seem "just like everybody else." The creation of secular institutes by Pope Pius XII in 1947 was intended to give these groups official standing in the Church.

Mary Lou Carr, who has studied secular institutes, described the phenomenon of "reserve" within these groups in a paper at Notre Dame College in Manchester, New Hampshire, in 1998:

> Another group of consecrated men and women, who wear no habit or outward sign of their consecration, are members of Secular Institutes. Their consecration and commitment is no less than that of religious brothers and sisters, but little is known of them. One of the reasons that these institutes are not well known is the principle of "reserve" or discretion. In the practice of this reserve, the member is discreet in making his or her membership known publicly. . . . In the strictest practice of reserve, the member refrains telling anyone from outside of the specific Institute of his or her membership. The purpose has been to provide the member with a greater freedom to interact in the secular world. The mission of Secular Institutes is to bring Christ to the marketplace, to change the world from within, to be hidden leaven in the world.

The United States Conference of Secular Institutes explains the custom of "reserve" this way: "The characteristic of a hiddenness or discretion occurs with about half of the membership in secular institutes. Some lay members do not mention their consecration in an institute to other people or groups in society because they do not wish 'to be set apart' from them. However, these members are expected to be known to their bishops and other officials within the Church."

The Missionaries of the Kingship of Christ push "discretion" further than Opus Dei does today. When I contacted the institute to request an interview, I was invited to pose questions through e-mail, even though the headquarters in Rome is not far from my office.

Today there are roughly twenty-seven secular institutes in the United States, eleven of diocesan right and sixteen of pontifical right. They include the Community of Saint John, founded in Switzerland by Hans Urs von Balthasar; the Crusaders of Saint Mary; and the Father Kolbe Missionaries of the Immaculata. There are more than two hundred secular institutes worldwide, with nearly sixty thousand members; some 80 percent of members are women. Most Catholics have probably never heard of them, in large part because of the "reserve." Members say the aim is not to be secretive, but to deflect the "glory" to God, and to be able to act as a "leaven" within the broader culture. If Opus Dei is secretive because it doesn't reveal its members, therefore, it's got company.

Telling Family Members

A special form of the concern about secrecy in Opus Dei is withholding one's affiliation from family members. No one disputes that over the years, this has happened. Matthew Collins, for example, is a computer programmer and systems analyst who has worked for a variety of medical agencies, and was a supernumerary in Opus Dei for almost twenty-seven years. He is still on good terms with Opus Dei and is now a cooperator. Collins has posted a Web site in question-and-answer format about his experiences in Opus Dei. Here's what he says on the subject of telling family members about one's decision to join Opus Dei:

> Another frequent criticism of the Work is that prospective members, especially numeraries, are sometimes advised not to tell their families for some time that they've joined the Work, or are considering doing so. When I joined Opus Dei I was given this instruction myself and it is sometimes still given. Frankly, I don't know why, and it seems kind of odd to me. Still, to put this in its proper context I think it might be helpful to remember that during its early development in Spain, the Work was viciously attacked by people who truly didn't understand what it was that Saint Josemaría was trying to do.

That Collins is correct about this advice having been given to Opus Dei members is a matter of public record. John Roche was an Opus Dei numerary from 1959 to 1973, eventually souring on the group. When he left, he assisted the *London Times* in publishing an exposé about what he had come to regard as the abuses and excesses of Opus Dei. One of his objections was that Opus Dei members were encouraged to conceal their decision to join from family members. A further example comes from the case of Tammy DiNicola, an American and former Opus Dei numerary for two and one-half years, who left the organization in 1990. DiNicola and her mother, Dianne, founded the Opus Dei Awareness Network, an anti–Opus Dei group that operates a Web site with testimonies of former members. Dianne told me in a May 2004 interview that when Tammy went to Boston College as a freshman, "For the longest time she seemed perfectly all right, and then she seemed to have a personality change. This was over a three-year period of time, and she was just becoming more alienated from us. She joined [Opus Dei] and did not tell us. That wasn't normal behavior for her."

Collins is also right that part of the historical logic was the memory of opposition from parents in the early days in Spain. This reality is documented in volume 2 of the Vázquez de Prada biography of Escrivá. For example, Vázquez quotes from a letter written in 1941 by a friend of an early member, Rafa Escolá, whose family was opposed to his membership. The friend quotes Escolá: "At my house, my mother and my five brothers look at me like [I am] a heretic on his way to perdition. All day they don't take their eyes off of me, and they study my smallest movements; everything I do seems suspect to them; if they see me sad, they say, 'It's natural, you're sad because you realize you're on the wrong path'; but if they see me full of joy and peace, they worry all the more; 'There's nothing more to do,' they say, 'there's no hope that he'll wake up, evil has put down roots inside him and he's now an inveterate heretic'; my mother can't talk to me or look at me without crying; between us now is an icy barrier." Such stories could be multiplied hundreds of times across Spain.

Resentment from parents about a religious vocation is hardly limited to Opus Dei. Some of the great saints in the history of the Church have had to overcome the opposition of their families; the parents and brothers and sisters of Saint Thomas Aquinas, for example, were so bitterly opposed to his joining the Dominican order that they locked him in a fortress for almost two years and, at one stage, sent up a woman to try to lure him away. Aquinas allegedly brandished a torch at her that he snatched from the fire, and in the end he joined up with the Order of Preachers, becoming one of the great Dominicans and great Catholic theologians of all times. The point is that sometimes parents and other family members try to block the vocational plans of their children, and so, Opus Dei members often say, there may occasionally be good reasons for counseling members to pick the right time and place to disclose their intentions.

Today a young person interested in joining Opus Dei can become a "aspirant" at the age of fourteen and one-half. According to Carlo Cavazzoli, a Argentinian numerary who serves on the governing body of Opus Dei in Rome, aspirants are instructed to tell their parents about what they're doing, and "the opinion of their parents is crucial in this stage of vocational discernment." Directors, Cavazzoli said, talk with the parents frequently.

Opus Dei directors, the ones responsible for giving someone permission to request admission, say today that they would be very hesitant in advising someone to withhold their decision from family members. Alvaro de Vicente, headmaster at the Heights School in suburban Washington, D.C., and an Opus Dei numerary, told me in a December 2004 interview that if a young man under eighteen approached him about joining Opus Dei, he would contact that boy's parents and discuss it with them. If they were opposed for whatever reason, he would tell the young man he had to wait until eighteen before "whistling," something that can legally be done as young as sixteen and one-half. "If he has a vocation at sixteen and a half, he'll still have it at eighteen," de Vicente told me. Beyond eighteen, the young man is an adult and cannot be forced to disclose anything, but de Vicente said he would "strongly urge" that the family be brought into the picture.

Not every Opus Dei numerary would necessarily be this absolute, and some would say that a person may occasionally have good reasons for not disclosing their choice right away. Whether this is secrecy or good judgment about nourishing a vocation when it is still fragile is, to some extent, in the eye of the beholder.

"Secret Statutes"

Father James Martin is a young, affable Jesuit with a keen sense of priestly service. After the September 11, 2001, terrorist attacks in New York, he immediately rushed to minister at the Twin Towers site. Out of his experiences working with the firefighters, police officers, and rescue workers came his book *Searching for God at Ground Zero,* published in 2002 by Sheed & Ward. He is a well-regarded writer on spiritual topics and frequently publishes in *America,* the American Jesuit magazine.

In the early 1990s he became curious about Opus Dei and volunteered to do a piece for *America.* Ironically, he said, his initial interest came from a sense that some of the criticisms of Opus Dei, including some he had heard within the Jesuit order, had to be exaggerated. In the end, despite attempts to be balanced and accurately present Opus Dei's positions, his February 25, 1995, article was widely seen as being critical.

Over lunch in New York in the spring of 2004, Martin told me that he began the piece with an open mind but became puzzled, then alarmed, at what he saw as the "secretiveness" with which Opus Dei officials responded to his questions. The straw that broke the camel's back came with his request to see a translation of the "Statutes," or the law approved by the Vatican that governs Opus Dei.

"I called them and said, 'I really want to understand you,'" Martin said. "'Why don't you send me a copy of your constitutions?' And they said, 'We can't give them out.' I put that in the article. When I asked 'Why not?' the response was, 'Well, it's a Church document.' They said canon law blocked them from doing it." In his piece, Martin quoted other canon lawyers who said that canon law did no such thing. All this led him to conclude that the refusal was a kind of sleight-of-hand to keep the "Statutes" away from public inspection.

"That kind of crap," Martin said bluntly, "really started to make me angry."

Martin is not alone in drawing the conclusion that Opus Dei has played something of a shell game with its "Statutes." The Opus Dei Awareness Network, on its Web site, claims that "these statutes have been kept in the shadow of a 'discretion' tantamount to secrecy for many years." Any quick Web search will turn up hundreds of references to the "secret statutes" of Opus Dei. The opuslibros Web site, a Spanish-language site critical of Opus Dei, has two volumes for sale entitled precisely *The Secret Statutes of Opus Dei*.

In truth, however, whatever the officials may have told Martin, the "Statutes" of Opus Dei had already been published, in full, by the time his article appeared. The 1982 edition of the "Statutes," which is the one currently in force, appears as an appendix to the book *The Canonical Path of Opus Dei*, published in English translation by the Opus Dei–affiliated Scepter Publishers and Midwest Theological Forum, in 1994. The Spanish original of that book appeared in 1989. In both cases the full set of 1982 "Statutes" of Opus Dei are included, along with excerpts from the 1950 edition, albeit in both cases in Latin. Moreover, a Spanish magazine called *Tiempo* published the "Statutes" in a Latin-Spanish translation in 1986.

The problem with the "Statutes" of Opus Dei is not so much their availability as the language in which they appear. Opus Dei has never produced an official translation from the Latin. When reporters or other observers ask to see a copy of the "Statutes," the best someone from Opus Dei can do is direct them to a copy in Latin, which, given the state of language study these days, is tantamount to giving them nothing. It cannot help but seem like a dodge. (The Opus Dei Awareness Network has posted an English translation of the 1982 "Statutes" on its Web site.)

One argument sometimes given by Opus Dei to justify the lack of an official translation, and it was the one cited by Martin, is that because this is a Vatican document, it is up to the Holy See to authorize translations. It's unlikely, however, that anyone in the Vatican would make a federal case out of it were a member of Opus Dei to produce a translation of the "Statutes" into the various languages.

The deeper logic, according to Opus Dei insiders, is that some essential terminological questions have not yet been settled in canon law. For example, is the relationship between a member and Opus Dei best described in terms of a "contract," or an "agreement"? In Spanish, the term "contract" has an almost exclusively commercial sense, and many canonists feel it's inappropriate for describing the nature of a bond in the Church. For that matter, is someone who is part of Opus Dei a "member," or part of the "faithful" of Opus Dei? Inside Opus Dei, the preferred term these days seems to be "faithful," to better reflect the fact that Opus Dei is part of the ordinary hierarchical structure of the Church. There is still a canonical debate about whether laity in Opus Dei can really be described as "members" in the full sense of the term. The hesitation about translation is mostly a desire to allow the canonical conversation to mature, officials say, and to not employ terms in haste that later will prove problematic, in the sense of dragging Opus Dei toward a canonical configuration that is not consistent with its own self-understanding.

At the same time, many members of Opus Dei can only roll their eyes at the fact that, after twenty-four years, a translation of the "Statutes" still has not been made. In fact, reading the informal English translation that ODAN makes available, or the Spanish version of the 1950 statutes on the opuslibros site, there does not seem to be much that is nefarious about either document. Both are largely overviews of the administrative structures, procedures for joining, and relationships among the various branches of Opus Dei already described in chapter 1, along with some brief comments about the spirituality of Opus Dei. From a public relations point of view, much of the "Statutes" actually reflect well on the organization, since they emphasize the need for humility and simplicity, and, as we have already seen, prohibit secrecy. Refusal to publish a translation therefore seems, at least to many observers, a case in which Opus Dei is avoiding an opportunity to improve its public image.

Other Documents

If the "Statutes" aren't really "secret," Opus Dei has other documents that are confidential. There is the *Catechism of Opus Dei*, now in its seventh edition. There is something called the *Vademecum*, a set of reflections written by the directors of Opus Dei centers and other facilities on their experiences of trying various programs, initiatives, and systems of organization. A copy is located in every Opus Dei center and updated periodically, so that members can learn from the experiences of others. Opus Dei also publishes two magazines, *Crónica* for the male members and *Noticias* for the female members; readership is restricted to members. Both are published in Spanish, the "official" language of the internal life of Opus Dei.

Different logics explain why these documents remain confidential. In the case of the *Catechism*, the argument is that it is for the formation of Opus Dei members, and its only application is internal to Opus Dei.

Moreover, it's not intended as a self-standing document, but rather a launching point for discussion with a priest or numerary. Absent that context, it could be misunderstood. Moreover, some officials in Opus Dei worry that if a book called the *Catechism of Opus Dei* were to circulate, it could reinforce impressions that Opus Dei has its own doctrinal system apart from the teaching of the Catholic Church.

As for the *Vademecum* (the technical name for which is *Experiences of Local Government*), it is a collection of texts, constantly updated, containing reports of initiatives that have been tried in various parts of the world, with analysis of what went well, what failed, and why. The aim is to draw lessons of general applicability for other Opus Dei members, especially directors of centers, so that members can learn from one another's experiences. In that sense the *Vademecum* is analogous to project reports produced for internal use by government agencies or corporations.

Aside from the concept of "collective humility," according to which Opus Dei is not supposed to have its own publications, the other argument given for restricting *Crónica* and *Noticias* to members only is that they were launched as a way of sharing the letters that Escrivá routinely received from members, originally from different regions of Spain and eventually from all over the world, updating him about their lives and activities. In that sense the magazines are a bit like a family scrapbook, containing personal anecdotes and experiences. The custom is for members to be identified only by first name, in part to protect their privacy, in part in keeping with the spirit of "humility" that is supposed to pervade Opus Dei. The overall idea is to strengthen the sense that Opus Dei is a worldwide family, with all members sharing in one another's ups and downs.

From 1938 to 1954 this communication took place largely in the exchange of letters between Escrivá and Opus Dei members. Later, the more formal instrument of a journal was adopted. Beginning in 1954, the basic structure has been for each issue to have the following sections: Favors of Our Father, meaning miracles large and small attributed to the intervention of Escrivá; news from the various apostolates of Opus Dei; Notes from Rome; spiritual readings; and commentary on current events.

The "favors" are sometimes miracles only in a rather loose sense; for example, someone had a hardened heart with respect to God and the Catholic Church, but after reading *The Way* has returned to the practice of the faith. Sometimes, however, the reports concern physical miracles.

In 1985, for example, a member wrote in *Crónica* that his car experienced a broken radiator during a long trip. He prayed to Escrivá, and the engine maintained its normal temperature as if the radiator were functioning.

Critics have charged that the journals are used to rewrite the history of Opus Dei. Tapia, for example, wrote that she observed Opus Dei members covering over or changing certain parts of *Noticias,* particularly when people pictured and written about were no longer members of Opus Dei. The "corrected" pages were sent to all directors, Tapia said, who were instructed to destroy the old pages and insert the new ones. The former members' existence within Opus Dei, according to her, was thereby effectively erased. On the other hand, Opus Dei members point that out that traces of at least some former members remain; old issues of *Crónica,* for example, still contain pictures of Raimundo Panikkar.

Whatever the case, Opus Dei makes the argument that *Noticias* and *Crónica,* since they are collections of the private experiences and memories of Opus Dei members, are intended only for "the family" and that it would be inappropriate to distribute them to the general public. They also note that some religious communities have their own in-house publications. For those interested in the goings-on inside Opus Dei, the organization publishes a semiannual journal called *Romana,* which is available on the Internet in three languages: English, Italian, and Spanish. Launched in 1985, *Romana*'s contents include documents from the Holy See, news about the spread of Escrivá's message, information about the activities of Opus Dei, the names of all directors of centers and national leaders, all diocesan positions entrusted to priests of the prelature, and details about apostolic initiatives undertaken by members of Opus Dei.

The "secrecy" that surrounds these publications is not impermeable. In the course of research for this book, I have seen copies of all of them. As I mentioned in chapter 1, I sat in on a formation course for supernumeraries at the Shellbourne Conference Center in Valparaiso, Indiana, in September 2004, where members were discussing chapter 1 of the *Catechism of Opus Dei.* I was handed a copy of the catechism and allowed to flip through it at my leisure. As for the *Vademecum, Noticias,* and *Crónica,* I was allowed to inspect copies of each at the Information Office of Opus Dei in Rome, just off the Piazza Farnese, near the library of the Opus Dei–run University of Santa Croce. Marc Carroggio, a Spanish Opus Dei numerary charged with relations with the press in Rome, told me that he had requested permission from his superiors for me to see each publication, and that it was readily granted. Of course, someone from Opus Dei selected which issues I saw, but they were from varying years and did not seem to be selected to present any particular image. I was not allowed to take the publications back to my office, but I was free to spend as long as I liked with them and could make whatever notes I wanted. In addition, Carroggio also brought samples of the letters Escrivá received in the early days that formed the basis for *Noticias* and *Crónica*. At Villa Tevere, I have also been to the small one-room office where the magazines are produced.

Frankly, there seemed to be very little that was exciting or explosive. Debate over whether it's wise to put out such publications even for internal consumption, and, if Opus Dei does feel the need for such publications, whether the demands of transparency in modern society ought to trump the need for confidentiality, will no doubt continue.

Why Not Call It an "Opus Dei Center"?

As presented in chapter 1, there are, in an informal sense, at least three categories of Opus Dei activity, which might be thought of in terms of concentric circles. In the inner circle are the "centers," where Opus Dei members live, where spiritual and doctrinal formation are offered, and where Opus Dei activities in a given area are coordinated. In the second circle would be the "corporate works," such as schools and social service activities, where Opus Dei takes responsibility for the spiritual life. Finally, there are activities in which Opus Dei members are involved, sometimes with other Opus Dei members and sometimes not, that in some general sense reflect the Opus Dei spirit, but in which Opus Dei has no formal role. An example is Lux Vide, an Italian TV production company whose founder and chief executive is an Opus Dei supernumerary. In all three cases Opus Dei is not the "owner" of the activity or its facilities, which are incorporated under civil law with their own boards of directors. Over the years, criticisms have surfaced with respect to all three that the link with Opus Dei is downplayed or hidden—in a word, "secret."

Even for activities within the first two circles, where there is a formal tie with Opus Dei, in most cases there are few external indications of it.

The world headquarters of Opus Dei, for example, is called Villa Tevere, not the "Josemaría Escrivá Center" or some such designation. The American headquarters, at Thirty-fourth and Lexington in Manhattan, is known simply as Murray Hill Place. Opus Dei schools don't carry names such as "Portillo Prep" and "Zorzano Academy," but have generic designations such as the Heights, Oakcrest, and Northridge Prep. Because of the lack of immediately obvious labels, some say it's possible to attend events at Opus Dei centers and not even know that's where you are. As Martin worked on his 1995 piece for *America,* he came to see this tendency to "fly below radar" as a conscious strategy for luring people into Opus Dei's sphere of influence before they are aware of what is going on.

Martin describes a typical experience for an unsuspecting college student:

"Someone comes up to him and says, 'How'd you like to come to a meeting? I belong to this Catholic group.' It's very vague," he said. "They never tell him what it is. He goes, he sees all these bright, interesting, well-educated Catholics talking about their faith. They have a Mass, and he goes a couple more times. The place is called something generic, like 'The Oak Center' or something. They're very friendly to this guy, and usually they meet these new people at parishes, at youth masses and stuff like that, or on campuses. With the best of intentions, they'll approach these people, get them interested in coming over. Then at some point, they'll spring it on them that this place is run by Opus Dei."

As seen from inside, the practice of assigning facilities generic names, often drawn from the name of the street or neighborhood, is part and parcel of Opus Dei's "secularity." As laypeople in the midst of the world, they do not want to mimic the patterns of religious orders, creating islands of ecclesiastical life named for saints or religious devotions. Further, Opus Dei members with whom I have spoken find it hard to believe that someone could visit one of these centers and not know it has something to do with Opus Dei, given the omnipresence of pictures of Escrivá and Opus Dei literature.

Yet even Opus Dei members sometimes can be baffled by how far the concept of "secularity" is pushed. Russell Shaw offers an example: "I recall the first time I went up to the headquarters building in New York. I was invited for a meeting to discuss public relations for the upcoming canonization of Monsignor Escrivá, in 2002. So we were having a conver-

sation, and after listening to a good deal of stuff that seemed rather ab-
stract, I finally said, 'You know, one thing we might do is put a sign on the
front doors, saying Opus Dei Headquarters.' " The comment, he said,
drew laughter, then silence as it became clear he was serious.

In fact, on at least this point Shaw seems to have prevailed. There is
now a small sign outside the building designating it as the location of the
American offices of Opus Dei. It reads: PRELATURE OF OPUS DEI / OFFICE
OF THE VICAR / FOR THE UNITED STATES.

Shaw said he finds the reluctance of Opus Dei to practice this sort of
disclosure frustrating. "It's the basic things, the simple things, things that
are very easy to do and that there are no reasons on God's earth for not
doing," he said. "Yet I find my dearly loved Opus Dei often refusing to do
them."

Finally, as for activities launched by Opus Dei members but not considered corporate works of Opus Dei, such as the Rome Reports TV
agency, the situation is even more complicated. Because these entities
have no formal connection with Opus Dei, it's rare for any acknowledg-
ment to be made. One will search in vain, for example, on the Rome
Reports Web site for any mention of the fact that founder and publisher
Santiago de la Cierva is a member of Opus Dei, or that some (though not
all) of the rest of the staff belong to Opus Dei. From the point of view of
these Opus Dei members, the natural question would be: Why should
we? If three or four members of the Elks go into business together, do
they make a point of it? If a CEO graduate of the Harvard Business
School hires fellow alums as his vice presidents, does that go in the corporate brochure? In many ways it is difficult to fault this logic. Perhaps
the difference in the case of Opus Dei comes more from the mystique
surrounding the organization than from the inherent reasonability of the
demand.

Change over Time

On the subject of Opus Dei and secrecy, one point about which there is
near-universal agreement is that the organization has become more adept
over time at responding to public curiosity. Today the Opus Dei numeraries in the Information Office in Rome—Giuseppe Corigliano, Juan
Manuel Mora, and Marc Carroggio—are recognized by most Rome-based

reporters as being very responsive, in some ways more so than spokespersons for many other organizations in the Catholic Church. Opus Dei puts out an annual document called "Informative Data" that provides basic facts and figures. There are Web sites, magazines, CDs, DVDs, and an ocean of literature. As one sign of this openness, I can repeat what I wrote in the introduction. Before launching this project, I secured a promise of cooperation from Opus Dei, and they held up their end of the bargain. I have never asked a question to which I did not receive an answer. In some cases the answer was "We don't know," but I never had the sense that this was a deception. There is some very basic data, such as a comprehensive membership list, that for its own reasons Opus Dei simply does not collect. There were also a few cases in which I was unable to ascertain the identity of a given Opus Dei member, but this was the choice of the member, not the information officers.

According to those who have watched Opus Dei develop, there has been a growing appreciation of the importance of "opening up." Alfonso Sánchez Tabernero, dean of the School of Communication at the University of Navarra in Pamplona, and an Opus Dei numerary, put it this way in June 2004 interview: "At the beginning we didn't explain ourselves very well. . . . The Founder used to say, 'We don't want to have prestige. We don't have to be well known, with everybody saying nice things about us.' The translation to real life was, 'Let's not speak about ourselves. Never, never.' . . . But all that is changing. I think that we are speaking more, becoming more open. We have to keep moving in this direction, otherwise people will remain suspicious. In Spain we had really bad coverage of Opus Dei for years and years. That has changed a lot, I think," he said.

As one small window onto the change, *America* magazine carried an article on Opus Dei by Jesuit father Thurston N. Davis on April 1, 1961, one of the first serious pieces about Opus Dei to appear in the American Catholic press. Davis quoted someone he described as "a minor Opus Dei official," who declared, "[Opus Dei] does not contemplate the establishment of anything resembling the standard American institution of a public information office." Whoever Davis's "minor official" was, he was not clairvoyant. Today Opus Dei has an Information Office in Rome and in most countries in which it is established, including the United States.

On the global level, the ferocious public reaction to the beatification of Escrivá in 1992 had significantly abated by the canonization in 2002. This contrast may have been in part due to weariness with the subject, but to some extent it reflects a growing communications savvy within Opus Dei. All this suggests that Opus Dei's commitment to transparency, not to mention its capacity to tell its own story, is increasing.

Juan Manuel Mora, who heads up the Opus Dei Information Office in Rome, acknowledges the ground Opus Dei has covered as well as the work still to be done.

"I've been doing this since 1991, first with Bishop Portillo, and now with Bishop Echevarría," he told me in January 2005. "I can say that in all these years not one day has gone by in which one or the other hasn't asked me to do more, or to do better. This is true of extraordinary situations, such as canonization or the General Congress, and the ordinary circumstances of everyday life. . . . Maybe the single most frequent instruction Portillo and Echevarría have given me is humility. They've made me see that often in our communications we confuse the aims of Opus Dei with our merits, and use a kind of language that can seem arrogant. To say, for example, that the faithful of Opus Dei sanctify their work would be wrong; we *try* to sanctify our work, with effort, but also with plenty of missteps and errors, because we neither are, nor think we are, better than anyone else.

"We learned a great deal from the beatification, especially from our mistakes and omissions," Mora said. "We found ourselves unprepared for an event on such a huge scale, and we tasted the consequences of insufficient communications. Since then I think a lot has changed, but there's still much that we have to improve.

"Our communications strategy is based on a principle: professionalism. Communications is an area of work with its own exigencies, and it needs to be done in a serious way. Opus Dei's spirit of the sanctification of work helps us with this. Among other things, institutional communication realized in a professional way demands attention not just to content, but also to attitude—openness, accessibility, sincerity.

"We're well aware that in this field you can't work on credit," Mora said. "Trust is something we have to earn with facts. We have to merit it."

Chapter Eight

MORTIFICATION

In the contemporary fascination with Opus Dei, at least in the English-speaking realm, no aspect of its life looms larger than "corporal mortification," meaning self-inflicted physical pain intended to "tame the flesh" and unite Christians with the suffering of Christ. In Dan Brown's novel *The Da Vinci Code*, in which his own mythologized version of Opus Dei plays a central role, nothing comes in for more dramatic treatment. The action begins on the novel's opening pages:

> *One mile away, the hulking albino named Silas limped through the front gate of the luxurious brownstone residence on the Rue La Bruyère. The spiked cilice belt that he wore around his thigh cut tight into his flesh, and yet his soul sang with satisfaction of service to the Lord.*
>
> *Pain is good. . . .*
>
> *Pulling his shades, he stripped naked and knelt in the center of his room. Looking down, he examined the spiked cilice belt clamped around his thigh. All true followers of The Way wore this device—a leather strap, studded with sharp metal barbs that cut into the flesh as a perpetual reminder of Christ's suffering. The pain caused by the device also helped counteract the desires of the flesh.*
>
> *Although Silas had worn his cilice today longer than the required two hours, he knew today was no ordinary day. Grasping the buckle, he cinched it one notch tighter, wincing as the barbs dug*

*deeper into his flesh. Exhaling slowly, he savored the cleansing rit-
ual of the pain.*

Pain is good, *Silas whispered, repeating the sacred mantra of
Father Josemaría Escrivá—the Teacher of all Teachers. Although
Escrivá had died in 1975, his wisdom lived on, his words still whispered by thousands of faithful servants around the globe as they
knelt on the floor and performed the sacred practice known as "corporal mortification."*

*Silas turned his attention now to a heavy knotted rope coiled
neatly on the floor beside him. Eager for the purifying effects of his
own agony, Silas said a quick prayer. Then, gripping one end of the
rope, he closed his eyes and swung it hard over his shoulder, feeling
the knots slap against his back. He whipped it over his shoulder
again, slashing at his flesh. Again and again, he lashed.*

Castigo corpus meum.

Finally, he felt the blood begin to flow.

One could, in the manner of a whole industry of "debunking" books
that have sprung up in response to *The Da Vinci Code,* spend time pulling
apart what's wrong with this scene. Most fundamentally, Opus Dei members say it is a gross exaggeration of what is actually a brief and mild experience. Some specifics: Not "all true followers" of Opus Dei, but only
the celibates, wear the cilice. Opus Dei members call their leader "the
Father," not "the Teacher." The organization is referred to by members as
"the Work," not "the Way." The item used for whipping is not a "heavy
knotted rope" but a rather small twine device called a "discipline." One
doesn't say a short prayer before administering the whip, but during—in
other words, it's over in the couple of minutes it takes to recite an Our
Father or a Hail Mary. There is no buckle and no strap on the cilice. Such
analysis could go on, but it would spoil the fun, because there is a seemingly unending appetite for sensational images such as those presented in
Brown's book.

Nor is this fascination confined to best-selling fiction. Much titillat-
ing commentary in the popular press plays up the physical discipline inside Opus Dei. A lavishly illustrated December 2003 article on Opus Dei
in *Gentleman's Quarterly,* for example, is entitled "Thank You, Lord, May

I Have Another?" The subtitle reads: "As the controversy over Mel Gibson's film 'The Passion of the Christ' rages on and the pope withers, a new breed of rigid, right-wing Catholicism is catching fire. Among the most powerful sects is Opus Dei, the secretive group at the center of the best-selling novel *The Da Vinci Code*. Why are so many influential Americans signing on, and what's with the whips?" The next page features a four-color image that looks enough like an actual photograph to fool someone who misses the credit for "photo illustration." It shows a middle-aged man, obviously a priest since his vestments are slung over a table and nearby chair, who is nearly naked except for a white loincloth. He's whipping himself ferociously with a wooden-handled whip in his right hand. His mouth is open, as if letting loose with screams of agony. From his left hand dangles a rosary, adding a touch of pathos. On his left leg is the cilice, a metal chain with spiked barbs turned inward, described above by Brown. Blood is flowing freely down the leg.

In fairness, the article that follows by freelance writer Craig Offman is not terribly sensationalistic. Even if it does lean in favor of the critics, Offman also quotes at least one Opus Dei member in its defense, Father C. John McCloskey. (In the interests of full disclosure, I should note that I am quoted in passing as a neutral observer in Offman's article, accurately, near the end, making the statement that, "In the English-speaking world, Opus Dei has become the lightning rod for the broader culture wars in the Church.") Yet the headline and illustration collectively create a sense of the lurid that's hard to beat in the category of attention-grabbing media elements: secrecy, religion, and self-inflicted pain.

It was not always so.

Back in the late 1930s and early 1940s, when the controversies surrounding Opus Dei first began in Spain, Escrivá and his small band of followers were accused of almost everything: heresy, destroying religious life, engaging in bizarre Masonic and cabalistic rituals, even having secret tunnels in which to hatch plots underneath their centers. Ironically, the one thing that no Spaniard of the day thought to impugn about Opus Dei was the practice of corporal mortification. It was so much a part of the spirituality of the era that it would have been tantamount to objecting that members of Opus Dei prayed the rosary. "Hairshirts," for example—garments made of rough cloth, often woven from goats' hair or inlaid with barbed chains and worn as undershirts or as girdles in order to inflict discomfort—were standard items in the spiritual repertoire of many Catholics, including great saints and theologians. Paul VI used a hairshirt, according to his secretary, until the day he died. When the famous Swiss ex-Jesuit theologian Hans Urs von Balthasar died in 1988, one of his close collaborators found a hairshirt in his closet. In the early twentieth century, when Opus Dei was taking shape, both Carthusian and Carmelite monks wore the hairshirt as a matter of rule. Other orders used the *flagellum,* or whip, basing this ritual in part on a famous essay written by Saint Peter Damian in the tenth century praising self-flagellation as an admirable form of spiritual discipline.

Given this history, Opus Dei members sometimes compare the cilice to the rosary. Neither, they argue, was invented by Opus Dei. Perhaps both have fallen out of favor, but that does not make them any less a part of the tradition of the Church and does not mean that they don't have a part to play in an authentic Catholic spirituality. "For God's sake, we in-herited the cilice," one numerary member in Italy said to me. "Why do people treat this like something that's unique to us?"

Yet times have changed, and as these practices have not merely fallen out of favor but come to be seen in many quarters as self-destructive and psychologically aberrant, the fact that Opus Dei clings to them has be-come one of the most riveting aspects of its story. This is especially so in Anglo-Saxon cultures, which sometimes lack the traditions of spiritual athleticism found in both Spain and Italy. For critics, the practices of mor-tification exemplify the inhumane approach within Opus Dei, which de-mands a kind of dominion over its members, body and soul. For admirers, there is something charming about the way Opus Dei refuses to tailor its spiritual program to suit the shifting fashions of an era's tastes.

The Reality

As noted in chapter 1, "mortification" is part of the daily spiritual program of all Opus Dei members. The practices that excite the public imagina-tion, however, are carried out only by the celibate members of Opus Dei, about 30 percent of the membership. Supernumeraries, mostly married laymen and women, do not go home at night and don the cilice or whip themselves during prayer. They're too busy getting dinner ready, helping the kids with their homework, cleaning the house, and paying the bills.

This does not mean that supernumeraries do not perform acts of mortification, but generally they take a simpler form—taking out the garbage when it's not their turn, for example, or refusing to be frustrated when a child makes a mistake for which he or she has repeatedly been corrected.

For the record, here are the acts of mortification as practiced by the celibate members of Opus Dei:

- **Cilice:** A spiked chain worn around the upper thigh for two hours each day, except for Church feast days, Sundays, and certain times of the year. It can leave small prick holes in the flesh, and some ex-members report that it makes numeraries tentative about wearing swimsuits wherever non–Opus Dei members may be, since the physical evidence of the practice might be off-putting. Numeraries have told me they tend not to wear the cilice when they leave their centers or offices, because it might attract attention to themselves and set them apart from colleagues and friends, which would be opposed to the spirit of secularity. They find time at home, in the mornings or the evenings, to wear it. On the other hand, one Opus Dei numerary who is a surgeon at the hospital connected to the University of Navarra told me that he sometimes wears it while standing up to perform surgery; among other things, he said, he finds that it focuses his concentration and reminds him that he's performing the surgery not just for the patient but for God.
- **Discipline:** A cordlike whip that resembles macramé, used on the buttocks or back once a week while reciting a brief prayer, usually either the Our Father or the Hail Mary. Numeraries can ask permission to use it more often, which apparently some do.
- **Sleeping:** Female numeraries generally sleep on thin boards placed on top of their mattresses, and will sometimes sleep without a pillow once a week. Male numeraries either sleep on the floor at least once a week or go without a pillow.
- **Meals:** Numeraries may practice a small corporal mortification at every meal, such as drinking coffee without milk or sugar, not buttering one's toast, skipping dessert, not taking

seconds, and so on. Opus Dei members fast on the Church's prescribed days for fasting (as, in principle, all Catholics are supposed to) but otherwise are encouraged to ask for permission to fast on their own. On the other hand, my experience of dining with innumerable Opus Dei members over the year in which I researched this book is that most do not appear to be especially fastidious about denying themselves food and drink.

• **Silences:** Each night after making an examination of conscience, numeraries are encouraged to maintain silence until after Mass the following morning.

At one point it was also customary among young numeraries to take cold showers, but in the 1980s the prelate of Opus Dei, at the time Alvaro del Portillo, clarified that there was no such requirement, although he did not prohibit the practice. Centers of Opus Dei have hot and cold running water, and members are left free to make their own decision.

Numerous references in the writings of Escrivá recommend these practices. In *The Way,* number 143, for example, he writes: "To defend his purity, St. Francis of Assisi rolled in the snow, St. Benedict threw himself into a thorn bush, St. Bernard plunged into an icy pond. . . . You . . . what have you done?" In number 227, Escrivá says: "If you realize that your body is your enemy, and an enemy of God's glory since it is an enemy of your sanctification, why do you treat it so softly?" In *The Forge,* one of his later works, Escrivá returns to the theme: "What has been lost through the flesh, the flesh should pay back: be generous in your penance."

Moreover, Escrivá's own acts of mortification could be strenuous. In a biography by Italian journalist Andrea Tornielli, the Vatican writer for the Roman newspaper *Il Giornale,* a moment is described in 1937, in Madrid during the Spanish civil war, when Escrivá and his early band of followers were stuck in the Honduran consulate. Typically, Tornielli writes, Escrivá would ask for the use of the bedroom alone when it was time for his spiritual practices. Once, however, his chief aide, Portillo, was sick and could not leave the room. Escrivá told Portillo to cover his head with his blanket. Portillo described what followed: "Soon I began to hear the forceful blows of his discipline. I will never forget the number: there were more than a thousand terrible blows, precisely timed, and always inflicted with the same force and the same rhythm. The floor was

covered with blood, but he cleaned it up before the others came in."
Members of Opus Dei are quick to add that while such acts were in accord with Escrivá's spiritual heroism, it's not something he recommended
for anyone else, nor is this the reality of what numeraries say they do.

Opus Dei members say that on this point, no one is encouraged to
emulate Escrivá. Tornielli does not quote the epilogue from Portillo:
"Nevertheless, he [Escrivá] always practiced the prudence of never directly compromising his health, and his advice was explicit on this point.
In a letter of January 22, 1940, for example, he advised: 'Do not perform
mortifications that can be damaging for your health, or that would embit-
ter your character; *discreet* mortification and *discreet* penitence are undoubtedly necessary; but the cornerstone is Love.' "

In fact, Opus Dei members insist that the practices of mortification
as they use them are not nearly so extreme. Joaquín Navarro-Valls, the
Vatican spokesperson, has said that he regards his regular workout in a
Roman gym as being far more demanding than wearing a cilice. In that
Gentleman's Quarterly article mentioned at the opening of this chapter,
McCloskey makes the same point. "I see people jogging on a summer
morning in D.C.," he said, "and that looks more uncomfortable to me."

Opus Dei members also insist that these practices of mortification
are not ends in themselves, but are intended to achieve spiritual goals.
This point was brought home for me by Jutta Burggraf, a German numerary and professor of theology at Opus Dei's University of Navarra. Though
she comes from a family of practicing Catholics, Burggraf said she was
fascinated by the Marxists when she was a university student, "because
they wanted to change the world." At the same time, she was getting to
know Opus Dei, and "whistled" in December 1973 at the age of twenty-
one, initially as a supernumerary. Five months later Burggraf became a
numerary. She studied theology and has gone on to become a noted theologian in areas as diverse as ecumenism, environmental spirituality, and
feminism.

I met Burggraf in her office, and one of the last points we touched
upon was "mortification." She told me that since the cilice and the discipline are difficult for many outside Opus Dei to understand, perhaps a
different kind of "mortification," such as a fast day once a week, would be
a better approach. A fast, she argued, could be a "more modern" form of
mortification, which might move people's attention from the act itself to

the spiritual end it is supposed to serve. (By "people," Burggraf meant people outside Opus Dei, whether in other circles in the Catholic Church or in the news media. By and large, she said, she's convinced that the members of Opus Dei themselves perform these practices with the proper spirit and understanding.)

As a footnote, I put on a cilice that came from an ex-numerary member of Opus Dei in the course of research, just to get a sense of the experience. While I suppose one gets used to it, in my case it seemed rather painful—not so much when standing up, but if I had to sit down, when the flesh on my thigh would push out, the barbs on the cilice bit down hard. On the other hand, it did not seem unbearable or masochistic, and running a mile, especially in my woeful physical condition, would likely produce greater hardship.

This is perhaps why, almost uniquely among the various myths and prejudices about Opus Dei, members often seem to become annoyed when asked about mortification. They insist that mortification forms such a small part of the "spirit of the Work" that all the public attention is badly misleading. One numerary told me that answering questions about the cilice is a much more painful form of mortification than actually wearing it.

The Theology

Much of the material in this section is drawn from the *Catholic Encyclopedia,* under the heading of "mortification."

Traditionally, Catholic theology has understood corporal mortification as being a form of asceticism, a means of training people to live virtuous and holy lives. The practice of asceticism has been, over the centuries, one of the qualities that made Catholic preachers credible to the outside world. Thomas Merton, the future Trappist monk and best-selling author, in 1948's *The Seven Storey Mountain,* described the impression made upon him by the priest who received him into the Catholic Church, whose gaunt, ashen face had been "hollowed out by ascesis."

Mortification is, first of all, a means of training the body to endure hardships. In that sense, one can think of it as a sort of spiritual workout, a way of toning one's spiritual muscles. Yet corporal mortification in this sense can be practiced even by people who aren't Christian or who don't necessarily believe in a supreme being. Parents will often encourage their kids, for example, to learn self-discipline by denying themselves certain pleasures. What makes mortification a Christian practice is the belief that divine grace will enable the person to endure the hardship, and that mortification is a means of responding to sin.

When one has sinned, mortification is believed to help awaken a sense of penitence and a desire to make things right. Mortification serves as a tangible reminder that when one sins it produces wounds—in the sinner, in the one sinned against, and in God. This doesn't mean that there's anything intrinsically wrong with the things someone might deny him- or herself. There's nothing sinful about taking hot showers, or using pillows, or having a second cup of coffee after dinner. Precisely because these things are good in themselves, the virtue of "offering them up" is all the greater. Mortification is supposed to be offered as a "reparation" for sin, a way of showing God that one is sorry and is determined not to sin again. (That's one additional thing wrong with the image spun above by Dan Brown in *The Da Vinci Code*. Silas, his albino Opus Dei assassin, has every intention of going out and sinning again—in fact, he's been given just an hour before going out to kill. If one has already scheduled one's next sin, it's hard to see anything that follows as being genuine reparation.)

At an even deeper spiritual level, the practice of mortification is believed to unite Christians with the suffering of Christ, especially his passion and death on the Cross. This doesn't mean that taking a cold shower is seen as the equivalent of Christ's death on Calvary. In orthodox Christian theology, only the "atonement," or the death of Christ himself, had the capacity to compensate for the effects of sin. The idea, however, is that individual Christians can add their own "expiations," or acts of suffering, to what Christ accomplished on the Cross, and doing so pleases God and contributes to the redemption of the world.

Celibates in Opus Dei often see corporal mortification as an opportunity to "give themselves" completely to God, including some physical exertion, in the same way that spouses in a marriage relationship give themselves to each other and their family. They stress, however, that "mortification" does not have to be a physical act, like sleeping on a board or whipping oneself. As many of the great spiritual writers of the Catholic Church have observed, the "real" mortifications are interior, things like disciplining one's pride, or overcoming hatred, or learning to love more unselfishly. External acts, they caution, are useful only if they promote this interior conversion.

Despite this logic, many Catholic spiritual directors today do not recommend corporal mortification. For one thing, they say, such practices can tempt true believers to extremes—if a little pain is good for the soul, then a lot must be better. For another, it strikes many directors as distracting. If one wishes to be united with the suffering of Christ, they argue, visit the poor or the sick. There's no need to wear a cilice. Some even believe that, as in the case of Dan Brown's Silas, it promotes a kind of cheap grace, a sense that one can cut corners in other areas of life and compensate for it with a whipping. Yet these directors generally concede that corporal mortification has a long pedigree, and that when used in moderation and with the correct intention, it may have beneficial effects for some believers.

Not Just Opus Dei

Opus Dei members are far from the only Catholics who engage in corporal mortification. In the twentieth century, famous saints such as Mother Teresa of Calcutta and Padre Pio have both worn the cilice and used the discipline. A 1999 dissertation from Rome's Angelicum University, "Spirituality of Mother Teresa of Calcutta and Its Transforming Influence on the Apostolate of the Missionaries of Charity for the Poorest of the Poor," quotes Mother Teresa on the use of the discipline: "If I am sick, I take five strokes. I must feel its need in order to share in the passion of Christ and the sufferings of our poor. When you see people suffer, naturally the image of Christ should come before you." The same book indicates that Mother Teresa asked her sisters to wear the cilice and use the discipline.

One would never know, however, that other Catholics do these things from scanning contemporary newspaper articles or TV news reports, which focus almost exclusively on the "whips and chains of Opus Dei." This is another instance, many members insist, in which Opus Dei is not proposing its own teaching or spirituality, but attempting to live the traditional spirituality of the Catholic Church in its fullness.

As proof that Opus Dei has no patent on the cilice, I came across a price list from the Discalced Carmelite Convent of Saint Teresa in Livorno, Italy, whose sisters craft cilices and disciplines by hand for clients all over the world. Opus Dei often orders its cilices from this community, but it is far from their only client. The items are cataloged under the general heading of "instruments of penance," and the list notes that the price covers both material and labor. The sisters stress that the figure given is more in the nature of a "suggested offering" than a hard-and-fast price; clients who can't afford that amount will be able to come to some arrangement.

Here's the price list for 1997, which was still current as of December 2004. I've converted the figures from the old Italian lire, as they were listed at the time, into American dollars.

Discipline made of rope:	$12.50
Cilice for the Upper Body:	$7.50 for one band with barbed spikes
	$12.50 for two bands with barbed spikes
	$15.00 for three bands with barbed spikes
Cilice for the Leg:	$5.00 for one band
	$7.50 for two bands
	$10.00 for three bands
Cilice for the Arm:	$2.50 for one band
	$3.50 for two bands
	$5.00 for three bands
Spiked Cross for the Chest:	$7.50

When one orders from the sisters, the shipment arrives with the simple designation of "religious objects" on the receipt where the courier asks for a description of the merchandise. Opus Dei orders the "cilice for the leg" with one band of the barbed spikes, meaning that it actually purchases one of the least imposing "instruments of penance" that the sisters have for sale.

Who uses these things? For one, the Discalced Carmelites themselves, since the sisters in Livorno make personal use of their handiwork. The Franciscan Brothers and Sisters of the Immaculate Conception, founded in 1965 and enjoying papal approval since 1988, use the cilice. It's also not just Mediterranean cultures; the Mother of the Church Monastery on Road 56, Victoria Garden City, in Lagos, Nigeria, also uses "instruments of penance." A scholar who works on the lives of the saints said that he recently read the official documents in the cause of beatification of a Spanish spiritual director who died in 1974, and who regularly distributed the cilice to the people to whom he gave guidance—priests, nuns, and laity. The reality is that the practice of corporal mortification in the Catholic Church is more widespread than many observers imagine.

Criticism

Sharon Clasen, introduced in the preface, is not your Hollywood version of an Old Testament prophet. A petite, soft-spoken mother of two girls, Phoebe, eleven, and Raina, eight, Clasen lives in Dumfries, Virginia, about thirty miles south of Washington, D.C., and could easily be mistaken for a prototypical "soccer mom." Yet she is a former numerary member of Opus Dei and a ferocious critic. She was the star witness for the prosecution in that December 2003 *Gentleman's Quarterly* article.

A good student in high school, she moved into Bayridge, a university residence in Boston run by Opus Dei, in 1981, when she was seventeen. Her father was Catholic but her mother wasn't, and Clasen was not raised as a practicing Catholic. She had been baptized, however, and by the time she got to Bayridge she was open to knowing more about religion. An Opus Dei member took her under her wing, and in December 1981, Clasen received her First Communion. (Coincidentally, she received it from Father José Luis Múzquiz de Miguel, the first Opus Dei priest to arrive in the United States.) She joined first as a supernumerary, and then, three years later, as a numerary.

Two years after that, in 1987, she left Opus Dei, bitter, full of guilt, and convinced that something was deeply wrong. "I released myself from that guilt because I read Steve Hassan's book, and that really changed my life, because he said that people don't join cults, cults recruit people. You realize that it wasn't my fault."

So Clasen regards Opus Dei as a cult?

"There's no doubt. I read Hassan's book about the Moonies, and everything is identical. It's so textbook," she said.

One of her complaints focuses on mortification, which she believes is symbolic of the annihilation of the self in Opus Dei, and which sometimes goes beyond the limits of the mild practices described above. Clasen said the cilice and discipline were presented to her in a small blue pouch shortly after she became a numerary. By this stage, she was living at a center of studies for female numeraries in Massachusetts called Brimfield. "They gave it to me on my second day," she said. "They took me into an office and closed the door and said, 'Here.' "

Prior to that, she said, she had never seen either item.

"I was a supernumerary for three years, and they used to give us classes on what to say if someone asks you about the cilice and the discipline. They never showed them to us, so we never saw them. But they would tell us how to answer the criticism. They would say, 'Well, it's like getting your body in shape.' And you read that in all the newspapers," she said. As noted above, it's an explanation commonly given by the Vatican spokesperson, Navarro-Valls.

Clasen said that when she began having doubts about Opus Dei, a female numerary told her the story quoted above about Escrivá in the Honduran consulate. "This girl told me about the blood on the walls," Clasen said. "She had me read a passage in this book about Escrivá. It talks about that story, about how he would put little razor blades and pieces of glass and pins and nails and stuff and hit himself. She was telling me that so that I would emulate it. Because I was having these doubts, and obviously I was sinful, or I should hate myself, so I should punish myself.

"And I did. Somewhere I got these little safety pins, and I opened them, and I put them into my discipline." But, Clasen said, she didn't do it very long, and it didn't change her mind about Opus Dei. "I wasn't good at hurting myself," she said. Clasen said that on the basis of her experiences in Opus Dei, she no longer thinks of herself as a Catholic. "I believe in God, but I just have problems with church, you know?"

Clasen told me this story at the home of Dianne DiNicola, founder of the Opus Dei Awareness Network in Pittsfield, Massachusetts. As we spoke, DiNicola brought out the cilice and discipline that her daughter, Tammy, had used as an Opus Dei numerary. Clasen said she threw hers away years ago. Seeing them on the table as she told her story, she began to weep. "I didn't think they'd have that effect on me," she said. "It's been years since I saw them."

This sort of report has surfaced from other former members of Opus Dei. John Roche, a numerary from Ireland who joined Opus Dei in 1959 and left in 1973, during which time he did a stint with Opus Dei in Kenya, also testifies that the practice was pushed to excess during his time: "Members flagellate themselves, wear a spiked chain, and the women sleep on boards nightly, practices no longer recommended by the Church," he wrote on September 7, 1982. "Members who are thought not to practice sufficient physical self-mortification, or not to be sufficiently active in proselytism, are sometimes criticized openly. Opus Dei abounds in stories of the Founder's bloodied discipline." Roche said in December 2004 that he stood by this account.

Agustina López de los Mozos, coordinator of the opuslibros Web site that is critical of Opus Dei, is a former numerary assistant. She joined Opus Dei at seventeen, in 1971, and left at twenty-five, in 1979. She describes her first introduction to the cilice, after she had just written her letter requesting admission: "One day, just by chance, I was in an office with a numerary, and I saw her take down a box of chocolates. I asked for one, and she told me the box was empty, but I could hear something inside it. Since I had already established a rapport with her, I asked what it was. She responded with a sly smile, saying that it really should be my director who explained it to me, but since the subject had come up, she would answer. She took out a very unusual belt, made of a chain with spikes turned outwards on the ends. Holding two strings of cloth at each end, she lifted it up and said to me, 'This is a cilice.'"

De los Mozos said that later she was given her own, and began to use it. How tightly one tied the cilice, she said, depended on what in Opus Dei was known as "generosity." Given the emphasis within Opus Dei on doing even the little things well, there was a tendency to tie the cilice tighter than one could stand and to go beyond the prescribed time limit of two hours. De los Mozos said she was instructed to wear the cilice for two hours each day, one day on one leg, the next day on the other. She said that when she took it off, small bits of skin would come off with it, leaving wounds on the leg that did not heal in twenty-four hours. De los Mozos said that during the summer, female numeraries would wear bathing suits "like those of grandmothers" in order to disguise these marks. At one point, de los Mozos said, she decided to tie the cilice around her waist, leaving less visible marks and being slightly less painful to wear. She said that the numerary who gave it to her, however, insisted that she put it back on the leg.

De los Mozos said the custom was to not wear the cilice outside the house. One reason, she said, was that if she had an accident and had to be taken to the hospital, the cilice would be "hard to explain." The danger of wearing it around the house, on the other hand, was that you might physically bump into someone. If that happened, she said, you were to force a smile and not abandon your cheerfulness. As far as the discipline is concerned, de los Mozos said she learned to say the Hail Mary so fast she could probably do one hundred in an hour, because she wanted to get the whipping over with as quickly as possible. De los Mozos said she also took cold showers and slept without a pillow (she used the telephone book). "On more than one occasion, I thought I was about to have a heart attack," she said, referring to taking a cold shower in wintertime. She said she had jokingly suggested doing so only in summer, to which the response of another numerary was, "What merit is there in that?" Also on the subject of cold showers, she said, "My personal hygiene probably wasn't all it could have been, because I tried to get out of the shower so quickly." Still, she said, "I survived."

Response

I recounted Clasen's story for Juan Manuel Mora, who heads the Information Office for Opus Dei in Rome. How, I asked him in December 2004, could such behavior be explained—pushing members to add harmful objects to the "discipline," or whip, for example, in order in inflict greater levels of pain as a way of overcoming doubts about Opus Dei?

"If someone indeed gave her that advice, it was an error," Mora said flatly.

"I can say with absolute confidence that if someone told her that, it wasn't a director. The directors continuously tell members exactly the opposite, that they are to do nothing extraordinary when it comes to mortification," he said. Mora said that he did not wish to pass judgment on

Clasen's experience, but that in twenty-six years as a director of various Opus Dei activities, he had never heard of anything similar.

Mora said that to do something like that, that is, to encourage members to go beyond the limits of normal mortification, would contradict the Opus Dei spirit. The concept of secularity, of not distinguishing oneself artificially from others, translates into an emphasis on being "natural" when it comes to the spiritual life. Pressing toward extremes in this area, he said, is not in the character of Opus Dei.

Other Opus Dei members make similar points. They observe that it would be rare to find members of Opus Dei who are devotees of private revelation, for example. You generally won't find members of Opus Dei at the latest Marian apparition, or trekking off to hear presentations about bleeding Eucharistic hosts, or rubbing rosaries in the hope that they'll turn to gold. Instead, they say, there is an emphasis on balance. As far as anything that smacks of extremism, members say there's a strong culture of disapproval.

Mora wanted to add one other point.

"The Work would not change at all if we decided not to do these things," he said, meaning the cilice and the discipline. "If we were to abandon the idea of sanctification of work, or of secularity, then we'd be something completely different. But these forms of mortification are secondary. They could be changed tomorrow without distorting the reality of Opus Dei in the least."

Sharon Hefferan, an Opus Dei numerary who at one stage was director of the Brimfield center, though not when Clasen was there, today runs the Metro Achievement Center in Chicago. Hefferan said she was not surprised to hear that Clasen received the cilice shortly after becoming a numerary.

"Supernumeraries were not always aware of the details of the lifestyle and dedication of numeraries, but would certainly be told about them should the topic be raised," she said. "One basic reason is that in Opus Dei emphasis is placed on generosity lived in daily simple sacrifices, not on the few additional and, until now, discreet penances practiced by celibate members."

Several Opus Dei members made the point that one benefit from the vast public discussion about corporal mortification in the wake of *The Da Vinci Code* is that at least no one will be able to claim in the future that they didn't know that these things happen in Opus Dei. For good or ill, it's a matter of public record.

Hefferan said that far from holding up Escrivá's personal practices as an example, the culture inside Opus Dei cuts in the opposite direction.

"Saint Josemaría used to say that his mortifications were *not* to be imitated," she said. "As Founder, he knew that God was asking him to practice more extraordinary and different penances. I was never advised, nor encouraged, nor have I ever heard of anyone being counseled to harm themselves. . . . In fact, I have never heard of anyone taking his example literally. If any director were to learn of someone doing so, she would be quick to advise her not to, as that approach would be contrary to the way that numeraries practice penance.

"The general public is now aware that individuals in Opus Dei choose to do penance in their attempt to imitate Christ," Hefferan said. "I think the challenge is to help people understand that self-denial is one way of participating in the sufferings of Christ, and that members of Opus Dei practice it with moderation and common sense."

Chapter Nine

WOMEN

Barbastro, where Escrivá was born in 1902, is a small city in a provincial part of Spain, and despite the renown of its native son, not accustomed to visits by foreign journalists. When I arrived in June 2004, a special dinner was arranged with the mayor, the vice mayor, and a couple of other local dignitaries. It helped that my guide, a Spanish numerary named Manolo Garrido, had lived in the area for a number of years as a public information officer for the nearby shrine of Torreciudad. In keeping with Spanish custom, our dinner was to start at 10:00 P.M.; and in keeping with Garrido's habits, a stroll across the town square to get to the restaurant took almost an hour, as every shopkeeper and bartender had to be greeted. The meal commenced close to 11:00 P.M., and finished somewhere in the wee hours of the morning.

I was seated near two individuals who were fluent in Italian, so that we could carry on a conversation over dinner. One was a male Spanish numerary, the other the female vice mayor of Barbastro, and a Socialist, Inmaculada Hervás. A charming and articulate young woman in her thirties, she was trying to make a good impression for her out-of-town guests. As the evening wore on, however, and especially as more superb red wine was consumed, our real personalities broke through. It emerged that although Hervás, like virtually every Spaniard from Aragon, is proud of Escrivá, she's not exactly sold on Opus Dei. In part, perhaps, this is because she sees it as being conservative politically. But her skepticism was also related to her perception that there is something inside Opus Dei that is hostile to women—a kind of fear of women, and of sexuality, that translates into a second-class citizenship for them.

This became clear when Hervás asked me what I had noted about women in Opus Dei. I described some of the women I had met, who seemed to be impressive people, but added that I was struck by the strong separation between men and women. The numerary picked up the challenge and began to explain the spiritual and canonical reasons why this is so, from the official Opus Dei perspective. When he finished, I turned to Hervás, an emancipated European leftist, and asked why she thought men and women were segregated inside Opus Dei.

"It's simple," she replied. "As far as the men of Opus Dei are concerned, they're still Adam, and we're still Eve."

The comment provoked a groan from the numerary, and the ensuing exchange lasted well into the night. The point, however, is that Hervás's statement crystallizes what many outside observers believe about Opus Dei—that there is a fear of women, as well as a male chauvinism, that generates separatism and a traditionalist subjection to men.

Members often find these questions over women puzzling, in part because a solid majority, 55 percent, of the 85,491 members of Opus Dei in the world are women. Further, they argue, women are by law equal to men inside Opus Dei, since there are two parallel systems of governance. In addition, women receive exactly the same theological and philosophical formation as men. Women in Opus Dei institutions sometimes hold administrative positions that make them the superiors of male Opus Dei members. At the University of Navarra in Pamplona, for example, the four departments with the largest budgets are all led by women.

Escrivá addressed the question of women's roles in the Church in a 1967 interview:

> For many reasons, including some derived from divine positive law,
> I consider that the distinction between men and women with respect to the juridical capacity for receiving holy orders should be retained. But in all other spheres I think the Church should fully recognize in her legislation, internal life, and apostolic action, exactly the same rights and duties for women as for men. For example, the right to do apostolate, to found and direct associations, to give their opinion responsibly on matters which affect the common good

of the Church. I fully realize that all this, which is not difficult to admit in theory when we consider the theological arguments in favor, will in fact meet with resistance in some quarters. I still remember the surprise and even the criticism with which some people reacted to the idea of Opus Dei's encouraging women who belong to our association to seek degrees in theological studies. Now, instead, they are tending to imitate us in this, as in other things.

On another occasion, Escrivá said that "without the women the Work would suffer an authentic collapse."

Nevertheless, there are a number of aspects of Opus Dei's internal life that fuel perceptions of an "antiwoman" mentality. This chapter examines each, seeking to establish the reality for women inside Opus Dei as well as how Opus Dei members see the role of women in the broader culture.

Numerary Assistants

Spanish ex-numerary Alberto Moncada, one of Opus Dei's leading critics, offers a common impression of the "numerary assistants," the women who devote themselves full-time to the domestic care of Opus Dei centers. In some circumstances this can mean cooking, doing laundry, and cleaning house for men. Moncada writes: "Escrivá shared the misogyny frequent in Catholic theology and discipline, and created a structure in which the primary activity of women was to care for houses and centers of the Work. . . . The result of this setup is that the numeraries are the last remaining males in Western countries, especially in Spain, who enjoy the prerogatives of traditional gentlemen, who do not get involved in household matters because that is the business of the women of the family or, in the present case, of his sisters in the apostolate."

It's not quite accurate to say that the domestic care of centers is the "primary" activity of Opus Dei women, since there are more than 47,000 female members and only 4,000 numerary assistants, which means that less than 10 percent of the women in Opus Dei are involved in this kind of work. The majority of female members of Opus Dei are supernumeraries, which means that they are often mothers in addition to being doctors, lawyers, journalists, university professors, hairdressers, and so on.

Among the female numeraries, many have full-time work outside Opus Dei while others work for the prelature. In addition, numerary assistants take care of centers of women as well, so their primary task is not necessarily picking up after the men.

Yet there is admittedly something startling about an organization in the twenty-first century that would have a whole class of members devoted to domestic service, and that this class would be composed exclusively of women. The Opus Dei Awareness Network has stated: "They are recruited from the poorer classes in society to do all of the cooking, cleaning and laundry for the centers of Opus Dei. They are told that this is their vocation from God, to give up the prospects of getting married and having children, in order to serve the needs of Opus Dei. They work extremely long hours, doing physical labor."

This is a perception roundly rejected by Opus Dei members. Numerary Lali Sánchez Aldana, director of the Shellbourne Conference Center in Valparaiso, Indiana, where a number of assistants work, said, "They're taking care of a family, not the men." Being a numerary assistant is not a job for women who have limited prospects in life, she said. "This is a work of administration and management that demands intellectual capacity and administrative skills."

One problem with this debate is that people tend to talk *about* the numerary assistants rather than *with* them. For that reason, I sat down in mid-September 2004 with Bernadette Pliske, twenty-three, and Andrea Feehery, twenty-seven, two numerary assistants at Shellbourne.

Pliske, soft-spoken and demure, grew up in nearby La Porte, Indiana, about forty minutes by car from Shellbourne, in a practicing, very traditional Catholic family. Her father, David Pliske, is an electrician for the local public utility company, and her mother, Linda, with the exception of a two-year stretch, has been a stay-at-home mom as well as a cooperator of Opus Dei. They named Bernie for Saint Bernadette, and told me that she was "always special." Though reluctant to talk about it, David said that Bernie had special religious experiences as a child, including visions of Jesus. At one stage the Pliskes moved to Canada to join a Catholic community organized around a visionary, though they later parted company when they found that it had been launched without the permission of the local bishop and was, in David's words, "in schism from the Church." When they returned to Indiana, they enrolled Bernie in the local Catholic high school, but both she and they were worried that she would evolve in an "earthly," worldly sense, which they said had happened to their two older children. They decided to home-school Bernie.

Bernie said she felt from an early age that she had a religious calling. "I knew I had a celibate vocation," she said. "I knew God was not calling me to be married." While at the high school level, she went to a training program at Shellbourne for girls who want to work at the center over the summers. Pliske said she "loved the people and loved the job." At around the same time, in January 1999, John Paul II visited St. Louis, and Pliske made the trip. She said that experience compelled her to think more seriously about a vocation. Over Easter she made the UNIV trip to Rome, an annual meeting with the pope for young people sponsored by Opus Dei. Upon her return, she said, it occurred to her that perhaps God was calling her to life in Opus Dei. She said she went into a chapel, knelt, and began to pray: "Okay, God, what do you want?"

Pliske said she knew "right then and there" that Opus Dei was the answer. A week later she made a retreat for high school students sponsored by Opus Dei and talked to an Opus Dei priest. He advised her that she had to speak to a director, which she did two months later. She decided to "whistle" as a numerary assistant. David, her father, said that he and Linda supported the decision. "Knowing that Opus Dei was approved by the Catholic Church meant everything to me," he said. "My daughter was not in a cult."

Feehery, a poised young woman with an infectious smile, grew up in Houston, Texas, in a Catholic family, and her father and mother are both supernumeraries. Unlike Pliske, however, she said she hadn't had much interest in religion. At one stage her parents took her to an Opus Dei event, and she said her reaction was, "I loved the food, but otherwise it didn't do very much for me." In 1995, however, she was looking for a summer job, and some friends recommended Shellbourne. She arrived with the intention of staying only three weeks, but passed the entire summer working at the conference center. She said she "made friends, had fun," but also grew spiritually. On the plane ride home, she said, she began thinking that she might join Opus Dei, "but when I was forty."

Part of Feehery's hesitation was that she had a boyfriend and had assumed that her future would involve marriage and children. She had toyed with the idea of becoming a dental hygienist. Moreover, she ran into resistance to Opus Dei at school. She was going to a Catholic high school in Houston and said that every time she would mention Opus Dei, "They would talk it down, saying it's a weird cult, that you shouldn't be doing it." That reaction, she said, came primarily from her teachers. Feehery said she took the comments with a grain of salt. "I knew what kind of lives these teachers were living, and I didn't think they were credible," she said. By the time she decided to join, "I knew what the controversies were about Opus Dei. I don't think I was very naïve."

None of this means that the step was an easy one. At one stage, she said, "I cried myself to sleep thinking about it." Out of desperation, Feehery said she did something that in retrospect she realizes probably wasn't the best spiritual response—she put God to the test. "I said, if you really want this, if you want me to give my whole life to you, you have to give me a sign. My boyfriend has to ask me, 'Isn't there something you want to tell me?' " Sure enough, she said, the boyfriend called her up and asked that very question. Feehery told him what she was thinking. She said he "blew up, hung up the telephone." Later, however, he called back to say, "I'm willing to give you up to God." She said the two have not kept in contact, but the relationship "ended on a good note." Feehery then told her parents, and a month later she "whistled."

Both Pliske and Feehery come across as bright, articulate young women. What did they think about signing up for a way of life that many people regard as a waste of their talents?

"I see it as an honor," Feehery said. "I like being the mother of every-one in the Work. I see it as a profession, but more and more I see it as be-ing a mother. My job is to see that people in the family have what they need, what they want. Our Lady did this for Our Lord. It's a great thing," she said. One might suspect that Feehery was simply doling out the party line, but we were speaking freely in a room by ourselves. In any event, Feehery did not seem the type who would allow anyone to put words in her mouth.

Pliske agreed.

"If I weren't a numerary assistant in Opus Dei, I'd be doing this sort of thing anyway," she said. "I'd be in a convent someplace, or having a family. Here I'm able to be a mother of a really big family. I absolutely love it. I think of my own mother, and of Our Lady in Our Lord's life." She said numerary assistants are "fully capable" of doing other things, so this life is a choice, not an act of desperation. She noted that in her center there were women who had been landscapers and interior designers. "It's not like we're uneducated," Pliske said. For anyone with that impression, she has a challenge: "I'd like to see them plan a meal for three hundred people," she said.

Feehery said she knows that lots of people outside Opus Dei "don't understand" her choice.

"Many people don't have a mother figure who cooks, cleans, and pays attention to the family," she said. "My mom stayed at home, and I saw later in life how important that was." Pliske said she hated the two years when her mother worked outside the home. "I locked myself out of the house," she said. "She wasn't there when I got off the bus." Therefore, she said, she looked upon her mom's decision to return to being at home as a "real gift."

Feehery said that she notices among her friends a tendency to value exterior measures of achievement. "I'll get these e-mails from them, and at the end they have to attach this long title," she said. "I always ask, why is that so important?" She said that contentment is "a grace you get from God." It's not that Feehery has shut off earlier interests. She had a budding passion for art in high school and still studies art in her spare time. Yet she said she has no regrets about roads not taken.

"I'm very committed," she said. "Everyone goes through a midlife crisis, and so I know those thoughts will come. But what makes a husband stay with his wife when that happens? In those moments, you just have to pray more."

Again, Pliske agreed.

"I know people who hate their work, but I never get bored," she said. "It's not just putting plates on a table, but it's what's behind that stuff. It's who I'm doing this for, and why I'm doing it. It makes that toilet look so much better," she laughed. "I can clean toilets for my parents, so they're always in my prayers."

Linda, her mother, said she supported Bernie's choice.

"I know she's going to scrub toilets," she said. "But I also know how Opus Dei understands the 'little things,' that scrubbing a toilet is just as important as anything else. All I want to know is, 'Is she pulling her weight?' I'm proud that as a mother, I was able to prepare her for the work she's doing."

To add another voice, in Rome I met Margherita Salas, thirty-six, a numerary assistant who for the last eight years has lived at Villa Sacchetti, headquarters of the women's branch, and who works in Villa Tevere. That means at least part of the time, Salas serves meals for the men, scrubs their hallways, and washes their clothes. At present, there are some fifty-four numerary assistants who live at Villa Sacchetti and serve the two facilities.

Salas comes from an Italian family in the north, near the border with Switzerland, and said that when she was growing up she loved to work in her parents' coffee bar. At seven and a half, when her parents allowed her to help out, she would stand on a stool so that she could work the coffee machine. After middle school, Salas went to a high school affiliated with Opus Dei in Milan that teaches young women the basics of the hotel, food service, and domestic service trades, where she lived for two years. She said she discovered at the school that service "could be not just a profession, but a vocation."

She was just fifteen and a half when she "whistled" as a numerary assistant. (Today one has to be sixteen and a half. Salas couldn't make a lifetime commitment until twenty-three.) I asked her if she felt she was too young. "I wanted to say 'yes' to the vocation I saw before me. I didn't want to put any limits on it," she said. And, she added, smiling: "I'm still here."

Salas said both her parents and her four older brothers were supportive of her choice, though her brothers teased her, saying, "Listen, if you want to cook dinner and clean house, why don't you come over here? There's plenty of work to do." Her parents, she said, never expressed regret that she hadn't chosen a more "prestigious" path.

"For one thing, I would probably be working in a bar if I weren't here, so the activity is not all that different," Salas said. "I suppose every parent has a dream for their children, but in the end what they really want is for the child to be happy. Luckily, my parents saw that Opus Dei is my family and my happiness." Moreover, Salas said, people from Opus Dei have reached out to her parents. For example, because she was in Milan on the day of their twenty-fifth wedding anniversary and couldn't make it home, some Opus Dei members in her parents' region took them a gift of silver-wrapped candies.

Salas said she does not see the fact that only women do this work as discrimination. "Women are different from men in their way of doing things," she said, "more intuitive, more concrete. In domestic work, I think women can give a little something extra. It's not a matter of the work itself, the material dimension, because there are also men who can do these things very well. In cooking, for example, there are more male professionals than females. But there's a sense in which a woman's natural vocation is for others. Women are mothers, they carry new life. I think when you're in a family, in a home, you see the difference between a woman's touch and a man's."

Salas said she's never felt pressured into doing the cooking and cleaning. "It's not that Opus Dei takes you and says, 'We need you to do this work,' " she said. "What Opus Dei adds is the idea of vocation, the supernatural significance of the work." Salas pointed out that there are a number of centers and other residences of Opus Dei where the domestic work is not done by numerary assistants, because there aren't enough of them to go around, and she said nobody in Opus Dei would compel a woman to become a numerary assistant just to fill a slot.

Many outside observers, sensitive to the way women have been oppressed over the centuries in the name of the noblest of ideals, might want to ask: Granted that being a numerary assistant is a vocation, one based on service and the sanctification of work, but why is it restricted to women? Why can't men do it, too?

Opus Dei members typically offer two answers. First, they say, this was the vision of Escrivá, so that's just how it is. "Opus Dei is not something made in a laboratory, designed at a table after a discussion among experts, but a historical phenomenon, that was born on a certain day and in a certain place, and that has developed with certain characteristics, and not others, among the many possibilities," Salas said. "Numerary assistants have always been women, and this is part of the foundational framework." In fact, she said, in the earliest years of Opus Dei, Escrivá assigned the domestic care of the centers to men, so it's not like he hadn't considered other possibilities.

Second, they argue, it is fatal confusion to think that there is no difference whatsoever between the two sexes. Women have an instinctive aptitude for creating and maintaining a homelike environment that most men lack. On this second point, Sánchez Aldana, the director at Shellbourne, was blunt: "Men just don't have the talent," she said. "Women have a certain quality they can add to the home, an attention to detail." Men, she said, "don't cut it."

Yet given that male/female differences are in part biological and in part socially constructed, could Opus Dei anticipate a day when men come into the women's centers to cook and clean, just as women today do for the men? Here opinions tend to divide.

María Ángeles Burguera, a Spanish numerary, said it could happen. "Men are doing more and more in the houses," she said, as traditional Spanish machismo gives way to a more democratic and collaborative spirit. "There was a time when the men did almost nothing, but today you find that some of the best cooks in Opus Dei are men," she said. "In some places that don't have numerary assistants, there are men's centers where the men do everything, including the cleaning. So maybe [the vocation of a numerary assistant] will change in the sense of tasks or material works, but I think there will always be some women of the Work looking after it, because it's just like being a mother in a family."

Other members are emphatic that the idea of a male numerary assistant is unthinkable.

Beatriz Comella Gutiérrez, a forty-six-year-old numerary and a professional historian currently working on a project concerning Escrivá's years in Madrid, said that a male assistant "simply was not part of the Founder's vision. He saw Opus Dei whole and entire, and this was not part of it," she said.

In any event, members argue, given the small number of numerary assistants, and the much smaller number of men who might be interested, this is more a question of symbolism rather than of practical reality. Finally, Salas said it's not like the men in Opus Dei don't do anything around the house. They take care of the sick, do repairs and maintenance, often work the door and the phone, and generally try to be helpful. For some, these are full-time tasks.

One final note about numerary assistants. Carmen Charo Perez de Guzman, a former numerary in Spain from 1972 to 1990, has charged that the numerary assistants, at least during her time, were not covered by insurance, pensions, or unemployment compensation, so they were left without any support should they decide to leave. I put the question to Pablo Elton, Opus Dei's chief financial officer, who said that today everybody has a pension and insurance, although the details differ by country and type of work.

"The numerary assistants are always covered," he said. "The way it works depends on the laws of the country and the place where they're employed. . . . For those who work in institutions such as university residences, conference centers, hospitals, and similar professional activities, forms of insurance and pension follow the rules of the sector, just like for the people who are not members of Opus Dei. For those who work in the small centers of Opus Dei, there are no particular legal requirements, since these are private residences. These numerary assistants have insurance and pensions analogous to those of domestic workers with nuclear families. The rights offered to domestic workers by this type of contract will depend on local legislation. In some cases the law requires compensation in case of unemployment, for example, and in others no. The bottom line is that all the numerary assistants have contracts and insurance in keeping with the country where they live and work. We don't follow in these cases a logic of 'savings.' "

Separation

One thing that strikes even casual observers of Opus Dei almost immediately is the strict separation between men and women in virtually every aspect of life. Male and female numeraries live in separate centers, and even when Opus Dei has a large building with multiple programs and offices, with quarters for both men and women, those facilities are completely separate, down to having separate entrances. This is the case at the American headquarters at Thirty-fourth and Lexington in Manhattan, for example, and at the Rome headquarters on Viale Bruno Buozzi. In Rome the facilities have separate names, Villa Tevere and Villa Sacchetti, though in reality these are simply two doors, one around the corner from the other, that lead into the same building. When Opus Dei offers retreats or evenings of recollection or get-togethers, men and women are always separated. Opus Dei–affiliated schools are not merely boys-only or girls-only, but only female instructors teach in girls' schools, and only male instructors teach in boys' schools (though the support staff is often mixed). As noted in chapter 1, Sarah Cassidy, an English numerary who sits on the Central Advisory Council, the top organ of government for the women's branch, said that if they have a question to put to anyone on the men's side, they would ordinarily do so in writing, not by means of a phone call or personal visit.

Father James Martin, the Jesuit who wrote the 1995 article on Opus Dei for *America* magazine, tells a story about how far the emphasis on separation goes: "I had a friend who worked on the information systems and the electrical stuff in the building at Thirty-fourth and Lexington," Martin said. "The Opus Dei people told him. 'We want separate phone systems, and we want separate computer systems, and we want separate everything.' And he said, 'Why would you want that?' And they said, 'We want to treat it like two separate buildings.' And he said, 'That doesn't make any sense. You're going to be talking to each other.' They said that was okay. And he said, 'It'll cost you twice as much money.' Their response? 'No problem.'"

"What is that?" Martin asked rhetorically. "It's either that women are dangerous, which is the worst of theology, or they're a sort of lower status. It just totally baffles me. If you're trying to be a lay organization, and 'being a lay organization' I assume means being in this contemporary culture, this separation just flies in the face of all that."

Even Catholics who don't necessarily share Martin's perspective often find the separation puzzling. A prominent American Catholic laywoman, who said she didn't want to be identified because she's supportive of Opus Dei, told me during a recent visit to Rome that because she works with both men and women in her professional life, she finds the segregation inside Opus Dei "a little odd." On a practical level, she said, she is often invited to give talks to Opus Dei, and having to do it once for the men and again for the women means "double the work."

To round out the picture, however, there is no taboo against men and women interacting inside Opus Dei. In some offices of Opus Dei, men and women numeraries work together. For example, men and women collaborate at the University of Navarra in Pamplona, and in many other corporate works of Opus Dei. On social occasions, at Mass, at congresses and symposia, and in a myriad of other settings, men and women mix. Further, the vast majority of members of Opus Dei, the supernumeraries, are typically married with children, and they live in mixed male/female environments.

Still, no one denies that the accent on separation inside Opus Dei is strong. Members offer four reasons to explain it.

First, it's how Escrivá set it up. "It's part of the charism the Founder received from God for the Work," Pat Anderson, head of the women's branch in the United States, told me. "You have to come at this thing spiritually, that's the whole point of it. It's hard to understand it otherwise."

Second, in terms of doctrinal and spiritual formation, there are advantages to having the men and women separate. The women can talk about being mothers, for example, in a way that would be difficult if the men were also present. Sports references tend to go down better when it's just the guys. Further, the separation facilitates a certain administrative clarity, so that the women's branch is responsible for women's events, and the men's branch for men's activities.

Third, at least as far as the numeraries are concerned, these are men and women who have committed themselves to celibacy, and a certain degree of prudence is justified by way of avoiding temptation. As laypeople in the world they are obviously going to come into contact with the opposite sex, but at least when it comes to living quarters and one's spiritual life, some degree of separation means that numeraries face fewer circumstances in which they might struggle with their commitments.

Finally, there is a historical logic. Church authorities, especially in the Vatican, have long had doubts that there could be a single body within the Catholic Church in which men and women share the same vocation and apostolic activities. With the Dominicans and the Franciscans, for example, there are men's and women's communities that are both "in the spirit" of Saint Dominic and Saint Francis, but institutionally and juridically they are separate from one another. The traditional fear was that mixing men and women in the same community would promote "promiscuity." Over the years, Opus Dei has sometimes faced the prospect that it would be split into two separate realities, one for men and the other for women, thereby destroying the organic unity that Escrivá had envisioned. In this context, Opus Dei members say, the only way that Escrivá felt he could reassure the concerns of some in the Vatican was to raise a wall of separation so high as to make any fears of "promiscuity" appear ridiculous. In other words, Opus Dei members say, the near-maniacal emphasis on separation was the price that had to be paid in order to keep the Work intact.

New Feminism

The Congregation for the Doctrine of the Faith, the Vatican's chief doctrinal agency, put out a "letter to the bishops of the Catholic Church on the collaboration of men and women in the Church and in the world" on May 31, 2004. The letter criticized tendencies in modern thought that create an "opposition between men and women, in which the identity and role of one are emphasized to the disadvantage of the other, leading to harmful confusion regarding the human person, which has its most immediate and lethal effects in the structure of the family." The document cited "radical feminism" as the source of this confusion.

Many Catholic feminists were immediately critical. Benedictine sister Joan Chittister charged that the document "demonstrates a basic lack of understanding about feminism, feminist theory and feminist development" and that "both the terms used and the theory appealed to in the argument is pitiably out of date and embarrassingly partial in its analysis of the nature of feminism." Her reaction offers in microcosm a version of the frequent alienation between the Catholic Church and many educated, emancipated women.

The response from female thinkers linked to Opus Dei, on the other hand, was much more receptive. Jutta Burggraf, for example, came to the Vatican's defense. "A genuine promotion [of women] does not consist in the liberation of woman from her own way of being," she said, "but in helping her to be herself. This is the reason it also includes a revaluation of maternity, marriage, and the family. If at present the social pressure of the past is being combated, which excluded women from many professions, why then is there so much fear to go against the present pressure, much more subtle, which deceives women, pretending to convince them that they will find fulfillment only outside the family?"

Burggraf said the Church is on the side of women.

"The Church is the largest institution in the world that is 'pro' woman," she said. "No UN institution has so many collaborators in all the continents—from the smallest villages in Africa to the most remote islands of the Pacific—that exert themselves as does the Church to give women formation and to help them live in dignity."

Another voice came from Pia de Solenni, an American Catholic laywoman who works as director of life and women's issues for the Family

Research Council, a pro-family organization founded by conservative Christian spokesperson James Dobson. De Solenni is not a member of Opus Dei, but she received her doctorate from the Opus Dei–run University of Santa Croce in Rome and has been going to priests of Opus Dei for spiritual direction for eight years. Her dissertation, on developing an integral feminism in light of Thomas Aquinas, won the Pontifical Prize of the Academies, a prestigious papal award, for 2001. De Solenni comes across as a dynamic, intelligent, and occasionally brash young woman, well-suited to the fast-paced media culture of Washington, D.C. When the Vatican's "Letter" appeared, she took a positive approach to it in a guest column for the *National Catholic Reporter*.

"Unfortunately, the effort to defend women's rights took a downward turn within the Church about forty years ago and spiraled into a bitter match of women versus men. The debate was reduced to a power grab that has created a temporary illusion of having it all, only to find that various conquests have slipped through our fingers, leaving us with no lasting victories," she wrote. "Competition and retaliation have created a stalemate. Thus, the letter is not about women, as much of the media coverage suggests. It's about both women and men and their relationship in civil society and within the Church."

These comments capture the tone of much thinking among women connected to Opus Dei when it comes to questions of gender, feminism, and relations between the sexes. By and large, Opus Dei's brand of feminism is much closer to John Paul II than to Gloria Steinem.

Consider, for example, Janne Haaland Matlary, a mother of four who is also the former vice minister of foreign affairs for Norway and professor of international relations in the faculty of political science of the University of Oslo. Matlary, a dedicated Catholic who represented the Holy See at the 1995 United Nations Conference on Women at Beijing, is a cooperator of Opus Dei and a frequent speaker at Opus Dei events. She has written a book titled *A Time to Blossom: A New Feminism*.

Matlary tells a story from her own experience to illustrate the need for a "new feminism," one that values motherhood and family. When she applied for her present position at the University of Oslo, she was shortlisted with a male candidate. They were told that both were equally qualified, yet the man was six years her junior. How on earth could he have achieved the same as she had, Matlary wondered, given the age difference? Matlary sat down and reasoned as follows: She has four children, and nine months' pregnancy for each made three years; four children times nine months' breast-feeding, another three years. Pregnancy and nursing in infancy alone came to six years. In addition, Matlary calculated she had passed at least two more years at home with her babies. In short, she had accomplished more than her male competitor when all the time spent in childbearing and child-rearing was subtracted. She made this point to the committee, and got the job.

In a 2000 address in Ireland, Matlary developed her ideas:

> There are very few [feminists] who talk about the importance of motherhood in practical-political terms, or even in more profound terms. In this sense modern feminism is very impoverished in its anthropology—or rather, in its lack of such. Instead of exploring what it really can mean to be a woman—what womanhood is—in an ontological and existential sense—feminism seems to assume and offer an aggressive view of man where the two sexes are engaged in a power struggle. . . . Modern feminism is silent on the question of what women are in their essence, and therefore has nothing to say on the importance of motherhood.

For another example of an Opus Dei voice on women's issues, there's Marta Manzi, who also goes by her maiden name, Marta Brancatisano. An Italian supernumerary, Brancatisano was the spokesperson for the organizing committee for the 2002 canonization of Saint Josemaría Escrivá. She and her husband met while both were in university, and they have seven children. She's published several books on issues of femininity and family, including *The Great Adventure* and *The Gospel Explained to My Son*. One of her most systematic treatments came in 2004's *Approach to an Anthropology of Difference,* published by the editorial house of Opus Dei's Santa Croce University in Rome.

Brancatisano is critical of much "classic" feminism.

"In the revolutionary fog" of the sexual liberation movement of 1968, Brancatisano wrote, "women started moving down the masculine path of expressing themselves and acting, aligning themselves in everything, often in an exasperated fashion, with that masculine mentality that instead needs to open itself to feminine coexistence. Thus we've created not merely a struggle of the genders—in the streets and in the media, as in the parliaments and the private homes—marked by violence and the desire for domination, but also rapid and progressive mutation of dress and of styles that has been irradiated, with an uninterrupted progression, by theoretical proclamations, even down to fashion, language and physical posture."

In an essay delivered at a 1998 roundtable, Brancatisano argued that, instead, women should enter the workforce not as "one more" but as a "different one," given that "the only ontological difference among human beings is determined by the sexes," and that care for the family and the home are "eminently feminine."

"The feminine specificity stands out by the capacity/aptitude of the woman to receive the other," she said, "which is written in her body and irradiates her whole personality. For her, contrary to man, the other is not a mystery but something of her own, somebody about whom she knows everything because she has carried him inside herself. Nobody like her can 'manage' persons and interrelate with them; she knows how to do it, wisely and with a special grace. . . . This know-how belongs to her, through a genetical law, no matter how varied the environmental and cultural conditions could be." Thus, Brancatisano argues, there is a uniquely feminine approach to being a politician, pilot, or scientist "in a surprisingly different way and not as a clone of man." She insists that only in this fashion will society come to value, as it should, the contributions of women as homemakers and caretakers of families. "We cannot expect that governments will value work in the house if we are not women who keep the profound conscience of what it means, not only of its usefulness, but of its dignity and full gratification for us women," she said.

The kinds of concerns Opus Dei women such as Burggraf and Brancatisano express reflect Escrivá himself, who said in a 1967 interview:

> I think that if we systematically contrast work in the home with outside work, retaining the old dichotomy which was formerly used to maintain that a woman's place was in the home, but now asserting the exact opposite, it could easily lead to a greater social mistake than that which we are trying to correct, because it would be a more serious mistake for women in general to give up the work of looking

after their loved ones. Even on the personal level one cannot flatly affirm that a woman has to achieve her perfection only outside the home, as if time spent on family were time stolen from the development of her personality. The home—whatever its characteristics, because a single woman should also have a home—is a particularly suitable place for the growth of her personality. The attention she gives to her family will always be a woman's greatest dignity. In the care she takes of her husband and her children, or, to put it in more general terms, in her work of creating a warm and formative atmosphere around her, a woman fulfills the most indispensable part of her mission. And so it follows that she can achieve her personal perfection there.

Bishop Javier Echevarría, the current prelate of Opus Dei, addressed the feminist issue directly in a 1996 interview with *El Mercurio* in Chile: "At the heart of true feminism there has to be, as is obvious, an increasing awareness of women's dignity," he said. "This is very different from those other, usually aggressive, types of feminism that try to claim that a person's sex is a purely physical thing, with no deeper human or social relevance." Women should be given the same opportunities as men, Echevarría said, and noted that women in Opus Dei pursue all types of careers. He quoted John Paul II to the effect that, in this sense, the feminist movement has been "substantially positive." With equal opportunities, he said, "a woman can retain her identity and not fall into the trap of thinking she will find her true identity by aping men or imitating their ways and gestures." Women, Echevarría said, should rebel against pornography as well as against "the sorry, misguided claim that abortion should be a right, and against divorce, which can only be described as a social disaster, quite apart from being an offense against God."

It would be both unfair and inaccurate to reduce the ideas of Burggraf, de Solenni, Matlary, or Brancatisano to the Opus Dei influence, as they are very much their own persons. De Solenni and Matlary are not even members of Opus Dei, and de Solenni made it clear in a November 2004 interview that she has no intention of becoming one. Moreover, no one in Opus Dei told either Burggraf or de Solenni what to say when the Vatican's letter appeared.

It's also not that figures such as Burggraf are insensitive to the traditional concerns of the feminist movement. Burggraf said that when she returned to Germany after her university studies in the 1980s, a center of Mariological research asked her to make a public criticism of feminism. They wanted a young female theologian, and she fit the bill. "I had read all the books of feminist theology, and I thought some of them were a little superficial," she said. "So I issued a terrible criticism, without any sensibility for the problems they were facing, without any effort to put myself in their place. I gave talks on the subject, and got invited all over the place because this was exactly what the conservatives wanted to hear. My writing on the subject spread to other countries. Today, I almost die of shame when I see it. When people started to criticize me, I thought, 'These women are right. They've suffered a lot, and I wasn't sensitive to that.' Now I think of myself as a Christian feminist, obviously without compromising Christian principles, but sensitive to what women have suffered."

Yet the women of Opus Dei nevertheless represent a climate of opinion that cuts against the grain in terms of the approach to women's issues in the broader culture. They tend to be supportive of the Catholic Church's ban on the ordination of women, leery about classic versions of feminism that they believe level differences between women and men, and they regarded John Paul II as an authentic feminist. It's certainly not just members of Opus Dei, or Opus Dei–educated women, who hold these views. Nevertheless, the relative compactness on these issues inside Opus Dei is in contrast to much of the rest of the Catholic Church, to say nothing of the outside world.

Big Families

Though Opus Dei keeps no statistics on the subject, as an anecdotal matter, families in the Work tend to be big. When I visited the Chicago home of supernumeraries Doug and Shirley Hinderer in September 2004, for example, I met most of their nine children when we gathered around the table for dinner. An American Opus Dei numerary named David Gallagher had gone with me, and he explained to the Hinderer children that he came from a family of thirteen kids. In London, I visited two supernumerary households: Jim and Theresa Burbidge, who have five children, and John and Jane Phillips, who have ten.

At the Opus Dei–run Oakcrest School for girls in McLean, Virginia, one of the students I chatted with was a sixteen-year-old junior named Meghan Hadley. She comes from a family of ten kids, and she told me that it's a running joke at Oakcrest that everyone is somehow related to everyone else, since many students come from other large families whose members have intermarried. It's not uncommon for a student to be the first or second cousin of several other students, to say nothing of having older or younger sisters on campus at the same time. This isn't always the case, since neither of the other two students I met came from large families, but there's just enough truth to it to make the joke funny.

The sociological reality of large families, coupled with the "Christian feminism" described above, means that there is a greater-than-average likelihood that female supernumeraries, at least at some point in their lives, will be stay-at-home moms. Some see this as an instance of Opus Dei promoting a traditionalist view of women, though supernumeraries with whom I spoke seem to find it consoling and fulfilling.

Linda Roth, a supernumerary in the Chicago area, said she was working for Price Waterhouse as a CPA, handling a number of high-profile accounts, when she began to have children. Many of her female colleagues pressured her to prioritize her career over her family. Yet Roth felt that being at home was "best for me and an important choice," and decided to shift to part-time status. She found support for that in Opus Dei, and "whistled" in 1984. The emphasis on sanctification of work within Opus Dei, she said, "elevated trivial things at home into something just as important as auditing Anheuser-Busch."

It would be facile to reduce the tendency toward large families to the fact that Opus Dei supernumeraries generally observe the Church's ban against birth control, although that's true enough. Matthew Collins, a former supernumerary and now a cooperator, says this is not a children-at-all-costs mentality.

"We must exercise our own judgment about the number of children to have," he said. "If, in our own conscience, formed in the privacy of our own prayer, we believe we have a serious reason to limit the number of children, we enjoy the same freedom other Catholics have to use natural family planning. It's good for all Catholics to consult a priest in this matter when making this decision, but the decision belongs to the couple alone. The decision should be made taking into account the financial, physical, and emotional needs of the spouses and the children they already have. This includes the likelihood of being able to provide a suitable home and an adequate education."

As a footnote, there is a trend among many Catholics with large families toward home-schooling, and some Opus Dei supernumeraries have made this choice. Sometimes Catholic home-schoolers can be judgmental when it comes to existing Catholic education and ambivalent about relationships with the institutional Church, but these are attitudes one finds less frequently in Opus Dei circles. My first encounter with an Opus Dei member came at a conference on Catholic independent schooling at the Franciscan University of Steubenville, Ohio, in 1998. In a room full of educational insurgents, the two Opus Dei representatives, layman Jim Stenson and Father Malcolm Kennedy, both longtime veterans of Opus Dei schools in the United States, loomed as the voices of moderation.

"We've always had very, very cordial relations with the diocese in our cities," Stenson said. "We never saw ourselves as a protest operation at all. I know some of these people do, unfortunately. I don't quite understand where they're coming from. Who are we to judge the job that other people are doing? We know there are many ways of looking at things in the Church, there's great diversity of opinion, people have many, many approaches that lead to God."

Governance

Opus Dei spokespersons often argue that women are more emancipated inside the Work than in many other areas of Church life, since female numeraries receive the same theological education as males (including candidates for the priesthood), and they have their own authority structure to administer their affairs in virtually autonomous fashion. Critics, however, frequently object that this autonomy is a sham, since in the last instance it's a priest—either the regional vicar for local affairs or the prelate on the international stage—who calls the shots.

Even Opus Dei members understand how people might form these impressions.

"I can understand why people are skeptical," said María Ángeles

Burguera, the numerary in Madrid introduced above. "Sometimes people think that because, well, the guy in charge is the bishop, it's a man running things. And there are the vicars of the prelate in every country."

Yet the women of Opus Dei insist that in practice, their autonomy is real. Marlies Kücking, the German numerary who heads the women's branch, explains how the system works. "Things from the regional governments come here, and there are departments that take care of issues concerning married couples, the young, theological/philosophical studies, formation, and so on," she said. "I see almost everything, in order to distribute them to the departments. They study them and propose a solution. All this work is done by women. The important things come to me, and then to the prelate. He may ask questions, but generally he approves whatever we've proposed, saying you know the issues better, even if he knows the reality perfectly well." The bottom line, she said, is that she "feels perfectly listened to and taken seriously."

Pat Anderson, head of the women's branch in the United States, was even more emphatic. "Opus Dei is one entity, but it really does have two foci, the men's branch and the women's branch," she said. "Each one is independent, even though we share a spirit. We're independent." When I asked about relations with the men's branch, her terse if good-humored response was, "What do I need them for?"

I asked if there was any sense in which women in Opus Dei are subservient to men, which elicited a similar "snappy answers to stupid questions" reply.

"Subservient?" she snorted. "How? I have nothing to do with them."

"Personally," she added, "I think the priests serve us. They are totally at our beck and call." They go to women's centers when asked, perform the duties they're given, receive the compensation a female director decides to provide, and lodge in the quarters they're assigned, Anderson explained. There is no sense, she said, that when a priest arrives, he's in charge.

In many cases, women use this autonomy to foster activity that empowers women. Susan Mangels, for example, is a forty-year-old numerary who serves as president of Lexington College. A convert from Lutheranism, she said that ironically, when she tried to explain to her father what Opus Dei was—a group of laypeople using their freedom to redeem the world—he drew the conclusion that it was "a Commie pinko organization."

Mangels said that Lexington, which teaches service industry skills and management to young women, was "founded in the 1970s to promote the prestige of women working in service industry." Looked at from the outside, Mangels said, one might see it as Opus Dei promoting a traditionalist conception of a woman's role. The reality, she said, is different. "There are many areas in the service industry sector that are male-dominated . . . cooking, for example. Our agenda is to turn out educated women who are skilled managers, skilled service professionals, who can think, who know their own dignity as a person." Mangels said she runs Lexington in tandem with the largely female staff, without any men from Opus Dei looking over her shoulder.

Strong Women

For concrete examples of strong Opus Dei women, consider two Kenyans I met in September 2004.

Frankie Gikandi, a numerary, directs the Kimlea Technical Center for girls outside Nairobi, which has about 150 girls full-time, and some 200 girls and older women in part-time programs. The center's Swahili motto is *Kazi Huvuna Matunda,* or "Work produces fruit." The girls who come to Kimlea are generally from the poorest areas around the coffee and tea plantations that ring Nairobi, and at first they think of the school as a house for *musungus,* meaning "whites." In fact, they are so intimidated that it takes Gikandi two months just to convince them to use the flush toilets inside. The center teaches girls basic skills, such as sewing and cooking. The area around the plantations gets cold, so Gikandi said it's easy to sell sweaters, and the income can make a huge difference.

Due to a high percentage of Kenyan men abandoning the family, along with poverty, and certain cultural traditions, many women in the Kiambu District, where Kimlea is located, are obliged to work on the plantations in order to support their children. As money becomes scarce, only the sons are sent to school, in the hope that the daughters will be taken care of by their husbands. This lack of education means that women often have no other option beyond picking tea leaves. They work from 6:00 A.M. to 6:00 P.M., for which they receive less than two dollars, barely enough to put food on the table. The resulting vicious cycle is difficult to break. Kimlea offers adult women courses in literacy, accounting, and other basic subjects, enabling them to choose less exhausting and more profitable work. Many have set up a sewing business, a food business, or small vegetable gardens, which have improved conditions for their families and communities. The girls also master trade skills in addition to basic academic subjects.

Gikandi's creativity seems to know no bounds. She has a beekeeping project at Kimlea, for example, so that the girls can make some extra income from the honey. In addition, she told me, the honey can be used for medicinal purposes. Gikandi also shows us waist-high bags of soil in which small crops are growing, a technique Kimlea teaches the girls for raising small amounts of food to feed families that don't have their own plots of land. The crops include something in Swahili called *Sukuma wiki*, or "Push the week," the idea being that it'll get you through lean weeks when food runs short.

Gikandi comes from a family of sixteen brothers and sisters, but not because her parents had anything to do with Opus Dei. Her father was a polygamist, with two wives, so some of her brothers and sisters are from one wife, some from the other. After Gikandi converted to Catholicism, eventually all sixteen of her brothers and sisters followed. Her father separated from his second wife, making arrangements for her to live on a separate farm and providing for her financial upkeep. He too converted to Catholicism and got married in the Church to his first wife. Gikandi seems to have a special talent for evangelization; she says every year at Kimlea, about one-half of the girls start out as Catholics, and by the end of the year it's usually up to two-thirds.

Gikandi is an articulate, no-nonsense administrator. She wants to found a clinic, for example, to treat the infections and viruses that circulate in the villages around Kimlea. For now, she's organized a mobile service utilizing a donated van that drives two doctors into the villages to administer medicine. The clinic would also be able to treat at least some of the effects of malnutrition and HIV/AIDS. She's constantly prowling for resources to cover the twenty-five dollars a month it costs to educate each girl. She's set up a Friends of Kimlea foundation to try to generate support.

Around Kimlea, there's no question who's boss. When Gikandi ambled out of the main building toward the gate, the security guard gave her a smart salute; as we walked around the small campus, a groundskeeper who had been lounging under a tree suddenly came to life, raking with the zeal of a convert. Out here, there is no male numerary or priest to call the shots—Gikandi hires and fires, pays the bills, and deals with the outside world.

I wanted to push Gikandi about her curriculum. "You're a strong, successful career woman," I said. "Why not teach these girls math and literature and science, and not just housekeeping and trade skills?"

"The objective is to train them in income-generating activity," Gikandi said. "It's not like, in most cases, that it's a choice between sewing or physics. Most of these girls come here because they want to help their families, and because they want to be mothers. Our aim is to help them be a good housewife, but also to learn skills that can generate income, so they're not completely dependent upon their husbands. You have to look at their capacities and possibilities, and decide where you can really make a difference."

Somewhere near the top of the list of impressive Kenyans would have to be Dr. Margaret Ogola, an Opus Dei supernumerary who heads the Commission for Health and Family Life for the Kenyan bishops' conference. Ogola is a pediatrician, a mother of four, and medical director of the Cottolengo Hospice in Nairobi for HIV-positive orphans. In her spare time she writes prizewinning novels. Her 1994 novel *The River and the Source* won the 1995 Jomo Kenyatta Prize for Literature and the 1995 Commonwealth Writers' Prize for Best First Book.

She met Opus Dei in 1990, she said, and was attracted by the fact that they "take laypeople very, very seriously." She "whistled" eleven years ago. Listening to her describe her experiences, it was obvious that Ogola does not check her intelligence at the door when she walks into an Opus Dei environment.

"Once I went to a gathering, the point of which was to know the faith," she said. "The statement was made that for people who have AIDS, it's their own fault. It's not considered good manners to stop someone, but I couldn't allow that to pass. As a physician, I had to say something. That day I had just left a five-year-old in the hospital who was fighting for her life, and I just could not accept that she was somehow culpable.

"In that sense, the approach can be a little oversimplified," Ogola said. "People who open their mouths need to think deeply, and to be empathetic. Christianity is about the Cross. Who am I to demand crosses of other people that would be too heavy for me to carry?"

At the same time, she said she valued Opus Dei's emphasis on "doing the little things." She said she has "a robust family life, active children," and that she appreciates being able to see all that from the point of view of sanctification. In addition, she said, she needs a little spiritual discipline in her life. "The plan of life can be pretty tough," she said. "They hold you to account."

Since Ogola is an HIV/AIDS expert, we spent some time on the subject. Kenya has at least 200,000 AIDS sufferers who should be on antiretroviral treatment, but only 20,000 actually get the medicine. Ogola knows how important ARV therapy can be; at her clinic, she's watched it make the difference between life and death. Yet she says the question Western journalists always ask—Why aren't more people on ARVs?—misses the point. "It's futile to think that ARVs will solve the problem of AIDS," Ogola said. For one thing, she said, people with empty stomachs can't absorb the toxicity of the medication and either vomit it up or don't take it. For another, deciding who gets ARVs, and monitoring their use, requires complex laboratory workups that Kenya's medical infrastructure, depleted in the 1980s by World Bank–mandated structural adjustment programs, can no longer manage.

Without "serious efforts at poverty eradication," she said, the AIDS crisis will continue. Among other things, she said, poverty has broken down traditional African social structures that surrounded sexual promiscuity with taboos.

Since Ogola works for the Kenyan bishops, I brought up the inevitable topic of condoms. She wearily expressed frustration that so much good work by the Catholic Church on AIDS has been overshadowed by the condoms debate, handing me a list of ninety-three Catholic charitable homes and community-based programs in Kenya. Ogola also acknowledged, however, that many African priests quietly counsel married couples in which one partner is infected and the other is not that the use of condoms in such circumstances can be tolerated. Ogola doesn't believe condoms are the solution. Noting that "it's the one gadget in medicine you have to use correctly each and every time," she said only "massive public education" followed by changes in behavior holds real promise.

Ogola said that as a physician, one of her main worries about the AIDS crisis is the way it falls disproportionately upon women. Because of social customs such as wife inheritance, in which a husband's oldest brother inherits his widow, women are dependent upon men and thus less able to protect themselves from infection. Because women are considered men's property, it's a rare African woman who can say "no" when her husband demands sex, even if he's infected. Moreover, when children are infected, it is the woman who cares for them. Ogola thus comes across as a strong African woman, interested in the fate of other African women.

Chapter Ten

MONEY

In his 1997 book Their Kingdom Come, *which describes Opus* Dei as a "world of deceit and dissimulation, crowded with holy manipulators and regulated by unscrupulous interests," Canadian journalist Robert Hutchison says he initially became intrigued with Opus Dei through rumors about its finances. "I first heard of Opus Dei in the 1960s when a Swiss banker friend informed me that it was one of the major players in the Eurodollar market," he wrote. "A religious association speculating in overnight Francs and next week's Dollars? That did not sound right at all." Hutchison writes that although Opus Dei is younger than General Motors, "its assets are said to be much larger." He also says that Opus Dei "professes bewilderment when accused of running a vast earthly empire." Hutchison crafts a comparison between Opus Dei and the Knights Templar of the Middle Ages: "The worldly resources of the Knights Templar sparked the envy of European princes, until finally the Templars were crushed. Having studied and even imitated the Templars, Opus Dei would be careful to avoid a similar fate."

Anyone familiar with journalistic sleight-of-hand will recognize that there's not a direct statement in any of these sentences. Hutchison does not assert that Opus Dei *in fact* plays the international financial markets, merely that a banker says it does, though he leaves the impression that he is onto something. He doesn't state that Opus Dei has more money than General Motors, merely it "is said." One can argue that this sort of maneuver is irresponsible, since it relieves a reporter of the obligation to establish the facts. That aside, Hutchison gives voice to a widespread public impression.

Speculation about Opus Dei secretly hoarding sums of money and building a clandestine financial empire has long been a feature of its mystique.

In fact, as will be detailed in this chapter, such perceptions are overblown. General Motors in 2003 reported assets of $455 billion. Even the most liberal estimate of Opus Dei's worldwide holdings, encompassing everything that could even remotely be identified as an Opus Dei operation (in ways that distort Opus Dei's own self-understanding), would come to $2.8 billion, a little over 1 percent of the figure for GM. This estimate for Opus Dei assets is based on data reported in financial statements for programs in Rome, Spain, the United States, the United Kingdom, Kenya, Peru, and Argentina.

The emotions that surround this issue are not just a matter of prurient curiosity. What's at stake, in the eyes of many Catholics, is nothing less than the soul of the Church. For Catholicism's progressive wing, the Vatican II document *Gaudium et Spes,* which proclaimed solidarity with "the joy and hope, the grief and anguish of the men of our time," signaled a new era in which the Church would align itself with the poor and marginalized. In the 1970s this came to be known as the "preferential option for the poor." There has been resistance to this transition from sectors of opinion that see a more exclusively spiritual mission for the Church. Questions about Opus Dei's wealth are therefore quickly swept up into this debate, reflecting a fear that Opus Dei may be leading the Church back into a cozy alignment with the status quo. The late Penny Lernoux, a Catholic journalist who specialized in Latin America, wrote in her book *People of God* that Opus Dei "is an efficient machine run to achieve worldly power." She linked this with a concern that as Opus Dei's influence grows, the Church will lose its prophetic edge. The "wealth of Opus Dei" debate is thus a marker for deeper Catholic struggles.

Nowhere is the contrast between what the outside world believes about Opus Dei and what Opus Dei believes about itself stronger than on the question of finances. Spokespersons say that Opus Dei has no desire to be an economic juggernaut. In fact, they say, Opus Dei wishes to own as little as possible, reflecting both detachment from earthly wealth and the secular "spirit" of Opus Dei. "We are not a holding company," said Pablo Elton, chief financial officer in Rome.

As a matter of civil law, "Opus Dei," in the limited sense of the central office in Rome, owns only Villa Tevere and Villa Sacchetti (the headquarters of the men's and women's branches), and a cemetery where numeraries are buried. Its annual budget for 2003 was $1.7 million. To get some sense of scale, the annual operating budget for the Vatican is $260 million; the University of Notre Dame in South Bend, Indiana, $500 million; and Harvard University, $1.3 billion. In some countries, "Opus Dei," in the sense of the regional government for that country, may own only its own headquarters. In other countries, not even that belongs to Opus Dei, because it's part of a multi-use facility that belongs to an independent local foundation. In the United States, for example, despite reams of newsprint to the contrary, the building at Thirty-fourth and Lexington does not "belong" to Opus Dei, in the legal sense, but to a foundation called "Murray Hill Place," which is also the name of the building.

All the "corporate works" of Opus Dei, meaning its schools, universities, social activities, university residences, and so on, are owned and operated by the laypeople who founded them, not by Opus Dei. The University of Navarra does not "belong" to Opus Dei, but to an independent, civilly incorporated board of directors (though many members of the board belong to Opus Dei). The same is true of Strathmore University in Nairobi or the University of Piura in Peru, or the Midtown Center in Chicago, or the South Bronx Educational Foundation, or Netherhall House in London, and so on through the list of Opus Dei–affiliated activities. Opus Dei insists that this is the logical consequence of its emphasis on secularity and freedom; critics see it as a shell game designed to conceal Opus Dei's true financial profile.

The obvious questions are: What assets do these various Opus Dei activities generate, regardless of who owns them? Who keeps track of them? What do they buy?

Most of the research for this chapter, and much of the writing, was done by Joseph Harris, a noted American analyst of Church finances, at my request. Harris is not an Opus Dei member or cooperator and does not work for them. It represents the first time someone has taken such a detailed, careful look at how Opus Dei programs are financed.

General Principles

Pablo Elton, general administrator for Opus Dei in Rome and more or less its chief financial officer, is a Chilean numerary who studied civil engineering at the Catholic University in Santiago. For seven years he worked at a consulting firm in Santiago, where, among other things, he helped produce a new design for the city's subway system. From 1988 to 1992 he sat on the boards of two Chilean companies involved in electricity and mineral extraction. Then in 1992 he was called to Rome to assist with the financial management of Opus Dei, and since 1998 he's been on the General Council, the men's chief governing body. If anyone knows Opus Dei finances, it's Elton.

He's not at all skittish about talking facts and figures; in fact, he laughingly told me that "my biggest enemies inside Opus Dei are the PR people," meaning that sometimes he is tempted to step outside the comfort zone of the communications experts, who worry that too much candor will fuel more Opus-bashing. Elton, however, insists that "we have nothing to fear from the numbers." We sat down with him for an interview in June 2004 at Villa Tevere. Elton told us that if you want to understand the approach within Opus Dei to economic questions, there are three core principles to grasp: secularity, freedom, and temperance.

As applied to financial questions, Elton said, secularity means that just as teachers in an Opus Dei school are expected to meet the highest professional standards as educators, those who handle the finances for Opus Dei operations are expected to be similarly qualified. The idea is not that financial decisions will be made at central headquarters; Opus Dei is not the Wal-Mart Corporation, which controls the lights and thermostats in its stores from a centralized company computer. Instead, trained laypeople will make business decisions, and Opus Dei will restrict itself to providing the doctrinal and spiritual underpinnings for their activity. Among other things, this means that the "corporate works" of Opus are independently owned and operated. Further, any other business activity of an Opus Dei member, whether a barbershop or a *Fortune* 500 company, is perforce beyond the purview of Opus Dei officials.

This distinction, between the activities of its members and Opus Dei itself, is one that some people don't buy. Michael Walsh, for example, in his 1989 book *The Secret World of Opus Dei,* rejected it. "It is a sophistry to distinguish either of these kinds of enterprise from purely Opus Dei ones," he wrote. "First, all profits made by numerary members in whatever capacity accrue to Opus itself. That is the consequence of the obligation of poverty which they have taken upon themselves. Even supernumerary (or married) members are under pressure to give as much as possible to the organization. Secondly, no numerary member certainly, and probably no supernumerary member either, will enter upon a business enterprise without having discussed it at length with his or her director; the obligation to be entirely open with the director applies in this sphere as in any other."

Yet Elton insisted this is not how it works in practice. He offered a concrete example from 1989, when he was the regional administrator, or financial officer, for Opus Dei in Chile. Some members of Opus Dei, in concert with some nonmembers, proposed the idea of creating an Opus Dei university, which eventually came to be called the University of the Andes. The new university signed an accord in which Opus Dei agreed to be responsible for pastoral and spiritual care and doctrinal formation. At a certain point, Elton said, the board of the university began to search for land upon which to build the campus, and an Opus Dei supernumerary who sat on the board and was an expert in real estate in Santiago took a lead role in scouting sites. Eventually one was found and construction began.

The point of the story, Elton said, is that to this day he has no idea how much the University of the Andes paid for that land, even though he was the chief financial person for Opus Dei in Chile at the time. It was a decision made by the board with the advice of this supernumerary, he said, in which the government of Opus Dei had no role to play. That, he said, is the spirit of secularity. Opus Dei takes care of the spiritual part, but everything else is up to the judgment of members. Opus Dei did not contribute any money to the purchase of the campus or the construction of the university.

"This supernumerary, by the way, is a good friend of mine," Elton said. "Yet he's never told me how much they paid. There's no reason why he should. It's something that's a matter for the board."

Elton added another example, also from Chile, of a university residence where he sat on the board of directors. The chair was a supernumerary who happened to be a senior partner at Price Waterhouse. "Now, what was I going to do? Go up to this guy and say, 'I'm the regional administrator, and I say we ought to spend our money on this or that'? This guy would say to me, 'Listen, I know my business much better than you do. I do this kind of thing for my clients, which include some of the biggest companies in the world, so just sit down.' He would have been right, too. So I felt free to give my opinion on that board, knowing that in the end, they would make the decision not because of what I said, but what their business logic and understanding of the spirit of the Work told them to do."

This logic of secularity is one of the reasons that it's difficult for journalists and others to get even basic financial information out of Opus Dei. While the outside world would consider the University of the Andes, or the University of Navarra, or the Shellbourne Conference Center as part of the "Opus Dei system," that's not how they're seen from within. They are regarded as independent, self-regulating activities, and the only responsibility Opus Dei has is to ensure that Christian doctrine is taught and spiritual formation is given. Elton's office doesn't collect annual financial statements, let alone detailed reports, from these activities. He genuinely doesn't know how much they're worth, what they bring in over a given year, or what they spend. That may be difficult for others to believe or comprehend, but he insists that it's the reality.

Privately, Opus Dei officials say there is a second, though much less fundamental, reason why Opus Dei is reluctant to "own" anything: to lower the risk that someone inside Opus Dei might have access to large sums of funds that could be misused. It's part of oral tradition that many years ago, a numerary in Portugal absconded to Brazil after emptying the bank accounts of various Opus Dei operations in that country. By diversifying ownership, and ensuring that funds are professionally monitored and controlled rather than being stuck in a director's desk drawer, Opus Dei builds in a precaution against corruption.

Elton's second principle is freedom.

It would be contrary to Opus Dei's emphasis on the free judgment of its members in secular affairs for headquarters to try to dictate how to make decisions on matters such as investments and expenses, Elton said, except in the rare cases when a matter of Church teaching or the spirit of Opus Dei itself is at stake. "The people who run these activities are there because they're good at their jobs, and because they understand the spirit of the Work," he said. "Our nature is to respect their liberty of conscience."

At the same time, Elton said, fidelity to Church teaching does impose certain limits. "It's a path," he said. "Some can go faster, some slower, some can take the scenic route and others the express lane, one can even walk or ride a bike, but the important point is to stay within the boundaries of the road." Liberty of conscience, he said, does not mean "the freedom to do whatever you want." At a very basic level, to take one example, it might be seen as good business practice to invest in a company that makes contraception, but it would not be consistent with being a "coherent Christian."

His third premise for a discussion of Opus Dei finances was "temperance," what in another context might be referred to as "poverty of spirit."

"Temperance would be austerity, also poverty, in the sense that Christians are supposed to imitate Jesus," he said. "So, how does a member of Opus Dei live this virtue? He or she has to exercise it according to one's condition in life. It will mean something different, for example, for a numerary than a supernumerary. A supernumerary with a family has a different economic condition, and will have different material needs. But the point is, nobody should be consumed by the desire for accumulation of material things. The point of the virtue is to be content with a moderate style of life, whatever that means."

The virtue of temperance applies to Opus Dei as an institution, Elton said, which is one of the reasons it doesn't want to "own" properties. Opus Dei, he said, also has to be content with moderate means. For this reason, he said, the sort of activities alleged by authors such as Walsh and Hutchison—involvement in international financial markets, real estate deals, and banking swindles—would not only be difficult to pull off, but contrary to the ideals to which Opus Dei aspires. He stressed that these are basic Christian virtues, "not something invented by Opus Dei."

Poverty of Spirit

Visitors to Opus Dei centers can be forgiven for occasionally straining to see the "temperance" that Elton describes. The houses are often, though certainly not always, located in upscale neighborhoods, and the furnishings and interior designs are well appointed. The chapels are usually impressive, and they don't look like they were constructed on the cheap. Over the years, impressions of wealth and privilege given off by the centers have often fueled images of Opus Dei "elitism," of a white-collar ethos, not in keeping with what has traditionally been meant by poverty of spirit. One critic phrases the question this way: "They may serve the poor, but are they, like Christ, willing to be with them, and to be one of them?"

Members usually make three points in response.

First, they note, not all centers are situated in posh neighborhoods. Numeraries who live in the South Bronx, for example, or in the Rimac neighborhood of Lima, or in the Tiburtino area of Rome aren't in swank parts of town. Further, as American numerary David Gallagher explained, sometimes the real estate market drives Opus Dei into higher-priced areas. When members are seeking a location to open a center, their needs are fairly unusual—a house with perhaps six to ten bedrooms, a large common room for "circles" and "get-togethers," and at least one other large room for a chapel. Often the properties that meet those requirements are in high-income neighborhoods, so Opus Dei has little choice but to bite the bullet and pay a premium price.

Second, members say, attention is paid to the "little things" in Opus Dei, which means that one's home should look nice. It would not be in the "spirit of the Work" to have a shabby reception area, for example, or to hold circles in rooms in which the paint is peeling, or to have people sit on broken chairs. Often, they insist, the appearance of opulence is just that—an appearance, born of savvy in knowing how to get the most out of limited means. For example, the Braval Center, in a low-income neighborhood of Barcelona called Raval, where one-third of the population is unemployed, has a living room for talks. Walk into this living room and it looks upscale. Yet Josep Massabeu, the numerary in charge, delighted in explaining to me the various dumps, street corners, and secondhand sales where he had picked up virtually everything in it. That, too, is what "paying attention to the little things" means in the world of Opus Dei—using whatever resources one has to offer God the very best. What can look to the outside world like ostentation feels from the inside like a consistent ethic of excellence.

Third, members say, this effort to keep up appearances is most obvious in the public areas of Opus Dei centers. Go back to the private quarters, and things become much more spartan. Most members' rooms are small, with little more than a bed and a writing desk. In many cases members share a bath. Moreover, members do not typically have private cars or televisions. At Villa Tevere in Rome, for example, there are roughly eighty members in residence, with seven or eight cars in common and four to five televisions. The point is that while Opus Dei strives to put on its best face for guests, most members are living modest lives.

Moreover, the flip side of Walsh's critique—that numeraries are expected to turn over their earnings to support Opus Dei activities—is that they're not getting rich themselves. If roughly 20 percent of Opus Dei members are lay numeraries, and if perhaps 60 percent of them work outside the government of Opus Dei itself, and assuming an average annual salary of just fifteen thousand dollars (allowing for differences in compensation between the developed and developing worlds), and assuming on average that they turn a third of their earnings over to Opus Dei, that's $51 million a year from numeraries' personal income to support programs such as the ELIS Center in Rome or the Kimlea Technical School for girls in Kenya and to help defray the expenses of the centers in which they live.

As for the supernumeraries, while a few have reached the peak of their professions and make comfortable incomes, most seem to scrape by on fairly modest middle-class means. This is especially common given the tendency among supernumeraries to have large families, which means that income is spread around a larger-than-average household.

For one example, consider Doug and Shirley Hinderer of Chicago, Illinois. Doug is senior vice president for human resources of the National Association of Realtors, and he and Shirley have nine kids. They'd like to have more, but so far no luck, and in order to keep the rhythm of new life in the house flowing, the family got a dog, Hunter. When the dog came down with parvovirus in 2004, however, the Hinderers didn't have the $2,000 it would have cost to have him treated by the veterinarian. Doug said that if they had a spare $2,000 sitting around, it would have gone to their oldest daughter in college, not to the dog. Instead, Shirley, a nurse, found an inexpensive medicine on the Internet, ordered it, and administered it to the dog herself. Happily, Hunter staged a full recovery.

Nobody in the Hinderer household is starving. Shirley said there's no Nintendo or Game Boy in their house, but that seems as much a moral choice as a financial one. Still, as Hunter can attest, the Hinderers are not living economically privileged lives. That, according to many Opus Dei members, is poverty of spirit.

Another example comes from supernumerary José "Pepe" Mercado, fifty-four, whom I met in Lima, Peru. He works as an agronomic engineer and draws a modest civil service salary. He and his wife, Mirta, have had nine children, of whom four have died. Covering the medical costs, plus supporting the five children who survived, has put an enormous strain on the family budget. Mercado said that when he first came into contact with Opus Dei, some friends told him it was "like the CIA," that it was an "ultra right-wing faction of the Church." As he began to explore Opus Dei, however, he said he discovered that it helped him organize his life and have confidence that despite his limited means, he will be able to provide for his wife and children.

"Some people ask me, how do you get by economically with such a large family, and all these problems?" Mercado said. "I tell them, with help from above."

For an application of "temperance" at the institutional level, Japan offers an interesting case in point. Opus Dei arrived in the country in 1958 and has only about 300 members and 12 priests, but operates 14 centers in five cities, along with primary and secondary schools, a well-known language institute, and centers for instruction in cooking and health care. Opus Dei as such, however, owns none of those properties. The only thing Opus Dei owns is one small chapel within the Oku-Ashiya Study Center in Ashiya, Japan. Even the central offices of Opus Dei in Japan are rented from a foundation.

I asked Father Soichiro Nitta, Opus Dei's regional vicar for Japan, to explain why that is.

"We don't want to own anything," he said. "We don't need to accumulate property in order to do the spiritual and doctrinal work we're called to do." In fact, he said, the only reason Opus Dei even owns the chapel is because under Japanese law, in order to be a legal personality, one has to have some physical address. The chapel satisfies that requirement and is registered in Nitta's name. Beyond that, everything belongs to lay members, along with other interested parties, who make up the boards of directors for the various activities.

Opus Dei says it wants to have the means to carry out its mission, and to do it well, but does not seek accumulation of wealth for its own sake. We'll test that theory by running the numbers in the United States.

Financial Profile in the United States

The United States provides an ideal test case for gauging Opus Dei wealth, because every nonprofit corporation in the country has to file a detailed annual report with the Internal Revenue Service, referred to as a 990. Based on these documents, Opus Dei activities appear to be organized in a network of seventy-four distinct corporations, operating in thirteen states and the District of Columbia.

By analyzing these reports, we can put a figure on the wealth of Opus Dei activities in the country. At the end of 2002, Opus Dei–affiliated foundations and other institutions controlled $344.4 million in assets. This includes a $69 million, seventeen-story headquarters in Manhattan, several university residences, schools, and conference centers around the country, plus stocks, bonds, and other investments. Opus Dei institutions also owed creditors a total of $24.4 million.

That $344 million in assets breaks down this way: Opus Dei centers and conference centers control $66.5 million, while fund-raising and investment comes to $84.4 million. A foundation to subsidize the University of Santa Croce in Rome, and two others that fund programs in Mexico and South America, have assets of $83.6 million. Administrative assets come to $69.5 million. Finally, Opus Dei's five elementary and secondary schools are worth $40.3 million.

To put this $344 million in context, in 2001 the Office of Communication for the United States Conference of Catholic Bishops published a report called the *Catholic Information Project*. If one adds up the financial data it provides, estimated revenues for Catholic programs in America for 2001 come to $102 *billion*. Hospitals and schools were the major players, at $59.7 billion and $28.3 billion respectively, dwarfing the total wealth of Opus Dei. The St. Vincent de Paul Society, all by itself, reported income—including donations, earnings from thrift stores, grants, income from real estate, and the monetary value of volunteer services— of $355 million. St. Vincent de Paul, in other words, *made* in one year as much as Opus Dei activities *own*.

To provide another frame of reference, the Archdiocese of Chicago, the second-largest archdiocese in the country in terms of population, regularly publishes financial statements that include assets for its pastoral center, parish churches, and elementary and secondary programs. On June 30, 2003, it had cash, investments, and buildings valued at $2.472 billion. The Archdiocese of Los Angeles reported administrative assets of $626 million. The Diocese of Joliet in suburban Chicago put its total program assets at $117 million, while the administrative center of the Archdiocese of Seattle controlled assets of $182 million. Opus Dei's profile is thus analogous to the holdings for a midsized diocese in the United States.

The financial activities of Opus Dei represent a growing, but relatively small, presence in the total picture of American Catholic Church activities.

Control

The theory, as described by Elton, is that Opus Dei doesn't "own" anything, and that all it provides for its affiliated schools, social service operations, and so on is spiritual and doctrinal formation. The reality, however, to judge from the United States, is that there is a layer of national coordination that may not be tantamount to ownership, but it's more significant institutional involvement than the official rhetoric might lead one to believe.

For example, the Information Office of Opus Dei in Manhattan lists the Association for Educational Development on North Keating Street in Chicago as a program affiliated with Opus Dei. The association sponsors philosophy, theology, and doctrinal classes along with youth camps and clubs and sports activities. The association listed six officers in 2002, led by John Wildes, president. Opus Dei officials insist that it's Wildes who has to worry about leaky roofs, since he owns the buildings. In reality, however, nobody actually "owns" a nonprofit, since under American law the community-at-large owns its assets. Control, however, is another matter. Somebody may control a nonprofit organization without owning it; usually, a board of directors runs the show.

A look at the board membership of the Association for Educational Development suggests a system of "dual control," meaning a balance between local administration and national oversight. A majority of the board members comes from the community and is responsible, at a practical level, for keeping things running. At the same time, the national headquarters plays a role in the person of Tim Hogan, a board member in

Chicago who also sits on the Council of Advisors for the United States. Hogan is the chief financial officer for Opus Dei in the States.

This pattern is replicated across the country. The assets of Opus Dei activities are managed through a cluster of one administrative and five fund-raising foundations, headquartered in New York. These foundations oversee investment management, fund-raising activities, real estate, and the distribution of several million dollars in subsidies to corporations that sponsor centers and conference centers. Examining membership on the boards reveals that a rather small group of members actually calls the shots. There are 30 total positions available for officers; a total of 24 were filled at the end of 2002. Five members of Opus Dei occupied 17 of the 24 positions. John Haley was president of five of these foundations, including the Woodlawn Foundation (which specializes in fund-raising), and he is also a member of the national Council of Advisors, the governing body for Opus Dei in the United States. Hogan filled four positions. Together these six boards control $139 million, or 41 percent, of the total assets of the Opus Dei activities in the United States.

Opus Dei may not own these activities, therefore, but it is involved in their administration. In this regard, Opus Dei leaders more or less mirror the management practices of most American bishops. Short of bankruptcy, bishops leave pastors to run their parishes as they see fit, but they like to have some idea of what's going on.

There's much less involvement in local affairs from Rome, again mimicking the practices of American dioceses. Officials in the States report only the financial activities of the national Opus Dei office to Villa Tevere, which for 2002 came to $207,762. Thus Rome has no clue as to the extent of the fiscal footprint of Opus Dei activities in the United States. In fact, when Pablo Elton and other officials in Rome were presented with the numbers in this chapter, they said it was the first time they'd ever seen them. Elton said, however, that based on what he could see, the accounting seemed correct.

Income and Expenses

The foundations that manage Opus Dei activities run a successful fund-raising program, which in 2002 produced a net income of $10.1 million. About half of this sum supported program budgets, while half was added to investment holdings to augment an endowment. Contributing to an endowment has allowed the foundations to avoid a pitfall common to non-profits, which is waiting for the boiler to explode before asking people to contribute to fix the heating system. Because of their endowment, these foundations have funds available to patch roofs.

Expenditures for 2002 clustered into four general categories:

- Elementary and secondary schools, $18.4 million
- The 61 centers and 7 conference centers, $18.1 million
- Support to programs in Mexico and South America, $3.6 million
- Fund-raising and the administrative portion of the Manhattan headquarters budget, $5.589 million

Opus Dei–related foundations control 46 corporations that sponsor 61 centers in 13 states and the District of Columbia, with a combined total of $40 million in assets. Thirty-five of the 46 corporations that sponsor centers are located in New York (7), Illinois (7), California (6), Massachusetts (6), Texas (5), and the District of Columbia (4). The Opus Dei presence is relatively nominal outside of these six states.

Opus Dei's activities in the United States are in the relatively uncommon position of having sufficient funds to retire both short- and long-term debt without selling any fixed assets. As a group, their philosophy is generally to own the sites rather than to go into debt.

When a center runs a deficit, it generally turns to a national fund-raising program called the Woodlawn Foundation. For 2002 the directors of Woodlawn provided approximately $4 million in grants. The funds came from donations or investment income. Woodlawn actually provided subsidies for 29 of the 46 corporations that sponsored centers. These grants represent about one-third of the total fund-raising revenue generated by the national program at the Woodlawn Foundation.

Cash management for conference centers is about as conservative as humanly possible. Conference centers average a cash balance of $115,721 and a minuscule average of $1,116 in unpaid bills. Program managers pay bills about as swiftly as they can open the morning mail. Opus Dei–related facilities carry a debt of $2.385 million for conference centers, about half of which is carried against the Shellbourne Conference Center in Valparaiso, Indiana. As with study centers, the managers of Opus Dei–related foundations believe almost exclusively in financing purchases from income, not through a mortgage.

Retreat programs generated $3.1 million. They obtained a relatively small portion of that revenue from contributions—about 15 percent. The great bulk came from fees charged to participants, most of whom were Opus Dei members. The total cost of operating the various retreat centers amounted to $4.075 million. Conference center programs operated at a cumulative deficit of $969,337 for 2002.

Fund-Raising

Several Opus Dei–related fund-raising efforts support programs both in the United States and abroad. A foundation called Woodlawn and Affiliates raises and allocates funds, mostly for men's activities. In addition, the woman's section operates a fund-raising program called Rosemore. There is also a small program called the Pontifical University Foundation to support Opus Dei's University of Santa Croce in Rome.

The Woodlawn Foundation functions as the fiscal hub for Opus Dei in America. Its staff solicits contributions from around the country, and in some cases around the world. They manage investments through the directors of the Rockside and Sauganash Foundations. Woodlawn directors transfer millions in funds to various Opus Dei programs. These grants represent a transfer of cash to subsidize the operation of centers, conference centers, and the national headquarters at Murray Hill Place.

Opus Dei activities have been successful at raising money, one measure of which is an increase in net assets from $16.2 million to $61.7 million over the past six years. The audited statements indicate that Opus Dei–related institutions received $133 million in contributions between 1997 and 2002.

Between 1997 and 2003 the Woodlawn Foundation raised $163 million. It transferred $113 million in grants to subsidize residence and conference centers, and to complete the construction of Murray Hill Place. In addition, Woodlawn directors added $45 million to the investment holdings of Opus Dei activities.

The Woodlawn Foundation and similar entities also have a system of grants, where proceeds are routinely transferred as subsidies to study and conference centers around the country. These grants amounted to $10.3 million for 2001–2002. Between 1997 and 2002 the Woodlawn Foundation and its affiliates made grants of $112 million to other Opus Dei corporations around the country, to acquire real estate, and to subsidize programs.

The directors of Woodlawn instituted an audit program in 1997, which is limited to the fund-raising activities. Auditors from Ernst and Young, LLP, have consistently stated that the financial statements for the fund-raising program present, in all material respects, the consolidated financial position of Woodlawn Foundation and Affiliates since 1997. The auditors don't look at other programs.

Investments

Opus Dei foundations have maintained an average balance in their portfolio of $60.9 million. They have changed their investment philosophy over the past six years, shifting from a ratio of 80:20 between low-risk investments over closely held corporations, to a position of 45 percent in mutual funds and publicly traded securities, and 55 percent holdings in limited partnerships and closely held corporations. Total investment and dividend income amounted to $10.239 million over the past six years. Gains totaled $20.779 million for the same period. (Most of that, however, came from a single transaction, discussed below.)

Centrally Organized?

The mythology about Opus Dei in the United States, as elsewhere, suggests that it's a well-organized and rigidly controlled financial machine. Jesuit father James Martin offered his assessment in a recent interview in the *National Catholic Reporter*. "What makes Opus Dei different is that it is very well organized, very influential and very wealthy. The group is centrally organized." In fact, the research for this chapter suggests that Opus Dei is not all that rich and is fairly decentralized. It seems to be as inefficiently run as many dioceses in the United States.

In many ways, in fact, Opus Dei operates a lot like an average American diocese. In theory, a bishop has total control. Since a bishop's theoretical span of control often includes several hundred personnel, the practical reality is for the bishop to run the chancery and for pastors to manage parishes as they see fit. While there is some national coordination through a few numeraries who sit on key boards, this layer is relatively thin.

National leaders do not regularly collect fiscal data from the various operations around the country. For example, Opus Dei programs generated a surplus of $3.9 million for 2002. This surplus was added to investments to increase savings. This key statistic, however, is not reflected in any report. Opus Dei programs generated $49.1 million in revenue and cost $45.9 million to operate during 2002. These statistics represent the first comprehensive description of Opus Dei finances in the United States, and have never been collected as such by Opus Dei officials.

Nor is comprehensive financial data relayed to Rome. This point does not apply, by the way, just to the United States. In the course of research for this chapter, Opus Dei officials in Rome were asked for financial statements for all the corporate works of Opus Dei in the world. As it turns out, they did not have this information in their files. They were happy to provide addresses and contact information for the various corporate works, and in every case for which a request was made, the information was forthcoming. The point is not that they were trying to hide anything, but rather that they don't collect the data. It's not a question of failures in administration or shortfalls in staffing; they simply don't want to know.

Wealthy?

Measuring wealth is a tricky business. At first blush, the $102 billion in revenue for the Catholic Church in the United States might seem like tremendous wealth, yet the bulk of that figure is tied up in schools, churches, and hospitals. If you tried to persuade a bishop that his diocese is "wealthy," he would likely tell you that few schools, and virtually no churches, turn a profit, and that the existence of independently controlled Catholic hospitals does nothing to pay his light bill.

In a fund-raising setting for nonprofit organizations, "wealth" generally means raising money beyond the reasonable needs of the organization. Saving for saving's sake might be a fair description of a wealthy endeavor. The story of Boys Town in the early eighties is the classic nonprofit tale of wealth. Two-thirds of the funds Boys Town raised at the time were not needed to fund the operation of the facility. The program at the time certainly qualified as "wealthy."

Opus Dei activities operated with a 6.6 percent surplus margin for

2002. They raised $49 million, and spent $46 million to operate all programs. The surplus was added to an endowment fund. A total of 31 percent of their total assets are invested in savings intended to protect against future problems. Opus Dei activities maintain current assets, mainly cash and cash equivalents, to pay their bills for seven months should their fundraising efforts not generate an additional dollar. These fiscal characteristics are consistent with a profile of a careful and cautious organization that could weather many adversities and still be able to pay its bills.

Opus Dei in the United States, measured by the available evidence, is not at a stage where it is raising money with no plausible purpose in mind. In general, funds seem to be going to expand programs and facilities that constitute the core apostolate of Opus Dei. They operate an increasing number of residence and retreat centers. It would seem a mistake, therefore, to call this careful and cautious approach to fiscal management "wealthy."

Murray Hill Place

The single largest gift to Opus Dei in the United States, and by most accounts the largest gift to Opus Dei anywhere, came with the donation of $60 million worth of stock in Ben Venue Laboratories on August 29, 1997. By the time the stock was sold a few months later, revenue amounted to $78 million. That one gift, all by itself, made the construction of the $69 million headquarters at Thirty-fourth and Lexington in Manhattan possible.

Ben Venue Laboratories, a pharmaceutical manufacturing firm located in Bedford, Ohio, founded in 1938 by R. Templeton Smith, was instrumental in the development of synthetic estrogen and freeze-dried human blood plasma. From 1943 to 1945, Ben Venue operated a penicillin production plant as part of a massive effort to bring penicillin within the economic reach of the world's population. In subsequent years Ben Venue scientists developed more than four hundred pharmaceutical products. The Ben Venue stock, which had been transferred to the Opus Dei–affiliated Woodlawn Foundation, was sold on December 1, 1997, to the Boehringer Ingelheim Corporation, a German pharmaceuticals conglomerate, for $78,558,354. Among other things, Boehringer Ingelheim is the maker of the Rhinospray decongestant for colds and the flu.

Opus Dei has refused to comment on who made the gift, but it's a matter of public record that before the transfer of the stock, Ben Venue Laboratories was owned by the descendants of R. Templeton Smith, the founder. His son and the CEO of Ben Venue, Kennedy Smith, died in January 1996. Smith was a convert to Catholicism in 1995 and a parishioner at Holy Spirit Byzantine Catholic Church in the Shadyside neighborhood of Pittsburgh, Pennsylvania. During the 1960s and 1970s he was a city magistrate in Pittsburgh, the only Republican to hold elected office in Allegheny County at that time. The Smith family was close to Opus Dei, since, at the time of Kennedy's death, they asked that in lieu of flowers, gifts be made to the Grandevue Center, a women's center of Opus Dei in Pittsburgh. Formally, however, the Woodlawn Foundation declines to name the Smith family as the source of the gift, citing a policy of protecting the confidentiality of its donors.

In 2001, John Haley underscored the importance of the national headquarters when he described Murray Hill Place, now known jokingly in Opus Dei circles as the "tower of power," as "a tangible expression of faith." Prior to the erection of the new facility, the American Opus Dei headquarters had been located in New Rochelle, New York, making it difficult for people who wanted to participate in the means of formation offered by Opus Dei.

The development of a national center had been a dream of Opus Dei for many years. Initial fund-raising began in 1982. An artist's rendering at that time depicted a relatively modest three-story building located in what appeared to be a suburban setting. The 2001 audit document portrays a detailed sketch of the final building, a seventeen-story office and residence complex located in midtown Manhattan, on some of the most expensive real estate on earth. The contrasting images of the small three-story building in 1982 and the seventeen-story final result in 2001 illustrate how the fiscal fortunes of Opus Dei changed with this massive gift from the Smith family.

The foundation that built the facility acquired the Manhattan property, the land upon which the building was erected, in 1993 for $5.095 million. The purchase was financed principally through a loan of $4 million from the Association for Cultural Interchange, a New Jersey–based Opus Dei foundation that normally provides grants and loans for programs outside the United States. In this instance, apparently all Opus Dei programs concentrated their resources to build a national headquarters. Construction began in 1995 and continued through 2001. The total building cost was $57,486,320, and the principal construction funds were disbursed from 1998 to 2001. Furnishings cost an additional $6,543,966. Total value for the headquarters was given in 2002 at $69.125 million.

This office and residence complex performs several functions, with its seventeen floors divided into five zones. The bottom floors house a Center of Studies, where young numeraries receive instruction and training, and also living and working spaces for the women who provide the services of food preparation and cleaning for the entire building. The middle floors function as the national headquarters of Opus Dei, comprising office and living spaces. It's divided into two areas, one for the men and one for the women. The top floors function as a conference center, including classrooms, sitting rooms for informal get-togethers, and guest quarters for participants. As noted in chapter 9, because men and women live and work at Thirty-fourth and Lexington, the building is divided into two, with one half for the men and the other for the women, including two separate entrances.

In addition to these practical uses, most observers say the headquarters also has a symbolic value. It makes a clear statement that Opus Dei in the United States has "arrived," that its presence is permanent, and that it will be a force to be reckoned with on the American scene.

Financial Profile Worldwide

Because of the vagaries of reporting requirements in other countries, coupled with the fact that Opus Dei itself does not collect detailed financial data from its corporate works, we can provide only a best-guess estimate for the size and scope of the total worldwide wealth of Opus Dei activities.

One country for which similar data does exist is the United Kingdom. There are twenty-six Opus Dei facilities in England and Scotland:

London
Netherhall House, residence for male students
Ashwell House, residence for female students
Lakefield, catering and hospitality school

Dawliffe Hall, residence for female students (and headquarters for the women's branch)

Kelston, club for boys

Westpark, club for boys

Tamezin, club for girls

Woodlands, club for girls

Hillcrest, club for girls

Wickenden Manor, conference center (for courses and retreats)

Orme Court (a center that includes the headquarters of the men's branch)

Elmore (center for men)

Pembridge House (center for women)

Brentor (center for women)

Crosmore, nonresidential facility in the city

Oxford
Grandpont House, residence for male students

Winton, residence for female students

Manchester
Greygarth Hall, residence for male students

Coniston Hall, residence for female students

Langsett, catering and hospitality school

Thornycroft Hall, conference center (for courses and retreats)

Pine Road (center for men)

Rydalwood (center for women)

Glasgow
Dunreath, study center for men

Glenalvon, study center for women

Hazelwood House, retreats center

Opus Dei activities in the UK have total assets of $72,869,807, but also liabilities of $42,498,599, which means its net worth is only $30,371,208. Unlike in the United States, where Opus Dei is virtually debt-free, Opus Dei in England is up to its eyeballs in debt. This means that it must make mortgage payments every month and cannot sell assets that are pledged as collateral. Its ability to borrow further funds is nil. This rather striking contrast in philosophy seems to confirm what Opus Dei officials in Rome such as Elton say, which is that there are no "directives" from the home office on such matters. Opus Dei's various regions, and programs within those regions, are more or less free to do as they see fit.

Opus Dei programs in England in 2002 garnered income of $6,310,237 and expenses of $4,885,879, for a net surplus of $1,424,358. This too is a striking difference with the United States, because the English programs, at least in terms of percentages, generate a much larger surplus than those in the United States, 22 percent on average to 7 percent. As noted in a previous chapter, there are about five hundred members of Opus Dei in all of the United Kingdom, out of a Catholic population of some 4 million.

Based on this complete data for the United States and the United Kingdom, and partial data from other countries, we can fashion an estimate of total revenue and assets for the 325 corporate works listed in chapter 1. The Opus Dei administration at Villa Tevere identified 36 elementary and secondary schools, 166 university residences, and 97 vocational/technical schools as corporate works. An average school in the United States operated with a budget of $3.5 million. University residences cost an average of $296,000. We assume that vocational/technical schools generated an average program revenue of $500,000. In most instances total assets were three and one-half times greater than operating revenue. These 299 programs generated an estimated total annual revenue of $233 million and controlled assets worth $781 million in 2004.

In addition to schools and residences, Opus Dei recognized fifteen universities around the world as corporate works. Programs in Spain and Rome enrolled approximately 25,000 students. Financial statements for the University of Navarra in Pamplona gave a per student operating revenue of $10,904. This estimate excluded the cost of the university hospital. We assumed that this statistic was typical of all European universities and the University of Asia and the Pacific in Manila. Total revenue for these programs amounted to $315 million, while assets amounted to $1.1 billion.

Opus Dei also recognized seven universities in Central and South America as corporate works. A total of 47,000 students were enrolled in these programs. We assumed that the per student revenue for the university in Argentina was typical for all schools. We also assumed that the two African universities fit this category. Total revenue amounted to $224 million, while assets totaled $782 million. Finally, we estimate revenue for the eleven business schools at $50 million, and assets for these programs at $175 million.

These regional estimates can be combined to a global estimate where 325 corporate works generated $822 million in annual revenue and involved total global assets of $2.8 billion.

To be clear, $2.8 billion is not pocket change. Two points, however, need to be kept in mind. First, these assets are not at the beck and call of the prelate in Rome, and precious little of these funds reaches him. The vast majority of these assets do not belong to Opus Dei in anything other than a metaphoric sense, and most funding is spent on schools, hospitals, and social service projects. They are not "liquid" assets. Second, by the standards of other groups in the Catholic Church, this is a moderate figure. If one wanted to add up the total assets of most religious orders that have a worldwide profile, for example, no doubt similar figures would result.

Octopus Dei

Some observers of Opus Dei would extend their inquest beyond the assets of Opus Dei's centers and corporate works, and point to secular enterprises with which Opus Dei members are involved as evidence of a much wider sphere of financial influence. Hutchison, for example, cites numeraries such as Spaniard Pablo Bofill de Quadras, who sat on the board of a company named Condotte Española, and an Argentinian supernumerary named José Ferrer Bonsoms, whose family had extensive property holdings, to suggest that in some sense these properties too belong in the Opus Dei ledger. Connecting the dots in this fashion, one can easily generate astronomical sums that have an "Opus Dei" fingerprint. Hutchison called this phenomenon "octopus Dei," the implication being that Opus Dei has its tentacles wrapped around all sorts of financial enterprises.

No doubt there is some merit in the exercise, if only to demonstrate that some Opus Dei members do have positions of importance in the worlds of commerce, international finance, banking, and so on. As noted in chapter 1, Luis Valls, a seventy-eight-year-old Spanish numerary member of Opus Dei, recently stepped down as executive chairman of Banco Popular, Spain's third-largest commercial bank with $47.9 billion in assets—a figure all by itself four times more than the estimate provided above for the total assets of Opus Dei activities worldwide.

Michael Walsh, another journalist critical of Opus Dei, wrote in 1989 that Opus Dei is "significantly connected to" 479 universities and high schools, 604 publications, 52 broadcasting stations, 38 press and publicity agencies, and 12 film production and distribution organizations. Those numbers come from a confidential report submitted to the Vatican in 1979 by then-father Alvaro del Portillo, Escrivá's successor as head of Opus Dei, concerning the hoped-for transformation into a personal prelature. The report was leaked to *El Pais,* the leading Spanish daily, and published on November 8, 1979. Portillo had cited the numbers as a way of indicating the penetration of Opus Dei members into all walks of secular life. He meant that Opus Dei members worked in 479 universities and high schools, 604 publications, and so on, not that Opus Dei owned or controlled those institutions.

Elton argues that treating an institution as being Opus Dei–controlled simply because some members work in it isn't fair. "It doesn't correspond to reality, just as it's not reality to say that a parliament or a basketball team is 'Catholic' just because there are Catholic parliamentarians or owners," Elton says. In 1989, he points out, when Walsh recycled the data from Portillo's report, Opus Dei actually had only six "corporate work" universities in the world: Navarra in Spain, Panamerican University in Mexico, the University of Piura in Peru, Sabana University in Colombia, the University of the Andes in Chile, and Austral University in Argentina.

Given the emphasis on sanctification of work inside Opus Dei, which in part translates into an emphasis on excelling at one's profession, it's likely that Opus Dei members are disproportionately represented among successful bankers and corporate CEOs. Certainly, that gives Opus Dei entrée into a circle of favorably inclined donors when it comes time to raise funds for capital campaigns or building projects. Elton said, for example, that from time to time he has approached wealthy Opus Dei members to request help for specific initiatives. In a serious crisis, one imagines that Opus Dei would have access to sufficient resources to weather the storm.

Yet this logic carries one only so far, for two reasons. First, it is an article of faith inside Opus Dei that just as members should not exploit Opus Dei by wearing their affiliation on their sleeve, so Opus Dei should not exploit members by asking them to favor Opus Dei in their professional responsibilities. It's fair to assume that, human nature being what it is, things don't always work this way, but nevertheless the rhetorical emphasis within Opus Dei on this point is strong, and it no doubt has an effect. In general, the prelate of Opus Dei has no influence on the economic activity of banks, companies, and law firms in which members work.

More important, if this logic is valid for Opus Dei, then it has to work for other groups as well. One could connect the same dots for the Knights of Malta, for example, an international association of Catholic laymen that includes nobles and industrialists who have relatively fat bank accounts. Legatus, an association for Catholic CEOs founded by the former Domino's Pizza executive Thomas Monaghan, numbers several hundred members across the United States, including executives of some of the country's largest banks, financial companies, and advertising agencies. Membership in the "executive level" requires that one's company have at least a $1 million annual payroll and $10 million in net worth. Certainly if one wished to add up the assets of all the companies represented by the members of Legatus, the result would be an impressive financial colossus, with a membership base much smaller than that of Opus Dei. The same could no doubt be done with the Knights of Columbus, an association for American laymen, or for that matter in dioceses that have a high socioeconomic profile. Indeed, there's no reason to restrict this exercise to Catholic groups. If one were to add up the net worth of all the graduates of Harvard University who are active in the corporate world, another "octopus" would appear.

In all these cases, however, there's no guarantee that these assets will ever be of use to the organization. Any fund-raiser for a university, for example, knows how difficult it is to convince alumni to come to the aid of their alma mater. Perhaps Opus Dei members feel a stronger attachment to Opus Dei than the average Harvard alum does to the university, but even so, one can't draw a straight line from the wealth of the companies in which members work, or even their personal assets, to support for

Opus Dei. If that were the case, for example, it's unlikely that Opus Dei in England would be carrying so much debt.

Perhaps owing to images of vast wealth, it has sometimes been rumored that Opus Dei's prominence under the pontificate of Pope John Paul II was due in part to financial muscle—support for the Solidarity movement in Poland, for example, or a "bailout" of the Institute for the Works of Religion (IOR), informally known as the Vatican Bank. For the record, these rumors have been repeatedly denied by Opus Dei and the other principals cited. Opus Dei's relatively modest financial profile would, in any event, raise doubts about whether it really has the resources necessary to provide money on the scale these rumors suggest.

Moreover, there are numerous examples of Opus Dei projects in various parts of the world that have had to be scrapped for lack of resources. For example, the Escuela Agraria El Pla in Spain's Catalonia region, an Opus Dei–affiliated school for farmers, recently had to close because its promoters couldn't find the money to keep its doors open. In Rome, the Scuola Petranova, an Opus Dei–affiliated institution, recently had to shut down part of its activities despite repeated efforts of parents, alumni, and Opus Dei cooperators and supernumeraries to raise enough funding to keep it going. They managed to save the primary school, and they hope that if economic conditions change, they may be able to reopen the high school after a few years. If Opus Dei's access to corporate wealth really were unlimited, this sort of thing shouldn't happen.

While the "octopus Dei" image has an undeniable literary appeal, it probably has little utility in assessing Opus Dei's financial situation.

Chapter Eleven

OPUS DEI IN THE CHURCH

Three years ago I published a book called Conclave: The *Politics, Personalities, and Process of the Next Papal Election,* and prior to Pope John Paul II's death in April 2005, I was often invited to give talks about the election of the next pope. I cautioned listeners that the trash heaps of Church history are littered with the carcasses of journalists who have tried to predict such matters, but that didn't stop anybody from wanting to hear about the papal sweepstakes. Whenever I made such a presentation, regardless of what part of the world I was in or the ideological composition of the audience, there was one question sure to surface. Occasionally a brave soul would raise it during Q&A, but more commonly someone would pull me aside afterward and, speaking in a hushed voice, ask: "Who's the candidate of Opus Dei?"

There were two assumptions bundled into this question: 1) that Opus Dei had a candidate, that is, that Opus Dei had an agenda and was seeking to elect a pope who could advance it; and 2) that whoever the Opus Dei candidate was would be a strong contender, because Opus Dei has a formidable power base in the Church. Both assumptions are debatable, but given Opus Dei members' knack for being in the right place at the right time, one can understand why people find them plausible.

Consider:

- No group in the Catholic Church enjoyed more obvious signs of papal approval during the pontificate of John Paul II. John Paul transformed Opus Dei into a personal prelature in 1982, beatified Escrivá in 1992, and canonized him in 2002. John Paul has met every year with Opus Dei university students for the UNIV encounters. Many in the Catholic Church and in the popular press have come to regard Opus Dei as a kind of papal "shock troops."

- In September 2001 the Vatican's Congregation for the Doctrine of the Faith set off a firestorm by releasing a document called *Dominus Iesus*, which insisted that other religions are in a "gravely deficient" situation with respect to Christianity. Seated next to Cardinal Joseph Ratzinger, then the Vatican's top doctrinal official and now Pope Benedict XVI, at the press conference to present *Dominus Iesus* was Monsignor Fernando Ocáriz, a consultor to the Congregation for the Doctrine of the Faith, one of the main authors of *Dominus Iesus*—and the vicar-general of Opus Dei.

- In the early 2004 contretemps over whether Pope John Paul II did or did not say "It is as it was" with respect to Mel Gibson's movie *The Passion of the Christ,* it emerged that the assistant director of the film, Jan Michelini, is the son of prominent Italian politician and journalist Alberto Michelini, an Opus Dei supernumerary. The young Michelini was the first child John Paul baptized as bishop of Rome. Moreover, the Vatican official who had seemed, at least indirectly, to confirm that the pope made the statement was Joaquín Navarro-Valls, a Spaniard who runs the Vatican press office. Navarro is a numerary of Opus Dei. That connection led some people to suspect an Opus Dei plot to "cook up" a papal quote. (For the record, Mel Gibson is not an Opus Dei member.)

- In September 2002, during the peak of the sexual abuse crisis in the Catholic Church in the United States, *America* magazine printed an explosive essay by an official in the Vatican's Congregation for Bishops arguing that homosexuals should not be ordained as priests. The article was written by Father Andrew Baker, a priest of the Allentown, Pennsylvania, diocese who is also a member of the Priestly Society of the Holy Cross—in other words, a member of Opus Dei.

- When the Vatican had a problem in the Diocese of Sankt

Pölten in Austria, where some forty thousand pornographic images were discovered on a computer in the diocesan seminary, John Paul II sent in an apostolic investigator who subsequently has been dubbed to take over as bishop, cleaning house in the seminary. The new bishop is Klaus Küng, former bishop of Feldkirch in Austria—a member of Opus Dei.

String together enough of these high-profile intersections between the Vatican, Opus Dei, and "conservative" causes, and one can begin to understand the popular perception that Opus Dei is "taking over." It's not just public cases, either. Church insiders can catalog a whole series of unpublicized incidents in which Opus Dei played a role, usually on what would be perceived as the "conservative" side.

To take but one instance, there's a community of roughly 440 religious sisters with branches in Spain, Peru, Guatemala, El Salvador, and Mexico, called the Daughters of Our Lady of the Sacred Heart. It's an outgrowth of the Sacred Heart family of religious communities founded in France in the nineteenth century by Father Jules Chevalier. In the post–Vatican II period, one wing of the women's community began to liberalize, but another felt that too much tradition was being squandered. The leader of this second faction was a Spaniard named Sister María de Jesús Velarde, a personal acquaintance of Portillo, and she turned to him for help when her group decided to break away. According to the regional superior in Chaclacayo, Peru, Sister Maria Goretti, the fledgling community was "under the umbrella of Opus Dei" until its canonical status was resolved in September 1998, with Opus Dei providing formation, priests, confession, and retreats. After the community was duly erected, it became en masse a "cooperator" of Opus Dei. In the seminary in the territorial prelature of Yauyos in Peru, for example, entrusted to Opus Dei, the sisters take care of purchasing, cleaning, cooking, and laundry. Cardinal Juan Luis Cipriani of Lima, a member of Opus Dei, has given the community assignments in a parish and a school in Lima.

Perceptions of Opus Dei's ecclesiastical reach generate continual rumors about its next conquest. It is widely believed in Rome that Opus Dei is gunning to take over Vatican Radio, currently administered by the Jesuits. Vatican Radio, with four hundred employees and daily broadcasts in forty languages, is enormously expensive, and because of its policy against commercial advertising, generates no revenue. Given perceptions of its vast wealth, it's no surprise that Opus Dei is seen as a potential white knight. In similar fashion, the former rector of the Jesuit-run Gregorian University, Father Franco Imoda, said that during his term, he heard rumors that Opus Dei was out to take over the Gregorian, the flagship Jesuit university in Rome, though he stressed that he filed these rumors in the category of "fantasy." For the record, spokespersons for Opus Dei in Rome deny that Opus Dei has any desire to hijack either Vatican Radio or the Gregorian, stressing that the lone interest of Opus Dei is, in the words of Escrivá, "to serve the Church as the Church wants to be served."

This chapter examines the most frequently cited instances of an allegedly expanding Opus Dei influence within the Church, to establish how much reality lies behind those impressions.

John Paul II and Opus Dei

John Paul was in a sense "the pope of the movements," a leader who strongly encouraged a wide array of new religious orders and lay groups in the Catholic Church—the Focolare, Comunione e Liberazione, L'Arche, Sant'Egidio, the Neocatechumenate, the Legionaries of Christ, and the Daughters of Charity, to name some of the most prominent. Even in this galaxy of new ecclesiastical life, no group was more prominent than Opus Dei. The pope paid special tribute to Escrivá in his spring 2004 book *Rise: Let Us Be on Our Way!*—a look back over his years as a bishop: "In October 2002 I had the joy of inscribing in the album of saints Josemaría Escrivá de Balaguer, founder of Opus Dei, zealous priest, apostle of the laity for new times," he wrote. Yet one should not exaggerate how much political capital this chemistry provided Opus Dei. For everyone in the Catholic Church who was impressed by it, there was probably also someone who resented it.

Moreover, Opus Dei is not a "creature" of John Paul II. He was not even the first pope to carve out a new category in canon law with Opus Dei as its first beneficiary. That was Pius XII, who on February 2, 1947, issued an apostolic constitution called *Provida Mater Ecclesia*, which created "secular institutes," and on February 24, 1947, three weeks later, issued a decree entitled *Primum Institutum*, which approved Opus Dei as the very first secular institute. Pius XII also came to the rescue when forces in the Vatican were considering splitting Opus Dei into separate men's and women's branches and removing Escrivá as superior.

Subsequent popes also smiled on Opus Dei, even if they were cautious about its juridical status. John XXIII, pope from 1958 to 1963, once told his private secretary that Opus Dei "is destined to open up undreamt-of horizons of the universal apostolate in the Church." As noted in an earlier chapter, there was a cooling-off in the later years of Paul VI's reign, but at the same time Pope Paul used *The Way* in his private meditations. John Paul I, the pope of thirty-three days, was an Escrivá fan, saying that while Saint Francis de Sales had developed a spirituality for the laity, Escrivá forged a lay spirituality.

Yet at the level of public relations, the identification between John Paul II and Opus Dei was so strong that in many cases, judgments about one became judgments about the other. In the English-speaking world, this tendency was especially strong given that the first wide-scale public discussion of Opus Dei came in 1982, with the erection of the personal prelature. Prior to that, one can find scattered references to Opus Dei in English-language newspapers, magazines, and other media, but the interest was episodic. Beginning in 1982, however, the debate over Opus Dei in the Anglo-Saxon world began to heat up, and it was in roughly the same historical moment that opinions about John Paul II began to harden.

An analysis prepared by an Opus Dei official for this book argues that there are deeper reasons than political convenience for the affinity between John Paul and Opus Dei. The document cites ten examples of a "spontaneous convergence" at the level of "ideas, visions, and judgment on priorities in the dialogue between the Church and modern society." They are:

- The universal vocation to holiness
- The freedom and pluralism of Christians
- Unity of life and coherence
- The apostolate of the laity
- The gospel of work
- The family
- Trust in youth
- The sacramental life

- Charity and justice
- Loyalty to the Church

Opus Dei did not arrive in Poland until 1989, so Cardinal Karol Wojtyla of Krakow, who became John Paul II, did not meet it there. Prior to his election as pope, however, Wojtyla had been invited to give a series of conferences for a center of studies for priests in Rome operated by Opus Dei, called Centro Romano Incontri Sacerdotali, or CRIS. His talks were printed as a book under the title of *La fede della Chiesa, The Faith of the Church*. On October 13, 1974, at the Residenza Universitaria Internazionale (RUI), also operated by Opus Dei, he spoke on "Evangelization and the Inner Person." Wojtyla asked: "Will the true development of the human person, that is, the person's spiritual maturity and personal morality, be able to keep pace with the progress of technical means that we will have at our disposal? In what fashion, in other words, shaping the face of the earth, will human beings be able to shape their own spiritual face?" In response, Wojtyla said that Escrivá offered an answer: "We could respond with a very happy expression, already familiar to people around the world, which has been spread for years by Monsignor Josemaría Escrivá de Balaguer, the founder of Opus Dei: 'Everyone sanctifying their own work, sanctifying themselves in work, and sanctifying others with work.' " Given Wojtyla's interest in a spiritual and personalist interpretation of work, as an antidote to materialistic Marxist conceptions, his attraction to Escrivá seems natural.

Before the first conclave of 1978, the one that elected Cardinal Albino Luciani of Venice as John Paul I, Wojtyla made a visit to Villa Tevere to pray at Escrivá's tomb. He was accompanied by his Polish compatriot Bishop Andrzej Maria Deskur (later to be made cardinal), who was working at the time as the secretary of the Pontifical Council for Social Communications. The visit came on August 17, 1978. After his election, John Paul II had an important conduit for information and perspective on Opus Dei in Deskur, who had been in the Roman Curia since 1973 and had become friends of both Portillo, Escrivá's top lieutenant, and Herranz, an Opus Dei priest who would later become a cardinal and senior Vatican official under John Paul II.

"I met Bishop Wojtyla, who was then an auxiliary of Krakow, during Vatican II, when Deskur introduced Alvaro and myself to him," Herranz said. "When Wojtyla came to Rome, he would often stay at the home of Deskur, who was very enthusiastic about Opus Dei and explained many things about it to Wojtyla, such as the sanctification of ordinary work." Herranz said Deskur's first contact with Opus Dei came through Father Salvador Canals, an Opus Dei priest who worked with Deskur on a document on the cinema.

Herranz said that when the pope appointed him secretary of the office he now heads, he brought John Paul a small donkey as a present, a symbol frequently invoked by Escrivá to represent the idea that one should carry Christ so all can see him, then disappear. The pope, he said, began to ask questions about Escrivá's spirituality, and twice waved away his private secretary, Stanislaw Dzwisz (whom Pope Benedict XVI has named archbishop of Krakow), so they could continue the conversation.

John Paul II met with young people who took part in the Opus Dei–sponsored UNIV trip to Rome over Easter, and on every occasion he gave an address. In the early years, when the pope was able to be more spontaneous, John Paul would often banter with the crowd, and those moments give some insight into the pope's attitude. Opus Dei has collected these images on a DVD called "Twenty-five Years with John Paul II." In 1987, for example, he noted the irony that Opus Dei youth began visiting the pope in 1968, "a particularly resonant year in the university world"—a reference to the student uprisings of 1968, a metaphor in Europe for a generation of leftist, anti-institutional activism that Opus Dei has resisted. At another point John Paul refers to the fact that one Opus Dei young person said he had read the pope's letter to youth, but added that it was a little long. "If these guys from Opus Dei think it's long," the pope joked, "what are the others going to say?" In another moment the pope refers to the sacrament of reconciliation, at which point applause breaks out. He looks up, seemingly surprised, and says, "That's wonderful, to applaud for confession."

The emphasis on individual confession within Opus Dei, in an era when some Catholics had abandoned the practice, was something John Paul II always admired. In an interview for this book, Joaquín Navarro-Valls, head of the Vatican press office, said he had precious few exchanges with the pope about Opus Dei over the years. One such instance occurred, however, when Navarro referred to the sacrament of confession in the context of an unrelated discussion. "Ah," John Paul quipped, "now you're talking like a member of Opus Dei."

Over the years John Paul spoke or published reflections about Opus Dei at least eleven times, including the decree establishing the personal prelature, homilies for both the beatification and canonization of Escrivá, and a message to a 2002 congress marking the centenary of Escrivá's birth.

One of John Paul's most reflective meditations on Escrivá came in an October 14, 1993, address on the occasion of a congress on Holiness and the World organized by Opus Dei. The pope said:

> *The profound awareness with which the Church of today feels itself at the service of a redemption that concerns every dimension of human existence was prepared, under the guidance of the Holy Spirit, by a gradual intellectual and spiritual progress. The message of Blessed Josemaría . . . constitutes one of the most significant charismatic impulses in this direction, departing from a singular realization of the universal irradiating force that the grace of the Redeemer possesses. . . . On the basis of this conviction, Blessed Josemaría invited men and women of the most diverse social conditions to sanctify themselves and to cooperate in the sanctification of others, sanctifying ordinary life. In his priestly activity he perceived deeply the value of every soul and the power of the Gospel to illuminate consciences and to awaken a serious and energetic Christian commitment in defense of the person and the dignity of the person. What power this doctrine has in the face of hard work, and at the same time how attractive it is in the new evangelization to which the Church is called! . . . Josemaría Escrivá de Balaguer, like other great figures in the contemporary history of the Church, can be a source of inspiration for theological reflection. In effect, theological research, which forms an essential mediation in the relationship between faith and culture, progresses and enriches itself by paying attention to the source of the Gospel, under the impulse of the experience of the great witnesses of Christianity. Blessed Josemaría without doubt is among them.*

John Paul II thus saw in Opus Dei not just a politically expedient group of loyalists, though there may well have been that element to their relationship, but as the carrier of an insight about the "universal irradiating force" of grace, with consequences in all areas of Christian life.

Benedict XVI and Opus Dei

Benedict XVI has had considerable interaction with Opus Dei over the years, working closely at the Congregation for the Doctrine of the Faith with a number of key Opus Dei members, and has always expressed admiration for its spirituality and apostolic activity. It is to be expected, therefore, that the support for Opus Dei under John Paul II will continue, even if Benedict is likely to put more emphasis on the revitalization of traditional forms of religious life alongside the flourishing of "new ecclesial realities" such as Opus Dei.

Shortly after the new pope's election, the prelate of Opus Dei, Bishop Javier Echevarría, put out a statement that alluded to Benedict's contacts with Opus Dei: "The new pope is well acquainted with the prelature's mission, and knows he can count on the cheerful efforts of the priests and laypeople who form part of it in order to serve the Church, which was St. Josemaría Escrivá's only ambition," Echevarría said.

As head of the Congregation for the Doctrine of the Faith, then-cardinal Joseph Ratzinger called three members of Opus Dei to serve as theological consultors: Monsignor Fernando Ocáriz, vicar-general of Opus Dei, and thus the number two official in Opus Dei after Echevarría; Monsignor Angel Rodríguez Luño; and Monsignor Antonio Miralles. All three men teach in the theology faculty at the University of Santa Croce, the Opus Dei–run institution in Rome. Ocáriz has been an especially prized collaborator of the doctrinal congregation. As noted above, he was one of the principal authors of the 2000 document *Dominus Iesus*, on the subject of the relationship between Christianity and other world religions, a theme at the heart of the pope's theological concerns.

While still a cardinal, Ratzinger took part in several public events at Santa Croce, including an April 9, 2003, roundtable on "the commitment and behavior of Catholics in political life," a session moderated by an American Opus Dei priest named Fr. Robert Gahl. Ratzinger also delivered an address at a 1993 congress on the theological teachings of Escrivá.

Ratzinger was awarded an honorary doctorate by the Opus Dei–run University of Navarre in Pamplona, Spain, in 1998. On that occasion, he delivered a lecture titled "What in Fact Is Theology?" on the nature of theology as an academic discipline, recently published in a collection of his works entitled *Pilgrim Fellowship of Faith: The Church as Communion* (Ignatius Press). In his address, Ratzinger praised the work of Monsignor Pedro Rodríguez, an Opus Dei priest and dean of the theology faculty at the University of Navarre, for his critical edition of the original manuscript of the *Catechismus Romanus*, the catechism of the Council of Trent. Ratzinger said this critical edition was of "great significance" for his own work on the *Catechism of the Catholic Church*.

"You are a member of a faculty that, in the relatively short period of its existence, has won a significant place in the worldwide discussions of theology," Ratzinger said. "Thus it is a great honor and a joy to me, through this doctorate, to belong to this faculty, to which I have already long been bound by personal friendships as also by academic discussion."

During an October 1995 event in Rome to mark the thirtieth anniversary of the Vatican II decree *Presbyterorum Ordinis*, the council's decree on priestly life, Ratzinger made a passing reference to Escrivá:

> I recall a little episode which happened in the first years of Opus Dei. A young woman had the opportunity to go and hear some talks by the Founder of Opus Dei. She was very curious to hear such a well-known speaker. However, after participating in the Mass he celebrated, as she related afterwards, she no longer wanted to hear a human speaker: she only wanted to discover God's word and his will. The ministry of the word demands of the priest a sharing in the kenosis, the self-emptying of Christ: rising and sinking in Christ. The fact that the priest does not talk about himself, but brings another's message, does not mean indifference on the personal level, but just the opposite: when he loses himself in Christ he takes the path of the Paschal mystery, and so truly finds himself, and finds communion with the One who is the Word of God in person.

In March 2002, Ratzinger participated in the presentation in Rome of a book entitled *Opus Dei—The Message, The Works, The People*, by Italian author Giuseppe Romano. On that occasion, he delivered his most extensive public comments on Escrivá.

Ratzinger began by reflecting on the name Escrivá chose for his new reality, "Opus Dei"—God's work, not his own.

While I was pondering this fact, there came to mind the words of the Lord reported in the Gospel of John: "My father is always working." These are words spoken by Jesus in the course of a discussion with some religious specialists who did not want to recognize that God could act even on the Sabbath. This is a debate that is still going on, in a certain way, among people and even Christians of our own time. Some people think that after creation God "retired" and no longer has any interest in our everyday affairs.

According to this manner of thinking, God could no longer enter into the fabric of our daily life. But the words of Jesus affirm the opposite. A man open to the presence of God discovers that God is always working and still works today: We should, then, let him enter and let him work. And so things are born which open to the future and renew mankind. . . .

In this sense, the theocentrism of Escrivá de Balaguer, in accordance with the words of Jesus, means this confidence in the fact that God has not retired from the world, that God is working now and we ought only to put ourselves at his disposal, to be ready, capable of reacting to his calling. This, for me, is a message of greatest importance. It is a message which leads to overcoming what could be considered the great temptation of our times: the pretense, that is, that after the "big bang," God retired from history. . . .

From all this I have better understood the inner character of Opus Dei, this surprising union of absolute fidelity to the Church's great tradition, to its faith, and unconditional openness to all the challenges of this world, whether in the academic world, in the field of work, or in matters of the economy, etc. The person who is bound to God, who has this uninterrupted conversation, can dare to respond to these challenges, and no longer has fear. For the person who stands in God's hands always falls into God's hands. And so fear vanishes, and in its place is born the courage to respond to today's world.

Ratzinger's remarks were later published in *L'Osservatore Romano,* the official Vatican newspaper, the day before Escrivá's October 6, 2002, canonization.

In addition, the new pope has one other source close at hand for insight into the world of Opus Dei—his private secretary, Father Georg Gänswein, who is not a member of Opus Dei, but who taught on the faculty of canon law at Santa Croce for five years. His area was the *munus docendi,* or the teaching office of ordained ministers in the church. He published articles in the bulletin of the canon law faculty, including one on the procedures for doctrinal investigation in the Congregation for the Doctrine of the Faith. (Friends of Gänswein say that of the things he appreciated about Santa Croce was that, in contrast with the typically relaxed Italian attitude to punctuality, the schedule is much more precise, thus better suited to his German instincts.)

In general, Benedict's papacy is likely to continue John Paul II's policy of supporting the so-called "new movements," such as Focolare, Neocatechumenate, Sant'Egidio, L'Arche, as well as the wide range of other groups that have flowered in the period after the Second Vatican Council, including Opus Dei. As a pragmatist, Pope Benedict is aware of the criticism of these groups. He knows that they are capable of exaggeration, of disconnecting themselves from the broader Church, of a kind of uncritical "cult of personality" around their founders. He will encourage them to mature and to deepen their intellectual and theological foundations. At the same time, however, he will see them as precious models of community based on truth.

In 1997's *Salt of the Earth,* Ratzinger said: "One can always raise objections to individual movements such as the Neocatechumenate or the Focolarini, but whatever else you may say, we can observe innovative things happening there." In 1984's *The Ratzinger Report,* he was enthusiastic: "What is hopeful at the level of the universal Church—and that is happening right in the heart of the crisis of the Church in the Western world—is the rise of new movements, which nobody had planned and which nobody has called into being, that have sprung spontaneously from the inner vitality of the faith itself. What is manifested in them—albeit subdued—is something like a Pentecostal season in the Church."

At the same time, the traditionalist side of Pope Benedict's personality means that he will be conscious of what some established religious communities in the Church, such as the Benedictines, Franciscans, and Jesuits, took as a neglect of religious life under John Paul II in favor of the new movements. In their more bitter moments, men and women religious sometimes felt as if John Paul had given up on them, having decided that the future belonged to the newest movements. Pope Benedict, who chose to name himself after the founder of monasticism, will see a genuine renewal of religious life as an important ambition of his papacy.

Power in the Vatican

Among Italian observers of Vatican affairs, whenever a new official is named or promoted, the most commonly asked question is *Di quale parrocchia è?*—which translates as "What parish is he from?" The point is not whether the new man is from St. Michael's or St. Monica's. "Parish" here has a metaphorical sense. It means "What circle of friends and patrons does this man depend on?" The premise, very much in line with traditional Italian assumptions about how the world works, is that behind the scenes in any institution are informal networks of alliances whose members grease the wheels for one another and who seek to expand their influence.

That bit of context perhaps helps explain the fascination with Opus Dei's presence inside the Holy See. The assumption among Vatican watchers is that members of Opus Dei who work in the Vatican form their own *parrocchia,* and as their numbers and prominence grow, so the control exercised by Opus Dei over the Vatican, and over the Catholic Church, expands. Many Catholics assume that by now the penetration of Opus Dei is near total, and that Opus Dei was more or less "calling the shots" in the waning days of John Paul II's papacy. It's not just the rank and file who hold this impression. When I interviewed one member of the College of Cardinals in the course of research for this book, who had generally positive things to say about Opus Dei, he added that he had just one concern: "As an outsider not living in Rome, I wonder about the extent of their influence in the Curia."

In fact, Opus Dei's presence in the Vatican is limited. There are only three Opus Dei members who hold the top job in a Vatican department (out of nine congregations, eleven councils, three tribunals, and assorted other offices): Herranz, a Spaniard, is president of the Pontifical Council for the Interpretation of Legislative Texts, which is charged with interpreting the meaning and implications of the Code of Canon Law; another Spaniard, Joaquín Navarro-Valls, heads the Vatican press office; and Italian layman Giò Maria Poles directs the Office of Labor for the Holy See, which is more or less the personnel department. Poles was still in office as of this writing, although he was beyond retirement age. Navarro, by the way, said that he does not believe that being an Opus Dei member was directly responsible for his appointment as the Vatican spokesperson. More relevant, he said, was the fact that he had twice been elected head of the Foreign Press Association in Rome, a sign of esteem among his colleagues. His being in Opus Dei, he said, was perhaps a "guarantee" for the pope that he had a solid formation in Catholic teaching.

Beyond these three, the seven priests of Opus Dei who worked in the Vatican as of December 2004 were the following:

- Monsignor Francesco Di Muzio, a *capo ufficio*, or midlevel manager, in the Congregation for the Evangelization of Peoples, the Vatican's missionary agency
- Monsignor José Luis Gutiérrez Gómez, a *relator*, or official, in the Congregation for the Causes of Saints
- Monsignor Miguel Delgado, *capo ufficio* in the Pontifical Council for the Laity
- Monsignor Stefano Migliorelli, an Italian official in the Secretariat of State (Migliorelli works in the First Section, which deals with internal Church affairs and is organized into language desks)
- Monsignor Osvaldo Neves, an official in the Secretariat of State (Neves works in the Second Section, which deals with diplomatic affairs)
- Father Mauro Longhi, a lower-level official in the Congregation for Clergy, which deals with the affairs of diocesan priests around the world
- Monsignor Ignacio Carrasco de Paula, chancellor of the Pontifical Academy for Life

In addition to Navarro, two other lay members of Opus Dei work in the Vatican press office: Miguel Castellví Villaescusa, head of the Vatican Information Service, and Alfonso Bailly-Balliere, an editor.

There are also eight priests who work in the Vatican who are members of the Priestly Society of the Holy Cross. While remaining priests of their diocese, they are also considered members of Opus Dei. It should be noted, however, that arrangements for these priests to work in the Vatican were made through the local bishop, and in some cases the Vatican office may not have been aware that the priest was a member of the Priestly Society. They are:

- Archbishop Justo Mullor, president of the prestigious Accademia Ecclesiastica, the school for Vatican diplomats
- Monsignor Nguyen Van Phuong, a *capo ufficio* in the Congregation for the Evangelization of Peoples
- Monsignor Jacques Suaudeau, an official of the Pontifical Academy for Life
- Father Francisco Vinaixa Monsonís, an official in the Pontifical Council for the Interpretation of Legislative Texts
- Monsignor Celso Morga Iruzubieta, a *capo ufficio* in the Congregation for Clergy
- Monsignor José María Yanguas Sanz, a *capo ufficio* in the Congregation for Bishops
- Father Andrew Baker, an official in the Congregation for Bishops
- Father Gregory Gaston, an official in the Pontifical Council for the Family

One point about this list is that it would be impossible to put together simply by relying on the *Annuario,* the annual Vatican yearbook that lists officials of the various departments. If you look up the name of a priest from the clergy of Opus Dei in the index in the back of the *Annuario,* it will say "Opus Dei." This is not true of the lay members of Opus Dei in the Vatican, however, or of members of the Priestly Society of the Holy Cross. In both cases there is no indication that these people are Opus Dei members. This lack of labels reflects the principle of secularity, but it also adds to the air of mystery. Interestingly, it's often a mystery also to other members of Opus Dei; most of the Opus Dei members who work in the Vatican told me they were unaware of how many members there were in the Vatican, or where they worked, when I interviewed them. Most could name six or seven others, including high-profile figures such as Navarro-Valls and Herranz, but none had a sense of the whole. They insist that they do not meet as a group, or pursue a common strategy.

Totaling the above names, as of December 2004 there were 20 members of Opus Dei who worked in the Vatican. In order to put that in context, the Roman Curia (the formal name for the papal bureaucracy), had 2,659 employees in 2004, which means that 0.7 percent of the total Curial workforce was Opus Dei. That's a somewhat misleading index, however, because the majority of those 2,659 employees answer phones, issue entrance passes, and perform routine administrative tasks. There are perhaps 500 policy-level positions, so by that standard, Opus Dei had 3.6 percent. One further note is that in the world of the Vatican, the most important office is the Secretariat of State, which acts as a coordinator for the work of the rest of the departments. Opus Dei has two priests there, one in each of its two branches, though neither is a "superior," meaning someone authorized to make decisions. The next most important departments are the "congregations," which are empowered to make legally binding judgments in their areas of competence, such as doctrine and liturgy. No Opus Dei member is currently a "superior," or decision-maker, in one of the congregations.

One other way to put these numbers in context is to compare them to those for the Jesuits, a religious order that, for both historical and political reasons, is often seen as a "rival" of Opus Dei. As of December 2004 the Jesuits had nine priests who work in the Vatican, excluding Vatican Radio. When one includes the 17 Jesuits at Vatican Radio, the total soars to 26. This number includes one Jesuit who works in the Secretariat of State and two who are heads of offices. Father Pasquale Borgomeo is the head of Vatican Radio, and Father Czeslaw Drazek is the head of the Polish-language edition of *L'Osservatore Romano*. It is difficult to make the argument, in other words, that Opus Dei is overrepresented in the Vatican with respect to at least one other body in the Church.

Beyond staff, the Vatican also relies on a wide network of "consultors"—priests and laity who do not work full-time in the Vatican but are called upon to give expert advice. Opus Dei has two such consultors of special prominence, both of whom assist the Congregation for the Doctrine of the Faith: Monsignor Fernando Ocáriz, the vicar-general of Opus Dei, and Monsignor Angel Rodríguez Luño, a professor of moral theology at Santa Croce. The Jesuits, too, have powerful Vatican consultors, including Father Karl Becker of the Gregorian University, also a consultor for the Congregation for the Doctrine of the Faith. Any number of other religious orders, lay movements, and Catholic groups number consultors to Vatican departments among their members.

In an interview for this book, conducted before the death of Pope John Paul II, Herranz, who has worked in the Roman Curia for forty-four years, denied that there is an "Opus Dei bloc" within the Vatican.

"There's no lobby, no kind of 'white Masonry.' I've heard these things, but no," he said. "In all these years, I've only gone once to the Office of Labor, not to see Poles but because there was a question I had to deal with. I see Navarro every now and then. My prelate is not the prelate of Opus Dei. My prelate is called John Paul II. I receive orders from him, the pope, and I execute them."

Herranz added that he has never discussed Vatican business with the prelate of Opus Dei.

"I've never asked the prelate for advice on what to do," he said. "If I need that kind of advice, we have fifty-five consultors from all over the world who are experts in the questions we handle. . . . This is something that has caused Opus Dei to suffer much, because some people haven't understood it. They've mistaken Opus Dei for a kind of political party, or an ecclesiastical party."

Bishop Javier Echevarría, the prelate of Opus Dei, dismissed the impression that Opus Dei is a growing power in the Vatican: "I remember that when someone would approach Escrivá to suggest somebody from Opus Dei who might be able to do a job in the Vatican, he would always say, 'Okay, but I want you to send me the request in writing, because I don't want anybody to think that I'm the one trying to get these people into the Vatican for my personal interests.'" Echevarría said he could state "categorically" that Opus Dei has never acted on its own initiative to place a member in a Vatican position. Further, he said, he does not discuss Vatican business with the members of Opus Dei who work there.

One way of measuring Vatican influence is to note what happens to someone who ends up on the bad side of a particular *parrocchia*. Part of

Opus Dei's reputation for Vatican power is reflected in what happened to Italian archbishop Luigi De Magistris, who started his curial service as a protégé of famed Cardinal Alfredo Ottaviani of the Holy Office. De Magistris had been head of the Apostolic Penitentiary, a confidential Vatican court, and was expected to be among the new cardinals named by John Paul II in October 2003. His name did not appear, however, and a few weeks later he was out of his job, replaced by American cardinal Francis Stafford. At seventy-seven years old, an age when many senior churchmen are still going strong, De Magistris is retired and seemingly unlikely to receive a cardinal's red hat. Rumors in Rome had it that this was long-delayed payback for 1992, when as a judge within the Congregation for the Causes of Saints, De Magistris was one of two to vote against the beatification of Escrivá. Opus Dei spokespersons deny having any role in De Magistris's exile, and some Vatican sources say that De Magistris had run afoul of power brokers within the Secretariat of State for other reasons. But that doesn't stop observers of the Vatican from taking his fate as a cautionary tale about crossing swords with "the Work."

On the other hand, Opus Dei members do not win every showdown. Take the case of Monsignor Joaquín Llobell, a Spanish Opus Dei priest and professor of canonical procedure at the University of Santa Croce in Rome. He's a widely respected canon lawyer who sits on the Apostolic Signatura, the Vatican's supreme court, as well as the Court of Appeal for the Vatican City-State. He once served as a judge *ad causam* for penal cases handled by the Congregation for the Doctrine of the Faith, including accusations of sexual abuse against priests, in some instances from the United States. Llobell also was a member of the commission that prepared a set of norms for handling "grave delicts," including sexual abuse, called *Sacramentorum sanctitatis tutela*, issued on April 30, 2001.

While Llobell is a loyal son of the Church, he is also a stickler for due process of law, and he felt that the rules under which the Church was processing sex abuse charges were flawed. In March 2004 he gave a public lecture in which he argued that canon law seeks rehabilitation of the offender, and proportionality between crime and punishment—meaning that "one size fits all" penalties are foreign to canonical tradition. Both points cut against the "one strike" policy called for by the American bishops and approved by the Vatican. He also criticized revisions to the sex abuse norms approved by John Paul II in February 2003, which removed the statute of limitations, allowed the Congregation for the Doctrine of the Faith to defrock a priest using nonjudicial means, and prevented appeal of the congregation's decision. Llobell has objected that within the congregation, the tribunals handling sex abuse cases are run by that office's "promoter of justice," in effect the lead prosecutor. No system of justice can be fair, he said, where the prosecutor selects and supervises the judges. It's not that Llobell is "soft" on clerical sexual abuse; in the late 1980s he voiced the opinion within the Roman Curia that the American bishops should bring penal cases against abuser priests under the Code of Canon Law. His position, however, is that the Church should not remedy one injustice with another, and he believes the current norms are, from a procedural point of view, unjust.

These views did not sit well with some, including the promoter of justice in the Congregation for the Doctrine of the Faith, Monsignor Charles Scicluna, a Maltese priest whose job it has been to coordinate the Vatican's canonical response to the American crisis. Maybe these norms aren't perfect law, Scicluna has told colleagues, but the Church found itself in a crisis and needed to react. Moreover, on Scicluna's watch decisions have been reached in a relatively quick amount of time. Of more than 700 cases that reached the Vatican in the wake of the American crisis, by spring 2004 some 550 had been processed and returned, a remarkable result given the tendency of the Vatican to "think in centuries."

Llobell and Scicluna are friends and colleagues, so there is no suggestion of personal antagonism, and Llobell had already stopped working for the Congregation for the Doctrine of the Faith before Scicluna arrived. Yet the two men nevertheless represent different canonical approaches, and Scicluna's is the one that has prevailed. Since his work on the 2001 norms, Llobell has never been asked back to assist the congregation, despite the tidal wave of penal cases that washed through its offices in the wake of the American crisis. The story is all the more illuminating given that the highest-ranking Opus Dei member in the Curia is Herranz, whose area of competence is precisely canon law. His views on due process and the legitimacy of the sex abuse norms are much closer to Llobell's than Scicluna's. If there really were an unstoppable Opus Dei juggernaut in the Vatican, one would have expected this policy dispute to go the other way.

The bottom line, therefore, is that while Opus Dei does have people in powerful positions in the Vatican, it is not "running the show." If the question is whether these Opus Dei members have what the Italians call *una voce in capitolo,* meaning that they have some degree of influence, the answer is certainly "yes." If the question is whether Opus Dei can always bend the system to its will, the answer seems to be "no."

Opus Dei and the College of Cardinals

Rules for papal elections put into place by Pope Paul VI and confirmed by John Paul II require that a cardinal be under eighty years of age to vote. As of the death of John Paul II on April 2, 2005, there were 183 cardinals in the world, 117 of whom were under eighty. It often surprises people to know that only two of them come from Opus Dei: Cardinal Juan Luis Cipriani Thorne of Lima, Peru, sixty-one, and Herranz, seventy-five. In the conclave of April 2005, 115 Cardinals actually voted, and Herranz and Cipriani were among them.

Other cardinals who are not members of Opus Dei are sometimes linked with it. Cardinal Diogini Tettamanzi of Milan, for example, has been described as "close" to Opus Dei. In 1998, on the group's seventieth anniversary, Tettamanzi published an article praising Escrivá as being comparable to Saint Benedict and Saint Francis of Assisi in terms of launching new movements within the Church. Tettamanzi also wrote the preface to a biography of Escrivá published by Italian journalist Andrea Tornielli, saying that the life, teachings, and works of Escrivá are "a true light in the path of the Church in our time." Likewise, Cardinal Joachim Meisner of Cologne, Germany, recently contributed a chapter to a book in honor of Escrivá. His contribution was entitled "The Charism of Opus Dei in the Church."

Another cardinal with historic ties to Opus Dei is the former archbishop of Boston, Cardinal Bernard Law, currently archpriest of Saint Mary Major in Rome. Law met Opus Dei while a student at Harvard in the 1950s, when an early group of members came to the campus from Spain. Law, born in Mexico, spoke Spanish fluently and befriended them. When he left Harvard in 1953, he asked a friend, William Stetson, to keep an eye on the Spaniards. Stetson went on to become a priest of Opus Dei, living for a period at Villa Tevere in Rome, then serving as vicar in Chicago. Today he runs the Catholic Information Center in Washington, D.C. Stetson and Law have remained friends, and when Law was designated by the Vatican to handle cases of Episcopalian clergy who wish to be received in the Catholic Church, Stetson served as his aide. In 1985, when Law was made a cardinal, he invited the prelate of Opus Dei, Alvaro del Portillo, to his honorary dinner in Rome. According to Stetson, Portillo later said that he'd never been treated as generously by another cardinal. Law's reputation, however, was badly damaged by his resignation from Boston amid a sex abuse scandal, facing accusations that he had ignored evidence that several of his clergy were abusing children.

Other cardinals who are seen as being "Opus friendly" for one reason or another include: Giacomo Biffi, emeritus of Bologna; Darío Castrillón Hoyos, prefect of the Congregation for Clergy; Nicolás de Jesús López Rodríguez, Santo Domingo; Alfonso López Trujillo, president of the Pontifical Council for the Family; Camillo Ruini, vicar of the Diocese of Rome; and Johannes Adrianus Simonis, Utrecht.

Even if one were to add up all the cardinals who have some sort of historic connection with or even a remote affinity for Opus Dei, however, it would be nowhere near two-thirds of the College of Cardinals, which is what it took to elect John Paul's successor. Moreover, the Opus Dei cardinals denied that they organized or acted as an interest group to influence the outcome.

"I know they [some other cardinals] do it," said Cipriani in a July 11, 2004, interview at his residence in Lima. "I don't care a bit for it. I can give an opinion, but my first opinion is that this is not an example of being a good son of the Church. If you're a good son of the Church, pray for the Holy Father, pray for holiness. If you see somebody who might be a pope in the future, pray for him. Try to help him be a good fellow, to work well. When the time comes, he'll be prepared."

Before the 2005 conclave, I asked Herranz if, when the time came for the conclave, he would call the prelate of Opus Dei for advice.

"You can rest assured that I won't make that call," he said. "I know with whom I have to talk. I'll go, as for many other things, to the Tabernacle, and I'll ask the Lord the question. I'll talk with him, examining the human qualities [of the candidates] . . . the cultural formation of the person, the pastoral experience he may have, age, health, many things. I believe in the Holy Spirit, and I have extremely clear certainties of moments in which the Holy Spirit has illuminated me. He'll be the one to reveal it to me, in that moment. It's him I'll ask."

Opus Dei and the Bishops

There are twenty bishops in the world who come from the clergy of Opus Dei, in addition to three emeriti, or retired bishops, for a total of twenty-three. In the United States, the lone bishop who comes from the clergy of Opus Dei is the archbishop of San Antonio, José Gómez.

The Opus Dei bishops are:

- Antonio Arregui Yarza, archbishop of Guayaquil, Ecuador
- Juan Luis Cipriani Thorne, cardinal of Lima, Peru
- Alfonso Delgado Evers, archbishop of San Juan de Cuyo, Argentina
- Antônio Augusto Dias Duarte, auxiliary bishop of São Sebastião do Rio de Janeiro, Brazil
- Javier Echevarría Rodríguez, prelate of Opus Dei
- Ricardo García García, prelate of Yauyos, Peru
- Luis Gleisner Wobbe, auxiliary bishop of La Serena, Chile
- José Horacio Gómez, archbishop of San Antonio, Texas
- Juan Ignacio González Errázuriz, bishop of San Bernardo, Chile
- Julián Herranz Casado, cardinal, president of the Pontifical Council for the Interpretation of Legislative Texts
- Philippe Jourdan, apostolic administrator, Estonia
- Klaus Küng, bishop of Sankt Pölten, Austria
- Rogelio Ricardo Livieres Plano, bishop of Ciudad del Este, Paraguay
- Rafael Llano Cifuentes, bishop of Nova Friborgo, Brazil
- Anthony Muheria, bishop of Embu, Kenya
- Francisco Polti Santillán, bishop of Santo Tomé, Argentina
- Hugo Eugenio Puccini Banfi, bishop of Santa Marta, Colombia

- Jaume Pujol Balcells, archbishop of Tarragona, Spain
- Fernando Sáenz Lacalle, archbishop of San Salvador, El Salvador
- Juan Antonio Ugarte Pérez, archbishop of Cuzco, Peru

The emeriti are:

- Juan Ignacio Larrea Holguín, emeritus archbishop of Guayaquil, Ecuador
- Luis Sánchez-Moreno Lira, emeritus archbishop of Arequipa, Peru
- Francisco de Guruceaga Iturriza, emeritus bishop of La Guaira, Venezuela

In addition, there are fourteen bishops from the Priestly Society of the Holy Cross, meaning that they were not incardinated as priests into the prelature of Opus Dei and therefore are not under Echevarría's jurisdiction, but they are nevertheless considered members of Opus Dei. They are:

- Isidro Barrio, bishop of Huancavelica, Peru
- Mario Busquets, prelate of the Territorial Prelature of Chuquibamba, Peru
- Marco Antonio Cortez Lara, coadjutor bishop of Tacna and Moquegua, Peru
- Nicholas DiMarzio, bishop of Brooklyn, United States
- Robert Finn, coadjutor bishop of Kansas City–St. Joseph, United States
- Gilberto Gómez, auxiliary bishop of Abancay, Peru
- Francisco Gil Hellín, archbishop of Burgos, Spain
- Gabino Miranda Melgarejo, auxiliary bishop of Ayacucho, Peru
- Jesús Moliné, bishop of Chiclayo, Peru
- Justo Muller, president of the Accademia Ecclesiastica, Rome
- John Myers, archbishop of Newark, United States
- Isidro Sala, bishop of Abancay, Peru
- Jacinto Tomás de Carvalho, bishop of Lamego, Portugal

- Guillermo Patricio Vera Soto, bishop of the Territorial Prelature of Calama, Chile

There are also four bishops emeriti of the Priestly Society of the Holy Cross:

- Enrique Pélach y Feliu, emeritus bishop of Abancay, Peru
- Alberto Cosme do Amaral, emeritus bishop of Leiria-Fatima, Portugal
- William Dermott Molloy, emeritus bishop of Huancavelica, Peru
- Jesús Humberto Velázquez, emeritus bishop of Celaya, Mexico

This adds up to a grand total of forty-one Opus Dei bishops. That number represents 0.9 percent of the 4,564 Roman Catholic bishops in the world at the end of 2004.

Based on this list, it's clear that the vast majority are Latin American. There is only one Opus Dei bishop in Africa, and there are four in the United States, and, outside Rome, only six in Europe. There are none in Asia. In Latin America, Opus Dei counts one cardinal and four archbishops. Thirty percent, meaning thirteen bishops, are in Peru alone, a phenomenon resulting from the decision of Pius XII in 1957 to entrust Opus Dei with the territorial prelature of Yauyos. The move gave Opus Dei the opportunity to develop clergy and become a presence within the bishops' conference. Few of the assignments given to Opus Dei bishops would conventionally be considered "plums."

One term of comparison is offered by the Jesuits, who in December 2004 had seventy-four bishops in the world and nine cardinals, the highest number in the history of the order. In fact, Jesuit officials privately say they are forever asking the Vatican *not* to name their members bishops, because they are needed for Jesuit ministries. John Paul II, in fact, named a larger proportion of bishops from religious orders than many of his predecessors. The Salesians of Saint John Bosco had 111 bishops worldwide in December 2004, including six cardinals. The number of Opus Dei bishops thus does not seem out of line with the pope's treatment of other groups in the Church, nor does it represent a significant chunk of the episcopacy.

In the one country where Opus Dei bishops would have a realistic opportunity to act as a bloc, Peru, Cipriani denied that it works this way.

"One of the main points of Opus Dei is that we will not act as a group, ever," Cipriani said. "If someone does it, we'll call him on it very harshly, asking him, 'What are you doing? What are you looking for?' " Further, Cipriani said, it's a fact of life in the Peruvian bishops' conference that Opus Dei bishops are not elected to important positions. "It's quite strange, but we cannot do anything in the national bishops' conference. We have no power whatsoever," he said.

When I asked if, as cardinal, Cipriani controls the church in Peru, he laughed and responded: "I would jokingly say, 'I would like to control the Church, but I can't!' I do my best, but I just can't."

Personal Prelature

On November 28, 1982, John Paul II issued the apostolic constitution *Ut Sit,* erecting Opus Dei as the first "personal prelature." The issuance of *Ut Sit* marked the climax of a fifty-four-year struggle to find a canonical "home" for Opus Dei, one that would protect its identity as a single body of clergy and laity, men and women, all sharing the same vocation. Members of Opus Dei like to repeat the comment attributed by Escrivá to a Vatican official in 1946: "You have come a century too early!"

The creation of the personal prelature was also, for many English-speaking Catholics, their first introduction to Opus Dei. At the time, and ever since, it has been seen in some quarters as a raw act of political muscle. In Michael Walsh's book *The Secret World of Opus Dei,* he devotes three chapters to the juridical evolution of Opus Dei, reading it in terms of hunger for ever greater forms of privilege. Among other things, the prelature was seen as being an end-run around the authority of local bishops. Opus Dei denies this, arguing that the authority of Opus Dei extends only to its spiritual aims; for all other matters, members are still regular Catholics, under the authority of the local bishops. For example, if members of Opus Dei want an annulment from a marriage, they can't get it from the prelate—they have to go to their local bishop.

Prior to 1982, Opus Dei had been variously classified as a "pious union," a "priestly society," and a "secular institute," and each category posed problems in terms of how Opus Dei saw itself. The core problem was that each designation tended to drag Opus Dei into the orbit of religious orders, distorting what it sees as its secular identity. As Escrivá's German biographer Peter Berglar put it, "Opus Dei was anchored to the Barque of Peter, but not in the proper port." Escrivá developed a saying to describe his attitude at each point that he accepted a juridical solution he felt was less than fully adequate: "To give in, without giving up, eager to win it back."

To take one example of the headaches that arose, a Vatican decree of March 22, 1950, banned clerics, religious, and members of societies of common life from taking part in business activities. The decree specifically stated that "the members of the recently established secular institutes," of which Opus Dei was the first, were not exempt. This meant that supernumeraries involved in any sort of business career were technically in violation of Church law. As late as 1958, in the lead-up to the synod of the Diocese of Rome called by Pope John XXIII, preparatory materials would have included members of secular institutes along with priests and religious in bans on entering bars, engaging in business, or going to the movies. To cite another point, canon 500 of the 1917 Code of Canon Law stated that within institutions that profess the "state of perfection," men and women must be juridically separate. The decree creating secular institutes in 1947 included this criterion, so there was the ever-present threat that Opus Dei would be split into separate male and female branches. In that sense, Opus Dei canonists argue, the transition to a personal prelature was justified by the need to carve out a new category that did not carry the "baggage" of being an extension of religious life.

Yet many observers cannot escape the sense that, whatever the canonical logic, Opus Dei ran a full-court press to get what it wanted. Some historians have even suggested that Opus Dei was more cunning than has generally been realized, that it laid the foundations decades ago in the Second Vatican Council. One of the council's lesser-known documents, *Presbyterorum Ordinis,* or the *Decree on the Ministry and Life of Priests,* issued on December 7, 1965, contains a passage that reads: "Where the nature of apostolate demands this . . . there can with advantages be set up some international seminaries, special dioceses or personal prelatures and other institutions to which, by methods to be decided for the individual undertaking, and always without prejudice to the rights of the local ordinaries, priests can be attached or incardinated for the common good of the whole Church." It was the first Church document to explicitly mention the possibility of personal prelatures. The secretary of the commission that prepared *Presbyterorum Ordinis* was Portillo. Herranz, too, worked on this commission. Some critics have charged that Opus Dei, in effect, "doctored" the document in order to prepare its own elevation.

Herranz denied that this section of the document was crafted specifically for Opus Dei.

"Someone might think that Portillo was the one responsible for this text," Herranz acknowledged. "No. He was simply the secretary of the conciliar commission, and I was an aide to the commission. There were twenty-five members who were cardinals and bishops selected by the conciliar fathers from all over the world. Then there were also twenty consultors, including [Dominican father] Yves Congar and many others. Portillo had secretarial duties . . . keeping minutes of the meetings, convoking the meetings, but the decisions and the texts were worked on by the members and the consultors."

As for the prelature itself, Herranz insists that the Vatican's motives were far broader than resolving a particular problem for Opus Dei.

"This was a much vaster problem. In the law, there was already a personal parish, some based on a rite, such as the Armenian or the Syrian. With the sociological variations in the contemporary world, things were less static than when the Code of 1917 was prepared, whose laws were based on an agricultural society. . . . People now move from one place to another, change their home continually. They are obligated to go abroad for work, and so forth. One can see that pastoral care can't be just territorial, but also personal."

Pressures for the Church to recognize new forms of pastoral organization had been building since the early twentieth century. In 1938, Pope Pius XI commissioned one of the most dynamic Italian Catholic leaders of the day, Franciscan father Agostino Gemelli, founder of the Catholic University in Milan, to preside over a congress in St. Gall, Switzerland, of leaders of twenty-five Catholic groups pressing to realize new possibilities for evangelization and apostolic work. Most of these groups hoped to find ways for laity to live a religiously serious, committed Christian life without thereby ceasing to be laity. The congress in Switzerland requested juridical recognition for new forms of life and mission. In the aftermath of the congress, Gemelli wrote a memorandum arguing for such recognition. Pius XII's apostolic constitution *Provida Mater Ecclesia,* which created the category of "secular institute," was a direct response. As noted, Opus Dei was recognized as the first secular institute shortly thereafter. Yet from Escrivá's point of view, even this category contained too much risk of confusion with religious orders.

Herranz said there was already a precedent for the personal prelature in the form of the Mission de France, a group of missionary priests and laity who worked to reevangelize lapsed Catholics in France. It had been approved as a nonterritorial prelature in 1954. "They were dispersed in all of France," Herranz said. "They would make a contract for working in the various dioceses. It was more personal than territorial. Also, there were laity who worked for the Mission de France, because their statutes also allowed this, so it was more like a personal prelature."

Yet even if this was clear to Herranz, it was not to others. On May 22, 1960, Escrivá's first request to transform Opus Dei into a prelature was rejected by the Secretariat of State. A letter from Cardinal Giovanni Cicognani said such a move would present "almost insurmountable juridical and practical difficulties." In 1969, Opus Dei convened a general congress to study the question of juridical status, and the conclusion was in favor of a personal prelature. Escrivá continued to work on the question until his death in 1975, when Portillo took over. The Vatican's concerns, however, did not go away. In 1980 a draft of the new Code of Canon Law contained norms for personal prelatures, even though at the time none yet existed. In the draft, the norms appeared in the same section as those for territorial dioceses, suggesting an equivalence between the two, and treated the prelate as analogous to a diocesan bishop. In a meeting of cardinals in 1981, however, this formula was rejected. The cardinals feared that treating a personal prelature as the equivalent of a local church would spawn a "church within the Church." In the end, the canons appeared under the heading for "Christ's Faithful" in the 1983 Code of Canon Law, not under the section on "The Hierarchical Constitution of the Church."

Herranz was part of a mixed commission of Opus Dei canonists and Vatican officials who studied the question during twenty-five sessions between February 1980 and February 1981, meeting in the Sala di

Congresso of the Congregation for Bishops. He said the single greatest challenge was to clarify the relationship between Opus Dei and the diocesan bishop. "We studied carefully the juridical attributes Opus Dei had in the moment of requesting this transformation, and what it would have afterward," Herranz said. "It was seen that it was not at all in the mind of the Founder to withdraw from the bishops' authority. This was more an impulse of religious orders. The laity of Opus Dei had to continue to be faithful of the dioceses in which they live."

Prior to the creation of the prelature, documentation was sent by the Vatican to two thousand bishops in the countries in which Opus Dei was present, inviting observations and suggestions. Herranz said that there were "maneuvers" to try to mobilize the bishops against the move, though he said he does not know by whom. In an article in *L'Osservatore Romano* accompanying the publication of *Ut Sit*, Monsignor Marcello Costalunga of the Congregation for Bishops commented on the response: "Numerous replies from bishops manifested their satisfaction with the manner in which, in perfect harmony with the norms applying the Second Vatican Council, the desired solution to the institutional problem of Opus Dei had been reached. There were also letters, though much fewer in number, which contained observations or requests for clarification: following an attentive examination they were all taken into due account, and all requests for further clarification were satisfied."

Whatever one makes of "due account," the mere fact of the consultation makes this one of the most collegial acts of John Paul's papacy. It would be difficult to name another decision in recent times for which the Vatican solicited reactions from two thousand bishops around the world.

It was clear from the beginning of his papacy that John Paul II wanted to solve Opus Dei's problem and to do it as quickly as possible. Herranz said the pope followed the proceedings closely, and at least on this point there is third-party testimony. Cardinal Sebastiano Baggio, at the time head of the Congregation for Bishops, has said that when he visited the pope in Rome's Gemelli Hospital after the May 13, 1981, assassination attempt, one of the things John Paul asked about was the resolution of Opus Dei's juridical status. The pope, he said, wanted to bring things to a close.

"When the decree erecting Opus Dei as a personal prelature came out, Baggio published two articles in *L'Osservatore Romano* saying clearly

that this was not only an act directed at resolving a problem of one institution of the Church, but at putting into practice a norm of the Second
Vatican Council," Herranz said. "Those articles were inspired by the pope,
and I know this because Baggio told me. The Holy Father said this puts
into action an idea of the council. Yes, it resolved an institutional problem
of Opus Dei that dated back to 1928, but that was an accessory. The
Second Vatican Council anticipated new pastoral institutions for new
times. . . . The pope wanted it said that this decision should be seen in a
much wider context."

Many canonists believe that part of the mystique surrounding the
personal prelature is that Opus Dei, after twenty-three years, is still the
only one, and perhaps not a very typical example of the pastoral problem
the "personal prelature" was intended to resolve. Some canonists believe
that in the not-too-distant future, other personal prelatures could be
erected, which would have the side effect of making Opus Dei seem less
privileged. For example, one proposal is to create a personal prelature for
the large population of Filipino immigrants on the Arabian peninsula, allowing Filipino clergy who speak the language and know the people, but
who are not incardinated into that territory, to deliver pastoral care under
the direction of a prelate. Once a few other personal prelatures of this sort
exist, the category may look less like a special favor for Opus Dei.

Finally, it's worth noting that Opus Dei is not the only organization
in the Catholic Church granted a new legal status under John Paul II,
despite controversy. On June 28, 2002, the "Statutes" of the Neo-
catechumenal Way, founded in Spain in the 1960s by two lay Catholics
named Kiko Argüello and Carmen Hernández, were given a provisional
five-year approval by the Pontifical Council for the Laity. It came despite
the fact that the Neocatechumenate does not fit in any of the recognized
categories in canon law—it is not an association of lay faithful, a movement, or a religious order, to say nothing of a personal prelature. Further,
the thirteen-volume "catechetical directory" at the heart of the Neocatechumenate, which consists of the teachings of Argüello and Hernández,
has not been made public. Despite objections similar to those leveled
against Opus Dei—that the leaders of the Neocatechumenate invade the
consciences of their members, that internal documents are secret—the
group now enjoys official legal status. The same point can be made of
other "new movements," such as the Focolare movement, which received

Vatican authorization as a lay association with the right to enroll priests as members, and which, as a matter of policy, will be led by a woman even after the death of founder Chiara Lubich. The favorable response to Opus Dei's request is therefore not quite as singular as it seems and perhaps illustrates Opus Dei's political power less than John Paul's desire to see these new groups flourish.

Beatification and Canonization

Another case where Opus Dei's alleged ecclesiastical muscles were flexed was the beatification of Escrivá in 1992 and, to a lesser extent, his canonization in 2002. The beatification set off an international uproar, in part due to charges that it was done in unseemly haste, ramrodded through by Opus Dei's money and political connections.

"He should enter the ranks of the saints with an asterisk," said Kenneth Woodward, at the time religion editor at *Newsweek* and author of *Making Saints,* a book about the canonization process. Woodward said the Vatican had not given a hearing to Escrivá's critics. In a 1996 letter to the Catholic publication *First Things,* Woodward wrote, "Opus Dei subverted the canonization process to get its man beatified. In a word, it was a scandal—from the conduct of the tribunals through the writing of the *positio* to the high-handed treatment of the experts picked to judge the cause." Similar comments, though less vociferously expressed, surfaced at the time of the 2002 canonization.

Rivers of ink have been spilled on all sides of this question. Here we can hope merely to establish a factual baseline, and sketch the views of how to interpret those facts.

Some facts:

- Escrivá's beatification was rapid by historical standards; seventeen years passed from his death in 1975 to the ceremony in 1992, and another ten from the beatification to the canonization, for a total of twenty-seven. Joan of Arc waited some six hundred years.
- The process was expensive. Father Flavio Capucci, the postulator, or official responsible for Escrivá's cause, once told me that for the beatification, the process of collecting testimony and

preparing documents cost around $150,000, and the ceremony itself in St. Peter's Square cost $500,000. The canonization cost less, since only one additional miracle needed to be established, though once again a massive ceremony had to be organized. The total for both events was slightly over $1 million.

- Some critical voices were excluded from the process. As noted in chapter 2, ex-members María Carmen del Tapia, Miguel Fisac, and María Angustias Moreno all volunteered to offer their memories of Escrivá. The tribunal in the Madrid archdiocese determined that all three had demonstrated what is known in canon law as "public hostility" toward Escrivá, and the requests were refused. This was a decision of the tribunal, not of Opus Dei. Ex-member Alberto Moncada, also a critic, was heard but judged to be "untrustworthy."

- There was opposition inside the Vatican. De Magistris, one of two judges on the nine-member beatification panel who voted against Escrivá, has already been mentioned. The other was Monsignor Justo Fernández Alonso, the only Spaniard, who was disturbed that critical witnesses had not been heard.

How can these facts be explained?

For critics such as Woodward, it's straightforward. Despite reservations about Escrivá, Opus Dei's money and influence drove the result home. It was a scorched-earth effort, in this reconstruction, blocking at every turn voices that might have raised questions. In that sense it was the ultimate demonstration of Opus Dei's power, the ecclesiastical equivalent of Caligula making his horse a senator.

Eamon Duffy, an English Church historian, has written: "The canonization of the founder of Opus Dei is the most striking example in modern times of the successful promotion of a cause by a pressure group, in order to extend and legitimize the objectives of that group; here the saint becomes a mascot and a means to an end for the group who venerate him."

Capucci, the Opus Dei postulator, sees things differently. As for the "haste" of the process, he argues that Opus Dei had good luck with the timing. "This was the first cause opened under a reform John Paul II introduced in 1983, making the process less cumbersome," he said. That reform, among other things, dropped the number of required miracles and eliminated the office of the "devil's advocate."

He cited a number of cases that moved along even more quickly in the wake of the 1983 reform: "The cause of Padre Pio lasted just nineteen years. The same norms facilitated the beatification of 'El Pelé' in 1997, four years after his cause began in 1994; the Italian couple Beltrami Quattrocchi in 2001, seven years after their cause opened, and Carlos Manuel Rodríguez, the first Puerto Rican to reach the altars, in 2001, nine years after his began." Capucci might also have added Mother Teresa, who broke all modern speed records with her beatification; she died in 1997 and was beatified in 2003. John Paul II waived the normal five-year waiting period before a cause after someone's death, a step not taken with Escrivá.

As for expense, there's no ducking the point: Beatifications and canonizations cost money. There's no evidence, however, that Opus Dei spent money on anything other than the process and the ceremonies. In this sense the difference with Opus Dei is that it was willing to divert personnel and resources to the task. Though not as wealthy as is sometimes believed, Opus Dei had deeper pockets than many other lay organizations or religious communities. As for the suggestion that Vatican personnel were bought off, Capucci said: "A question like this is offensive not just for the alleged giver of the money, but also the receiver. Anyone who asks it doesn't know Opus Dei or the Congregation for the Causes of Saints."

As for the critical voices of ex-members, Capucci says he wishes they had been heard, and that he himself proposed doing so. It was the tribunal, not Opus Dei, that excluded the critics. Naturally, he's confident that the scrutiny of Escrivá's life would have survived whatever they had to say.

It's a matter of fair debate as to whether Escrivá merited beatification and canonization. The speed with which these took place, however, seems less a testimony to Opus Dei's political manipulation than to its work ethic. On this point there is an independent witness, Augustinian father Rafael Perez, who once held the job of "devil's advocate" before it was suppressed. He was a judge in the Madrid phase of Escrivá's beatification.

"It would be almost impossible [to bring pressure to bear], and ineffective if there were any, since numerous individuals participate in each of the distinct phases of the cause," he said. Perez said the two factors that tend to make the most difference are the intrinsic merits of the case and how good a job the postulator does.

"A cause goes ahead when the postulators know what they are doing and dedicate a lot of time to it, all the time that the cause requires," he said. "If some causes go slowly it is because those that promote them are not really interested, or because the postulators have more causes than they can handle. It can also be for a lack of competence on somebody's part. Once the evidence has been gathered and submitted to the congregation for the decision-making phase, a good deal of work is still required of the postulation office so that the evidence can be studied." Perez said he once came across a cause where the postulator had died and nobody had the funds to find a new one, and so he encouraged the local bishop to get on the ball. In the end, the cause moved forward.

"Money will never succeed in making a saint," Perez said. "But without resources it is not possible for a cause to move ahead, because those who work on it are not discarnate spirits. Officials of the congregation, translators, consultors, lawyers, doctors, printers, and so on have to receive a just wage."

Perez seems, however, to have left one item off the list: papal interest. Mother Teresa wasn't beatified in six years simply because her postulator did a good job. It was clear that John Paul II wanted it to happen. Similarly with Escrivá, the pope's long track record of support and devotion, including his visit to Escrivá's tomb in 1978, left no doubt where he wanted the process to end.

That, in fact, is probably the single most telling argument against the hypothesis that Opus Dei "bought" or "manipulated" the beatification and canonization. There was no reason why they had to. John Paul was positively inclined, and was just waiting for the paperwork to reach his desk. To get it there as quickly as possible, Opus Dei deployed all the resources necessary, including a top-notch postulator and support staff, and there were no shortfalls in funding to convene meetings or get documents translated. The most defensible conclusion seems to be that Opus Dei may have played hard and fast, but they played by the rules.

Opus Dei in the Parishes

Most Catholics pay little attention to the sorts of matters rehearsed in this chapter—how many people Opus Dei has in the Vatican, or the politics behind the beatification of Escrivá. If they have a sense of Opus Dei at all, it's probably from watching a "CNN Presents" special on *The Da Vinci Code*. A few, however, have developed impressions out of personal encounters with members, either priests or laity. When that experience is positive, it can undo prejudices. When it's negative, it can reinforce them.

To the extent that "pew Catholics" have a complaint, it's usually that Opus Dei is "divisive." To some extent, this can be a matter of selective perception. Supernumeraries who show up at Mass with their kids and help out around the parish without making waves go unnoticed, and "Opus Dei" as such gets little credit. When something goes wrong, on the other hand, "Opus Dei" gets the blame.

Perhaps the most emblematic case in point concerns Father C. John McCloskey, today the highest-profile Opus Dei priest in the United States. When he was stationed in Washington, D.C., as director of the Opus Dei–run Catholic Information Center, McCloskey became something of an inside-the-Beltway phenomenon, emerging as a "talking head" on American television on matters where religion and politics intersect. As of this writing, McCloskey had returned to the States from a sabbatical in England.

In 1986, early in his career, McCloskey was appointed assistant director at the Aquinas Institute, the Catholic campus center at Princeton University. It was a stormy period, which ended with his dismissal in 1990. Critics say McCloskey was a polarizing figure, counseling Catholic students about which courses to avoid, and even which priests would be best for confession, something he denies. To some extent, judgments about McCloskey's tenure come down to matters of interpretation. Everyone agrees that McCloskey promoted individual confession, for example, including sometimes telling students that certain things needed to be confessed. Some saw this as "spiritual bullying," others as good pastoral care.

There's no doubt that McCloskey could be blunt. Addressing parents seeking a Catholic college for their children, he once wrote, "If you encounter words like 'standard,' 'belief,' 'maturity,' 'conviction,' 'commitment,' 'marriage,' 'family,' 'evangelization,' 'culture,' 'character,' 'truth' and 'knowledge,' take a closer look. On the other hand, if you encounter words and phrases like 'values,' 'openness,' 'just society,' 'search,' 'diversity,' and 'professional preparation,' move on." He added: "If the university harbors any well-known 'dissenters,' the case is closed. . . . Do not be fooled by those who purport to be Catholic and whose livelihood and retirement depend on protecting this fiction."

Defenders say McCloskey was simply trying to encourage Princeton students to be serious about holiness. Moreover, they say, some of the charges against him were false. For example, McCloskey never had an index of forbidden courses. Instead, he once sent out a list of recommended courses, with this warning: "Remember, everything depends on the outlook of the teacher giving the course. The latter may seem quite interesting and stimulating, but if it is given by an anti-Christian, its impact is counterproductive." The opposition to McCloskey could be remarkably nasty. At one point McCloskey objected to an on-campus skit designed to promote safe sex, which included having female students stretch oversized condoms over the heads of male students. In response to McCloskey's objection, an undergraduate wrote in the school newspaper: "Perhaps the Princeton community and society at large should advise McCloskey to take to drinking nothing but the semen of AIDS patients."

The point here is not to sort out the rights and wrongs, but rather to observe that for many students and faculty at Princeton, McCloskey *was* their experience of Opus Dei, and reactions varied. Some were turned off, while others were impressed. In the latter category, for example, are two current seminarians at the North American College in Rome, preparing to be diocesan priests, who met McCloskey at Princeton.

To take another example, David Pliske, whose daughter Bernie is an Opus Dei numerary assistant, was introduced in chapter 9. The Pliskes come across as a kind, loving couple, and, defying the stereotype of stand-offish Opus Dei types, are very involved in their local parish. "I take pride in our church, and I love our parish," David said. "We like to help out."

Pliske has been a sacristan at Saint Stanislaus Church in Michigan City, Indiana, for the past thirteen years. In that capacity, one of his responsibilities is to train altar servers. In our interview at the Shellbourne Conference Center, he bluntly told me, "I won't train girls." It's not that Pliske has anything against girls, but rather that in light of Church teaching against women priests, he doesn't think it's appropriate. Some may find Pliske's position rigid, others courageous. In any event it's the kind of thing that in many parish settings can lead to division, especially if the perception is that someone with attitudes such as Pliske's is connected to Opus Dei.

Not every Opus Dei member is as provocative as McCloskey, or willing to draw the same line Pliske does. Yet the percentage of Opus Dei members likely to ask critical questions about parish practices, challenge things they don't like, and stand up for what they see as principle is probably a bit higher than in the general Catholic population. For one thing, these are typically serious, motivated parishioners. For another, the doctrinal formation they receive in Opus Dei gives them the intellectual tools to defend positions that might otherwise remain at the level of "gut instinct." Finally, they tend to be more "conservative" than the average Catholic, which means the odds that they're going to find something they don't like in a typical parish are probably a bit higher. It's no surprise that sometimes people find the arrival of Opus Dei members into their parishes a bracing experience.

On the other hand, this is far from the only experience of Opus Dei. Parish communities often find Opus Dei members, both priests and laity, a breath of fresh air. They are frequently motivated, hardworking, cheerful, and, if they really take their cues from the concept of Christian freedom, charitable and nonclericalist in their attitudes.

Father Jerome Kisch, for example, is pastor of Saints Peter and Paul Parish in Naperville, Illinois, in the Diocese of Joliet. He is also a member of the Priestly Society of the Holy Cross, the association for priests sponsored by Opus Dei. He said he met Opus Dei in college, but has really come to appreciate it after ordination. "In the seminary, everything is right there for your spiritual life, but when you're ordained, you're responsible for doing it yourself," he said. "No one is giving you grades. It's helpful to have a regular meeting with a spiritual director."

Kisch said that in his experience, far from being a divisive element, Opus Dei helps him to be more patient with his parishioners and fellow priests. "People don't always agree on things in the Church," he said. "Without the direction we get from Opus Dei, I could tend to be more dismissive. It helps me recognize that the other priests in the presbyterate are my brothers, that we're in the same family. I need to live this in a spirit of true charity."

At the same time, he acknowledged, things can sometimes get complicated. For example, some Opus Dei parents in his area recently started their own school, the Kingswood Academy. They wanted strong character formation for their children, Kisch said, and began with an enrollment of one hundred kids. The problem is that his parish already has its own school, so some people are likely watching him to see where his real loyalties lie. "When I help out on the [new] school, I do it on my day off, so it doesn't really compete," he said.

Father Joan Costa is a parish priest in Barcelona, Spain, and also a member of the Priestly Society of the Holy Cross. Out of a total of perhaps 600 priests in the Barcelona archdiocese, Costa says about 60 belong to the society, and he acknowledges that it never set especially well with the former cardinal, Ricardo María Carles Gordó. "He thought that if all the diocesan priests are only diocesan priests, without attachments to any other groups, the unity will be stronger," Costa said.

"But I think it's false. I try to have a lot of friendships with the other priests. I try to spend time with them, to go the mountains all together. As a member of the society, one of the points in our spirituality is to join all priests in friendship. Saint Josemaría Escrivá had a very beautiful expression, that the distance between a priest of Opus Dei and another priest is less than a thin piece of paper. In other words, we're basically the same. That's how I try to live, and it's also how I try to approach the people in my parish. I'm not above them."

Emily Kloc is a veteran parishioner at Saint Mary of the Angels Parish in Chicago, which since 1991 has been the only parish in the United States entrusted to Opus Dei. Born in 1933, she's been active at Saint Mary's all her life, from back when it was an almost homogeneous Polish parish to today's multi-ethnic mix. "I have the greatest respect and admiration for the Opus Dei fathers," she said. "These priests always have time for people. I don't know how many hours they sit in the confessional." She singled out for special praise Father John Debicki, the pastor, a Pole who says Mass once a week in the mother tongue. Kloc said that under Debicki's care, there have been no divisions in the parish because of the Opus Dei presence.

"We always had devotions here, the Our Lady of Perpetual Help, Saint Therese, and so on," she said. "Now we also have Saint Josemaría. What's the problem? The vast majority of the parishioners are not just satisfied, they're thrilled. I see them becoming more religiously serious, I see more going to confession. How can you argue with that?"

Given that there are only 85,491 members of Opus Dei in the world, and 1.1 billion Catholics, the odds are that if a given Catholic meets anyone at all from Opus Dei, it's likely to be just one or two people. Much of popular opinion about Opus Dei at the local level comes down to this—whom did they meet? Was it McCloskey, or Kisch? Was it Pliske? Was it Costa? How did they react to what they saw and heard? Did they react, for example, like Kloc at Saint Mary of the Angels, or like some hostile students at Princeton? Perceptions of whether Opus Dei is "divisive," and to what extent, often hinge on such chance encounters.

Opus Dei and the Jesuits

Opus Dei's university in Rome, Santa Croce, occupies a building just off the Piazza Navona that once belonged to the Jesuits. Pope Julius III (1550–1555) gave the Church of Sant'Apollinare and its adjoining buildings, including what is now Santa Croce, for the use of the German College launched by Saint Ignatius of Loyola, founder of the Jesuits. Today, Sant'Apollinare is the main church used by the University of Santa Croce, and in the foyer one finds a place for devotion to Escrivá. Farther along the main nave, however, before the altar rail, one finds two side chapels to the left and right, holdovers from the days before Opus Dei arrived. One contains a statue of Ignatius, the other of his great Jesuit collaborator and patron of missionaries, Francis Xavier.

Let it never be said that God doesn't have a sense of humor, since this means that virtually every day a big chunk of the Opus Dei brain trust finds itself worshiping under the gaze of Jesuits.

The rivalry between Opus Dei and the Jesuits is in a sense ironic, because Escrivá himself had a great personal devotion to Ignatius. One gets the sense that the two men, separated by centuries, nevertheless understood each other. Both were Spanish, both passionate, both capable of levelheadedness and organizational skill in one moment, feats of poetry and spiritual excess in the next. As a matter of fact, the very name "Opus Dei" came from a Jesuit, Father Valentín Sánchez Ruis, who was Escrivá's confessor for a period of time and once asked him in offhanded fashion, "How's that Work of God going?"

In the late 1930s and early 1940s, however, Opus Dei's relationship with the Jesuits came off the tracks in Spain, when a Jesuit, Father Ángel

Carrillo de Albornoz, began criticizing Opus Dei, in part because it was peeling off young men from the Marian Congregations, pious associations that were traditionally "feeders" for Jesuit vocations. More deeply, Carrillo saw Opus Dei as a quasi-Masonic sect pursuing its own agenda. The increasingly acrid back-and-forth between Carrillo and Escrivá, reflected in their correspondence as reproduced in the Vázquez de Prada biography, was one of those cases of an immovable force meeting an irresistible object. Both men were proud, each convinced the other was deluded.

Carrillo had been a brilliant government lawyer in Spain before he entered the Jesuits, and by all accounts he was a handsome, imposing man with a magnetic personality. Spanish Jesuits who were novices in the 1940s talk about how much their vocation was influenced by his preaching, his spiritual direction, and his personality. He had been a chaplain for the Nationalist forces during the civil war and at one point was left for dead after a raid. A doctor somehow discovered he was a Jesuit and decided to operate. The experience left a piece of platinum in his body that often gave him serious pain. When Carrillo said Mass, he would sometimes cry out in agony. He was considered a hero, and it's no surprise that many Jesuits followed him into battle against Opus Dei. His motives may have been in part competitive, but Carrillo was also convinced that something was wrong with Opus Dei, that it was secretive, anti-Catholic, and dangerous. The dispute between him and Escrivá was not theological, as Carrillo was an orthodox, conservative Catholic.

After a stint in Rome at the Jesuit Curia, Carrillo stunned his Jesuit brothers by leaving the order in 1951. In somewhat mysterious fashion, he wrote the superior general of the order from Switzerland, returning money the order had given him for the trip there. He ended up in Paris, where an entrepreneur (and alleged dealer in contraband) named Martorell hired him as head of his business operation. After receiving his decree of laicization, Carrillo married Martorell's daughter, Maria Teresa Martorell, in a Protestant church in Paris. He died in Paris in 1981, with no indication that he returned to the Church or requested the sacraments. Nevertheless, a group of former members of the Marian Congregations in Madrid organized a Mass in his memory, so deep was the impression he had made.

The antagonisms between Opus Dei and the Jesuits forged in those early years never went away, and they were given a fresh burst of energy in the period after the Second Vatican Council. Many Jesuits all around the world plunged with vigor into the postconciliar tide, joining base communities of the poor gathered to study scripture and analyze their situation in light of it, writing liberation theology, challenging authority inside the Church and out, and pressing the "preferential option for the poor" as both a political and personal imperative. Opus Dei was more likely to swim against this tide—insisting that the proper role of the Church is not to advance a political program, but to pass on the spiritual and doctrinal traditions that are its primary reasons for existence.

Escrivá's new Jesuit foil, at least at the level of public perception, became the order's superior general, Father Pedro Arrupe, born five years later than his fellow Spaniard, in 1907, and who died in 1991 after a long convalescence. If Arrupe symbolized the new post–Vatican II ethos, calling his Jesuits to be "men for others," which in practice sometimes meant joining movements for peace and justice and engaging in gospel-centered activism, Escrivá walked another path, insisting on the primacy of traditional forms of prayer, devotion, and the sacramental life. It's not that Jesuits didn't pray, or that Opus Dei members didn't serve the poor; but it was a question of thrust and emphasis. In Latin America especially, the Jesuits became identified as the leading champions of the "liberation theology" movement of the 1970s and 1980s, which attempted to break the Catholic Church's traditional embrace of the ruling elite. Opus Dei, though by no means the only or even the most animated source of opposition to liberation theology, took another approach. Social change would be the product of changing one heart at a time, reflecting Escrivá's spirituality in *The Way*: "I'll tell you a secret, an open secret: these world crises are crises of saints."

Just as some Jesuits were adopting a more critical stance toward authority and tradition, motivated by deep love for the Church and a desire to see it realize the best version of itself, that same love impelled Escrivá and Opus Dei to cling to authority and tradition all the more resolutely. At a personal level, the two men got along amicably—Arrupe made a point of being at Escrivá's funeral in 1975. But they were leading their communities in different directions.

Nothing crystallizes this tension better than the fact that in one thirteen-month period, from October 1981 to November 1982, John Paul first delayed Arrupe's request to call a General Congregation of the Jesuits and appointed his own delegate to prepare the meeting, and then erected Opus Dei as a personal prelature. Both were decisions that had complex histories and consequences, but to the public eye it seemed like a clampdown on the Jesuits and an elevation of Opus Dei—almost as if a torch were being passed.

However exaggerated such perceptions may have been, there were just enough concrete instances to keep the flames of conflict lit. To take one small but revealing episode, in Peru in July 1990, then–auxiliary bishop Juan Luis Cipriani of Ayacucho (today the cardinal of Lima), a member of Opus Dei, shut down the archdiocesan Office of Social Action, at the time led by a Jesuit missionary named Father Carl Schmidt. The Jesuits took this as a sign that Cipriani, and by extension Opus Dei, did not want to challenge the status quo; Cipriani insists that the office's radical political stance carried it dangerously close to complicity with terrorism.

Though both Opus Dei and the Jesuits emphasize that at a personal level there are many friendships between members of the two groups, there's no denying the frequent sense of being on different planets. When I visited Opus Dei's center at the University of Notre Dame, called Windmoor, in September 2004, I sat down with a group of young men who for various reasons found themselves attracted to Opus Dei. Each one told me his story. When it was time for David Cook, twenty-one, to speak, he happened to mention that he had attended a Jesuit high school, which set off a round of derisive chuckles in the room. Meanwhile, when I was in Peru, I met with a Jesuit who works for that country's bishops' conference. When I asked him his view of Opus Dei, he said it was negative. When I asked why, he responded, "I'm a Jesuit." The suggestion was that no further explanation was required. Two of the sternest critics of Opus Dei in English-language Catholicism—Michael Walsh, author of *The Secret World of Opus Dei*, and Peter Hebblethwaite, the late Vatican writer—have been former Jesuits.

In a previously undisclosed episode, there was a potential turning point in the relationship between the Jesuits and Opus Dei in the late 1960s and early 1970s that went unrealized. In an interview for this book in December 2004, the current prelate of Opus Dei, Bishop Javier Echevarría, revealed that during that period of time, Arrupe hoped to extend an olive branch to Escrivá. Concretely, Arrupe proposed that the Jesuits and Opus Dei launch a new university together. The idea would be not only to combine resources for educational ends, but also to overcome their differences, and thus help bridge the growing gap in the Catholic Church that the breach between the Jesuits and Opus Dei symbolized. Arrupe no doubt felt that given the historical commitments of both the Jesuits and Opus Dei to evangelizing the intellectual class, this project would have been a natural outgrowth of their respective missions.

As Echevarría tells the story, Escrivá turned down the proposal.

"He told Arrupe, 'There's a risk here for you,'" Echevarría said. "The Jesuits were becoming too much like laity, wanting to do too many things in the world, and were in danger of losing their identity as religious. Escrivá felt that if we mixed in this way, either Opus Dei would become more religious, or the Jesuits would become more secular. Either way, it would do damage to one of us. It would be like lawyers and doctors trying to work out of the same office."

Thus the proposed Jesuit/Opus Dei university never came to pass.

Whatever the logic, any Catholic with imagination cannot help but feel a sense of lost opportunity about Escrivá's response. Not only would such a university have been a marvelous experiment in dialogue within the Church (I would have paid real money to attend those faculty meetings!), but, on an academic and professional level, it almost certainly would have been a first-class institution of higher learning.

Today, most observers say the old rivalries have calmed. The current superior general of the Jesuits, Father Peter-Hans Kolvenbach, told me that he knew Bishop Alvaro del Portillo and considered him an "excellent man," and said that as far as he is concerned, there are "no problems" between the two groups. There's evidence of this on the ground. In Lima, Peru, fifty-three-year-old David Kuomán, a supernumerary, said that when he first began to feel a tug to Opus Dei, he went to his confessor, who was a Jesuit. "If you've found your path there, follow it," the priest gracefully told him. Yet even in 2005, tension can still be found, albeit in a muted, less explosive form. The capacity of both Jesuits and Opus Dei members to imagine creative ways of overcoming these lingering divisions will be an important test for the possibilities of healing in the broader Church.

The Future

Officials in Opus Dei insist that the organization has no "agenda" for the Catholic Church, and within the limits of Church teaching, members are free to take whatever positions they wish on debatable issues. In the vexed question in the United States of whether pro-choice politicians should be denied Communion, for example, one will find Opus Dei members on all sides. I recently lunched with an Opus Dei priest in Washington, D.C., who told me that he would need to know more than someone's voting record before denying them Communion, and opined that "all the intelligent people" he knows in Opus Dei take a more liberal position on such questions. I've met intelligent Opus Dei members who would dispute that, but the point is that there is a genuine pluralism.

Yet the distinction commonly made among Opus Dei members between "Church teaching," which is beyond debate, and "open questions," which are not, is not as simple as it seems. Many theologians, to say nothing of average Catholics, believe in the possibility of forward movement in teaching, as the Church reflects more deeply on the gospel, on tradition, and on human experience. This is what the nineteenth-century English cardinal John Henry Newman called the "development of doctrine," with his memorable phrase that "to live is to change, and to be perfect is to have changed often." Thus Catholic thinkers find themselves pressing forward all the time, pushing the Church to rethink some traditional positions on human sexuality, on non-Christian religions, on papal authority, and a host of other questions. This is not a prescription for relativism, such thinkers argue, but rather a more thoughtful fidelity. Freezing "Church teaching" at a given stage in development risks making an idol out of one way of phrasing a doctrine that may not yet have reached Newman's stage of perfection after much change.

In the tension between conserving the faith and pondering whether the community has fully grasped what particular points of the faith mean, many Opus Dei members lean more toward the first, more "conservative" pole. Consider this extract from an essay written by McCloskey, in which he imagines himself in 2030 writing to a freshly ordained priest:

As you may have learned, there were approximately 60 million nominal Catholics at the beginning of the Great Jubilee at the turn of the century. You might ask how we went from that number down to our current 40 million. I guess the answer could be, to put it delicately, consolidation. It is not as bad as it looks. In retrospect it can be seen that only approximately 10 percent of the sixty or so were "with the

program." I mean to say only 10 percent of that base assented whole-
heartedly to the teaching of the Church and practiced the sacra-
ments in the minimal sense of Sunday Mass and at least yearly
confession. . . . The Catholics we do have are better formed, practice
their faith in the traditional sense at a much higher level than ever,
and are increasingly eager to share that faith with their neighbors.
Dissent has disappeared from the theological vocabulary. . . . Upon
that fulcrum we can transform the world if we stay the course.

The course described by McCloskey is one that more liberal
Catholics would probably not wish to stay.

This is not a matter of Opus Dei having a "line" or an "agenda"—as
McCloskey himself would concede, he speaks for no one but himself—
but it reflects, to some degree, the sociology of Opus Dei members. This
is a reality, and it suggests painful collisions ahead with Catholics of a
more "liberal" or "progressive" outlook. This is the real sense in which one
might say that Opus Dei is "divisive," in that asking hard questions always
is. Discussion about this reality, however, is likely to be more productive
if it focuses on the issues: Where should the limits of acceptable discussion be set? How do we understand the implications of fidelity to Church
teaching? How do we handle conflicts when they arise? How can
Catholics learn to listen to one another before passing judgment? In
themselves, these questions have nothing to do with Opus Dei, though
Opus Dei members will be important parties to the conversation.

Chapter Twelve

OPUS DEI AND POLITICS

From January 8 to January 11, 2002, a massive international conference was held in Rome on the one hundredth anniversary of the birth of Saint Josemaría Escrivá, entitled the Grandeur of Ordinary Life. The event drew twelve hundred people from fifty-seven countries, with an impressive number of VIPs, and was streamed live on the Internet. At such a gathering, devoted to the memory of a Catholic saint, one would expect theologians, historians, priests, and nuns—and indeed, such folks were present in spades—but the presence of a U.S. senator, who is not even a member of Opus Dei, takes a bit more explaining.

U.S. senator Rick Santorum, Republican of Pennsylvania, was on hand to take part in a panel discussion on the role of religion in public life. Santorum, a Catholic, is a big fan of Escrivá. He quoted with approval a famous line from *The Way*: "Have you ever bothered to think how absurd it is to leave one's Catholicism aside on entering a university, or a professional association, or a scholarly meeting, or Congress, as if you were checking your hat at a door?"

Anticipating much of the debate that would erupt in the United States around the 2004 election between President George W. Bush and Sen. John Kerry, Santorum criticized any distinction between private religious conviction and public responsibility. He took special aim at John Kennedy's famous speech in Houston in 1960, when Kennedy said he would not take orders from the Catholic Church if elected president. That approach, Santorum said, has caused "much harm in America. All of us have heard people say, 'I privately am against abortion, homosexual marriage, stem cell research, cloning. But who am I do decide that it's not right for somebody else?' It sounds good," Santorum said. "But it is the corruption of freedom of conscience."

Addressing himself to Catholics in public life, Santorum argued that it isn't good enough to say that one privately upholds Church teaching on matters such as abortion or gay marriage, but won't "impose" these views through civil legislation. That's a kind of moral schizophrenia, he charged. In that regard, Santorum made the bold assertion, again anticipating the rhetoric of the 2004 election, that George W. Bush is "the first Catholic president of the United States. . . . From economic issues focusing on the poor and social justice, to issues of human life, George Bush is there," Santorum said. "He has every right to say, 'I'm where you are if you're a believing Catholic.' "

On June 26, 2002, Santorum was back at it, appearing on a panel at the John Paul II Cultural Center in Washington, D.C., along with Jean DeGroot, a philosophy professor at Catholic University, as well as the noted Dominican theologian Father Romanus Cessario. The theme was "The Christian in the Secular World: Aspects of the Thought of Blessed Josemaría Escrivá." Santorum is sometimes identified in the press as an Opus Dei member, and although that's not accurate, reporters can be forgiven for making the leap.

The old joke about the Church of England dubbed it "the Tory Party at prayer." From an external point of view, it would be easy enough to draw a similar conclusion about Opus Dei in various parts of the world. In the United States, links between members of the Republican Party and certain members of Opus Dei are well documented. A number of American conservatives, such as Robert Bork, Robert Novak, and U.S. senator Sam Brownback, none of whom are members of Opus Dei, nevertheless were brought into the Catholic Church through the efforts of Father C. John McCloskey. In the American press, Supreme Court justices Antonin Scalia and Clarence Thomas are frequently identified as Opus Dei members. Though neither man is a member, the fact that it's the most conservative justices of the Court who attract such speculation says something. The Opus Dei–affiliated Catholic Information Center on K Street in Washington, D.C., has become a crossroads for conservative Catholics involved in lobbying and public policy on the Hill; the daily noon Mass sometimes collects a "Who's Who" of that world.

In Spain, the government of former prime minister José María Aznar, of the conservative Popular Party, featured three members of Opus Dei. Federico Trillio, a supernumerary, served as minister of defense, while Jesús Cardenal, also a supernumerary, was a top finance official. (Cardenal is not a member of the Popular Party, but an independent.) In addition, the former national police chief, Juan Cotino, is an associate. In the government of Socialist prime minister José Luis Rodríguez Zapatero, there are no ministers from Opus Dei. In Peru, the only Opus Dei member involved in national politics is numerary Rafael Rey, a member of Congress and a conservative opponent of that country's current center-left president, Alejandro Toledo. In Italy, journalist Alberto Michelini, an Opus Dei supernumerary, has served as a member of parliament for Forza Italia, the conservative party launched by Italian media tycoon Silvio Berlusconi.

In Poland, Roman Giertych, leader of the conservative League of Polish Families, is a supernumerary. Giertych says he wants to defend a "Christian Poland," and is therefore strongly anti–European Union. His ambition is to build a political force that will resemble "Aznar's Popular Party in Spain or the British Conservative Party." In Chile, the mayor of Santiago and leader of the right-wing Independent Democratic Union is Joaquín Lavín, a supernumerary. Lavín was a presidential candidate in 1999, but lost to Richard Lagos in a runoff. He is expected to be a candidate again in 2005.

One could go on multiplying examples, but the point should be clear: To the extent that Opus Dei members or supporters are involved in secular politics, they tend to cut to the right. Especially on matters pertaining to the "culture wars," one will find prominent Opus Dei voices. This reality has led many outside observers to conclude that Opus Dei is, in itself, a "right-wing" or "conservative" force in secular politics.

Very quickly, however, a distinction has to be made. There are two senses in which an organization can be said to be "conservative." The first is sociological, that is, that many of its members are conservative; the second is institutional, that is, that the organization has a policy or "line" that can be described as conservative. As will be unfolded in this chapter, there's little question Opus Dei qualifies in the first sense, though there are exceptions. In the second sense, however, Opus Dei does not have a corporate political stance, and while one can talk about the "conservatism" of members, that language goes awry when talking about the institution itself.

Opus Dei and a "Party Line"

As noted already, there is a strong aversion within Opus Dei to group activity. A famous saying of Escrivá has it that "Opus Dei does not act; its members do." As one application of this idea, Escrivá was implacably opposed to the idea of a Catholic political party. "It seems substantially better to me," he wrote in a letter of June 16, 1960, "that there be many highly qualified Catholics who, while not posing as 'official' Catholics, work within the political structure from positions of responsibility to create a true Catholic presence, sustained by an upright love for their coworkers." This emphasis on not posing as an "official" Catholic helps explain why members who are active in politics often don't like to talk about their affiliation with Opus Dei. It's not always a matter of secrecy so much as Escrivá's insistence that their positions should rise or fall on their own merits, not because they pose as the approved Catholic response to some political question.

For Escrivá, the need to keep Opus Dei out of politics arose from two motives. The first was to respect the principles of Christian freedom and secularity, the second to prevent internal divisions within Opus Dei. An early member of Opus Dei, Juan Jiménez Vargas, has spoken about the way Escrivá's approach influenced his followers: "The unity of the Work came first. Each of us took part in the elections in a normal way, with great prudence so as not to take part in any activity that could harm the Work or give grounds for identifying it with any political view, or uniting it to any political faction."

Escrivá could be ferocious on this point. "If Opus Dei had ever played politics—even for a minute—I would have left the Work at that very moment of error," he declared in 1970. "For, on the one hand, our means and aims are always and exclusively of a supernatural character. On the other hand, every single member, man or woman, possesses in secular matters an absolute personal freedom—respected by all—as well as the personal responsibility that follows as a logical consequence. Therefore it is impossible that Opus Dei would ever be associated with undertakings which are not of an explicitly spiritual and apostolic nature."

Opus Dei and Christian Democracy in Spain

The case of the Vatican's attempt to forge a Christian Democratic Party in Spain at the end of the Franco era, and Escrivá's refusal to be enlisted in the project, offers a classic illustration of his insistence on the political independence of his members. Giovani Benelli was one of the most remarkable men ever to serve in the Roman Curia. A graduate of the Accademia Ecclesiastica, the Vatican's elite school for diplomats on the Piazza Minerva in Rome, Benelli served as the chargé d'affaires in the Vatican embassy in Spain prior to being consecrated a bishop in 1966. He was sent as nuncio, or ambassador, to Senegal, where he served until June 1967, when he was called back to Rome to become the *sostituto,* or the official in the Secretariat of State in charge of day-to-day Church affairs. In that capacity he was Paul VI's right-hand man, and wielded a kind of power that few Vatican officials have before or since. He was a tireless worker, so much so that he had to take on two secretaries who could split shifts for the eighteen and twenty-hour days Benelli was accustomed to working.

Benelli had been ordained to the priesthood during the carnage of the Second World War, in 1943. After the wreckage, with a devastated economy and an angry, desperate population, there was a real fear that Italy was poised to elect a Communist government in 1948 and thus provide the Soviets with a long-sought beachhead in Western Europe. Knowing what Communist rule could mean for organized religion, the Catholic Church threw its institutional weight behind the new Christian Democratic Party, which was in effect the "official" Catholic party, and by most accounts the Church made the difference. One symbolic illustration: One of the few times that Padre Pio, the Capuchin stigmatic and visionary, ever left his convent at San Giovanni Rotondo was to vote for the Christian Democrats in 1948.

Contemplating the end of the Franco era in Spain, Benelli was convinced that pent-up frustration might lead to a similar danger of a Communist victory there. He thus wanted the Church to help prepare a transition to a stable, democratic post-Franco era. Italian church historian Alberto Melloni has noted that when Benelli was in the papal embassy in Spain during the Second Vatican Council, he was troubled by what he saw as the philo-Franco line of the Vatican under Cardinals Alfredo

Ottaviani, in the Holy Office, and Cardinal Giovanni Cicognani, the secretary of state. When Benelli arrived in the Vatican, he was determined to change course, and wanted Spanish Catholicism to fall in line.

The solution Benelli favored was the "Italian model." Spain should create the basis for a Christian Democratic Party, and the Spanish Catholic Church should support it. Though it's not clear that he ever communicated his expectations to Opus Dei explicitly, it was widely understood that he wanted Opus Dei, along with the rest of Spanish Catholicism, to be politically engaged. Escrivá, however, refused to commit to Benelli's project; as indicated in chapter 2, he wrote to Paul VI explaining that he was opposed to the creation of a "Catholic" party in Spain. From the point of view of Opus Dei, Escrivá said he could not impose a political choice on his members.

Cardinal Julián Herranz, president of the Pontifical Council for Legislative Texts and an Opus Dei member, has worked in the Roman Curia for forty-four years, and he remembers the days of conflict with Benelli.

"One could see that he was interested in creating in Spain, as in Italy, a kind of Christian Democrat Party," Herranz said. "The thing was, how to do it? Some members of Opus Dei were inclined to do it, others weren't, for the reason of political liberty." Escrivá, Herranz said, declined to "get Opus Dei members in line," and that obviously disappointed Benelli.

One episode in particular illustrates the chill that settled in between Benelli and Opus Dei. The ambassador of Spain to the Holy See during this period, Antonio Garrigues Díaz-Cañabate, organized a lunch between Benelli and Escrivá in an attempt to air out their differences. During the lunch, according to later recollections from Portillo and Herranz, Escrivá asked Benelli what error or injustice he had committed, so that he could correct it or ask forgiveness. Benelli responded that he had nothing to say on the subject. Escrivá then asked him, "Monsignor, why are you holding us hostage?" The reference was to the fact that Escrivá had been unable to arrange an audience with Paul VI, and no progress had been made on Opus Dei's request for transformation into a personal prelature. Again Benelli did not respond.

Still, Herranz said, Benelli retained a personal respect for Escrivá.

"I saw Benelli the day after the death of the Founder. He didn't understand some things about Opus Dei in terms of politics, but he said to me, 'This afternoon we'll have an article published in *L'Osservatore Romano* to memorialize Monsignor Escrivá.' He had interrupted an audience with an ambassador to receive me. He told me that he had always admired the figure of Monsignor Escrivá as a man of providence. Benelli said, 'What Ignatius of Loyola was for the Council of Trent, Josemaría Escrivá was for the recent Ecumenical Council. He was born so that the Second Vatican Council could become part of the life of the Church.'"

The Benelli story offers a good case for testing whether Escrivá was serious about Opus Dei having no political agenda. If ever there was a set of circumstances propitious for a "power grab," this situation presented them. The end of the Franco reign meant that a vital transition was looming for Spain. Escrivá's 1964 letter to Paul VI makes clear that he too was worried about a Socialist/Communist takeover, so that must have been a compelling argument for political engagement. Further, he had the full blessing of ecclesiastical authority. Had Opus Dei led the way in the creation of a Spanish version of Christian Democracy, it's imaginable that its total of eight ministers in thirty-six years under Franco would have been swamped by its representation in a new Spanish government.

Moreover, the towering reality is that in the late 1960s and early 1970s, Escrivá was desperate to resolve Opus Dei's canonical status and had a powerful motive for not alienating the most powerful man in the Vatican short of the pope himself. In spite of all that, he declined to use the institutional weight of Opus Dei, or his own personal authority, to back Benelli's project. In that light, one can only conclude that Escrivá meant what he said, that Opus Dei must not become a partisan political force.

Even as fierce a critic on other points as John Roche, an English numerary from 1959 to 1973, absolves Opus Dei on this one. In a letter to the *Times* (London) written on November 19, 1979, Roche wrote: "In fairness to Opus Dei I must say that during my fourteen years of membership (until 1973), living in Ireland, Kenya, Spain and England and holding positions of some responsibility, I failed to detect any party political intention." He goes on to say, however, that at the sociological level certain instincts seem widely diffused. "Its members loosely share a spread of political attitudes which result from its anti-Communism, its right-wing religious outlook, its peculiar blend of God and Mammon, and of course its historical origins in Spain."

The Conservative Tendency

This is perhaps the most obvious instance in which outside observers, hearing members of Opus Dei insist that the Work has no political agenda, are likely to be perplexed. The evidence seems overwhelming that most Opus Dei members, in matters of secular politics, are conservative.

As one window onto this, I found myself in the parking lot of the Heights, the Opus Dei–affiliated boys' school, located in Potomac, Maryland, in suburban Washington, D.C., on December 1, a few weeks after the November presidential elections in the United States. I arrived early for my appointment, so I decided to see what the bumper stickers might tell me about the sociology of the Heights. Bear in mind that Maryland is a "blue state" that went 53 percent to 39 percent for Kerry; the nearby District of Columbia went overwhelmingly for Kerry. One wouldn't know it, however, from this parking lot. I counted at least twenty Bush/Cheney stickers to one for Kerry/Edwards. In fact, Kerry was tied with Michael Peroutka, presidential candidate of the Constitution Party, who lambasted Bush and the Republicans for being soft on the abortion issue and whose bumper sticker was emblazoned on a station wagon. There were also a healthy number of SUPPORT OUR TROOPS and THE NATURAL CHOICE IS LIFE stickers.

Granted, there's only so much one can tell from bumper stickers. I tested my perceptions with Vera Golenzer, a parent who has a twelve-year-old girl at Oakcrest, the Opus Dei–affiliated girls' school in McLean, and a ten-year-old son at the Heights. Her reading? "Most of the families here are Republicans," she said. "They have strong political views." She said her kids carpool with children of another family whose parents were Kerry supporters, and one of their boys got into a scuffle with a friend who told him he couldn't come to school with a Kerry sticker on the car. One other indicator of the climate is that the Heights has educated the sons of a number of Republicans, including U.S. senator Chuck Hagel, a Republican from Nebraska, and U.S. senator Mel Martinez, Republican from Florida. One has to reach back to Edmund Muskie, who ran for president in 1972, to find a prominent Democrat who sent a son to the Heights. At the same time, Golenzer stressed that "there is no political line being pushed" at the Heights, "either from the teachers or from Opus Dei."

This example comes out of the American political context, and depending on what part of the world one is talking about, Opus Dei's political profile can differ. Yet in much of Latin America and Europe, the tendency toward conservative parties is unmistakable. In Asia, with the exception of the Philippines, Opus Dei is not a large enough presence to have developed a reputation; within the Philippines, however, it is seen as tilting right. William Esposo, a Catholic journalist in the Philippines who is associated with the Focolare movement, said of Opus Dei's profile: "It is perceived as centrist with a capacity to go right. The Opus Dei image can never be seen as left or left of center."

How is one to explain this phenomenon, if Opus Dei as such has no program and leaves members free to make up their own minds? Doesn't there have to be some sort of internal "line" to explain the apparent unanimity? In fact, as will be documented in a moment, that unanimity is not absolute—there are leftist members of Opus Dei. At the same time, the tendency to the right is clear, but it does not require the hypothesis of a hidden agenda.

First, let's define what we mean by "conservative." For many classical theorists, three cardinal principles of conservatism are: 1) limited government, 2) the free market, and 3) a foreign policy premised on national security. If those are the points of reference, it is not clear that members of Opus Dei, even in the United States, are overwhelmingly "conservative." One will find Opus Dei libertarians and Opus Dei statists, Opus Dei capitalists and Opus Dei believers in government intervention, and some Opus Dei members have a slightly more "internationalist" bent than the typical American, if only because they take membership in a global family of faith seriously, which tends to give them a broader horizon.

This pluralism is clear outside the United States. One example comes from Spain, where, as mentioned above, supernumerary Federico Trillio was minister of defense in José María Aznar's conservative government and hence involved in the policy that took Spain into war in Iraq alongside the United States. His position was ferociously criticized by Spanish journalist Pilar Urbano, a numerary of Opus Dei, who publicly argued that the war was based on "lies." (Urbano also asserted that the incursion in Afghanistan was a "vendetta" rather than a specific response to a terrorist threat.) Llúis Foix, an associate of Opus Dei and a columnist for *Vanguardia* in Barcelona, has criticized Trillio on similar grounds. In Italy, Alberto Michelini, a supernumerary, may be aligned with the conservatives, but Mario Maiolo, also an Opus Dei supernumerary, is on the other side of aisle. He's vice president of the province of Calabria, in southern Italy, and a member of the center-left Margherita Party. The president he serves under comes from the Refounded Communists.

To take an American example, in the December 14 Web edition of *New Republic Online,* Andrew Sullivan posted a piece blasting Robert Novak, whom he described as "a convert not just to Catholicism but to its most hard-line sect, Opus Dei." Aside from the fact that Novak told me on December 20, 2004, that he is not a member of Opus Dei and no one has asked him to become one, the piece amused an Opus Dei priest I know, who said the irony was that he agreed with Sullivan and not Novak (the point at issue was whether President Bush's refusal to meet Rocco Buttiglione, an Italian Catholic politician and European Union critic, on a recent trip to Washington was an act of cowardice, in an effort to "make nice" with Europe).

In recent years, however, the key markers of conservatism in the West have become less questions of statecraft or economic policy, and more cultural questions, especially the three neuralgic matters of abortion, gay marriage, and stem cell research. On those questions, the emphasis within Opus Dei on "thinking with the Church," and the sociological fact that most people attracted to Opus Dei accept traditional Catholic positions, produces a near-uniformity in favor of "conservative" views. Moreover, many Catholics regard these positions as nonnegotiable. The typical Opus Dei member will see these questions as being more politically decisive than tax policy or budget levels. In practice, at least in the United States and Europe, this generally means they vote conservative. It is an interesting thought experiment to ask what the "Opus Dei vote" in the United States in 2004 might have been if, instead of John Kerry, the Democrats had nominated someone like Robert Casey, the former Democratic governor of Pennsylvania, who had a strong pro-life stand. This is not an entirely hypothetical exercise, since there is an American Opus Dei priest, Father

John Wauck, who teaches communications at Santa Croce in Rome, who when still a layman was once a speechwriter for Casey.

The conservative instinct, driven by cultural issues of special Catholic concern, is by no means restricted to Opus Dei. In the 2004 general election in the United States, Bush captured 52 percent of the Catholic vote to 47 percent for Kerry, and among Catholics who attend Mass at least once a week, the margin was 56 to 43 percent. Many of these Catholics were not necessarily supportive of Bush policies on the environment, or the United Nations, or even Iraq, but felt compelled to vote for the Republican candidate because the Democrat held what were seen as unacceptable stances on the cultural issues. In that sense, Opus Dei is perhaps a particularly concentrated form of a general tendency in Western politics, which is that a significant portion of religiously serious voters feel themselves driven to the right. If these cultural questions could somehow be removed from the agenda, the pluralism among Catholics, and the pluralism among Opus Dei members, might be more clear.

Opus Dei's Image Problem: The Case of Peru

A factor that further skews perceptions is that most Opus Dei members who have managed to achieve public prominence are identified with the right, and impressions of these high-profile figures are transferred to Opus Dei itself. Perhaps nowhere in the world is this process as clear as in Peru, where the term "Opus Dei," for most Peruvians, is coterminous with Cardinal Juan Luis Cipriani of Lima.

To his critics, Cipriani embodies an authoritarian model of leadership and a right-wing political stance. In 2003, Peru's Commission of Truth and Reconciliation, set up to investigate violence in that country from 1980 to 2000, concluded of Cipriani, "He never questioned the violations of human rights that were committed by the forces of order, and on the contrary, he maintained constantly and sharply that 'it cannot be said Peru is a place where human rights are not respected.'" Cipriani roundly rejected that criticism. In a July 2004 interview for this book, Cipriani said of nongovernmental human rights groups such as Amnesty International and Human Rights Watch, "They didn't speak about human rights, they came to mess around with terrorism." He once accused these groups of "speaking about [a kind of] human rights that is a *cojudez*," meaning, roughly, "bullshit."

Cipriani started out as an auxiliary bishop in Ayacucho, one of the poorest zones of Peru and birthplace of the Shining Path movement. The Shining Path was a Maoist revolutionary movement that aimed to transform Peru into a socialist state. It was bitterly opposed by the Peruvian military and security services, especially under former security chief Vladimiro Montesinos. Most analysts say both sides in the long-running conflict were guilty of human rights abuses.

"I had very good relations with the self-defense groups, the *rondas*," Cipriani said. "To me that's human rights. They have the right to live on their own places, to defend their family and their cattle and children and property. It was not the military—they, the peasants themselves, defeated the Shining Path, not the army. . . . I don't defend the ideology of human rights, I respect human rights that start from the dignity of being sons of God. I don't care for these NGOs that come here to play around with the terrorists," he said.

Cipriani admitted to being fed up with critics who didn't face the same risks he did at the peak of the violence.

"Nobody wanted to be elected mayor, there were no candidates, because they were killed," he said. "Nobody wanted to be the governor, because they would be killed. Nobody would say a word against Shining Path, because they would be killed. My voice was the only voice to stop this violence, but I didn't follow the divine path of the NGOs. That was, for them, a mortal sin. I didn't play around with poverty and with human rights. I went directly to the places where there were problems. I would go to the army and say, 'What happened in this place, why are people speaking about these things?' The ideological approach can make for beautiful speech, but I never saw those people from the Truth Commission in Ayacucho. Not once, in all those years. Now they are the gurus of peace."

Cipriani is widely seen in Peru as an ally and supporter of the exiled former president Alberto Fujimori, whose strong antiterrorism campaign broke the back of the Shining Path, but whose undemocratic and corrupt administration ended in disgrace. Cipriani refuses to distance himself. "I think the demon is more Montesinos than Fujimori," he said, referring to the widely hated former head of the security services under Fujimori. "I will not say that Fujimori's not a friend of mine. They say that hurts my image. I don't care, I care for the truth."

Cipriani is also the ultimate antimatter to liberation theology, the Latin American current that sought to align the Catholic Church with progressive movements for social change. He minces no words on the subject: "It's an ideology, not a theology. They created a system of pastoral work that is now inside of the Church, and not only in Peru. Desacralization, making social work the first thing to do, criticizing the magisterium, involving priests in politics . . . that whole system is part of what liberation theology left here in Peru and Latin America, also with the 'Indian theology' in Mexico or the 'African theology' in Africa. It's a system, a parallel magisterium to the real magisterium. They were defeated in the doctrine, because that was easy, to study the books and see their errors. But the way of doing the Church, the pastoral work, is still going on and is quite difficult to change."

In our interview, Cipriani said that he has been the object of a blackbag campaign hatched by forces within the Catholic Church, including some of his fellow Peruvian bishops. In 2001, the then–minister of justice in the Peruvian government, Fernando Olivera, secretly carried three letters to the Vatican, one allegedly written by Cipriani, the others by the papal nuncio. The alleged Cipriani letter was addressed to Montesinos and purportedly showed Cipriani asking for the "elimination and incineration" of secret videotapes showing him with Montesinos. The letters, however, turned out to be fakes, concocted using scanned copies of a letterhead stolen from the offices of the Peruvian bishops' conference.

On September 13, 2004, an anticorruption prosecutor in Peru accused Bishop Luis Bambarén, a Jesuit and former president of the Peruvian bishops' conference, of conspiring with Olivera in the letters scandal. Bambarén told Peruvian radio that the charges are "absolutely false," and as of this writing no charges have been brought. Meanwhile a court case was under way against another Peruvian bishop, Jorge Carrión of Puno, for his alleged role in the plot. Despite all of the controversies, according to one recent poll, Cipriani had a 52 percent approval rating, far higher than Peru's embattled president.

"They are making me a saint, with lies, with envy, many times from inside of the Church. For me this really hurts," he said, breaking into tears. "I'm sorry, but it's quite painful. I have to shut my mouth because I love the Church, the unity of the Church. But I mean . . . many of these lies come from inside, not from outside. It's one lie after another, for sixteen years. They don't stop."

Cipriani was blunt, not hesitating to criticize human rights groups, liberation theology, or elements within the Peruvian government. All this makes him good copy, and it explains why he has so often made headlines in Peru. Yet on all these matters, Cipriani was speaking for himself, not as a member of Opus Dei. Technically, as a bishop, he's no longer under the jurisdiction of the prelate of Opus Dei. Yet most Peruvians, and most Church-watchers around the world, cannot help but connect the dots between Cipriani's public utterances and the Opus Dei "line."

Exceptions

The conservative instinct in Opus Dei, however overwhelming, is not universal, as a few examples will illustrate.

Squire Lance

Squire Lance is a Democratic political activist in Chicago, who in November 2004 managed the successful candidacy of a Democratic candidate for a judgeship in Illinois. An African-American, his first taste of political organizing came as a protégé of Saul Alinsky, the legendary radical and community organizer who believed in getting down to the grass roots rather than working through institutions; he once famously said, "The only movement worth anything is a bowel movement."

As executive director of Alinsky's Woodlawn Organization, Lance directed almost 60 percent of the civil rights activity in Chicago in the 1960s. After the tumult of the 1968 Democratic National Convention in Chicago, an Illinois assemblyman named Dan Walker approached Lance and asked him to help do some legwork for a panel investigating what had happened. Contrary to popular impression, Lance found that very few blacks had taken part in the street violence. When Walker ran for governor in 1972, Lance organized African-American support for him, and when Walker's liberal platform prevailed in a huge political upset, he brought Lance to the statehouse.

Lance was Walker's personal liaison with five state agencies, including responsibility for Amtrak, highways, and mental health issues. He was the arm of the governor, with power to hire and fire, and was making a very comfortable living. "I had real authority, I loved my job, and my community was excited about my responsibilities," he said during a September 2004 interview in his Chicago home. "I was not just a 'spook by the door.'"

In 1976, however, Walker was unseated in the Democratic primary by a candidate backed by the Richard Daley political machine, and suddenly Lance was out of work. He finally landed a job at the Cook County Medical Examiner's office handling dead bodies, a position that involved a 60 percent pay cut. "Emotionally, I took a complete dive," Lance said. "I was totally depressed. There was no way I could handle it." Lance had grown up a Catholic, but had stopped practicing the faith. This crisis, however, drove him back to the Church. "When you're living in an environment in which you're a complete and total victim, you put a great deal of faith in God. I said, 'I've got to find God again.'"

Lance went to a Sunday Mass at Saint Philip Neri parish, where he grew up. As it happens, he had not been to Mass since before the Second Vatican Council, and was stunned to find the liturgy in English, with the priest facing the people. It made him "extremely uncomfortable," he said, since he thought of himself as a "very orthodox Catholic." At around the same time, the *Chicago Sun-Times* published a negative piece on Opus Dei, and ironically, the description of it as a pre–Vatican II style of Catholicism sounded exactly right, so he sought it out. (This is not how Opus Dei sees itself, but that's another matter.)

"Listen, I had been a pagan, pure and simple," Lance said of his years in politics. "I paid little attention to my family. I was pretty nearly a workaholic. Outside of that, I paid little attention to anything but my social life. I went out drinking on Friday nights, and watched sports. I needed something to shake all that up."

Lance got in touch with an Opus Dei priest, who explained the basics—sanctification of work, divine filiation, and so on. Lance said he didn't really understand much at the time, but the guy "asked all the right questions," wanting to know the birthdays of his wife and children and how Lance approached his role as a father. He began attending Opus Dei events, and in 1978 he became a supernumerary. "At the human level, I discovered that I could order my day with little difficulty, I could make decisions about what was important," Lance said of the impact Opus Dei had. "A discipline required of me in the Work helped me be more attentive to my family. I'm much more at peace."

How does he reconcile his left-wing politics with being in Opus Dei?

"It's my choice, I want to be a Democrat, and I want to be in Opus Dei," he said. "There is nothing in Opus Dei that says that's a contradiction." Yet Lance acknowledged this makes him something of a rare bird. When I asked if he knows any other Democrats in the Work, he said, "Maybe I know one other guy who votes Democratic . . . not very many." His primary reason for being a Democrat, he said, is "because of where Democrats stand on the question of race."

Being in Opus Dei, he said, gives him a chance to push his Democratic friends on questions of values. "When I sit in a room with the mayor and state's attorney, who are both Irish Catholics, I can say to them, 'Okay guys, I'm from Opus Dei and you got to get your virtue shit together,'" he laughed.

Ruth Kelly

At the time of this writing, the most prominent Opus Dei member in the world to occupy a cabinet-level position in a national government was Ruth Kelly, a supernumerary and the education secretary in England. That makes Kelly a rising star in the Labor Party, historically the main left-of-center party in British politics.

Kelly is only thirty-six, meaning her political career has been on the fast track. She's a mother of four and was a journalist for the *Manchester Guardian,* widely considered the leading left-wing daily in Britain, from 1990 to 1994. She worked for the Bank of England before going into politics. Her parents were a pharmacist and a teacher, and she represents the Bolton West District. According to political observers in the United Kingdom, Kelly has been especially adept at navigating the rivalry between Prime Minister Tony Blair and Chancellor of the Exchequer Gordon Brown, being one of the few Labor politicians who enjoys respect in both camps. She was economic secretary in 2001 and financial secretary in 2002 before joining the Blair cabinet in 2004.

Kelly is also known as part of a breed of younger British politicians who take a strong moral line on issues such as parenting and antisocial behavior. She is staunchly anti-abortion and anti-euthanasia, and said that she would speak her mind on those subjects in party debates, although she made clear in a January 23, 2005, interview on the *Breakfast with Frost* program that she would uphold whatever policies the government develops in her department. Kelly grew up a Roman Catholic in Northern Ireland, and her family moved to England when she was fifteen, just in time for the recession of the early 1980s under Prime Minister Margaret Thatcher. The resulting social unrest helped propel Kelly into politics. "I had a very strong feeling that it was unjust and that, if I could do anything to help, I should be doing it," she said.

Kelly also holds the record for most children born to a sitting member of the English parliament. She married Derek Gadd in 1996 and within a month of Labor's landslide a year later, she had given birth to her eldest son, Eamonn. Within the past seven years she has had Sinead, now five, Roisin, now three, and Niamh, now one. While the family pays for a nanny, Kelly takes her responsibilities as a mother seriously, and is known as one of the few ministers who doesn't take work home at night (not because she's lazy, but because she's remarkably focused).

"The family imposes a discipline on me. If I didn't have a family I would probably be a work junkie like lots of other ministers. I just don't have that choice. I have four kids seven and under, and they want their mum," she said.

Although her own children attend Catholic schools, Kelly is known as a strong supporter of public education. In general, she is seen as a strong Blair loyalist, meaning a centrist on most questions, and some have suggested her as a future candidate for prime minister.

When Kelly's links to Opus Dei were revealed in December 2004, it caused a brief flurry in the British press, most of it negative. She compounded the problem by refusing for almost a month to discuss it at all, leaving Opus Dei in the awkward position of not being able to either confirm or deny her membership. Finally, she said: "I, along with any other politician, am entitled to a degree of privacy in my private life. I do have a private spiritual life and I am completely open about that. People know that I am a Catholic and that I take it seriously."

Xavi Casajuana

Don't try to tell Xavi Casajuana, an Opus Dei supernumerary in Sabadell, just a few miles outside Barcelona, that he's a Spaniard. "When I have to go around the world with my Spanish passport, I detest it. I don't want to be considered Spanish," he told me during an interview in his Sabadell apartment. "I'm Catalan. I have my own language, Catalan. I prefer to go to a Catalan Mass than a Spanish Mass because I always pray to my father, God, in Catalan, not in Spanish. I speak Catalan and three foreign languages—Spanish, French, and English."

As one piece of evidence of how emphatic Casajuana is about being Catalan, he told me that when he drives around in Europe, he puts a sticker that reads CAT for Catalonia over the place where the Spanish license plate has E for *España*. "I'm not Spanish," he said. "I want to fight for my country, and my country is Catalonia." In the midst of saying this, Casajuana reached into his billfold and pulled out two items: the flag of an independent Catalonia, and a holy card of the Madonna.

Casajuana, thirty-two, works as computer technician for a factory that makes electric motors, but his passion is politics. He belongs to a leftist regional party, Esquerra Republicana de Catalunya, which supports independence for Catalonia. In Spain, the conservative parties, such as the Popular Party, are generally nationalistic, which leaves those who push for greater regional autonomy with no choice but the left.

Don't try telling Casajuana either that as an Opus Dei member, he should support the former Spanish prime minister José María Aznar, widely assumed to be friendly to Opus Dei. "Aznar is the last man in the world who I desire to see. As a Catalan, I know that Aznar wants to destroy my country. He wants to destroy my language. He wants to destroy my culture. He wants to destroy the history of my country," Casajuana said, becoming more emphatic with every syllable.

"I expect that one day Catalonia will take part in the Olympic Games, with its own soccer and basketball teams," he said. "I want to have a Catalan passport. I want to have my language recognized in the European nations, of course, because it's the eighth most spoken language in Europe."

Casajuana said that he doesn't really feel that he has a stake in the national political debate in Spain, because neither the Popular Party nor the Socialists seem inclined to help Catalonia. But if he were to choose between them, he said he would vote for the Socialist prime minister, Zapatero, rather than Aznar. He said he doesn't like the expectation that, as a Catholic, he should vote a certain way; that, he said, would be a return to the "national Catholicism" of the Franco era. He added for good measure that he "detests" the political line followed by Federico Trillio, Aznar's minister of defense—and, like Casajuana, an Opus Dei supernumerary.

Casajuana said many of his friends and colleagues are surprised to hear that he's both Opus Dei and on the left. "When they knew that my wife had a boyfriend, her family always asked her, 'Is he a member of Opus Dei?' And my wife responded, 'Oh, I don't know.' I mean, she knew. But they really expected to find in me a person of the Popular Party, a really Spanish person, a conservative person. So they don't understand anything."

A Social Conscience

Opus Dei has a reputation for being "elitist," and certainly it aspires to have an impact on professional and intellectual circles. That's one of the reasons that the first place Opus Dei usually sets up shop is near a university. This does not mean, however, that it's an exclusively white-collar spirituality. There are barbers and bus drivers and mechanics who belong to Opus Dei. Further, it does not mean that Opus Dei lacks a social conscience. The bulk of Opus Dei's "corporate works" are designed to serve the poor and excluded. Escrivá wrote: "A man or a society that does not react to suffering and injustice, and makes no effort to alleviate them, is still distant from the love of Christ's heart. Christians should be united in having one and the same desire to serve mankind. Otherwise their Christianity will not be the word and life of Jesus; it will be a fraud, a deception of God and man."

As examples of Opus Dei's social conscience, consider the following:

- The ELIS center in Rome, which is an Italian acronym for "Education, Work, Instruction, and Sport." It's designed to give low-income young men from Rome's Tiburtino neighborhood an opportunity to develop trade skills and thus lift themselves out of poverty while also helping them develop academically and giving them a chance to play sports. The premises include a hall of residence for 150 people, most of them students at the ELIS Higher Training School; a building used for training programs for traditional jobs such as mechanics, goldsmiths and watchmakers, and new technologies; a business "nursery" (helping with premises, equipment, and consultations) to favor the birth of new small-scale enterprises; a sports club with 500 members; a library of 10,000 books; and three study rooms. So far, about twenty young businesses have been set up because of help from the ELIS "nursery," and 95 percent of the boys who have attended the training courses have found jobs.

- The Midtown Center in Chicago, which serves some 350 young men during the regular school year in after-school and Saturday programs, and 60 over the summer. Through a combination of classes, one-on-one mentoring, and sports, the idea is to keep the kids out of gangs and equip them to finish school. Seventy-two percent of the students are Hispanic, 25 percent are black, and the rest fall into "other." At least 85 percent of the students come from low-income families. One index of the difference Midtown makes is a survey that found 95 percent of its students graduate from high school, and 75 percent go to college. The general numbers for the inner-city area in which Midtown is located are that 60 percent of male students graduate high school and 15 percent go to college.

- Moluka, a medical-social dispensary in the Congo, which is a subsidiary of the Monkole Hospital. Doctors and nurses offer health care to people who would otherwise find it unattainable. In addition, the dispensary provides programs of physical hygiene and nutrition, home and neighborhood sanitation, family health, child care, literacy work, finance, domestic science, and creation of productive activities. The dispensary aims to take care of a population of 30,000 people.

- Condoray rural training center for women, in Cañete, Peru, about ninety miles from Lima. More than 20,000 farm women, in one of the poorest regions of Peru, have been trained in literacy and trade skills. In this area, some 83 percent of women between nineteen and thirty-nine are illiterate, while 70 percent of the families are so poor that they cannot provide basic necessities. In the opening days of the literacy courses, indigenous women forced down from the Andes by poverty and violence are taught how to pick up a pencil and make marks on paper, something few of them have ever done.

• The Informal Sector Business Institute in Nairobi, Kenya, which aims to teach basic business skills to poor men who participate in Kenya's vast "informal," meaning off-the-books, economy, selling candy, shining shoes, or peddling used car parts. The idea is to help men improve the living standards of their families, making it possible to leave their kids in school. Points covered in the training include basic bookkeeping techniques, inventory management, sales techniques, and scheduling.

What difference do these programs make?

Juan Carlos Ocon, thirty-one, went through the Midtown program while he was a young Hispanic growing up in inner-city Chicago. His family had just arrived from Mexico, and his mother thought Midtown would give him focus. Ocon's father had died six months after the family arrived in the United States, and his mother, with three kids to take care of and speaking no English, found one job at one factory, and a second job at another factory. Ocon said he got involved with the sports programs, became the star on the soccer team, and that gave him greater confidence in the classroom. As a bonus, he said, his teammates on that soccer team are still his best friends. As evidence of the impact Midtown can have, of his three closest friends from those days, one is an information technology specialist, one is an accountant, and one is an engineer. All three come from impoverished immigrant families in the inner city.

Ocon went on to Northridge Prep, the Opus Dei–affiliated boys' school, but did not become a member of Opus Dei. He is instead a cooperator. Today, Ocon is a teacher in the Chicago Public Schools system, at Juarez Academy, and in training to become a principal. He also wants to be a leader in the Hispanic community, helping engineer what he calls a "cultural revolution. . . . Many of us forget why we came here, which was to give our kids a better opportunity," Ocon said. "We're in survival mode, not focused on education. We need a kind of activism to get ourselves back on track."

Of Midtown, Ocon said: "I think they're genuinely concerned with helping inner-city youth become better students and better people through character formation," he said. Today, he said, he tries to connect students from Juarez Academy with Midtown. "It made a huge difference in my life," he said.

John Mathenge, thirty, is taking the program from the Informal Sector Business Institute, located in the heart of Nairobi's slums. He makes bed frames, upholstery, and wardrobes and sells them to locals. He told me that before he took the course from the institute, he had no concept of even elementary bookkeeping techniques. He thought all the money he made from a sale simply went into his pocket. Now he knows that he has to put some of it back into the work, buying timber and other materials. This way, even when there isn't an immediate order, he doesn't stay idle. He now has three men working for him, and the business has expanded. The institute has also taught him basic computer skills and even given him some talks on being a good father.

"I owe them a lot," he said. "I'm able to provide more for my family." As one outgrowth of the experience, Mathenge said, he's determined that his children will finish school.

Mathenge said he was born Catholic, but has since switched to Presbyterianism. He goes to church every Sunday morning, from 8:45 to 10:45 A.M., and said he enjoys the "praise and worship." Despite rumors of aggressive Opus Dei recruiting through its corporate works, when I asked him what he thought of Opus Dei, he looked at me and said: "What's that?" It turns out that after several months of attending courses, no one, at least not yet, had told Mathenge that this activity was sponsored by Opus Dei.

Summary

As already noted, there's a strong tendency for Opus Dei members to be politically conservative, especially when it comes to cultural questions such as abortion, contraception, and homosexuality. The vast majority of members did not acquire these views from Opus Dei; they had them before they got there, or would have developed them from the social and ecclesiastic circles in which they move in any event. What Opus Dei adds, perhaps, is a doctrinal formation that gives people more confidence in advancing these positions publicly, and a greater sense of personal obligation to be coherent in their choices. For people and organizations that take a different view on cultural questions, Opus Dei members sometimes represent formidable adversaries, and a robust debate in terms of what public policy should be is entirely legitimate. The debate, however, will make more sense if it's pitched at the level of the issues rather than Opus Dei's allegedly covert role in stoking right-wing activism.

There is a risk for Opus Dei as well, which is that the nature of contemporary Western political alignments, in which the conservative parties tend to be the carriers of traditional "Catholic" positions on cultural matters, will over time drag Opus Dei precisely where Escrivá never wanted it to go—treating one political party as the "Catholic" party, and identifying Opus Dei with it. In the United States, some conservative Catholics, and certainly not just those from Opus Dei, flirted with this position in the 2004 Bush/Kerry presidential election, treating a vote for Bush almost as a commandment of the faith. While a Catholic can conclude that one candidate is superior to another on issues of importance to the Church, no party is ever perfectly in accord with Church teaching, and there is always room for debate about which mix of positions is preferable. That is precisely why Escrivá wanted to leave Opus Dei members free to make up their own minds. In their zeal to be coherent Catholics and "think with the Church" in matters of public policy, which are entirely noble instincts in themselves, the challenge for Opus Dei is to avoid becoming the "Popular Party at prayer," or the "Republicans at prayer," an outcome that would have perhaps disappointed no one more than Escrivá.

Chapter Thirteen

BLIND OBEDIENCE

*David Clark's professional title is "thought reform consul-
tant,"* but his specialty is getting people out of cults. He is a former member of a Bible-based/occult group in Southern California, a court-certified
cult expert, and has been an exit counselor for more than twenty years.
He was a contributing author to the book *Recovery from Cults: Help for
Victims of Psychological and Spiritual Abuse* (W. W. Norton, 1993). One
of his most high-profile cases was Tammy DiNicola, a numerary of Opus
Dei who lived at the Brimfield center of studies in Massachusetts when
her family solicited Clark's help. In 1990 the family asked DiNicola to
come home for a party to celebrate her graduation from Boston College,
and afterward they asked her to speak with Clark. DiNicola eventually
left Opus Dei and went on to found the Opus Dei Awareness Network,
an anti–Opus Dei group, with her mother, Dianne.

DiNicola is not the only Opus Dei member with whom Clark has
worked over the years. Asked how many contacts he's had, he said perhaps twenty families with members involved in Opus Dei have made inquiries, and maybe he's worked with twelve members. I spoke with him
in a May 2004 interview about his perceptions of Opus Dei.

"The organization has a public face of belonging to the Catholic
Church and acting as a defender of the faith," Clark said. "They take a
conservative theological line, and in fact this is a very serious part of what
they are. But their inner world is hard for outsiders to perceive. There's a
tremendous internal political effort to keep outside people from seeing

what's really going on, based on the feedback of former members, former leaders, and their documentation," he said.

Clark, who is not Catholic, said that he did not set out to target the group. "I wasn't out there beating the bushes," he said. "I heard about it through families that were deliberating about what to do, struggling with what they were seeing happen to their sons and daughters."

From 1972 to 1974, Clark belonged to what he called a "charismatic cult" that was an offshoot of the "Jesus movement" in the 1970s. He trained in a Reformed Episcopalian seminary in Philadelphia, so he has a theological background, and when he first began to hear about Opus Dei, he felt he recognized some of the same distortions and techniques that were familiar from his own experience. In the end, he said, based on his observations, he concluded that Opus Dei exhibits "more of the cult dynamic than the church dynamic."

In general, Clark said, the profile of the members he's met is that they are "sincere, and adapt well to what Opus Dei is presenting. They tend to be true believers, and quite submissive." He said their families are often initially supportive of Opus Dei membership, "because they know it's supported by the Catholic Church." But they begin to sense something is wrong, Clark said, when they find their family members can't come home for the holidays, have only limited time to spend on the phone, and numerary members report that they turn their money over to Opus Dei. Based on his conversations with members, Clark said he believes Opus Dei exerts "undue influence" on young people to join the group, "so that it is a battle of fully informed choice."

To what extent does Opus Dei resemble a cult?

"Well, it upholds the teaching and authority of the Roman Catholic Church," he said. "Normally a cult involves a turning away from tradition, while Opus Dei is in a sense very traditional. But the practice is different. One's freedom of conscience is compromised, and it can be very stifling. Often people can't speak freely, and the interactions are very controlled. It's like a science fiction movie, people become like symbiotic clones." In that sense, Clark said, members often learn more about Opus Dei after leaving than they did while they were inside.

Opus Dei, Clark said, is "one of the more sophisticated" groups he's encountered. "One group they go after is the cream of the crop, the professionals," he said. "It's very scary, almost militaristic." Moreover, Clark said, he's heard concerns expressed not just by families, but by voices from within the Catholic Church. They typically involve one or more of four points, he believes: that Opus Dei exercises "mind control" over members; that it disrupts families; that some people have great difficulty separating from the organization; and that it injures the Church.

Clark said these are not just dated impressions. In the past year, he said, he's had inquiries from parents. "It's very difficult to do anything," he said. "You have little or no access typically to these people. It's hard to find a time window when you can be with them."

Clark said he believes Opus Dei has to "move more into the mainstream," with a system of "checks and balances" to monitor its internal life and a new commitment to "transparency." He drew a parallel with the lessons learned from the sex abuse crisis in the United States. "It's about oversight and accountability," he said. "That's what needs to happen with Opus Dei."

Pluralism

By most accounts, one of the hallmarks of cultlike behavior is rigid uniformity and unthinking deference to authority. Members of Opus Dei insist that this hardly describes their internal reality, where they say great pluralism reigns. Aside from the examples given in chapter 12 on politics, such as in Peru where two numeraries belonging to opposing liberal and conservative parties lived together in the same center, perhaps a couple of other illustrative instances are in order here.

An Opus Dei–related foundation in Rome called ICEF (an Italian acronym for "Cultural, Educational, and Family Initiatives") organized a conference in Rome in 2003 on the controversial Mel Gibson film *The Passion of the Christ*. The vice director of the film, Jan Michelini, is the son of a well-known Opus Dei supernumerary in Italy, Alberto Michelini, a journalist and politician, and it was in part through his intervention that Pope John Paul II watched a copy of the film in December 2002. An Opus Dei numerary, papal spokesperson Joaquín Navarro-Valls, was among the leading supporters of the film inside the Vatican. Many observers, in Italy and elsewhere, assumed there was a uniform pro-*Passion* line within Opus

Dei. The fact that many Catholic conservatives around the world were supportive also fueled this impression.

Yet at the ICEF event, an Italian supernumerary, Alessandra Caneva, raised what many later referred to as a "rumpus" by delivering a sharp critique of *The Passion*. Caneva is a screenwriter and author (among other things, she was part of the writing team for the wildly successful Italian TV series *Don Matteo*, about a priest-detective), and Caneva criticized the Mel Gibson movie from an artistic as well as theological point of view.

"The dramatic arc is unbalanced in favor of crude suffering," she said of the movie. "The deep reasons for [the suffering], and the consequences of the sacrifice of Christ, are missing, and this is something that not only agnostics but many of us Christians have forgotten. These points are touched only through dialogue, and in the context of that ocean of blood in the film, words are a weak cinematic element. . . . The deep feeling is missing that alone can make me feel infinitely loved, despite my—despite our—sins." Other members of the audience, some belonging to Opus Dei and others not, leaped to the movie's defense, and a spirited debate ensued.

To take another example, in 2004 the Opus Dei–sponsored University of Santa Croce organized a conference on Poetry and Christianity, which included a roundtable on that cornerstone of Italian literature *I Promessi Sposi* by Alessandro Manzoni. Two contrasting views came from two Opus Dei numeraries—Cesare Cavalleri, editor of the Italian journal *Studi Cattolici*, and Professor François Livi of the University of the Sorbonne in Paris. For Cavalleri, Manzoni's novel was a preeminent expression of Catholic literature. For Livi, on the other hand, *I Promessi Sposi* reflects "the imprint of the culture of the Enlightenment, of a Christianity often reduced to popular devotion." In fact, Livi said, the book cannot be defined as "a Catholic novel," words that for an Italian audience are tantamount to heresy. Again, lively debate followed.

Such episodes, for many Opus Dei members, give the lie to the notion that there is anything inside Opus Dei that resembles science fiction, or that turns people into "symbiotic clones." In fact, they argue, one of the cardinal principles of Opus Dei is precisely its respect for the liberty of conscience, so that the kind of control over members that Clark describes would be virtually unthinkable.

A Catholic *Rashomon*

Listening to people talk about control inside Opus Dei, one almost has the sense of being in a Catholic version of *Rashomon,* the 1950 Akira Kurosawa film that depicts the same event seen from radically different perspectives. From the point of view of observers such as Clark and critical ex-members, Opus Dei is a dangerous, cultlike group that subjects members to strict oversight, isolates them from the outside world, and programs them to devote absolute obedience to the group and its leadership.

One ex-numerary, Spaniard Alberto Moncada, points to the Spanish-language Web site www.opuslibros.org, which has posted negative testimonies from scores of ex-members of Opus Dei, some of which are signed by name and some of which are not. "There is no ecclesiastical organization whose ex-members attack it so deeply," Moncada says. Indeed, Sharon Clasen, the ex-numerary introduced in chapter 8 who has since left the Catholic Church, said her biggest criticism of *The Da Vinci Code* is that it was, if anything, too soft on Opus Dei. "It failed to capture the essence of the mind control in this. . . . You didn't see all the manipulation," she said.

Others see a very different reality. As already noted, there are 85,491 members of Opus Dei in the world, not to mention 164,000 cooperators, meaning nonmembers who support Opus Dei through prayer and other forms of assistance, and an estimated 900,000 who attend Opus Dei evenings of recollection, get-togethers, and other events. Even by the most generous estimate, the number of embittered ex-members is dwarfed by these current members and supporters. Further, there are plenty of ex-members who are not angry with Opus Dei, who left for various personal reasons but who have remained on good terms. Three of them will be introduced in this chapter. While much of the negative commentary comes from ex-members, that does not mean that all ex-members have negative things to say.

Neither is it just members or cooperators who have positive impressions of Opus Dei. Members of the hierarchy of the Catholic Church often come away with favorable reactions.

Consider Archbishop Ndingi Mwana'a Nzeki of Nairobi, Kenya,

whom I interviewed in September 2004: "For me, they are doing wonderful work," Nzeki said. "They definitely penetrate the society. They are very faithful to the Church, to the Church's teaching. They receive the sacraments and they organize seminars and workshops for young people, for married couples, for all kinds of people. . . . Personally I support them, very much. They have been very, very straight with me. I don't agree with those who criticize them. I don't see them pushing at all, pushing for control," he said.

Or consider the testimony of Cardinal Cormac Murphy-O'Connor of Westminster, England, the same diocese where the late Cardinal Basil Hume issued guidelines for Opus Dei in 1981 out of concerns over secrecy and recruiting. Here's how Murphy-O'Connor describes his experiences: "I think they've taken on board the criticisms while maintaining their charism, and have become more open," he said during a November 2004 interview. "In a real way, rather than notional, they've been very cooperative in wanting to work with local bishops. There's no sense that they want to work in opposition. . . . The Catholics I've met in Opus Dei have clearly been very dedicated Catholics, very committed to the particular path that is described by Escrivá, which is the mission of laypeople in their professional fields."

The bottom line, according to Murphy-O'Connor, is that "I'm very content to have Opus Dei in the diocese." In January 2005, Murphy-O'Connor entrusted Saint Thomas More Parish to the clergy of Opus Dei, located near their Netherhall university residence in London.

For the outside observer attempting to be objective, Opus Dei thus presents a singularly challenging subject. On the one hand, critical voices who have had firsthand experience of the group can't be dismissed; on the other hand, the satisfaction of thousands of members, and official approval even from bishops who may not share Opus Dei's spirituality, cannot be set aside either. In this chapter, the most common complaints about excessive control over members will be examined, in an attempt to ascertain where the realities lie. Then we'll try to understand how people can perceive those realities so differently.

One note: Virtually all of the criticism concerning alleged "control" in Opus Dei focuses on the numeraries, that 20 percent of the membership who make promises of celibacy and live in Opus Dei centers. Even on a logistical basis, it would be difficult to exercise control over supernumeraries, who have jobs and families and live in their own homes. Much of what follows is therefore focused primarily on the numeraries.

Blind Obedience

Some young people who have considered a vocation in Opus Dei report that the controls to which they were expected to submit were not adequately explained in the beginning, so that the nature of life as a numerary only became clear once they had already made a commitment. John Schneider, for example, is a Notre Dame undergraduate who began attending events at the Windmoor Center his freshman year, and "whistled" shortly thereafter. "If they had told me what would be required of me, and laid out the events that would have followed, I would have said, 'Thanks, but no thanks,'" Schneider said. "Instead, over the course of months, they told me bit by bit, bit by bit. Personally, I'm okay if you were to allow someone to direct your life in that way. I have no problem with that. My fear is that they do not properly draw people's consent as they draw them into the organization." Schneider eventually decided not to continue as a numerary.

Critics point to various techniques of control: that members are required to confess only to priests of Opus Dei; that members are obliged to take spiritual direction from numeraries; that they are required to admit their failings before the group; that, for numeraries, their mail is screened; that access to books and TV for numeraries is controlled; that because numeraries give much of their salary to Opus Dei, they are not financially independent; that the practice of "fraternal correction" amounts to a form of social control; that numeraries are encouraged to take their cues from directors and the community rather than thinking for themselves; and that members who want to leave are hounded and threatened.

Confession
Critics have charged that Opus Dei obliges its members to confess only to Opus Dei priests, so that the priests can "keep track" of members. In fact, as a formal matter, there is no such requirement. No such stipula-

tion appears in the "Statutes" or any of the other governing documents of Opus Dei. Such a regulation would be in violation of the Code of Canon Law, which states in canon 991: "All Christ's faithful are free to confess their sins to lawfully approved confessors of their own choice, even to one of another rite."

On the other hand, as a routine matter it is generally expected that members will confess to Opus Dei priests, on the assumption that those priests are in a better position to know the specific spiritual commitments that members have undertaken, to ask more penetrating questions, and to give more pertinent spiritual advice. In this regard is a quotation from Escrivá in *Crónica*, the internal magazine for male members:

> *You can go to confession with any priest who has faculties from the local bishop. In this way I defend freedom, but with common sense. All my sons and daughters have freedom to go to confession with any priest approved by the local bishop, and they are not obliged to tell the directors of the Work what they have done. Does a person who does this sin? No! Does he have good spirit? No! He is on the way to listening to the voice of bad shepherds. . . . You will go to your brother priests as I do. And to them you will open wide your heart— rotten if it be rotten!—with sincerity, with a deep desire to cure yourself. If not, that rottenness would never be cured. If we were to go to a person who could only cure our wound superficially, it would be because we are cowards, because we wouldn't be good sheep, because we would go to hide the truth to our own detriment . . . seeking a secondhand doctor who cannot give us more than a few seconds of his time, who cannot use the surgical knife and cauterize the wound, we would also harm the Work. If you were to do this you'd have the wrong spirit, you'd be unhappy. You wouldn't sin because of this, but woe to you! You would have begun to err, to make a mistake.*

The Spanish term for "secondhand doctor" is *un medico de ocasión*, which has the sense of a doctor who is not familiar with the patient's medical history. Some have taken this as a derogatory reference to non–Opus Dei priests, usually relying on a less precise translation, as "second-rate."

What Escrivá is arguing, according to Opus Dei interpreters, is that while members can go to any priest they like, if they routinely seek out priests who don't know them and don't know Opus Dei, it's probably because they don't want to be pushed too deeply. They're looking for a superficial experience that will satisfy the requirement for the confession of sin but will not really demand conversion of heart—what the German Lutheran theologian Dietrich Bonhoeffer called "cheap grace." Saint Teresa of Ávila once gave similar advice to her nuns, suggesting that whenever possible they should confess to a Discalced Carmelite friar, since he would be in a better position to guide them. Opus Dei members by and large regard this as a matter of common sense, since the point of belonging to Opus Dei is precisely to receive its spiritual formation.

Spiritual Direction
Members receive spiritual guidance from directors of Opus Dei centers, who are lay numeraries, or from other members appointed by the director. Critics have charged that directors demand that members divulge personal information, even the details of their sexual lives. Because these exchanges are not covered by the "seal of the confessional," meaning the requirement of confidentiality of the sacrament of confession, some believe that directors share this information with other Opus Dei officials as a means of monitoring members. María Carmen del Tapia, the ex-numerary who wrote *Crossing the Threshold,* said that when she was a spiritual director, she had to write reports about the people to whom she gave direction, and she sometimes received orders on what to tell them.

Opus Dei officials make three points in response. First, they say, if directors are to give spiritual guidance, they have to "get personal," talking about various aspects of members' lives. The sexual dimension is one of those aspects, and, at least in theory, should be neither exaggerated nor ignored. Second, they say, Opus Dei follows the general law of the Church on spiritual direction, which stipulates that no one can be compelled to make a "manifestation of conscience." In other words, no one can be ordered to talk about something they don't want to discuss. Third, they insist that directors do not discuss with anyone else the matters that come up in spiritual direction, unless it's a confidential matter of getting advice.

People inside Opus Dei say it generally works this way in practice, though some report that members who avoid certain topics in spiritual direction are accused of having "bad spirit." On the charge that spiritual direction is used to force members to bare their souls, at least one critic is willing to give Opus Dei a pass. Pointing to the case of Robert Hanssen, the American supernumerary who sold FBI secrets to the Russians, critical ex-member Alberto Moncada said: "This guy was supposed to be going for spiritual direction once a week for all those years. How on earth did they not figure out what was going on?" (In fact, at an early stage Hanssen admitted his crime to an Opus Dei priest, Father Robert Bucciarelli, but insisted that he had stopped and had not betrayed anything damaging. Bucciarelli counseled him to donate any money received to the poor, but not to turn himself in for the sake of his family.)

In addition, members say, attempts to use spiritual direction to "control" people probably wouldn't work in practice. Numeraries go to one another for spiritual direction, but the same two numeraries do not "switch hats" and counsel each other. Thus the network of who's talking to whom in a given center, or a given area, is fairly haphazard. "How this system could result in some uniform control is, simply from a logistical point of view, hard to imagine," an American numerary said.

Some have attacked the practice of spiritual direction on two other grounds: first that it is given by a layperson who may lack training; and second, that these directors are sometimes young and lack life experience.

On the first count, Opus Dei insists that numeraries are just as "trained" in spiritual matters as priests, since priests and numeraries, men and women, receive the same theological formation in Opus Dei. There's no reason a priori to assume that a layperson is any less qualified to give spiritual direction. In fact, one could make the argument, and people inside Opus Dei do, that to assume a priest is better suited for the job simply because he's a priest is a clericalist mentality, and that a layperson may be better able to appreciate the spiritual struggles another layperson experiences.

On the charge of youth and inexperience, some inside Opus Dei plead "guilty," especially in earlier periods of the group's history when it was not uncommon for a director to be in his early twenties. In some cases, members admit, youthful zeal outstripped a director's capacity to appreciate the human complexity of a given situation. One numerary, for example, spoke about a situation that came up when he was the director of a center in Spain. Another numerary fell in love with a woman, or at least thought he had. The director was only twenty-four when he found himself wrestling with this situation, and sometimes blames himself for the fact that his fellow numerary ended up leaving. Today, Opus Dei members say, it's less common for directors to be quite so young. Moreover, officials say they can always seek out help, with the member's permission, if they feel that they are in over their heads.

The Emendatio

The *emendatio* takes place in the weekly "circle," a roughly forty-five-minute meeting devoted to practical talks on the spiritual life, a commentary on a gospel passage, and a personal examination of conscience. The circle ends by praying the Preces, the only prayer specific to Opus Dei. The idea of the *emendatio* is that within the circle, a member admits some fault in living the "spirit of the Work," such as neglecting to say some prayers or mortifications, or a missed opportunity to evangelize. The stipulation is that this must be a "fault," not a "sin," which would be a more serious matter to discuss in confession. The formula for the *emendatio* is for the member to kneel down and say, "In the presence of God Our Lord I accuse myself of . . ." Similar practices used to be common in religious orders, though in the years since the Second Vatican Council they have largely been abandoned.

The *emendatio* is voluntary, members say, and not everyone does it every week. Some people may go years without doing one. Further, if a member is planning to do it, the idea is supposed to be discussed with the director first to make sure that it's appropriate for a group setting. The point, Opus Dei spokespersons say, is not for members to debase themselves, but to encourage a spirit of penitence in others as well as to reassure others that everybody struggles with the same problems. It also reinforces the sense that the Church is one body, in which one member's faults affect others, so that a member has a chance to ask pardon of the others. Both laity and priests perform the *emendatio*.

Screening Mail

It is often alleged that the mail of numeraries is screened by directors, in order to cut them off from anything that might challenge or weaken their commitment. Sharon Clasen was a supernumerary and then numerary from 1981 to 1987, living at the Bayridge center and then the Brimfield center, both in the Boston area. She said that when she lived at Brimfield, she received her mail pre-opened in a slot at the end of a hallway. She also said that she believes some of her mail never reached her, because she had been receiving letters regularly from an old boyfriend until she arrived at the center. Her outgoing mail had to be read by the director.

No one from Opus Dei denies that in the past mail was screened, as was common practice in religious orders, seminaries, boarding schools, and other institutions in the Catholic Church. In theory, they say, the point was not to exercise "control," but to be in a position to alert members if there was anything problematic with respect to their spiritual commitments. Moreover, it was a sign of the person's total giving of self, that they held nothing back from their superiors or from God. No doubt the practice was open to abuse, which is why religious communities by and large abandoned it, and Opus Dei spokespersons say they have as well.

Marc Carroggio, a spokesperson for Opus Dei in Rome, said he found "wholly implausible" Clasen's hypothesis that some letters from an old boyfriend were withheld from her.

Peter Bancroft, an American numerary, said that technological change would make screening impractical these days anyway. "Since the advent of e-mail and cheap long-distance telephone rates ten to twelve years ago, I don't write or receive many letters, nor do any of the young numeraries at the centers I've been director at," he said. "Once or twice someone has shown me a letter he has written, but I don't recall anyone ever showing me a letter he has received. I have heard that directors used to open mail—but did not usually bother to read it—just as a way of helping people understand that their life should be an open book. My understanding is that this practice was discontinued about fifteen years ago. Opening mail is really a nonissue."

Books, TV, and Movies

Another frequently voiced charge is that numeraries have to ask permission before reading books or watching TV programs. Clasen said that when she was a supernumerary at Boston College, she was asked to submit the required reading lists for her courses to her director to be checked. At Brimfield, she said, a roommate was not allowed to read some of the material on the required list for her honors program, and thus prayed to the Holy Spirit for "infused knowledge." Father Álvaro de Silva, a Spaniard who worked for Opus Dei in the United States for thirty-five years before leaving to become a priest of the Boston archdiocese in 1999, said that when he was in Opus Dei, he was discouraged from reading the work of Sulpician Father Raymond Brown, who served on the Pontifical Biblical Commission and was widely considered the leading Catholic Bible scholar in the United States until his death in 1998.

Opus Dei spokespersons reply that no one is "prohibited" from reading certain titles or authors. If members are in doubt about whether a particular book is worthy reading material, spokespersons say, they are encouraged to discuss the matter with their director or someone else knowledgeable in that subject.

Father Guillaume Derville, spiritual director of Opus Dei, said that Opus Dei has a "database" containing thousands of reactions to books by members over the years, which can be consulted when people want guidance on particular titles. "There are books that without even dealing with religious themes are impregnated with an anti-Christian ideology," Derville said. "Others reflect a deep consistency with the teachings of the gospel, others are immoral, others could be of great help for all types of readers, and so on." This database is not, Derville said, an "official list," and the judgments expressed in it are "by definition perfectible." Derville stressed that it is not an "index of forbidden books." The database also contains more formal reviews, along with reactions from professors and friends.

It is not obligatory to consult the database prior to reading something, Derville said, nor is anyone required to accept the judgments expressed in it. "The choice always falls to the individual," he said.

As time goes by, Derville said, this database could be made public in the form of a Web site. First, he said, it would need the attention of a professional editorial staff to make sure the judgments are balanced and reflect uniform criteria, that "simplifications and partisan stances" have been weeded out, and that the selection of themes is adequate. All that, he said, will require "people, time, and labor."

To be sure, judgments about what's appropriate reading matter inside Opus Dei may differ from sectors of opinion elsewhere. For example, David Gallagher, an official of Opus Dei in the United States, said that while nobody "controls" the reading material of members, if someone sees another member reading something they regard as problematic, they might approach that person. I asked Gallagher if, for example, reading the novels of John Updike might trigger such an intervention, and he said yes. The point is not that Updike is prohibited inside Opus Dei, and in fact I know members who like his books; the point is rather that this is an example of the way that "red flags" might go up inside Opus Dei a bit more quickly than in other environments.

Or, to take another example, the librarian at Strathmore University in Nairobi, Kenya, a supernumerary named Fidelis Katonga, told me that because he's responsible for the moral and spiritual development of students as well as their academic development, part of his job is to "keep these young minds away from harmful materials." Katonga said that one will not find on the open shelves of his library works by Marx, Engels, or Bertrand Russell. If students have a special need for these works, they have to submit a request, and the books will be brought out from the back so they can be consulted under guidance. The idea is that students should not be "misled."

"I have a duty of ensuring that these destructive publications don't spoil young minds," Katonga said.

Opus Dei members who publish books on subjects of faith or morals are also encouraged to request an expert opinion from a theologian or ethicist inside Opus Dei to be sure that there's nothing in the book contrary to Church teaching. Where Church law already requires a *nihil obstat,* meaning a formal declaration that there is nothing contrary to Church teaching in a publication, Opus Dei members are expected to go to the local diocesan bishop like everyone else. But if Church law does not require it, Opus Dei members are generally expected to ask for it from someone in Opus Dei, although spokespersons insist it's up to the individual what to do with the feedback received. Critics often see this as another instrument of control, though Opus Dei members say they see it as a way of flagging potential problem areas in their work so they can think about them.

On the subject of TV, the operating principle is much the same. Numeraries are not prohibited from watching television, and in fact every Opus Dei center I visited had a TV room. When I was in Barcelona, for example, on Saturday everyone gathered to watch an important soccer match. When I visited Netherhall, the Opus Dei university residence in London, several numeraries were making plans to watch the England and Australia rugby match on TV that afternoon. Nobody was asking anyone's permission. On the other hand, one suspects that if a numerary were sitting in an Opus Dei common room watching *Survivor,* and the motive wasn't a cultural anthropology project at the local university, someone would contemplate making a fraternal correction. Whether that amounts to "control" will depend, first, on what judgment one makes about the content of the program; and second, what one thinks the expectations should be of someone who is committed to the spiritual path marked out by Opus Dei.

Movies are a somewhat different story. The custom within Opus Dei from the beginning is that numeraries normally don't go to public entertainment such as movies and sporting events, unless there's some special logic in a given case. Gabriela Eisenring, a Swiss numerary who works for the government of the women's branch in Rome, said that this is for motives of "austerity, self-giving to God, and the giving over of one's time." Those numeraries whose work requires them to attend these events, she said, do so without any problem. Within centers, numeraries sometimes have a "movie night" together with a film picked out by the director.

Money

As described in chapter 1, numeraries are expected to give much of what they earn in their professional employment to support the center in which they live, and to underwrite the various corporate works of Opus Dei such as the ELIS center in Rome for young workers, or the Condoray center in Peru that teaches literary and trade skills to women. Opus Dei says this is how it works in a family, where members pool their resources to meet the family budget, even though in practice numeraries may retain control of a good chunk of their earnings in order to pay off personal expenses, taxes, and so on. Supernumeraries are encouraged to be as generous as possible; Russell Shaw, the American Catholic writer, gives two hundred dollars a month.

María Ángeles Burguera, a Spanish numerary who works as a journalist, described how it works. "I have my own budget," she said. "I study what I need this month. Maybe I need to have some sweaters and trousers, and I have to think about what I need to eat every day. Then I decide, maybe I'll give this much. I take a part for me, and I give the rest to the center." Burguera said she discusses her budget with the director of the center, to be sure that the needs of the center are covered. Her paycheck, she said, is automatically deposited in her bank account, and she goes to an ATM machine to withdraw the money that she then gives to the director. She said she also leaves some money in her account in order to pay off loans from college, and in case medical expenses arise. In any given month, she said, she probably turns over half her paycheck to her center, though she said sometimes it will be more and sometimes less.

An American numerary outlined how he apportioned his earnings in a year in which his salary was $40,000.

$13,000: Taxes, Social Security, retirement fund

$12,000: Basic food and shelter

$2,000: Costs of the annual course (three weeks) and retreat (one week)

$2,000: Car expenses

$4,000: Clothes, medical, travel, taxis, eating out, etc.

$7,000: Contributions to various apostolic works of Opus Dei

"Basic food and shelter" includes the costs of maintaining the center in which this numerary lives, which sometimes means paying off a mortgage. The car is probably a common car for the center, so that everyone chips in for gas, maintenance, and making payments. On the other hand, whether this person was a numerary of Opus Dei or not, he'd have to devote a roughly similar portion of income to housing and transportation. The specific "Opus Dei" element of his budget is for the annual course and retreat, and the contributions to apostolic works. That amount, $9,000, comes to 22.5 percent of his earnings.

Since numeraries do not generally build savings plans, some have suggested that this places them in a position of financial dependence and therefore discourages thoughts of leaving. In this regard Opus Dei is not unique; the same thing happens within religious orders, where members who leave often have to "start over" in terms of a career and planning for retirement. Further, because numeraries are expected to finish schooling and acquire professional employment, with all the requisite training and credentials in their line of work, they are arguably in a stronger position to support themselves than members of religious orders who have no outside experience, training, or contacts. Even numerary assistants typically study at centers for hospitality or cooking schools and receive some sort of certificate or professional credential.

According to Pablo Elton, chief financial officer for Opus Dei, numeraries have their own bank accounts and, in countries where credit cards are in common use, their own credit cards. Elton said the lone stipulation is that numeraries are encouraged to use their cards "with sobriety." In addition, numeraries are not obligated, as has sometimes been reported, to sign over their wills to Opus Dei, according to Elton. They are free to leave their money to whomever they wish, Elton said, and their wishes are respected. In point of fact, many members leave money to schools, residences, and other activities connected to Opus Dei—just as many Americans, Elton noted, leave money to the university they attended or to other causes dear to them.

Fraternal Correction

If a member of Opus Dei sees another member failing to live the "spirit of the Work" in a way that goes beyond the normal struggles, he or she may offer what's known as a "fraternal correction." According to Matthew Collins, a former supernumerary and now cooperator, the guiding principles are:

- The perceived fault in the other person is a fault or failing in the spirit of the Work
- The person receiving the correction doesn't get hit with the same thing over and over and over again

- If the directors of the Work are aware of some fact that makes it inopportune to make the correction, it isn't made
- A spirit of fraternal charity is the motivation for the correction
- The person receiving the correction is aware that the matter in question isn't simply the opinion of another member but is, in fact, an issue of the spirit of the Work

While critics charge that fraternal correction is another tool for keeping members in line, Opus Dei officials say the practice is based on the example of Jesus, who said in Matthew 18:15, "If your brother sins, go and tell him his fault between you and him alone. If he listens to you, you have won over your brother."

In theory, the person who observes a fault first prays about the issue, and for the person. He or she then goes to that person's director and confidentially mentions it. If the director agrees the correction should be made, permission is given. The person making the correction then confidentially tells the other person. The person receiving the correction is supposed to say "thank you" and receive it cheerfully. When the correction has been made, the person goes to the oratory to pray for the other, and then tells the director.

Carl Schmidt, a longtime American numerary who lives at the center on Wyoming Avenue in Washington, D.C., offers an example. He said he once overheard members in his house grousing about the liberal leanings of the *New York Times,* and made a fraternal correction. "I know it's got its biases, but the *New York Times* is one of the greatest newspapers in the world, and members of Opus Dei should be working in the *New York Times,*" he said. "If you keep talking that way, you're going to discourage anybody from getting a job there. You're acting as if he would be an enemy, and in fact he's your brother. You won't get brothers doing it with that kind of negativity."

Dependence on Directors

"Tim Coralto" is a pseudonym that journalist Jason Fargone of *Philadelphia* magazine invented for a young Philadelphia man, and devout Catholic, who's involved in what's known as the Journey into Manhood movement. In essence, it's a program for gay men to try to control their sexuality, not denying it but not acting on it, either. What caught my eye about Tim's story is that he is also a former numerary of Opus Dei. Through Fargone, I got in touch with him, and like Fargone, I agreed to protect his identity.

Tim, who is Hispanic, grew up in a Catholic family and met Opus Dei through his uncle, who was a numerary for eighteen years but has since left. He was a sophomore in high school when he was invited to his first Opus Dei event for boys. "I enjoyed connecting with a bunch of boys my age, getting some spiritual talks but also having fun doing skits, watching a movie, listening to a college-age numerary play 'Bye, Bye, Miss American Pie' on the guitar. I was very impressed," he said.

Later, as a senior, he began attending doctrinal formation courses. "Growing up in what I would call a modern, liberal parish, I felt my faith experience lacked substance and I was dying for something more meaningful, so I ate up what Opus Dei was teaching me," he said. Eventually he was asked by an older numerary to consider whether or not he had a vocation to Opus Dei. He prayed in front of the tabernacle, and the answer seemed to be a clear "yes."

Tim whistled in 1986. "My first two years in Opus Dei were like a honeymoon. I felt so close to God and to my brother numeraries. I remember pinching myself to make sure it was real, I couldn't believe life could be so good," he said. Then, he said, something began to change. The pressures of completing his professional training while also "doing apostolate," meaning working with youths and being available to the needs of his Opus Dei family, were overwhelming. He had a breakdown. As part of that experience, his homosexual feelings "returned with a vengeance," he said. Opus Dei put him in touch with a Catholic therapist, and eventually Tim reached the conclusion that it would be best if he left. "I believe the feeling was mutual," he said. In 1990 he moved back into his father's house, and on March 19, 1991, when he didn't renew his contract with Opus Dei, his exit was official.

What is Tim's evaluation of the experience today?

"I have mixed feelings . . . a love/hate thing," he said. "Overall my experience was positive, but I think there were some really unhealthy things, too. If I had to distill it down to the essentials, I'd say the sanctification of work and family life, the study of the teachings and traditions of the Church, and the universal call to holiness are the best parts of

Opus Dei. The asceticism in their spirituality, however, I think is dangerous. I think it is too negative and encourages one to be too hard on himself. The lifestyle is too controlled and rigid. I stopped thinking for myself
and left it up to my directors because I couldn't trust my intuition."

Tim, it should be stressed, is not angry with Opus Dei. He is close
to his aunt, a faithful supernumerary. In fact, before agreeing to speak
with me for this book, he spoke to the older numerary who had first
encouraged him to "whistle" to make sure he would not be injuring Opus
Dei.

Dennis Dubro, an American who was a numerary from 1973 to
1987, describes an incident from his time helping to run an Opus
Dei university residence named Warrane College in Sydney, Australia,
which illustrates Tim's point about the emphasis put on the authority
of directors:

> Some of the students in the dormitory were opening the fire doors
> and setting off the alarms. It was thought they were sneaking girls
> in, so the directors locked all the fire escapes of our eight-story 200-
> bed dormitory. We were told it was better for all of us to burn in this
> life than for a few to burn in Hell. One director said if there was a
> fire his Guardian Angel would wake him and he would go out the
> front door and run around the dormitory unlocking the fire doors
> from the outside. After a few days, the locked doors were reported to
> the university. The university said this was an unacceptable policy
> and told us to unlock the fire escapes. This was done, and we made
> a big public statement about how thankful we were that the univer-
> sity had noticed this oversight and assisted us in providing a safe en-
> vironment for our students. Then our director locked the doors
> again. A professor who was a member of Opus Dei and who had
> agreed to serve on our Board of Directors didn't believe the doors
> were unlocked. He decided to see for himself. Within a day, the uni-
> versity sent out another directive that the fire doors were to be un-
> locked and to remain unlocked permanently, but we heard
> immediately from the regional directors of Opus Dei that this mem-
> ber had no authority or business doubting the word of a director. We
> were told our directors were accountable to God alone for their ac-

tions, and members are supposed to choose to spend their time do-
ing apostolic work rather than checking the word of our directors.

Dubro tells the story to illustrate both the occasional eccentricity of
the climate inside Opus Dei as well as the emphasis on not challenging
directors, though it's worth noting that it was another member of Opus
Dei who decided the director was wrong and reported him to the university authorities.

Other members insist there simply is no such climate of blind obedience. Lucia Calvo, for example, is principal of the Besana School for girls
in Madrid's Pueblo Nuevo neighborhood, and draws its students largely
from recent low-income immigrant populations. She's been in the job for
three years. Prior to that, Calvo worked at an Opus Dei school in
Australia. In Madrid, she lives in a women's center with ten other numeraries, a couple of whom work for Opus Dei; several teach in universities,
and one works for a Spanish NGO. Another is a seventy-something professional artist. The center is approximately twenty minutes away from
her school by subway. She told me in a May 2004 interview that her life
is anything but "controlled," and that her director does not give her orders
about how to run her school.

"Thinking for myself is what I do every day, every minute of every
day, in this job," she said. "Nobody from Opus Dei looks over my
shoulder to tell me what to do. I have total freedom, inside the center
where I live, and outside." Calvo oversees a staff of 32 teachers at Besana,
and a student body of 400 girls ages eleven through sixteen. Calvo
conceded that there is an emphasis within Opus Dei on internal unity,
but stressed that in her view this is "not uniformity, but unity." If anything,
she said, her lifestyle as a numerary, without family commitments of her
own, makes her more "free" in her job than a married woman with a
husband and kids would be. "Sometimes I think of some of the teachers
here after school, they go to their house and they take care of their kids,
and they find that's very hard," she said. "In that sense, I have much more
liberty."

Members note that one thing that distinguishes Calvo's experience from those of "Tim" or Dubro is age. The level of oversight exercised

for young people in their late teens and early twenties is doubtless a bit more extensive, they say, than for someone like Calvo, who's in her forties.

Leaving Opus Dei

There are no reliable estimates of the number of ex-numeraries of Opus Dei, largely because Opus Dei officials say they do not track their "retention rate." From anecdotal accounts, however, it seems that perhaps 20 to 30 percent of people who "whistle" as members do not remain in Opus Dei. That percentage drops off after the "oblation," meaning formal incorporation into Opus Dei, and even more so after the "fidelity," meaning the permanent commitment six and a half years after whistling. One numerary who has served as director of three different centers over fourteen years, working with sixty-two numeraries over that span of time from ages eighteen to eighty-five, said eight of those numeraries left, roughly 13 percent. Whatever the global percentage, there is a substantial body of former members, numbering in the thousands, and they sometimes offer diverse accounts of their experiences of leaving Opus Dei.

Joseph I. B. Gonzales, a Filipino who whistled as a numerary in 1979, and who left six months before his "fidelity" in 1985, reports that enormous pressure is placed upon numeraries to not abandon their vocation, including warnings that leaving Opus Dei is a grave offense against God. "When I left, the priest told me to confess to mortal sin, and from what I understand, the same ludicrous imposition has been inflicted upon other former numeraries," he said. Gonzales today teaches management courses at the Ateneo Graduate School of Business in Rockwell Center, Makati City, Philippines, and works as a communications and research consultant.

Gonzales said the demand to confess was just the beginning of the pressures exerted on members whose commitment starts to waver. "Besides the threat of eternal perdition and the pernicious emotional blackmail engendered by the charge of betrayal of Jesus Christ, there are other forms of psychological pressure, in the form, perhaps, of peer pressure or cognitive dissonance arising from a real upending of the intensely cultivated Opus Dei Weltanschauung. Having invested many years of wholehearted service to the organization, it becomes very difficult for the numerary to acknowledge the folly of this investment, cut his losses, and pull out, to use a stock market analogy. It means acknowledging a terrible mistake—perhaps the most difficult psychological step—and spending many, many years afterward correcting the negative and sometimes traumatic consequences of the mistake," he said.

Alleged harassment has included phone calls, personal visits at home and at work, and letters. Moncada said that after he left Opus Dei in the mid-1960s, a member of Opus Dei approached his father, who was a supernumerary, and tried to convince him to disinherit Moncada (the father refused). At another point, Moncada said, a bank had asked him to do some sociological research, but at the last moment the project fell through, and a bank official told him it was due to the intervention of someone from Opus Dei. In both cases, Moncada conceded that he had no indication these individuals were acting on instructions from anyone in Opus Dei. Nevertheless, Moncada said that when someone left, at least in his generation, Opus Dei tried to organize that person's "civil death."

In September 1983, German ex-numerary Klaus Steigleder published *Opus Dei: An Inside View*. At age fourteen, Steigleder became part of a theater group at a Cologne youth club, without knowing it was Opus-related, and eventually "whistled." Then, when he exited Opus Dei at the age of nineteen, he reported that leaving is difficult for members because "their spirits are broken, and they have lost all touch with everyday life." Steigleder said it took him two and a half years to actually leave, even after he had made an initial decision to do so. "The difficulties were not of an institutional sort," he said, "but were due to tremendous moral pressure. For members who have interiorized the doctrine, mentality, and spirit of Opus Dei, it's extremely difficult to liberate yourself from it, and be able to see it and examine it in an objective manner."

Opus Dei spokespersons reply that in one sense, leaving Opus Dei is the simplest thing in the world. Prior to the stage of the "fidelity," or the lifetime commitment, all one has to do is not renew the contract on March 19, and one is automatically no longer in Opus Dei. It's therefore one of the few organizations that one can leave by doing nothing. After the fidelity stage, a member who wishes to leave is supposed to write a letter expressing his or her intentions. Some do, though others simply pick up and go. In either case, as will be documented below, at least some ex-members remain on good terms with Opus Dei.

Christopher Howse, who today edits the opinion page of London's *Daily Telegraph,* is an ex-numerary who reports that he was not traumatized by the process of leaving, which he elected to do in 1988 after having joined Opus Dei as a university student in the 1970s. Today he lives in an apartment near the residence of the archbishop of Westminster and is a widely respected journalist and spiritual writer. He said that he decided to leave Opus Dei because the apostolic tasks he was expected to perform weren't a good fit for his personality. "I found I was not suited to the way of life of a numerary in Opus Dei. They have to take on a teaching role, and almost a pastoral role—helping other people with their prayer life. I was not really cut out for it," he said.

No one from Opus Dei pressured him to stay, Howse said. He has gone on to defend the group in public debate in Britain; in January 2005, for example, around the time of the appointment of supernumerary Ruth Kelly as the country's education minister, he wrote: "I have never since met a group who are kinder, more patient or less motivated by personal ambition."

Elizabeth Falk Sather is a Chicago-area numerary who left Opus Dei in early 1983 after roughly five years. "I went on the Opus Dei Awareness Network Web site," she said, reading accounts by former members such as Moncada about what happened when they left. "I was shocked. I didn't experience any coercion, anyone locking doors on me. My director said, 'This has to be your free choice.' I didn't feel hounded. They saw I was being open and honest."

Virtually everyone agrees that for supernumeraries, exiting Opus Dei poses less risk of turbulence. Matthew Collins of Baltimore was an Opus Dei supernumerary for twenty-six years before leaving in 2003 and becoming a cooperator. Here's how he described his experience:

> While many people in the Work do not understand my decision, and perhaps even believe I "lost my vocation," I have been treated with the utmost charity and respect. Not a single person in the Work has in any way made me feel unwelcome. I was very open with the directors when I was considering leaving the Work, and my freedom

*was always respected. It was a very difficult decision for me, and at
times I would have almost welcomed pressure from them to stay in.
They never did so. On the contrary, the consistent message I received
from them was that it was their opinion that I had a vocation to the
Work, but that it was completely my decision, and that if I chose to
leave the Work, I would continue to be welcome at Opus Dei activities. Further, the advice I received was that if I did leave, I should
embrace my new path, that God would take care of me, and that I
should never look back and think I had made a mistake.*

Differing Accounts

How is one to reconcile such differing accounts?

For one thing, there is the basic psychological fact that some people
have a greater tolerance for structure than others. What one person experiences as a rigid, stifling environment, others will experience as orderly
and liberating. One could go through a similar exercise comparing the testimonies of former members of the armed services, or people who have
worked in corporate environments.

Second, since very little inside Opus Dei is spelled out in terms of
fixed procedures, a great deal depends upon the personality of a given director or priest. It may well be that both Gonzales and Falk Sather are accurately describing their own experiences, and both are naturally tempted
to think that their own experience is normative, whereas in fact both reflect the style of the directors each knew—one heavy-handed and authoritarian, the other understanding and flexible.

Third, there has been change over time, and Opus Dei has learned
from experience to be careful of anything that could seem like threats or
intimidation. Members say they regard the vocation to Opus Dei as a serious commitment before God, and hence they want to encourage both
those thinking of making that commitment, and those thinking of abandoning it, to think seriously. Yet today they seem better able to communicate that in the end, this must be a free choice.

Fourth, several of the ex-members who complain about the control
exercised over numeraries tend to be young men and women who left
Opus Dei after a short time, such as Schneider, Steigleder, and "Tim,"
meaning that they experienced the most intensive early period of training

and formation, but not much afterward. Every numerary spends two years in a center of studies, which can be a fairly rigorous experience, a bit like "boot camp" in the army. Numeraries are expected to continue their professions or university studies while also intensifying their spiritual formation, taking theology and philosophy courses and studying the "spirit of the Work." It's no surprise that many of the most critical ex-members left Opus Dei during or shortly after this period.

Older members say that the degree of personal freedom one enjoys tends to expand once one has gotten through the first few years, much like veteran soldiers enjoy greater autonomy than new recruits. Additionally, most observers of Opus Dei say the situation has changed considerably with time, and the degree of oversight and regulation that would have been considered appropriate twenty years ago, or sixty years ago, today would no longer be tolerated. One Opus Dei member said that the presence of older members in centers today means that there's a greater degree of maturity, life experience, flexibility, and a capacity to not overdramatize things that aren't terribly essential.

At the same time, most numeraries make no bones about the fact that theirs is a challenging life. They are expected to hold full-time jobs, lead various apostolic activities such as youth groups and formation programs for supernumeraries, and pass a considerable amount of time in social settings with the other numeraries who live in their centers. Members often struggle to balance the demands of work or school with their commitments to Opus Dei activities. There's not much "down time," and, as with any communal living situation, privacy is limited. The key question appears to be, how does one react? Satisfied members say they find this life enriching, while those for whom it doesn't "take" often say they found it rigid, an unacceptable surrender of their personal independence. Both the critics and the supporters may be describing the same reality, but seen from two different perspectives.

Families

A related charge regarding control in Opus Dei is that the organization alienates members from their families. In the late 1970s, a concerned English mother, whose son had become an Opus Dei numerary at age eighteen, began writing a series of letters to various Church officials, including Cardinal Basil Hume of Westminster. The letters have a pleading quality, focused on what she saw as her growing estrangement from her son. On August 24, 1978, the mother wrote a priest who had been designated by Hume to respond:

This should be prefaced by saying that had we been more vigilant as parents, then these problems may not have arisen. Without any information given to us as parents, we believe that [our son] was, by doctrinal teaching and spiritual direction, prepared for a decision at the age of about 17 and one-half years, so that by the age of 18 he was legally of age to assert his right. There was no contact with us as parents about this decision before or since on the part of Opus Dei. We are anxious, naturally, as parents, that he should develop fully in every way, according to his diverse gifts. . . . [Our son] is only home for brief spells, and we have been reluctant to mention study, even though it is we who finance it and we who have to sign the grant form as being responsible. . . . Under normal circumstances we would have, and should have, discussed with [him] at the end of term whether he should change to physics (where possibly he has greater facility). Unfortunately we do not really have access to him. Indirectly, intentionally or not, Opus Dei seems to have estranged him, or caused a withdrawal, from parents and school friends, and there is no contact with a parish or other groups in the Church. . . . Our three children are not brilliant, they are intelligent with quite wide interests. They have had, I suppose, a secure, structured setting in which to progress and therefore according to ability have done well. However, I do feel they need the support which now we are unable to give. Since we were both students we could give him the benefit of our experience, discussing with him how he should approach next year etc. It is not that we want to hinder any development toward a vocation, but we want to be sure that at this stage all avenues remain open to him. . . . I feel that as a Christian today one should be living fully in the role in which we are set, giving generously in our work, to friends and family inside and outside the Church, sustained and enriched by the sacraments and guided by the example of Our Lord in the gospels. (I have yet to see him read any other devotional book but The Way *by the founder of Opus Dei.) I am, therefore, deeply concerned at the separation, withdrawal, and narrowing that has taken place in his life. More than ever today the Church seems to be working to strengthen family units and to emphasize the role of parents, and this is my main criticism of Opus Dei. Is it to safeguard vocations? Whatever it is, I feel that [our son] is being denied his rights as the eldest child in his family, and we are unable to fulfill our duty toward him as parents. I must stress again, however, that we should not have allowed our sons to spend so much time at an Opus Dei center, even though it was a Church organization, before they were of an age to assess the situation maturely. We can only continue to pray about this situation.*

Similar letters appear in the archives of bishops' offices in various parts of the world. Given that Catholicism regards the family as a kind of "domestic church," this is a serious matter.

American Catholic J. J. M. Garvey, who has two daughters who are Opus Dei numeraries, was moved by his experience to write a fifty-eight-page pamphlet called *A Parent's Guide to Opus Dei* in 1989, and to found a group called Our Lady and Saint Joseph in Search of the Lost Child, an Ad Hoc Alliance to Defend the Fourth Commandment. Garvey, a staunchly orthodox Catholic, argued that Opus Dei reflects the pathology of a "sect" as described in a 1986 Vatican document on the subject, beginning with the way that young people "suddenly leave home to secretly affiliate with Opus Dei." Garvey writes of young people who join Opus Dei: "Their behavior becomes artificial and rigid, and their answers seem calculated to maintain a certain distance with their parents and close relatives. Normal communication with the family is significantly reduced. Even more, parents cannot receive credible information from representatives of the Work about these changes in personality and behavior." Today the Garveys live in Fredericksburg, Virginia. Their two daughters are still numeraries, one living in Washington, D.C., and the other in Chicago. Though the Garveys do not like to talk about their experiences, friends say they feel as if they have "lost" their children to Opus Dei.

Yet bishops who have heard this sort of complaint from parents also understand that throughout Church history, young men and women who have given themselves in vocations to God, in religious orders, in the diocesan priesthood, and in various lay movements and apostolates, have often faced resistance from their families. Trying to sort out legitimate concerns from overreactions, therefore, has been perhaps the most vexing challenge facing Church authorities.

Here is how the Opus Dei Awareness Network describes the approach to families within Opus Dei: "Numeraries are typically not allowed to go home for Christmas, attend family weddings or even tend to sick family members. They are told 'Opus Dei is your family,' and are made to feel guilty about spending time with their blood families because it takes away from your 'Work of God.' Every effort is made to transfer the feelings they have for their own families to Opus Dei; thus, pictures of family members are not allowed in their rooms, but there are plenty of pictures of the Founder, the Prelate, even the Founder's sister and parents. The end result is that the numeraries' emotion for their families is replaced with controlled emotion for Opus Dei."

This description doesn't match the reality as it's described by Opus Dei members. For example, when I met Beatriz Comella Gutiérrez and María Ángeles Burguera, numeraries in Madrid, both proudly produced photos of their families, and not in response to questioning but as a spontaneous gesture during conversation about their lives.

Burguera, who has nine bothers and sisters, pointed in the picture to two brothers who are priests, one a Salesian and the other a Franciscan currently working in Ecuador. She also pointed to one brother, a doctor, and another who is a manager of a company, smiling and saying, "Don't think we're all so religious . . . they don't go to Mass." Her mother is an Opus Dei supernumerary, while her father sometimes has had his doubts; as Burguera put it delicately, "They had conversations." Today, however, she said her father has come around, largely through watching the positive experiences of her older brother, who is a numerary, and her own. Burguera said that she sees her family often, though perhaps not as often as she would like. She goes home for major family events, and is in constant contact with family members over the phone and through e-mail. Comella Gutiérrez said the same thing is true in her case.

On the subject of pictures of family members, Carlo Cavazzoli, an

Argentinian numerary who serves on the General Council in Rome, said that in the common rooms of centers of Opus Dei there is an effort to keep things a bit generic, so that guests don't feel like they're in someone else's private space. In the rooms of numeraries, however, Cavazzoli said there's no prohibition on pictures of family members, and many display them.

David and Linda Pliske, parents of numerary assistant Bernie, introduced in chapter 9, say they have not lost contact with Bernie since she moved into the Shellbourne Conference Center in Valparaiso, Indiana.

"At the beginning, one of my anxieties was to realize that once she started being about Opus Dei, we might not see her very much," David Pliske said. "We love her dearly, and would miss her. I remember thinking, 'What do you mean Opus Dei is your family? We're your family.' At the same time, I know that these kids don't belong to us, they're God's, and we need to encourage them spiritually." After all, Pliske said, "When you get married, you start a new family. This was something I just needed to accept. The bottom line is, this was her choice."

Linda Pliske said she didn't share these worries. "I wasn't concerned. My attitude was, 'Wherever you go, I will find you,' " she said, laughing. "I was so happy for her. Bernie had looked at some religious orders, but we didn't see a lot of young people. There's a lot of youth in Opus Dei, so she has a much greater chance to make friends her own age."

Linda said that Bernie makes it home for birthday parties, funerals, and other family events, and that they make the forty-minute drive from their home to take her out to dinner at least once a month. Sometimes Bernie brings a friend from the conference center, other times it's just the three of them. They speak on the phone at least once a week. Twice a year, she said, the Pliskes invite the girls from the center to their home in the Indiana countryside. In the fall they go to a local pumpkin patch and organize a hayride. In the spring they organize a cookout and play volleyball.

David said that compared to some forms of religious life that Bernie might have chosen, they can't complain about the amount of contact they have with her. "I had two aunts who were cloistered nuns," he said. "They were allowed to come back home once every seven years for two days. Compared to that, this is fantastic."

The English mother who wrote to Church officials about her son in 1978, who spoke to me on the condition that her name not be used, may be typical of many parents who are neither as embittered as Garvey nor as enthralled as the Pliskes. I spoke with her in January 2005. Her son is still a numerary, and his mother said he has been "an extremely dutiful son," and by all appearances is "relaxed, happy, and fulfilled" in Opus Dei. They keep in regular contact, talking on the phone at least once a week and seeing each other over holidays, and the mother said a couple of times a year she usually attends Opus Dei events for families.

"Most of my friends, Catholic and non-Catholic, are apprehensive about Opus Dei, but when they meet my son they're totally disarmed," she said. The mother said that she has a "huge admiration" for most of the people she has met in Opus Dei, who seem "so saintly." She traveled to Rome for both the beatification of Escrivá in 1992 and the canonization in 2002, and described them as "very moving" experiences. At the same time, she said, she also came away confirmed that Opus Dei was not for her.

The mother said the "enormous anxieties" she and her husband, who died eight and a half years ago, experienced about what was happening with their son in 1978 don't really come across in the letter quoted above. As a result of her correspondence, the son was interviewed by Cardinal Basil Hume, and the mother met with Father Philip Sherington, at the time the head of Opus Dei in England (who later died in an accident in Ireland), whom she said she admired. After those conversations, she said, her son seemed to become more focused on his studies, and in general the situation improved. Nevertheless, the parents were still sufficiently worried that they pulled their second son from the local Opus Dei boys' club, and neither of their other children went on to join Opus Dei.

The mother said she has detected "huge changes" in Opus Dei's approach in the last quarter century, which she attributes in the first place to the guidelines for Opus Dei issued by Hume in 1981. "The cardinal was very brave, and people respected him," she said. "He could speak without any animosity, and somehow people knew he was right. His intervention started the change, toward less secrecy, less pressure on young people, and so on. Things are clearly different today."

The mother said she still worries that her son was induced into making a life commitment before he was ready, but acknowledges that some of his contemporaries in Opus Dei later moved on, so he could have taken other paths.

The discrepancies between the experiences of the Garveys, Pliskes, and this English couple, and thousands of other families whose children have become numeraries, may arise in part from a gradual "loosening up" in Opus Dei over the years. In part, too, the contrast may reflect differing instincts about how much contact with family members is appropriate for someone who has made the vocational choice implied in Opus Dei. Given the high level of demands on a numerary's time, no doubt there are occasions when families would like to see them that prove impossible. Is that the normal course of life, or is that isolation and control?

The Fourth Floor

Alberto Moncada, the ex-numerary who has written a number of critical books and articles about Opus Dei, says the stress and pressure is so intense on numeraries that they have an unusually high rate of psychological problems. In Spain, he said, when a numerary breaks down, it is common practice for them to be sent to the psychiatric department of the University Clinic at the University of Navarra in Pamplona, Spain, which is known around campus as "the fourth floor" because of its location in the medical building. There, Moncada alleges, the numeraries are treated, often with drugs, and then sent back out for duty. "The fourth floor is only for mad Opus Dei numeraries," Moncada said. "You can quote me."

The result, Moncada said, is " 'Opus gulag' in Navarra."

In order to see for myself, I visited the fourth floor, more formally known as the University Clinic of the Faculty of Medicine, on June 21, 2004. I met with Dr. Salvador Cervera Enguix, who holds a chair in psychiatry within the medical faculty at Navarra and has served as director of the clinic for thirty-three years. Cervera is former president of the Spanish Society of Psychiatry, the main secular body of professional psychiatrists in Spain, as well as the Spanish Society of Biological Psychiatry and the Spanish Committee for the Prevention and Treatment of Depression. All three bodies have no connection to Opus Dei.

Of the ten therapists who work in the clinic, Cervera told me, only two are members of Opus Dei. On the day we walked through the facility, he told me that no members of Opus Dei were among the twenty-five patients currently receiving treatment. In a year, he said, perhaps 2 percent of the patients the clinic sees would be Opus Dei members, which includes both numeraries and supernumeraries. Cervera said the clinic has two objectives: first, to treat mental illness "with techniques that are internationally accepted and scientifically proven"; second, to make the first objective "compatible with a Christian sense of life." In part, he said, that means respecting the belief systems of the clinic's patients, allowing for a spiritual as well as strictly scientific interpretation of their experiences.

Cervera said that it would not be ethically consistent to use his clinic to "recuperate" struggling members of Opus Dei, thereby imposing an objective other than valid medical treatment. He noted that the clinic was fully accredited and licensed by secular accrediting agencies, who, he said, "would not tolerate" such unethical conduct. Further, he noted, his election as president of several secular psychiatric bodies suggests that the clinic is operating within commonly accepted scientific norms.

"In my experience, numeraries do not experience psychological difficulties at a rate any higher than the general population," Cervera said. "It's no different than for any other group of people who are very dedicated, work hard, are very busy, and perhaps don't rest enough." If anything, Cervera said, membership in Opus Dei may help members cope with stress. "It's well established that a well-lived form of religious belief is a defense against psychiatric illness," he said.

Cervera said that when Opus Dei members come to the clinic for treatment, they receive the same care as any other patient. They are not prescribed drugs at a rate any higher than others, he said, and Cervera said he would never accept patients simply because they are experiencing "doubts" about a vocational choice. "If it is producing serious depression or anxiety, we would treat it," he said, "but not in the sense of predetermining the outcome. In some cases, it may well be that the healthy thing for that person to do is to choose another path." Further, Cervera said, the therapists at the clinic never discuss the treatment of patients who belong to Opus Dei with the directors of their centers. "Our relation is with the patient, not with anyone else," he said.

As a footnote, the Navarra clinic is the only one in Spain where patients are not segregated by sex—belying, in at least one instance, Opus Dei's reputation for rigid male/female separation. Cervera said he doesn't want patients to withdraw from the world, "just sitting in their rooms and taking their medication." He wants them to function, as much as possible, in normal social environments.

Satisfied Ex-Numeraries

Since much of the criticism of Opus Dei tends to come from ex-numeraries, it's worth noting that some former numeraries continue to be on good terms with Opus Dei and have positive perceptions of their experiences.

Joseph McCormack

Joseph McCormack, thirty-eight, is a public relations expert at a top-ten marketing agency in Chicago. He was an Opus Dei numerary for four years, then left, and eventually became a supernumerary. He said that what he most values about Opus Dei is that it helps him integrate his faith with his life. "Christ gets pushed out of this society that we live in," McCormack said. "How does he get back in? Opus Dei is the only practical thing that helps me." As an example, he said, "Maybe I'm going into a meeting with senior executives from Kodak. I want to do a good job for this client, help them meet their business objectives. That activity is totally consistent with the rest of my life, it's part of who I am as a Christian in the world."

McCormack met Opus Dei as a student at their boys' school in Chicago, Northridge Prep. At seventeen he went on the UNIV trip to Rome, an annual encounter with the pope for young people connected to Opus Dei, and "loved it." Afterward he decided to whistle as a numerary, and moved into an Opus Dei center while attending Loyola University of Chicago. "I was happy there," he said. "I didn't feel controlled or manipulated in the least." At the same time, McCormack said, he came to realize that "it wasn't for me. I knew there had to be a better fit out there." He left as a numerary in 1988, but continued attending activities sponsored by Opus Dei, and in 2000 rejoined as a supernumerary.

McCormack said he knows perhaps twenty ex-numeraries who left for one reason or another, and more than half are still on good terms with Opus Dei. "I found leaving Opus Dei very, very easy," he said. "No one hassled me, and no pressure was applied." Ironically, today much of his professional work is with companies that have some sort of image problem, something he acknowledges is true of Opus Dei as well. "Officials of Opus Dei asked me in to give some advice on this," he said. "I told them that the good news is, they're no worse off than lots of other people. Many big companies have no idea how to communicate, either."

Elizabeth Falk Sather

Elizabeth Falk Sather is a former numerary who today is a cooperator. She grew up in a "very devout, orthodox Roman Catholic household," she said, where Opus Dei was already familiar. Her mother wanted Elizabeth to get her religious education through Opus Dei, so she began attending events when she was twelve years old. She has a sister who is a numerary and a brother who is a supernumerary. Like McCormack, she took the UNIV trip to Rome during her senior year in high school, and she said it "opened up whole new worlds for me." Prior to that point, she said, Opus Dei had been basically her mother and a few friends.

Falk Sather whistled as a supernumerary at seventeen, just before she left home to study at Boston College. She began attending an Opus Dei center in Boston for the weekly spiritual formation and spiritual direction with a numerary. At one point the director asked her if she had ever considered life as a numerary. Falk Sather said she "thought about it, prayed about it," and in late 1977 decided to whistle again, this time as a numerary. She moved into the Bayridge center in Boston at the beginning of her sophomore year, and then into Brimfield in Newton, Massachusetts, the women's center of studies. In 1980, she said, she moved to Milwaukee where she got a job as a teacher and lived in an Opus Dei center for women there. Because her family lived in that area, she said she was able to see her mother a great deal, with no restrictions on their contact.

Around that time, Falk Sather said, she started to have doubts about whether or not life as a numerary was really for her. She spoke to her director about it. "They always told me, be honest, be open about how you feel about your vocation," she said. "They told me not to keep anything inside." Her primary issue, she said, was that she felt a tug toward getting married and having children. She said she went through a four- to five-month period of discernment, and then decided to leave.

Today Falk Sather is married with seven children, five girls and two boys. She said one of her daughters is involved with Opus Dei at Marquette, and that if one of them wanted to be a numerary, "That would be great, I'd be very happy." Her best friend, she said, is a former associate who is today a supernumerary of Opus Dei.

"They taught me how to pray," Falk Sather said of her experience in Opus Dei. "It made my faith more applicable to daily life, showed me how to be a good Catholic Christian in the middle of the world, nice and normal and fun at the same time. It helped me bring my kids closer to God, to live their faith as best they can. It's helped the Church tremendously."

Ignacio G. Andreu

Ignacio G. Andreu, forty-one, is a Spanish ex-numerary who teaches philosophy at a public university in Barcelona. He first met Opus Dei in a small Spanish town when he was still in high school, where he grew up in a devout Catholic family, although no one in his immediate family belonged to Opus Dei. Like McCormack and Falk Sather, Andreu went on the UNIV trip to Rome when he was seventeen. He decided to join shortly thereafter. The attraction, he said, was "the spirituality . . . and the freedom." Also, like many members of Opus Dei, Andreu said the idea of sanctification of work was a powerful draw. "I was impressed by the possibility of offering my study, and then afterward, my work to God."

After entering Opus Dei, Andreu briefly studied in Madrid and then came to Barcelona to study philosophy. He remained in and around Barcelona the rest of the time he was in Opus Dei, from the age of seventeen to thirty-five. At a certain stage, he said, he was assigned to work with a group of Opus Dei members in a small town outside Barcelona, where most of the members were older and, he said tactfully, "a little difficult." It was a stressful time, Andreu said, and he began to "drop his guard," letting his prayer life slide.

"In Opus Dei life is usually very easy, but it can become very hard if you don't pray," Andreu said. "When you are down, maybe temptations come more easily."

That temptation, Andreu said, came in the form of a young woman. At a moment of low self-esteem and spiritual emptiness, he said, not to mention exhaustion from overwork, it was an attraction too powerful to resist. He and the young woman began an affair. In a spirit of honesty, he told the director at his center what was going on. Rather than casting him out, the director suggested that he take a sabbatical to sort out what he wanted to do.

"In those months I never tried to enter into contact with that girl," Andreu said. "When I came back to Barcelona five months later, I phoned my center because I was still the vice director here, and the woman who answered the phone said, 'Oh, Señor Andreu, how are you? You have a phone call from Maria two days ago.' That was the girl, and it just brought everything back. I didn't have the strength to cut that relationship. I couldn't." He resumed the affair.

Next, Andreu turned to another director of another center and was told to move into a hotel room for a couple of months, both to buy time and avoid scandal. Eventually, he said, he decided to write a formal letter declaring his intention to leave. "That's the honest thing to do, because there are people who disappear and do not come back," Andreu said.

Two years later, the relationship with Maria was over. As some in Opus Dei had predicted, Andreu said, it turned out she was interested in him only because he was "forbidden fruit." Today he is in a serious relationship that may be heading toward marriage, and is also a cooperator of Opus Dei.

Andreu says Opus Dei did everything right, and that what happened was his own fault. "If you are humble, the directors will do everything to help you, everything," he said. "It doesn't make any sense for them to treat numeraries with a whip. They want to try to keep you happy, not drive you away." He said the trick is for numeraries to be honest with their directors. "The director may say, 'I want you to do five things.' You may know deep down that five is too much, that you can only handle two or three, that with five you will break. But your pride takes over, you want to be strong, so you say, 'I'll do all five.' But that's not the director's fault, that's pride and dishonesty. I should have been honest about what was happening in my life much earlier."

"Maybe if I get married, I will become a supernumerary," Andreu said.

Differing Interpretations

Ex-members such as Moncada, Clasen, DiNicola, and Roche, plus cult-watchers such as David Clark, describe a closed world inside Opus Dei, in which numeraries are cowed into submission, cut off from their families and the outside world, and controlled down to the most minute details, such as what they watch on TV or to whom they send letters. Examining the Opus Dei Awareness Network and opuslibros Web sites, it's clear that this is more than simply the perception of a handful of ex-members. There are scores of such accounts, by both men and women, covering decades of experience.

At the same time, another group of people, comprised of current and former members, testify to the freedom they feel inside Opus Dei. It's not just the high spiritual ideals—sanctification of work, being contemplatives in the middle of the world, and so on—that members praise, but also the genuine friendships that often last a lifetime.

Having spoken at length to people on all sides of this discussion, it's impossible for me to believe that one side is lying and the other is telling the truth. When ex-members recount experiences of isolation from the outside world, overwork, and censorship, the details of what happened to them generally ring true—but those same experiences can be interpreted as building a family environment, being dedicated to one's apostolate, and exercising good prudential judgment about what to read or watch. In other words, the most convincing explanation usually seems to be different frames of reference, not dishonesty. Of course, at the level of detail, some points cannot be so easily resolved. Opus Dei either does or doesn't send overstressed numeraries to the fourth floor at Navarra, for example; directors either do or don't report on what members say in spiritual direction. But at the level of overall impression, how one interprets the facts about Opus Dei seems to depend upon one's basic approach to spirituality, family life, and the implications of a religious vocation.

Reconciliation

Throughout the research for this book, when I brought up the subject of critical ex-members to veteran members of Opus Dei, I often sensed a pain that didn't come through in conversations about *The Da Vinci Code,* or the Vatican Bank scandal, or alleged plots to control the election of the next pope. Several members said that of all the public criticism of Opus Dei, the comments that sting the most come from the ex-members, because it is clear that, regardless of who is to blame, something about their experience left them bruised and hurt.

In one instance, I had an off-the-record conversation with a numerary who had been the director of a center where a well-known ex-member lived. When we finished our talk, in which the director largely defended Opus Dei's conduct, the director asked me: "If you speak to this person, please say that I'm sorry, will you? I'm sorry that it worked out this way." I had the sense that this was genuine emotion, and the tears that welled up in this numerary's eyes seemed to confirm the point.

I often had the impression that some people in Opus Dei hoped that this book might open a dialogue between them and the ex-members, albeit indirectly. Granted, the nature of the book has so far provided scant evidence of such a desire; more often, it has pitted the comments of critical ex-members against the testimonies of current members, and this has been unavoidable. There are real disagreements, and a "who says what" approach is essential to getting to the bottom of things. But that journalistic convention should not create a misleading impression; my sense is that the overwhelming majority of Opus Dei members, and at least some of the ex-members, do not want to fight. If at all possible, without compromising what both sides see as the truth, they'd like to make peace.

In that sense, perhaps the right tone upon which to end this chapter was set by Bishop Javier Echevarría, the prelate of Opus Dei, in our December 2004 interview at Villa Tevere. Speaking of the ex-members, Echevarría said: "I say this with all sincerity, and from the bottom of my heart. If we have hurt anyone, if we have failed anyone, we ask their forgiveness."

Old wounds, however, are sometimes the most difficult to heal, a point made clear by the story of attempts by Opus Dei to reconcile with one of its best-known ex-members, María del Carmen Tapia, who wrote the critical 1992 book *Beyond the Threshold: A Life in Opus Dei*. In the lead-up to Escrivá's canonization in 2002, Tapia contacted the Opus Dei Information Office in Rome with a transcript of an interview she had given to the Catholic News Service, in which she amplified some positive comments she had made about Escrivá in an interview with the Italian

news agency ANSA. This gesture led to a series of friendly contacts between Tapia and officials in Opus Dei, including a meeting in Rome with
the prelate, Echevarría. For a time, some in Opus Dei hoped that a real
healing might be imminent.

Tapia, however, laid down one nonnegotiable condition: statements
made about her by Opus Dei officials during the 1992 beatification
process, including a reference to "perverse behaviors on her part while
still a member of Opus Dei—statements which had become public
knowledge after having been leaked to a Spanish newspaper—must be
publicly retracted. Otherwise, Tapia argued, what she regarded as slander
would remain part of the historical record.

During the work on this book, I asked Opus Dei if it wanted to respond to Tapia's request for a public retraction. The following response
came from Juan Manuel Mora, of the Opus Dei Information Office in
Rome:

> Around the canonization of Josemaría Escrivá, the Information
> Office of Opus Dei in Rome had frequent, and I would say cor-
> dial, contact with Ms. Maria del Carmen Tapia. There were di-
> verse opportunities for collaboration.
>
> Everything began on December 24, 2001, the day on which
> she wanted to make a public declaration, which she repeated on
> other occasions, in a very serious tone: she desired to reaffirm
> that no one should use her book, or any other testimony, against
> the canonization of the founder of Opus Dei. In an important
> declaration to the [Italian] news agency ANSA, Maria del
> Carmen Tapia affirmed, among other things, that "the antici-
> pated and happy conclusion of the canonization of Monsignor
> Escrivá was for me a motive of joy, because several times after his
> death, I asked favors of him that, in truth, I can say many times
> he granted to me." Moreover, she added that, "I never considered
> his strong character an obstacle to holiness." She explained: "I
> also worked with him for many years, during which time I be-
> came aware that his commitment and his aim was the good of the
> Church and of souls. He had the extremely clear idea that he
> was, without doubt, an instrument in the hands of God for

spreading Opus Dei in the world." I think that, in that moment, Ms. Tapia was conscious of the fact that ten years earlier, in 1992, her book and her declarations were used by some to oppose the beatification of Josemaría Escrivá, and she wanted to avoid the repetition of this abuse.

It was precisely in 1992 that a very sad episode happened. In fact, a few weeks before the beatification, a newspaper published an article that contained some lines from a confidential document of the beatification process, which someone had unjustly given to the press. Some fragments were reported out of context, I would say betraying their meaning, and thus giving offense to Ms. Tapia. In my view, the subjects who distorted and spread these phrases were in fact involved in defamation of Ms. Tapia, whose image was hurt. I remember as if it were today the pain that episode caused to the people of Opus Dei who became aware of it: it almost seemed as if someone wanted to defame the founder, defaming at the same time other persons. It's necessary to recall that this was a matter of the process of canonization of Josemaría Escrivá, in which testimonies of the holiness of his life were studied; it was not a process about other persons, and no one else was being judged. I can affirm that, despite differences concerning some of the content of her book, no person of Opus Dei has ever wanted to do or say anything that could damage the reputation of Ms. Tapia.

Years have since gone by. Time and good will have helped to close the wounds. The beatification and canonization of Josemaría Escrivá were events that have helped millions of persons come to know the figure of this saint, also outside the Church, transmitting a truthful and attractive portrait. I retain, moreover, that during the canonization the reputation of Ms. Tapia, which had been unjustly damaged, was in a certain sense restored. Ms. Tapia merits the affirmation of her honorability. She herself wanted to decisively deny the impression of hostility against the saint; she has manifested appreciation with regard to members of Opus Dei, an appreciation which is returned with affection. In sum, I believe that it can be understood that Ms.

Tapia—and with her, other persons—was the victim of manipulation.

Despite Mora's intent of affirming the "honorability" of Tapia, she replied to me in July 2005 that she regards his statement as insufficient. In essence, she said, despite the irenic tone of Mora's words, he never acknowledges that Opus Dei officials falsely accused her of untoward behavior.

Tapia's response:

1. I stand by the statements that I sent to the ANSA agency. . . .

2. While in Rome, Opus Dei asked for and encouraged me to resign from Opus Dei, without knowing the concrete charges and without the benefit or opportunity to defend myself against these so-called charges.

3. I received photocopies of original documents—from a Spanish newspaper—that were allegedly prepared by a department within the Vatican. Those photocopied documents contained statements from Opus Dei directors, who represented on pages 610 and 611 from the *Summary of the Roman Process*, Article 2346 (p. 768)—without facts to substantiate their claims—that my behavior was "perverted." In Article 2347 (p. 769) of the same document, it was stated that "I tried to pervert some women with the worst deviations" and that "I was a person without conscience," among other things.

4. Since the public statements reflected (in the photocopied materials) are unfounded and not true, the document is slanderous. I have asked Opus Dei for a public rectification, and to this day my pleas have been without success. In the text you sent me, it is not clear, and it is much less concrete, which is the part of the document prepared in the Vatican that speaks about me that Opus Dei directors consider misleading, or which is the truthful document that they speak about. Although I understand the difficulty the Opus Dei directors met when they became aware of the misleading document, I am surprised I was not informed at that time.

5. I have direct and concrete knowledge that different people in Opus Dei have spoken derogatively about me. A few examples are the following:

a) A letter was written in 1966 by an Opus Dei Director and priest to my father. The letter to my father stated in part that, ". . . if you knew the behavior of your daughter, you would feel deeply sorry, since she did not only damage to herself, but in fact seriously damaged other souls . . . and my conscience does not allow me to return to you her personal documents related to her stay in Venezuela." The letter went on to say that if I returned to Venezuela, there would be very distressing facts revealed about me, but again, those so-called facts were not clear nor said.

b) Another lengthy letter, in 1992, was written about me by the Central Directress of Opus Dei to a Portuguese newspaper, which was also translated for other countries. The letter was very critical and negative and noted that my personal documents were retained in Rome; she also said that my behavior was such that "I realized facts of another kind"—without explaining what kind of facts.

c) A letter from the Regional Vicar of Italy was written on January 13, 1997. Without personal and direct knowledge of my life, he stated his amazement about my behavior, and also corroborated statements made by the Central Directress, which I have mentioned above.

6. Precisely because my attitude towards Opus Dei is not belligerent, I have forgiven; I do not hold any animosity towards the institution, and I pray for those members who openly accused me of wrongdoing. However, such public and serious slanders of my reputation and name deserve to be corrected, directly and clearly by a public statement, so as to restore my name and reputation as a person who has sought to live as one of faith and conscience in the Church.

All this suggests that goodwill alone will not suffice to achieve genuine reconciliation between Opus Dei and at least some of its ex-members, who want to see concrete admissions of fault by Opus Dei, as well as corrective measures. Opus Dei officials, meanwhile, often feel torn between reaching out to ex-members in a spirit of amity and continuing to debate the ex-members' charges, which officials sometimes regard as unfair or dishonest. The minefields these dynamics create will not, if the Tapia case is any indication, be cleared overnight.

Chapter Fourteen

RECRUITING

People find their way into Opus Dei in a variety of ways, but within that diversity, Louisa Shins, a Dutch supernumerary, followed one of the more remarkable paths. She was born in the south of Holland, where she attended a school for women looking to do domestic work. She met her husband while at school, and the two were married in 1961. They moved to Italy, where her husband pursued a career as a nuclear technician. They lived about forty miles north of Milan, in a town on Lago Maggiore. They had three children, two boys and a girl, all of whom went to international schools and grew up speaking Dutch, Italian, and French.

When their oldest son turned eighteen, he decided to go to Amsterdam for university studies. After about a year, the son called home and said he had found an international residence that he liked very much, where he could be with young men from Spain, France, and Italy, as well as the Dutch. That residence, it turned out, was operated by Opus Dei. Then their second son headed off to Amsterdam and repeated the pattern. After one year he phoned his parents saying he too wanted to move into the Opus Dei residence. Shins said she didn't know much about Opus Dei at this stage, merely that she had asked a Dutch Benedictine who had given Opus Dei a clean bill of health. After a while, however, she said she noticed changes in her boys, for the better. They didn't argue with each other, and they seemed more focused, more responsible, more adult. Finally the daughter left for Holland, and she decided not to mess around, moving directly into an Opus Dei residence for university girls.

Not long afterward, the Shinses took a family vacation together in

Spain. Louisa said she knew something had changed when one of her children proposed going to a weekday Mass, and the next day another proposed saying the rosary. Moreover, Shins said, she began to see changes in her daughter. She smiled more, she seemed content, and was always willing to help out around the house. "What a beautiful thing," Shins recalls thinking. At that stage she began attending Opus Dei retreats and get-togethers in Milan, despite having to travel some forty miles over foggy, dangerous roads.

At some point, she said, her children revealed to her that they planned to join Opus Dei as numeraries. She said she cried a bit and did not tell her husband because she didn't want him to know yet that the children would not be coming home. At this stage, she said, she wasn't quite sure what to make of Opus Dei, and her husband hadn't shown any particular interest. Then, out of the blue, in 1987, one of the children phoned and proposed that the following weekend all five of them meet in Rome. Louisa got off work from her teaching job, and her husband, already retired, was ready to go. When they met in Rome, two of the children took Louisa and her husband sightseeing, but the third said he needed to stay by the phone, because he had to call someone every hour. Shins thought that a bit odd, but didn't make much of it. When they got back, the son announced: "Tomorrow we're going to Mass with the pope." Louisa said she didn't sleep well that night with excitement, but wasn't worried . . . she had told the hotel manager that if they didn't wake her at 4:00 A.M., she wouldn't pay the bill.

The family went to the private Mass, and afterward everyone lined up to meet John Paul II. A Vatican aide told them they could make a bit of chitchat, so Louisa's husband decided to ask a question out of professional interest. "Holy Father," he asked, "what do you think of nuclear power?" It probably wasn't the usual postliturgical fare, but John Paul was unfazed. "Research is always for the good," he said. "We have to do a great deal of research. If something is clean and affordable, then it's a good thing." Her husband, Louisa said, was content with the response.

Then it was her turn, and Louisa decided to "pop the question." Pointing to her children, she said: "Holy Father, we have three children in Opus Dei, and we don't know much about it. We've heard some people with different opinions, some positive, some negative. Tell me what you think, because yours is the only opinion that really counts for me." The pope looked at her and said, "These are your children?" Louisa said yes, and the pope turned and began speaking with the three of them. He chatted for a few moments, obviously developing a positive impression, then returned to Louisa and her husband.

Looking at the parents directly, the pope smiled and said: "And you're not yet members?"

It was all downhill from there.

As a footnote, the next day the Shin family was in an audience with Bishop Alvaro del Portillo, the prelate of Opus Dei. Again, they were told they could ask a question, and so her husband decided this would be the ultimate test. Addressing himself to Portillo, he asked: "Father, what do you think of nuclear energy?" When Portillo responded with virtually the same words that John Paul II had used, Shins decided that Opus Dei was good enough for him. He and Louisa became supernumeraries shortly thereafter.

Elements of the Charge

Of all the complaints about Opus Dei, none is more recurrent than the impression that Opus Dei is a ferocious recruiting machine, using its centers and corporate works as "fronts" for attracting new members, especially among the young and impressionable. As in the story of Louisa Shins, from time to time Opus Dei finds that somebody else is willing to lend a hand, in this case no less a figure than John Paul II himself. In general, however, the impression is that Opus Dei rarely leaves things to chance.

The image of stop-at-nothing Opus Dei recruiting has become the stuff of Catholic legend. One anti–Opus Dei Web site, www.opus deialert.com, which reflects a staunchly conservative, traditionalist Catholic outlook, has even published a "cease and desist" order for presentation to Opus Dei members who make recruiting overtures. The text is as follows:

> *This cease and desist order is to inform you that your and the Opus Dei cult's harassing and intimidating actions against my fellow Catholics and I has become unbearable. Such anti-social behavior is completely in violation of all normal codes of decorum, law and*

*decency. This letter is to demand that your and the Opus Dei cult's
continuing involvement in, planning and encouragement of, high-
pressure recruitment, information gathering, harassment and intimidation must cease and desist immediately. Should you and the
Opus Dei cult continue to pursue these activities in violation of this
cease and desist order, we will not hesitate to pursue further legal action against you and the Opus Dei cult, including, but not limited
to, civil action and/or criminal complaints. [Insert specific harassment incidents here. Be sure to include date(s) and place(s) of oc-
currences(s).]*

*I and my peers have a right to remain free from Opus Dei's cul-
tic, intimidating, manipulative and high-pressure tactics, and we
will take the responsibility upon ourselves to protect that right. Note
that a copy of this letter and a record of its delivery will be stored.
Note, too, that it is admissible as evidence in a court of law and will
be used as such if need be in the future.*

*This cease and desist order demands that you immediately dis-
continue and do not at any point in the future under any circumstances do the following to me: speak to, contact, pursue, harass,
attack, strike, bump into, brush up against, push, tap, grab, hold,
threaten, telephone (via cellular or landline), instant message, page,
fax, e-mail, follow, stalk, disturb my peace, keep me under surveil-
lance, gather information about and/or block my movements at
home, work, social gatherings, religious functions and/or at any
Catholic Church–sponsored activities.*

When one asks members of Opus Dei about recruiting, they generally recoil at the very term. Membership in Opus Dei is a vocation given
from God, they say, and it's not something that can be artificially generated to fill a quota. Did Jesus "recruit" his disciples? Or is it that they
found something irresistible about him that compelled them to respond
to his invitation? In any event, they say, they have no interest in coercing
someone into joining Opus Dei. The last thing the world needs, they say
ruefully, are more embittered ex-members of Opus Dei.

That said, even if Opus Dei does "recruit," in itself there would be
nothing objectionable about it. The army recruits, and colleges recruit,
and law firms recruit, and McDonald's recruits. Virtually every Catholic

diocese in the world has a priest assigned as its "vocations director," and while most would not be so brazen as to use the term, their job is to recruit new priests. Religious orders do this, too. Indeed, it would be counterintuitive were there not some "recruiting" in Opus Dei, since members believe their vocation to be a precious thing, and one would expect a natural desire to share it with others. The negative perception of Opus Dei on this score is not so much that it recruits, but that it uses underhanded, manipulative ways of going about it.

These, then, are the three elements of the charge against Opus Dei on the issue of recruiting:

- That Opus Dei, as a matter of both policy and practice, is constantly seeking new members
- That Opus Dei is methodical, highly organized, and effective in its approach to recruiting
- That part of Opus Dei's effectiveness arises from deception, manipulation, and coercion

Does Opus Dei Recruit?

One can certainly find passages from Escrivá that give the impression of a single-minded focus on winning new members. For example, in *Crónica*, the internal Opus Dei journal for male members, in 1963, Escrivá wrote: "We do not have any other aim than the corporate one: proselytism, winning vocations. . . . Proselytism in the Work is precisely the road, the way to reach sanctity. When a person does not have zeal to win others, he is dead . . . I bury cadavers." Or again, from 1971: "Go out to the highways and byways and push those whom you find to come and fill my house, force them to come in; push them . . . we must be a little crazy. . . . You must kill yourselves for proselytism." And, from 1968: "None of my children can rest satisfied if he doesn't win four or five faithful vocations each year."

Even allowing for some slippage between "proselytism" in the sense of winning converts for Christ, and "proselytism" in the sense of bringing people into Opus Dei, the thrust of these injunctions seems clear: Members of Opus Dei should be serious about sharing their life with others. On the other hand, Opus Dei spokespersons insist that when

Escrivá said "force them to come in," it was a reference to an episode from the gospels in which Jesus talks about guests at a wedding feast. The idea is not that people ought to be coerced or compelled to enter Opus Dei, Escrivá's interpreters say, but rather that the force of the Christian example should be so strong that it exerts its own natural gravitational pull. They also say that his talk about every numerary bringing in five new vocations a year was understood by everyone to be hyperbole, not meant to be taken literally.

In the early days, the aim of winning vocations for Opus Dei loomed large. For example, I was given an opportunity to examine some early correspondence to the Rome headquarters from members around the world, drawn at random from the Opus Dei archives. One letter, dated January 8, 1950, was from an Irish numerary named Dick Mulcahy, who referred to himself as "the man who is holding the red light at the moment," a joking reference inside Opus Dei to the most recent member in a given center. The "red light" is the signal on the caboose of a train, and, at least in the old days, nobody wanted to hold it for very long. Mulcahy wrote, "Since tomorrow is the Father's birthday, it would be very nice to give him a present of two vocations."

In the course of this book, examples of Opus Dei's zeal for identifying prospects have already come up. Rafael López Aliaga, today an associate and the CEO of Perurail in Lima, said that when he ranked high in local qualifying exams for university placement in a regional city in Peru, a member of Opus Dei, whom he had never met, called him out of the blue to invite him to an event in another city. Dutch supernumerary Edna Kavanagh said that after she was named businesswoman of the year in Holland in 1984, Opus Dei approached her to invite her to events. Again, she had never met them before. In both cases, López and Kavanagh ended up grateful for the outreach, even if they were a bit taken aback.

Some observers say the desire to win vocations has developed into an exact science within Opus Dei.

"They say you should have a set of fifteen friends, and the first five should be close to joining," said Tammy DiNicola, the American ex-numerary who left Opus Dei with the assistance of anticult expert David Clark. "We would fill out statistics every night. You would discuss each person on your list with the director. And then you have to fill out a form every month. You say, 'I spoke apostolically with this person,' 'They went to confession with an Opus Dei priest,' 'They went on a retreat,' and so on."

DiNicola says there are even songs within Opus Dei that extol the virtues of recruiting. " 'La Pesca Submarina,' Spanish for 'Underwater Fishing,' is one of many songs written by an Opus Dei member for all the Opus Dei members to sing at their get-togethers," she said. "During the time I was a numerary, I sang this song many times." A sample of the lyrics: "When you see a fish, you position yourself at the same level, with maneuverability, with cleverness, you hurl the harpoon with aim, then you grab it, and that's it!"

Moreover, ex-members allege that events such as the annual UNIV trip to Rome, when young people associated with Opus Dei have a meeting with the pope during the Easter period, are designed to be "peak moments" in which a decision to join Opus Dei crystallizes. Recall that all three of the satisfied ex-members profiled in chapter 13, for example, reported that the key moment in their decision to join Opus Dei came on a UNIV trip. Sharon Clasen tells her story:

> They invited me to Rome, and I had no idea what that was about. One of my friends who actually became a supernumerary told me it was a numerary factory. That was during Easter in '82. They work in teams. This other woman who came along is the one they call in for the hard sell, like when you're buying a car. It was when I was in the crypt, at Escrivá's tomb, that she asked me. I didn't know what to say really. I said I'd have to think about it. My friend, the one who was supposed to be my buddy all week, got a migraine, because they were pressuring her to be a numerary, and she was from this big, large family, and she always wanted babies. She was crying and had this headache, and all week she was in bed. . . . The other woman yelled at me, that I was running away from my vocation, and I started to cry. So we talked about it, but I didn't join then. But I was heavily pressured.

A month later, Clasen said, she was in Opus Dei as a supernumerary. She later joined as a numerary and left after two years, in 1987.

Ex-members say other outings have a similar recruiting subtext. Charles Shaw, an American ex-numerary who "whistled" as a Harvard undergraduate during a five-week summer trip to Mexico in 1991, which had been presented to him as a social service outing rather than a recruiting expedition, describes what happened: "I remember being on one particular bus ride with the director, and he was giving me a 'talking to' about joining. He pitched the idea in a way that made it seem very monumental, and he particularly talked about the burden of my decision in light of my eternal salvation as well as his; that he had a duty somehow to show me the way, and that I had a duty to respond generously. It felt so momentous. But as I look back, it was all mind games. He wanted to leave the summer program having gotten someone to join. He'd just met me a few weeks before. He had certainly heard a lot about me, because that's another thing I learned; there is a lot of talk behind the scenes about possible members, much more than there should be, because I think there are serious betrayals of trust.

"I had no idea who this guy was before the trip, we'd never met, but he had heard from the director at the center near Harvard that I was a prime candidate," Shaw said. "The Work organizes these trips and work projects for college students as a means of getting members, and of helping prospective members move along in their decisions. The thing is, however, that you don't realize that's their purpose."

After fourteen months as a numerary, Shaw left in 1993. "What directors in the Work can sometimes lack is patience in helping guys discern a vocation, because of the pressure they feel to get new members," Shaw said. "It's almost like a mantra in the Work, to make friends with guys who could join as a numerary or supernumerary. It's pressure, all the time. So it's understandable, once you see that from the inside, that you could lack judgment in certain circumstances in pushing people along to join because there is the constant pressure to get more members. Understandable, but not excusable, and actually very harmful because you start down the path on what you think is your vocation and it's a struggle all the way, and you want to make it work, but it's not going to because it's not for you."

Opus Dei spokespersons usually say that all this has been lifted out of context, or expresses a youthful zeal that maturity has put in a different context. Given the respect for Christian freedom that is inherent to the "spirit of the Work," they say, it would be antithetical to "push" or "force" anyone into Opus Dei. "Recruiting," in the sense of convincing people to join Opus Dei when it would otherwise not occur to them, according to spokespersons, would be a distortion.

On the Opus Dei Awareness Network Web site, DiNicola has published a two-page, legal-size form that ex-member Ann M. Schweninger said was in use at the Van Ness Study Center in Washington, D.C., in 1987. Though it has no heading, it appears to be a form for collecting data about people involved in Opus Dei programs, asking about their human qualities, their study and work habits, and their attitudes toward the Church and Opus Dei. David Gallagher, an Opus Dei official in New York, said in January 2005 that "the use of something like this is not normal in centers of the Work." Gallagher said that he was director of the men's study center in Washington, D.C., in the late 1980s, and he used no such form. "If something like this came to the attention of the directors, it would normally be discouraged, precisely because it does not properly respect the privacy of the persons who are in touch with our apostolates," Gallagher said.

At least some Church officials with experience of Opus Dei say they don't perceive excessive recruiting pressure. Father Jacek Buda, a Polish Dominican, has been responsible for the Catholic campus ministry at Columbia University in New York since early 2003. He's encouraged participation from Opus Dei and said in a November 2004 interview at the Church of Notre Dame, near the Columbia campus, that he's never had reason to suspect a hidden recruiting agenda.

"Opus Dei always has this mythology around it," Buda said. "When I took over, I wanted to see if anything would happen here. Several priests warned me not to let them become too strong. I was ready to fight with them if I had to, but I realized there is nobody to fight with. . . . I was afraid they would be about trying to get vocations for themselves. Young communities are often like this, they try to grab as many young people as possible. But I found that Opus Dei is very serious intellectually about what they do. They work for the Church. For me, this is a key criterion. Do they work for the Church, or for the group? I've seen groups that carefully choose activities to support their own cause, but I didn't find that with Opus Dei."

María José Font, a Spanish numerary who works in a law firm in Barcelona, was introduced in chapter 3. "I was never recruited," he said. She conceded that she had been approached by Opus Dei members about her decision, but did not see this as pressure. "Yes, quite a lot of people talked to me about it," she said, making the classic Opus Dei distinction between "discernment" or "guidance," on the one hand, and "recruiting."

"Some asked me about joining, and my answer was always no," she said. "This is our approach. If we think a person may have a vocation, we say, 'Why don't you think about it, why don't you pray about it?' "

Font said she has followed this practice herself. "I've done this with a lot of my friends. I may have done it fifty times over the course of twenty-five years, but then I give a lot of talks and have a lot of friends. This is not 'recruiting,' because I would never do this out of the blue, without knowing the person." This, Opus Dei members say, is what makes their approach different from "recruiting" in the classic sense. Vocations arise out of friendship and family relations, they say, never "cold calls."

Font said that, "I've never felt any pressure from anyone in Opus Dei to bring in more people. But I love my vocation, and it's a normal thing to try to find more people who want to share it. If you have the best thing in the world, why not share it?"

Case Studies

To determine how young people experience the "recruiting" pressures in an Opus Dei environment today, let's look at two case studies, one from Africa and the other from the United States.

The Kianda School

The Kianda School for girls in Nairobi, Kenya, draws a fairly affluent clientele that would be most people's idea of the kind of up-and-coming young women Opus Dei would like to recruit. Kianda, which is a corporate work of Opus Dei, ranks among the top five schools in Kenya in national examinations and has a combined elementary and secondary student population of nine hundred. In September 2004, I sat down with five students from Kianda, none of them members of Opus Dei, out of the presence of any school officials.

Annie Kiuna, eighteen, said her experience is that "members of Opus Dei see it as their goal to bring people closer to God, not necessarily into Opus Dei." She said her Catholic faith has "grown and become stronger" by virtue of her experience at Kianda. She arrived at the school, she said, having heard rumors that Opus Dei is "a cult, not in the mainstream," but that this has not been her experience.

Betha Munuku, fourteen, said that she had similar fears, but that she has found Opus Dei to be a "nice organization." Munuku said that members are "really ordinary," and "not trying to force anything. They're just trying to serve God by what they do."

Elsie Oyoo, eighteen, said she wants to be a diplomat, and she gets to practice her skills at home, since she is the only Catholic in a household composed of evangelical Protestants. She said they're constantly questioning her about various aspects of the Catholic Church, and she appreciates the way Kianda has equipped her to withstand these challenges. She said that she's thinking about joining Opus Dei, and is trying to decide between becoming a numerary or supernumerary—but not, she says, because anyone from Opus Dei has pressured her. "From what I can see, they're just trying to share Christ's life, imitating Christ's footsteps," she said.

Hendrika Wanda, eighteen, whose mother teaches at Kianda, said she originally thought members of Opus Dei were "freaks who go to Mass every day, do benediction and meditation, and were just strange." Then, she said, she went to Rome for the canonization of Escrivá in 2002 and saw "people from all parts of the world," and thought "there has to be something about these people." She also saw "how the pope loves Opus Dei." She said, "I realized they're just ordinary people trying to be saints." Wanda said that no one used the occasion of her trip to invite her to join Opus Dei, and she's ambivalent about whether she would be open to it if they had. "Maybe Opus Dei is a good thing, but it's not for everyone," she said.

Wanda acknowledged, however, that sometimes the people from Opus Dei come on too strong. "I was going to a circle, and I wanted to quit," she said. "They just wouldn't let me go. There was pressure. The impression they gave was that if I didn't come to the circle, my spiritual life would go down the drain."

Kiuna said that in her experience at Kianda there is "some pressure," both to take part in the religious practices offered by the school and to consider a vocation in Opus Dei. "Sometimes they can make you feel that if you don't do what they're doing, you're going to go to hell," she said. "It's more of an attitude than anything they necessarily say to you. They can make you feel guilty. I think it makes some run away from Opus Dei," she said. Kiuna said, for example, that she was more or less forced to go to a number of meditations. "I had to sit there and listen to a priest for forty minutes, and I didn't want to be there. It gave me a bias against Opus Dei." Over time, she said, she's realized that "they're just trying to help you, because it's their work to bring people closer to God." Still, she said, the hard sell "sometimes pushes people away."

Susan Kimani, fifteen, said she too initially resented the way Opus Dei members were demanding in their insistence that she mimic their approach to prayer, but she's come to understand that they're trying to help her develop spiritually. "If you want to be a doctor, you've got to be serious about science, whether you like it or not," she said. "It's the same thing if you want to be a saint. The truth is, it's tough."

Oyoo, who is considering membership in Opus Dei, said the approach to "recruiting" as she's experienced it is paradoxical. "There's pressure and there isn't," she said. "There are all these signs that it's what they want you to do, and then when you bring it up, it's kind of pushed aside," she said. "They almost shut you down, tell you that you have to wait, to pray about it, to be sure." She said that in her view "the pressure is not excessive."

Kiuna said that another subtle form of pressure at Kianda is that those students who seem to be moving toward membership in Opus Dei sometimes receive "special treatment," though not necessarily in any calculated way. "You get closer to the teachers who are members," she said. "If you go to the center, you make friends, people start to take an interest in you." It's all very natural, she said, but it can have the effect of sending the signal that if you want to do well at Kianda, you should manifest some kind of interest in Opus Dei.

At the end of the day, all five girls said they were grateful to Kianda for what they saw as an excellent education, a good moral example, and the personal concern for the students. None said they found the "pressure" to consider a vocation in Opus Dei excessive, but all agreed that in some form, it's there.

Windmoor

Later in September, I visited the Windmoor Center at the University of Notre Dame, America's flagship Catholic university and another environment in which one would expect that Opus Dei would do its most aggressive trawling.

David Cook, twenty-one, said that "what pulls me here is friendships with people of virtue, not any recruiting by Opus Dei." He said that when he first started going to Windmoor, he mentioned it to the rector in his dorm, whose response was, "You have to be very careful. They're going to try to suck you in, make you feel bad about the way you're living." In fact, Cook said, in part that's true. "I was going to bars, getting drunk. Now I'm trying to live the virtues that Opus Dei talks about." In that sense, he said, he welcomed a little bit of "pressure" to clean up his act.

Sam Chen, twenty-four, offers a classic example of how "recruiting" within Opus Dei works. He's a Chinese graduate student who arrived at Notre Dame knowing virtually nothing about Catholicism. "I saw people wearing crucifixes and going to Mass, and I was totally lost," he laughed. At one stage he expressed curiosity about Catholicism to another graduate student, who suggested he meet a friend at Windmoor. Chen went to the center, and a guy "dressed really weird" answered the door. It turned out to be an Opus Dei priest wearing a cassock. Chen met the resident, and it turned out that because spring break was coming up, Windmoor was organizing a trip to the Appalachian Mountains. Chen was asked if he wanted to come along, and readily agreed. He had a good experience. "I liked them so much," he said. "They were so nice, they took care of me." Along the way, Chen said, he noticed that the people on the trip would say the rosary in the car, and were very patient in explaining to him what it was all about. "I was surprised at how disciplined these people were," he said. "They're so organized and so diligent."

When he returned from the trip, Chen said, he had to start thinking about housing for the next term. He asked somebody from Windmoor if he could live there, and the answer was, "Okay, no problem." Since then he's taken part in some of the means of formation and is thinking about becoming a Catholic. Is he also thinking about joining Opus Dei? "I like Opus Dei a lot, but I'm definitely not going to join," he said. I asked Chen if he ever sensed that the affection shown him was artificial, intended to lure him into Opus Dei. "Not at all," he said. "I think I would know. These are just nice guys, trying to be good people."

Tom Messner, twenty-six, is a third-year law student at Notre Dame who grew up with an evangelical Protestant background. When he arrived at Notre Dame he befriended someone from Windmoor, and he began attending events at the center. "The guys here did a lot of catechesis with me," he said. "It was through the Work that I learned about the Catholic faith." Messner was received into the Catholic Church in the fall of 2002. Far from feeling used by Opus Dei, Messner said that, if anything, "I'm the one who uses Opus Dei." He said he thinks of Opus Dei like "coming in for an oil change, and then heading back out into the world."

Becket Gremmels, twenty-one, a resident at Windmoor, said there is a kind of recruiting that goes on. "Every time there's something happening, you're supposed to bring friends to the circles, to meetings, to recollections," he said. "But I don't think it's any heavier than what goes on with campus ministry or the student clubs here. I certainly haven't found that."

Chen said that he hears all the time about recruiting in Opus Dei, but he hasn't seen it himself. "I had a friend who was a member, and then he decided to bail out," Chen said. "Opus Dei did not pressure him." Chen said he had another friend who was interested in joining, "and they told him to take his time. Eventually he decided not to join, and that was fine. They welcomed him back, and he's still friends with people here. Personally, I think that the guys here wouldn't seem so happy and relaxed if they were constantly under this big pressure."

Andres Valdivia, nineteen, comes from a Brazilian family, and he first met Opus Dei in Brazil. Later his family moved to Dallas. He recalls going to a Christmas party at an Opus Dei center where the kids watched *Little Drummer Boy*. In sixth grade, he went to an Opus Dei camp, where he returned for four years. He said he appreciated the "prayer life, the sense of prayer you get."

Valdivia said when he was about sixteen or seventeen, he took a walk with an Opus Dei numerary and felt "pressured to join." He said he was told, "I think you have a vocation to Opus Dei." Valdivia said the numerary "kept talking about it, telling me I should act quickly." He said it made him feel "kind of scared. I didn't want to be a numerary, but what Opus Dei offers me is priceless." In the end, Valdivia said that when he decided not to join, the numerary did not break off the friendship with him. "This guy really cared about me, and helped me grow a lot," he said.

The Recruiting Myth

One sign that an organization is getting a bad rap comes when people hold prejudices about it that, at a logical level, are contradictory. In the case of Opus Dei and recruiting, people tend to believe two things: first, that Opus Dei is well organized and highly efficient; second, that it recruits incessantly. If both were true, one would expect Opus Dei to be growing by leaps and bounds. In fact, however, the opposite is the case.

The 2000 *Annuario,* the official Vatican yearbook, reported a membership for Opus Dei in that year of 1,734 priests and 81,954 laity, for a total of 83,688. In 2004, the numbers were 1,850 priests and 83,641 laity, for a total of 85,491. This means that over four years, Opus Dei grew by 1,803 members, an average of 450 per year. In fact, the number of new members is slightly larger, because some 200 members of Opus Dei die each year, meaning that over four years roughly 800 existing members died, so to achieve a net growth of 1,803, some 2,603 new members had to be added. Hence Opus Dei probably adds a worldwide total of 650 new members each year.

If 20 percent of Opus Dei's membership is composed of numeraries, that means that in 2000, there were roughly 16,400 numeraries. If every one of them was supposed to bring in five new members a year, the quota suggested by Escrivá, there should have been 82,000 new members each year over those four years, for a total of 328,000 new members. In other words, the numeraries of Opus Dei fell short of their alleged target by a whopping 325,397 members. If this were a corporation and the numeraries were its sales force, most of them would be out looking for work.

In some parts of the world, there has been virtually no growth at all. American supernumerary Russell Shaw points out that if you asked an Opus Dei official in 1980 how many members there were in the United States, the answer was, "about three thousand." Ask today, and the answer is still, "about three thousand." There is no reason to think these numbers are deliberately underreported. Priestly ordinations are a matter of public record, and numeraries visibly live together in centers. Most organizations, if anything, tend to pad their membership rosters. The plain reality is, Opus Dei is not growing very fast.

One of these images of Opus Dei has to go: Either they really are not maniacal about recruiting, or, if they are, they're not very good at it.

None of this should call into question the conclusion advanced above—Opus Dei does "recruit," in the sense that members invite others to think about a vocation, and certainly they rejoice when someone feels the call and seems a good "fit." But whatever techniques or strategies they employ do not produce the bonanza of new members that some public discussion would lead one to expect.

Evidence for the point emerged everywhere I visited. At the Opus Dei–affiliated Besana School, located in a working-class neighborhood of Madrid, for example, the student population is 400. Out of that number, four have expressed an interest in joining Opus Dei, representing 1 percent of the student body. Pablo Cardona, an Opus Dei numerary and professor at the elite IESE business school in Barcelona, said that in the seven years he's taught at IESE, working with 1,400 students, four of them have gone on to join Opus Dei, meaning 0.3 percent. At the International University of Catalonia, an Opus Dei–affiliated school in Barcelona, roughly three students each year out of a student body of 3,000 become members of Opus Dei, or 0.1 percent of the total. At the Valle Grande Rural Institute in Peru, a center for formation both for area farmers and young men, the institute works with some 600 farm families and has 110 boys in its academic programs. Out of that total, approximately one to two each year join Opus Dei. At Strathmore University in Nairobi, which has a full-time student population of 1,500, vice-chancellor John Odhiambo told me that approximately 200 of those students are Catholic, and maybe 50 every now and then attend an event at an Opus Dei center. In a "good year," he said, perhaps four will join Opus Dei, representing 2 percent of the Catholic student population. At the Kimlea technical center for girls outside Nairobi, there are approximately 150 full-time students and 200 in part-time programs. Out of that total, two to three join Opus Dei each year, thus representing 0.8 percent.

Chicago's Midtown Center serves around 150 low-income students during the year and another 200 over the summer. Art Thelen, an Opus Dei member who's worked in and around Midtown since 1963, says he knows of one person who joined Opus Dei while still in high school and attending programs at the Midtown Center, and perhaps six to ten who joined later in life. Father John Debicki, pastor at Saint Mary of the Angels Parish in Chicago, since 1991 the only parish in the United States entrusted to Opus Dei, said that over that span of time he's not aware of a single member of Opus Dei who has come out of the parish. At the Metro Achievement Center, a program for girls similar to the Midtown Center, director Sharon Hefferan said that in five years, no vocations to Opus Dei came from among the roughly 300 girls who moved through the various programs. At Chicago's Lexington College, where some 200 women pass through its programs each year, maybe 20 have become Opus Dei members over twenty-seven years, according to President Susan Mangels, a numerary.

At the Crotona Center in the South Bronx, where numerary David Holzweiss works with 200 kids and 100 adults, one high school student has expressed interest in Opus Dei in seven years. At the companion Rosedale Center for girls, supernumerary Cathy Hickey said that in the sixteen years she's been at the center, during which time some 1,600 girls have taken part in its activities, there have been no members of Opus Dei. At the Heights, the Opus Dei boys' school in Washington, D.C., with a student population of 460, over the last five years only one has "whistled" while still in school, and six or seven joined later, according to director Alvaro de Vicente, a numerary.

The Baytree Center in London, which serves 800 people a year, mostly unemployed immigrant women, in thirteen years has not brought in one new member for Opus Dei. Peter Brown, director at Netherhall, a university residence that is the largest corporate work of Opus Dei in the United Kingdom, said he joined Opus Dei after being a resident. Of the roughly 100 residents there each year, Brown said, roughly one joins Opus Dei, either as a numerary or supernumerary. I asked Brown, if Netherhall did not produce any vocations for Opus Dei over a five-year period, would someone from headquarters call to see what was going on? "It doesn't work like that," Brown said. There is no "quota."

These reports cohere with the picture that comes from the worldwide numbers, which is that Opus Dei membership is growing at a very small clip. There is little evidence that Opus Dei schools, social service centers, and other corporate works are merely "fronts" for a recruiting operation—or, if they are, it's one of the least impressive recruiting operations on record.

When asked about these numbers, directors generally make three points. First, they say, there is a much larger number each year of baptisms among participants in Opus Dei programs, meaning converts to the

Catholic Church. At Kimlea, for example, director Frankie Gikandi says that each year about half of her enrollment of 150 students starts out Catholic, and by the end of the year usually about two-thirds are Catholic. Second, the directors say, these Opus Dei activities produce a number of vocations to the priesthood and religious life as well as to Opus Dei. Third, they say, the main purpose of these activities is not to generate recruits, but to accomplish their stated missions—educating students, helping the poor, and so on. In the context of the global Catholic picture, the fact that Opus Dei is growing at all may seem impressive in an era in which vocations to the priesthood and religious life are in decline, at least in the West. On the other hand, measured against public perceptions of a vast recruiting armada, Opus Dei in reality seems much less formidable than imagined.

How to explain the slow growth? Most observers attribute it to two factors. First, being an Opus Dei member is not easy, especially for a numerary. The commitment to a daily plan of life, to weekly confession and spiritual direction, and to other events on a weekly, monthly, and annual basis involves a serious allocation of time and personal energy that most people, most of the time, aren't willing to make. Further, the particular approach to spirituality and doctrinal formation of Opus Dei is not for everyone; recall the Guinness Stout image in the introduction to this book. Second, Opus Dei members say they try to ensure that particular candidates are right for Opus Dei before encouraging them to move forward. They have learned from bitter experience what can happen when someone has a bad experience of Opus Dei. It is not at all uncommon, members say, for someone to have to ask several times over a period of months before they are given permission to write the letter requesting admission.

Deception

The final charge against Opus Dei recruiting practices is that, however tame they may be, and whatever the actual number of members they produce, they are frequently deceptive. Young people are often drawn into Opus Dei's sphere of influence unawares, enticed by friendship with Opus Dei members, and pressured into joining before they understand what they're getting into. Moncada, the Spanish ex-numerary and leading critic of Opus Dei, said this is his most serious complaint. "I understand they're a conservative organization, fine," he said. "My main concern is for the kids."

In response, Opus Dei spokespersons usually point out that part of the logic for having a period of a year and a half between when someone "whistles" and the "oblation," the moment when they commit themselves to a contract with Opus Dei, is precisely to give them a chance to get to know Opus Dei from the inside. What some experience as a secret world, they say, is more like what anyone goes through in adjusting to a new family. Further, no one can make a permanent commitment to Opus Dei for another five years after the oblation, they argue, so by the time that moment rolls around, the person knows everything there is to know about the demands of the Work. Ex-members sometimes argue, however, that because the moment of "whistling" is generally experienced as being momentous, this sort of disclosure should take place beforehand.

The other element of the deception complaint is that Opus Dei members pursue friendships with potential members, at least in part, in the hope that they will end up joining Opus Dei, and sometimes distance themselves if it becomes clear that's not going to happen. Critics charge that makes these friendships artificial and manipulative.

Father James Martin said that in his research for his *America* article, he came across a number of stories of young men and women on college campuses who had been befriended by Opus Dei members, only to be abandoned once it became clear they were not interested in signing up. "This one guy I talked to basically got dropped, and when he tried to make contact, nothing," Martin said. "I mean, he assumed these people were his friends. He tried to call them afterward, and the response would be, 'Well, we really don't have any time for you.' I think that's pretty anti-Christian."

Faced with this kind of criticism, members typically respond that their friendships are sincere and generally survive whatever decision someone makes about whether or not to stay in Opus Dei. As noted in the previous chapter, former members such as Joseph McCormack, Elizabeth Falk Sather, and Ignacio Andreu testify that after they left Opus Dei, they retained strong friendships with members. Whether a friendship survives someone's exit from Opus Dei, they say, often depends on how they leave.

If it's on good terms, friendships often endure; if there were hard feelings, things can be more difficult.

Spokespersons acknowledge that sometimes at the *tertulia*, especially at centers where members work with youth, numeraries will talk about the young people who take part in the center's programs, and who among them might have a vocation to Opus Dei. They stipulate, however, that they would not discuss private matters and would never "craft strategy" to artificially entice that person to join.

To get a sense of how all this works in practice, I sat down with Juan De Los Ángeles, director of admissions at the University of Navarra, and Gonzalo Robles, secretary-general of the university. Both are responsible for recruiting, but in this case for the university, not for Opus Dei. Nevertheless, they are in direct contact with highly intelligent and motivated high school students all over Spain, which should be a classic breeding group for new Opus Dei recruits.

Nineteen percent of the student population at Navarra is drawn from the eighty-four Opus Dei primary and secondary schools across Spain, so presumably those students and families already know what they're in for. From everyone else, however, De Los Ángeles said the single most frequent question he gets about Opus Dei when he's on the road trying to sell Navarra is about recruiting: "If I come to Navarra, will you want me to become a member of Opus Dei?"

De Los Ángeles said he responds by trying to assuage any concerns about deception or underhanded techniques. "I tell them, 'Well, listen, this is a university. That means it's a place where everybody does whatever they want. This is a place for freedom. It's a real university, so nobody is going to go after you. On the other hand, maybe you'll find someone in your class who is a member of Opus Dei, and he wants you to come over or to do something. So he'll ask you to come with him for Mass, or for such-and-such an activity that is taking place in a center of Opus Dei, or whatever. It's his right to ask, and yours to say no. Simple as that,'" he said.

De Los Ángeles acknowledged that Navarra, as an Opus Dei institution, does have a clear "apostolic orientation," and in part that means that they'd like to see students attracted to Opus Dei. "We want to raise members and find people willing to join," he said. "We explain that clearly.

When people ask this, I say, 'Yeah, we want to find new members. Of course we want that, but we are not going to put too much pressure on you, because we want people to find this as a vocation, a free choice.'

"There are many people who don't even take part in one Opus Dei activity during all the time that they are at the university," De Los Ángeles said. "We would like it if more took part, obviously, but they are free to do whatever they want."

I asked De Los Ángeles and Robles why, if this is the policy, the university doesn't publish a brochure entitled "Recruiting for Opus Dei at the University of Navarra," which would outline what Opus Dei is, how students will be exposed to it, what to do if they're interested and if they're not, and who to contact if they feel that excessive pressure to join is being applied. The brochure could be distributed to students and parents, and that way everyone would be clear about what the rules of the game are. Isn't it possible, I asked, that some of the concern about deceptive recruiting techniques comes from the fact that there is no clear policy?

A moment of stunned silence followed the question, and then it became clear that I had stumbled into the cultural gap that separates Anglo-Saxon corporate thinking from the rest of the world.

"Maybe our policy is, well, the best way to find out is to come here and you can see. I mean, in the ordinary life of this university you can know perfectly well how people of Opus Dei go about things," Robles said. "The thing is, maybe we know the policy so well that we don't need to write it down," De Los Ángeles said. "Also, if there are abuses, we have something called 'fraternal correction,' and I suppose we would handle it that way." De Los Ángeles added, "A business consultant I know used to say that the stronger the culture the less need for structure. So I think that we are culturally strong, but the structure is very low."

Finally, both De Los Ángeles and Robles said that, ironically, from their point of view, the real challenge for Navarra is almost the opposite of overintense recruiting. Instead, it's that students can go through several years on campus and not seem in the least "infected" with the Christian values of the institution, let alone an interest in Opus Dei. At one point, they said, Bishop Alvaro del Portillo, former prelate of Opus Dei, met with all the members who work at Navarra and challenged them to be sure that students don't spend five years on campus and learn nothing about Christ.

Summary

In the end, the reality seems to come down to this: Opus Dei does pray for, desire, and encourage new vocations. They understand themselves to be doing so within the context of respect for freedom and liberty of conscience, but in specific cases, members with a particular zeal can push too hard, as in the case of Andres Valdivia, or Charles Shaw, who was cornered on a bus in Mexico. In that sense, one's perspective on "recruiting" in Opus Dei is often driven by the personal style of a particular member and dependent on how it was perceived by a potential recruit. For its own internal reasons, especially De Los Ángeles's point about the preference to resolve problems with culture rather than structure, Opus Dei resists adopting clear statements of policy that might have the effect of clarifying for both its own members and the outside world, what's appropriate in discussing a vocation with someone. Further, the vaunted Opus Dei recruiting machine turns out to be something of a myth, since the annual rate of growth is minuscule compared to some people's perceptions of what Opus Dei wants.

Among some observers there's a sense that whatever the difficulties over recruiting may have been in the past, things today seem calmer. In Martin's 1995 *America* article, for example, he quoted Donald R. McCrabb, at the time executive director of the Catholic Campus Ministry Association, who said there were complaints among campus ministers about Opus Dei concerning both recruiting practices and the controls exercised over members. In January 2005, I contacted Ed Franchi, who holds McCrabb's position today, to ask if things had changed. "While some of the concerns expressed by Don ten years ago are probably still valid, we actually hear very little about Opus Dei these days," Franchi told me. "Several other Catholic organizations with campus outreach have developed in those ten years, and the questions and concerns we hear about them are much greater."

On the subject of why Opus Dei doesn't have a "recruiting policy," Carlo De Marchi, an energetic young Italian who serves on Opus Dei's

General Council in Rome and is responsible for the apostolate with youth, said it just doesn't work that way.

"When I was eighteen," De Marchi said, "I told my friends about my vocation, what Opus Dei meant in my life, why I was thinking about not getting married . . . these are things that one shares spontaneously—my story, the gift I received from God. These confidences are impossible to formalize, to organize rigidly, because they're part of friendship. In that climate, a young person can ask: What if I too have this gift?"

SUMMARY EVALUATION

Chapter Fifteen

THE FUTURE OF OPUS DEI

It's time to draw some conclusions. What can one say, in summary form, in response to the typical questions that most people ask about Opus Dei, the most controversial force in the Catholic Church?

- Many of the charges leveled against the founder of Opus Dei, Saint Josemaría Escrivá de Balaguer—such as his alleged fiery temper, his vanity, and his disillusionment with the aftermath of the Second Vatican Council—are open to multiple interpretations, and in any event do not seem disqualifying in terms of personal sanctity. If they were, many other famous saints of the Church would have to be removed from the rolls. Other charges seem overdrawn, at least as usually formulated. Escrivá was not, for example, "pro-Franco"; the most that can be said is that he was not "anti-Franco," either.

- The ideals that Escrivá bequeathed to Opus Dei—such as sanctification of work, contemplation in the middle of the world, Christian freedom, and divine filiation—seem promising elements of sound Christian spirituality. Even if there is at times an overweening cult of personality around Escrivá, these are principles that for too long had been buried under clericalist and dualistic debris.

- Opus Dei is not especially "secretive." Opus Dei's officers and the locations of its centers are matters of public record, its activities are registered under relevant civil laws, and its information offices will answer virtually any question one puts to them. The fact that they do not answer a limited number of questions—most prominently, who's a member and who isn't—makes Opus Dei secretive no more than Alcoholics Anonymous. Other groups in the Church, such as secular institutes, also have policies of discretion about membership. Over the years there has been a steady progress toward greater levels of openness. The early controversies in Spain in the late 1930s and 1940s, when Opus Dei was accused of Masonry, bizarre rituals, and heresy, combined with the problems in the 1950s and 1960s of fitting Opus Dei into Church law, explain much of its traditional reticence.

- Practices of corporal mortification, whatever one makes of them, are not unique to Opus Dei. They have a long pedigree and accepted theological rationale, and do not generally seem to be taken to extremes. When there are exceptions, Opus Dei spokespersons make no bones about saying they were mistakes.

- Women in Opus Dei do not, for the most part, feel like "second-class citizens." In some cases there is a rather "traditional" understanding of gender roles, but the kind of person attracted to Opus Dei by and large is already comfortable with that vision. While ultimate authority inside Opus Dei rests with ordained men, the same is true of the Catholic Church in general. That aside, the women of Opus Dei have their own system of governance that in practice makes them quasi-autonomous. Female numeraries and supernumeraries around the world hold positions as lawyers, architects, journalists, and university professors. Numerary assistants, who do the cooking and cleaning for Opus Dei centers, do not seem to feel oppressed; they see their role as being "mothers" to the Opus Dei family.

- Opus Dei is not rich, at least by the standards of other organizations in the Catholic Church, and certainly when compared to giant multinational corporations. With exactitude, we can fix their total American assets at $344 million, and their assets in the United Kingdom at $72 million. (Opus Dei would not accept this consolidated figure because it does not "own" its various works; individual members and their boards of directors do.) Using the American and English figures as a baseline, we can estimate worldwide assets at $2.8 billion. To put these numbers in context, the United States bishops estimate the revenue of the American Catholic Church alone to be $102 billion. General Motors in 2003 reported assets of $455 billion. Opus Dei ranks in terms of wealth as a midsized American diocese.

- The profile of Opus Dei as "elitist" has some historical validity, given Escrivá's interest in evangelizing the intellectual and professional classes. Yet Opus Dei is not "elitist" in the sense in which people often invoke the term, meaning an exclusively white-collar phenomenon. Among its members are barbers, bricklayers, mechanics, and fruit sellers. Most supernumeraries are living ordinary middle-class lives, struggling to pay the bills and afford college tuition for their kids. There are some well-heeled Opus Dei members, but they are not typical. In Cañete, Peru, for example, I met a supernumerary named Isabel Charún, whose tiny two-room house for her large family doesn't even have a complete roof in the bedroom. Charún's circumstances are typical of a broad swath of Opus Dei members, especially in the developing world.

- Opus Dei's is not an exclusively vertical spirituality; it does have a social conscience. Many of its corporate works are aimed at helping the poor, from the Kimlea School for girls in Kenya, which teaches low-income girls from coffee and tea plantations basic trade skills, to the Valle Grande Rural Institute in Peru, which helps impoverished farmers protect biodiversity and get indigenous crops to market. What Opus Dei does not do, in an institutional way, is involve itself in struggles for social justice.

- Opus Dei is not "taking over" the Catholic Church. As of December 2004 there were 20 members of Opus Dei who worked in the Vatican, as compared to 26 for their historical rivals, the Jesuits. Opus Dei members occupy 3.6 percent of policy-making positions in the Vatican, mostly at the middle levels. The 41 Opus Dei bishops represent a tiny fraction, 0.9

percent, of the more than 4,000 Roman Catholic bishops in the world.

- Opus Dei itself, as an organization, claims to have no agenda for Catholicism. Members, however, tend to lean right on many theological and liturgical matters. The intellectual Rubicon to be crossed is this: Can teaching presented as authoritative by Church officials be wrong? If a Catholic answers "yes" to that question, he or she is unlikely to feel comfortable in Opus Dei, where there is a strong emphasis on "thinking with the Church."

- Opus Dei, as an organization, has no "line" in secular politics, either, and in fact one finds members of Opus Dei on all sides of many questions. Yet when it comes to abortion, divorce, gay marriage, and stem cell research, one will almost always find Opus Dei members on the right, since these are matters on which there is a clear "official" Catholic position. In that sense, the current fixation on these issues may distort the genuine pluralism that exists in Opus Dei on other matters.

- Opus Dei is not the voracious recruiting machine of myth, given the snail's pace of recent growth, averaging 650 new members per year worldwide the last four years. Most Opus Dei–affiliated institutions are lucky to generate one new member a year, out of the hundreds of people the institution might serve. While there have been episodes of excessive pressure applied to young recruits, these seem more characteristic of the past than the present and have not been so strong as to dissuade many people from saying "no."

- For the majority of Opus Dei members who are supernumeraries, there are very few instruments of control. For the 20 percent of members who are numeraries and live in Opus Dei centers, there is a higher degree of structure, an expectation of consultation with superiors, and prudential judgments about what's appropriate matter for reading and entertainment that some outsiders would find stifling. There's little evidence, however, that unwilling people are being subjected to this regime through "mind control." Most members who find the structure excessive simply leave.

- A substantial number of ex-members of Opus Dei, enough to suggest that they are more than isolated cases, report feeling damaged by their experience. While the nature of their complaints varies, the most serious charge is that these members felt manipulated into making a commitment to Opus Dei, pressured into sustaining it, and subjected to demands they found excessive. These reports suggest the need for care in vocational discernment, especially among the young.

- Given the zeal that accompanies a vocation in Opus Dei, sometimes individuals may come on too strong in terms of "recruiting" or oversight, exerting pressure or showing insufficient understanding for human weakness. Some of the critical testimony of ex-members comes down to the failure of certain officials of Opus Dei to use good judgment. As time goes on and Opus Dei matures, these episodes seem less frequent, and the internal climate seems more open. It's less common, though not impossible, to find critical ex-members who left Opus Dei in 2004, as opposed to the mid-1960s or mid-1980s.

Historical Perspective

Opus Dei likes to stress its singularity, and with reason. There has never been anything quite like it in Church history, a body of laity and priests, women and men, united by a common vocation and belonging to a single institution. In a chronological sense, however, Opus Dei can be seen as the latest in a series of Copernican shifts in Catholic spirituality that date back at least to the twelfth century. The Franciscans redefined religious life by demonstrating that it did not require the cloister, but could be lived in the city, cheek by jowl with secularity. The Jesuits demonstrated that religious life did not require common prayer or traditionally "religious" activity, but that every field of human endeavor could be lifted up to the "greater glory of God." Opus Dei, in effect, suggests that religious living does not even require religious life in the classic, canonical sense—that lay Christians, with no vows and no habits, in all external ways identical to everyone else, but infused with a sense of vocation, can work to transform the world from within.

Though Opus Dei is by no means a religious order analogous to the

Franciscans or the Jesuits, the common element in these developments is a progressive dissolution of "religion" as a separate category of experience, a realization slowly unfolding through the centuries that all of creation and all of human life is already suffused with religious significance, and a thrust to devise styles of living consistent with that insight. Opus Dei claims to carry this process to a new stage, announcing that evangelization and redemption is the work of all Christians in the places where they find themselves—in boardrooms and nurseries, in parliaments and post offices. While Escrivá said he revered religious life, his vision pushed off in another direction. It is the death knell of clericalism, a bold empowering of the laity as the primary ministerial corps of the Catholic Church in everything except the sacraments. Whatever one makes of Opus Dei as a carrier of this idea, it marks a sea change in ecclesiastical culture.

Every time a new form of life comes along in the Church, it struggles for acceptance. It is a commonplace about Opus Dei to observe that the Jesuits before them, and the Franciscans and Dominicans before the Jesuits, were also the targets of the most outlandish accusations. Historically, founders have responded to these slings and arrows with unwavering submission to the papacy, in order to demonstrate that their revolution is intended to serve the Church. The first time Pope Innocent III and Saint Francis met, in 1209, the pope is said to have told the mangy Francis to "go roll in the mud with the pigs," which is precisely what Francis did. Innocent was so taken with his obedience that he approved the Franciscan rule. Saint Ignatius of Loyola placed the Jesuits completely in the hands of Pope Paul III; asked what his reaction would be if the pope suppressed his new community, Ignatius responded, "A quarter of an hour of prayer, and I should think no more about it." So too with Escrivá, who once vowed that even if the cardinals were to elect a savage as pope, "I would immediately throw myself at his feet and tell him that the entire Work is at his unconditional service." In that context, Opus Dei's staunch loyalty to John Paul II seems of a piece with the birth pangs of something creative within Catholicism.

In many ways the post–Vatican II era was the worst possible moment for this new phenomenon to come into view, because the "culture wars" of the last forty years have meant that all many people see in Opus Dei is its deference to Church authority, its "traditionalism," not the new approach to Christian life this deference and traditionalism is meant to incubate. Opus Dei came on the scene in a historical period when Catholics were choosing sides, for or against traditional conceptions of doctrine and power, and every reality in the Church was subsumed into the rubric of being "progressive" or "conservative" in terms of that debate. With respect to Opus Dei, it is a bit like trying to perceive a three-dimensional object from a two-dimensional frame of reference; inevitably only bits and pieces come into view. Yes, on the question of *Roma locuta est*, Escrivá and his followers come down on the "conservative" side. But if that is all one sees in Opus Dei, something essential has been lost. The discussions that have loomed large in this book—about power, secrecy, and money—are all essential to clearing the air, but they are merely prolegomena to a thoughtful consideration of what Opus Dei is about.

Whether Opus Dei will be able to answer the questions that surround it, and then effect the paradigm shift in Christian thought and action it proposes, remains to be seen. The obstacles are formidable. When one says "prayer," most people still think instinctively of saying words to God rather than seeing how they live and work. When people speak of "spiritual life" or "interior life," the tendency is still to think of certain pious practices, of retreats, of events that take place in a church. When people speak of "apostolate," few think spontaneously of "sanctifying others through their work," or of personal friendship, or of normal social and family life lived in a Christian spirit. The idea that all the ordinary circumstances of one's life already *are* prayer, that they already *are* forms of the spiritual life and the evangelizing mission of the Church—this is heady stuff, and it will take time to absorb. In many ways, members of Opus Dei themselves are still trying to digest it.

The first seventy-five years of the life of Opus Dei have been spent trying to scratch and claw for a toehold within the structures of the Catholic Church, from whence this message could be launched. During that period, much about Opus Dei was misunderstood or only partially grasped, and this has bred an astonishing range of prejudices—sometimes due to ill will, sometimes due to mistakes and overzealousness on the part of Opus Dei members, but often because of the sheer novelty of it all, the sheer audacity of Opus Dei's claims about the secular world and the lay state. Perhaps, as Opus Dei members say among themselves, all the controversies will be forgotten in five hundred years. Perhaps, as Opus Dei's detractors quietly pray, Opus Dei itself will be forgotten in that arc of time. Without knowing the mind of God, it's impossible to say. What is clear, however, is that if Opus Dei fails, it should be on the basis of deficiencies in its spirituality—its particular approach to the sanctification of work, its members being contemplatives in the middle of the world—and not because of false steps in its infancy, and not because the idiosyncrasies of a particular historical epoch meant that the essential things about Opus Dei never got a hearing.

The Future: Reforms

We may not be able to peer five hundred years into the future, but at least under the pontificate of Benedict XVI, Opus Dei is on solid ground. Its fortunes may wax and wane, but Opus Dei has a solid juridical basis, a worldwide membership and network of related institutions, and a constituency within the Catholic Church to sustain it. A more forward-thinking question would be this: If Opus Dei wishes to do more than survive—if it wishes to thrive, assuaging the anxieties people sometimes have and thus opening new apostolic horizons, what steps might it take?

On the basis of this book, three steps seem the most compelling.

Transparency

John Paul II in 1984 said that the Catholic Church should be "a 'house of glass' where all can see what is happening, and how it carries out its mission in faithfulness to Christ and the evangelical message." Even if there's nothing inherently secretive about Opus Dei, it has not always realized this idea of being a "house of glass," in part because it has resisted self-promotion or anything that might transform itself into an "interest group." Yet to phrase the question exclusively in terms of Opus Dei's own self-understanding is, in a sense, too narrow. Opus Dei exists not just for itself and its membership, but for the Catholic Church and for the broader world. There is a legitimate public curiosity to which Opus Dei should (and, to be fair, increasingly does) respond. Moreover, negative public impressions of Opus Dei, nurtured in some cases by its struggles with transparency, inevitably become negative impressions of the Catholic Church. If there is something Opus Dei can do to ameliorate these impressions without sacrificing its identity, it arguably faces a moral obligation to do so.

What could Opus Dei do to appear more transparent? Several steps suggest themselves:

- Each region should regularly publish complete financial statements that describe its revenue, expenses, assets, and liabilities for all activities designated as corporate works. These statements should be accompanied by readable prose explanations in local languages and in English. The headquarters in Rome should collate short reports from every country that give totals, and publish descriptions of the scope of corporate works in all sixty-one countries currently reached by Opus Dei programs. The United States region currently makes an attempt, as the Woodlawn Foundation publishes an audited financial statement covering some of the financial activities in the country. The key word here is "some," because not all financial activities are included. Statements need to be complete to be usable. These reports could clearly make the point that a corporate work is not "owned" by Opus Dei, but is administered independently by the laity who make up its board of directors. There's a special imperative for financial disclosure with Opus Dei, since many observers consider Opus Dei to be fantastically wealthy. The recent construction of a seventeen-story headquarters in Manhattan only reinforced these misconceptions. Church observers believe that buildings like the "tower of power" could be paid for only from a hidden horde of mysterious Vatican bonds squirreled away in some dimly lit Roman vault. Reality is much less tantalizing. It is only by making such mundane facts more public than an obscure footnote in a tax return that Opus Dei will escape these undeserved perceptions.
- Clearly identify facilities linked to Opus Dei. When one walks up to the center on Wyoming Avenue in Washington, D.C., for example, or similar centers in Lima and Madrid and Helsinki, there should be a sign that reads, A CENTER OF OPUS DEI. Further, the link with Opus Dei merits more than a single sentence in the literature of its activities. In the style of the brochure for Oakcrest, the Opus Dei girls' school in McLean,

Virginia, there should be a prominent discussion of what Opus Dei is and how it influences the operation of this activity. Within that treatment, it can be made clear that Opus Dei is responsible only for spiritual and doctrinal formation, and that in all other matters the activity is administered by individuals exercising their own responsibility—Opus Dei is not a "brand name." Similarly, it should be a matter of policy that the first time a new person, especially a young person, attends an event at an Opus Dei center, that it is clearly explained that this activity is being sponsored by Opus Dei. For the most part this already seems to be the practice, but it bears spelling out.

• At least in the Anglo-Saxon world, Opus Dei might consider developing written policies on some of the most neuralgic points in its life and apostolate. For example, one will never get Opus Dei to put out a brochure on "recruiting," because to them that word smacks of coercion and artificiality. But a brochure on "Friendship in Opus Dei" might be more feasible, which could outline why Opus Dei members often invite friends and colleagues to activities and stress that no one sins or shows bad Christian spirit by saying no. It could also briefly comment on what to do if one ever feels excessive pressure is being applied to join Opus Dei. The same brochure could explain that an invitation to attend an Opus Dei event, such as a circle or day of recollection, has no hidden agenda other than sharing the life of Opus Dei with its friends. The brochure could be distributed to students, parents, and anyone else who is in an environment in which these concerns might arise.

• Similarly, a brochure entitled "Vocation as a Numerary" could outline in clear detail the expectations and obligations of a numerary, and what life will be like in a center of Opus Dei. Among many other points, it would, briefly and tastefully, explain the practices of corporal mortification, the financial expectations of members, and all the other aspects of life inside Opus Dei. It could be distributed to candidates before they "whistle," and, in the case of young candidates, to their parents, and to anyone who asks. Again, the point is not that any of these matters are currently secret. Certainly by the time most people join they've already developed friendships with numeraries and "know the score." Yet even some ex-members, such as Notre Dame undergraduate John Schneider, say they didn't know as much as they should have, and anything Opus Dei can do to lift that impression is to the good.

One can anticipate the objections to these suggestions within Opus Dei, that they would compromise the spirit of family, that they are not "natural," that they amount to an attempt to formalize something that should be spontaneous and informal. Perhaps so, but families too have their policies. Sometimes a bit of structure is the price to be paid for making the family work. In this case the cost to Opus Dei's self-understanding has to be weighed against the enormous public good to be accomplished by reassuring public anxieties.

- Opus Dei should consider making it part of its contract with members that under given circumstances, especially when it's a matter of a public figure, membership can be revealed by Opus Dei. This is admittedly a delicate matter, because everyone is entitled to a zone of privacy, especially when it comes to their spiritual life. Moreover, deciding who is a public figure is a notoriously tricky business, as case law in the area of libel and defamation will attest. Nevertheless, it is badly damaging to Opus Dei's image when it has to dance around questions of whether so-and-so is a member. The case of Ruth Kelly, the English education secretary, makes the point. When the British press reported that she had "links" to Opus Dei in December 2004, spokespersons for Opus Dei in England, constrained by the policy that it is up to the member what to reveal, were reduced to making statements such as, "She is 'in touch.' She has attended meetings." Those were public facts, and, strictly speaking, they were true. Nevertheless they created ambiguity, with some English papers reporting that Kelly was a member and some that she wasn't. In the end, these half-truths end up fueling suspicions of secrecy. This is a case, in fact, in which Opus Dei was not well served by one of its own members. If belonging to Opus Dei is nothing to be ashamed of, then when someone is prominent in public life, it seems fair that the organization should be able to respond openly and fully about that person's membership. After that, it's up to the individual what to say. This stipulation could apply to elected officials as well as to bishops of the Priestly Society of the Holy Cross and arguably also to its priests, who are public figures within the Catholic Church.

- Opus Dei members, and especially supernumeraries, need to realize that whether they like it or not, they are the ambassadors for Opus Dei in their social and professional environments. They should volunteer to speak about Opus Dei in parish council meetings, at Catholic schools and universities, and in any other setting where people might be able to ask questions and get things out into the open. Again, the point is not to seek publicity for Opus Dei, or to have individual members arrogate to themselves the right to speak in the name of Opus Dei. Rather they can speak out of their own experience, and in so doing help put a face on this group that most people know only through the media or watercooler gossip. One example is offered by Matthew Collins, the former American supernumerary and now cooperator in Baltimore, who maintains an informative and nonpolemical Web site in question-and-answer format about Opus Dei. Robert Duncan, a supernumerary in Madrid, runs a Web site in Spanish and English called Santificarnos, which, although its interests are much broader than Opus Dei, treats the subject in a reasonable, informative fashion. Such initiatives could be multiplied, and not just in cyberspace, assuaging public concerns about transparency and helping to create a different image for Opus Dei.

- Finally, Opus Dei needs to find creative ways to reach out to ex-members who had difficult experiences. Granted, some ex-members may not wish to reconcile; perhaps the scars went too deep, or perhaps their diagnosis of the flaws within Opus Dei is so sweeping as to make conversation difficult. Some may even have become professionally dependent upon being identified as "Opus Dei critics." Still, Opus Dei needs to make a transparent, public effort to reach out to these people, to say to them publicly what Bishop Javier Echevarría said in this book: "We're sorry." In no way does that imply that every charge made against Opus Dei is valid. Opus Dei might even invite in a panel of ex-members, some critical and some not, to discuss specific questions, such as how to smooth the transition out of Opus Dei for those who choose to leave. The fact of those discussions, and their results, could be made public, as a way of signaling Opus Dei's genuine desire for dialogue.

All of these steps would have the effect of making Opus Dei seem more open, more comprehensible to outsiders. Some Opus Dei members may be frustrated by such suggestions, feeling that Opus Dei has already bent over backward to be what member William O'Connor once called it in a response to Michael Walsh: "an open book." Anyone who takes the time to understand us, they insist, will find that there is nothing to hide. Yet in the image-driven world of the twenty-first century, a perceived problem is tantamount to a real problem. Bishops, pastors, and other agents in the Catholic Church would no doubt breathe easier if Opus Dei could find new ways to address these perceptions, which, however unfounded or unfair, often complicate discussion about its role and mission.

Collaboration

When I was in Kenya, I had dinner one night with a Jesuit friend who has been active in Church circles in that country for thirty-two years. When the topic of Opus Dei came up, he expressed a negative judgment anchored in several factors, but the most important for him was the charge of "elitism." I asked him about the activities of Opus Dei in Kenya with which he was familiar, and he cited Strathmore University and the Kianda School, both of which tend to draw the cream of the Kenyan crop. He was not aware of any other Opus Dei activity. When I explained that earlier that day I had been to a nursery school, the Gatina Nursery, located on a tea plantation outside Nairobi, where two part-time teachers supported by Opus Dei bring milk and cookies to the perhaps one hundred children in their care, and that this simple act has made the difference between life and death by malnutrition, my Jesuit friend was dumbfounded. "This is not the Opus Dei I know," he said.

The deep question to ask is, how is it possible that he did not know?

Kenya is a relatively small country, with a Catholic population of just 7.6 million. How could he not know about other activities in Kenya sponsored by Opus Dei, many of which contradict the impression of an elitist organization?

This is not an isolated instance. I could multiply examples all across the globe of Catholics involved full-time with the Church, especially members of religious orders, who don't know the most basic things about Opus Dei. Setting aside factors such as poor communications, or bad blood between Opus Dei and the Jesuits, the basic answer as to how my friend could be so much in the dark boils down to sociology. Opus Dei activities are led by laypeople who generally do not move in the same circles as men and women religious. They do not usually attend meetings or events sponsored by religious orders, and they're often not in the same networks of communication. At a personal level, many members of Opus Dei enjoy positive relationships with members of religious communities. Yet when the Union of Superiors General, the main umbrella group for male religious communities, convenes in Rome—or the International Union of Superiors General, for women—Opus Dei is not present. When religious men and women meet on the national, regional, and local levels, Opus Dei is not there. This is not because of standoffishness, but because Opus Dei is not a religious order, and has spent much of its institutional energy over seventy-five years making that point.

The consequence is that members of religious communities often do not know very much about Opus Dei. This is an especially serious matter given that historically, and to some extent still today, much of the criticism of Opus Dei has come from within religious life. The secular press has created a few of its own myths, but by and large it tends to recycle accusations that come from within the Catholic Church. Many times those accusations are based on prejudice that a better personal awareness of Opus Dei would do much to resolve.

One obvious step would be for Opus Dei to collaborate in a more systematic way with other groups in the Church, especially religious orders. We have already seen in chapter 11 that Escrivá spurned one such offer in the late 1960s from Father Pedro Arrupe, former general of the Jesuits, for Opus Dei and the Jesuit order to jointly sponsor a university.

Today could one imagine Opus Dei and the Jesuits jointly operating a social program analogous to Condoray in Peru or Kimlea in Kenya, educating low-income women in trade and literacy skills? Could one imagine Opus Dei and Catholic Relief Services working together on something like Nairobi's Informal Sector Business Institute, which teaches basic business skills to poor Kenyans involved in the vast off-the-books "informal economy"? Such joint undertakings would not merely provide valuable services, they would also create opportunities for other Catholics to get to know Opus Dei on an up-close-and-personal basis. From a broader perspective, in the context of a Church that is too often polarized and divided, such joint initiatives could promote dialogue among Catholics of differing temperaments and outlooks, which is a consummation devoutly to be wished.

When one asks members of Opus Dei about such possibilities, however, the overall impression is that it's not in the "spirit of the Work."

"We make a conscious effort to not move in religious circles or to horn in on their works. We tend to avoid going where they're already working. We don't want to create turf wars or animosity," said Father Tom Bohlin, vicar for Opus Dei in the United States. "Our prime message is going in another direction. It's a new approach to lay spirituality, so we're going on a different road. We're on two tracks, but we're working simultaneously in serving the Church."

When asked if there is something in principle to prevent the kind of joint projects described above, Bohlin did not duck the question: "On an institutional level, yes," he said. "We would insist that the operation has to be done by laypeople with lay spirit, as opposed to the religious spirit, because you put the two together and one will end up influencing the other." This was Escrivá's basis for rejecting Arrupe's proposal for a joint Jesuit/Opus Dei university: "You can't have doctors and lawyers working out of the same office."

Two other arguments are generally advanced for this position. One is that individual Opus Dei members are already engaged in myriad forms of collaboration. To illustrate the point, Echevarría, the prelate of Opus Dei, told me a story about Cardinal Giovanni Colombo, archbishop of Milan from 1963 to 1979. At one point Colombo held a diocesan synod in Milan, and afterward he complained to the vicar of Opus Dei in Italy that Opus Dei did not participate. The vicar pointed out to Colombo that, in fact, five of the people on the coordinating committee Colombo himself had appointed were members of Opus Dei. But in a sense, this anecdote crystallizes the nub of the problem. At the level of individual initiative, Opus Dei members are generally committed Catholics involved in their parishes, their dioceses, and other aspects of the life of the Church. Yet that activity is virtually invisible as something connected to Opus Dei; it does very little, therefore, to reassure those with concerns that Opus Dei is constructing a "parallel church."

It's not that even, in an informal way, Opus Dei institutions don't collaborate with others. To take just one of a thousand examples, numerary Frankie Gikandi, director of the Kimlea center for girls in Kenya, said that a group of Assumption Sisters looking to set up their own school have come several times to Kimlea to inquire about how to find staff and what sort of curricular materials to use, and even asked technical questions about utilities and licensing. Gikandi has been happy to help, as she has been with an archdiocesan home for the disabled ten kilometers up the highway. Yet this collaboration remains in the category of informal exchange; the Assumption Sisters and Opus Dei are not going to open a girls' school together. The outside world typically does not recognize this as an instance of "Opus Dei" collaboration.

Second, Opus Dei members will often argue that because Opus Dei guarantees the spiritual and doctrinal formation in its corporate activities, it cannot share that responsibility with anyone else. Given that, they say, the key is better communication between Opus Dei and other realities in the Church rather than institutional collaboration. But this too somewhat misses the point; collaboration *is* a form of communication. It says something about the role any group wants to play in the Catholic Church when it reaches out to others, searching for ways in which the ecclesiology of Communion, a favorite theme of John Paul II, can be translated into practical reality. At a psychological level, collaboration is a way of saying, "We don't have all the answers, and we don't think we're any more 'Catholic' than you are. Let's work together and see what we can accomplish."

The hard question facing Opus Dei would seem to be: Can they imagine creative ways to collaborate with other groups in the Church, especially religious orders, in a structural and institutional way, without doing damage to their spirit of freedom, individual responsibility, and a lay approach? Without "acting as a group" in the pejorative sense, is there a way for Opus Dei to envision joint initiatives and undertakings that would be visible as such to the rest of the world?

Institutional Self-Criticism

In the three-hundred-plus hours of interviews I conducted for this book, the most frustrating moment usually came when I would ask members of Opus Dei the following question: "Given that Opus Dei, like the Catholic Church itself, understands itself to have both a divine and a human side, it is always capable of being reformed. According to you, what are the reforms that Opus Dei needs today?"

The immediate tendency was to phrase answers in terms of personal conversion and self-improvement rather than say anything institutional about Opus Dei. Here, for example, is Echevarría's answer:

"When the canonization happened [in 2002], I made a connection. I said that, 'Canonization means the personal conversion of each one of us.' Therefore, place yourself before the Lord—and this was always the response of Josemaría—ask yourself what there is to reform in your own life. This is a very vast field of endeavor! Every day we have to convert ourselves anew in many ways, in the life of piety, in work, even in matters like punctuality or doing little things well. We have to be more attentive to the needs of others. If we don't live this spirit, we're lost.

"Saint Josemaría used to say that the Work doesn't need external reforms, because we are men and women in the middle of the world, and thus we walk with the world. Opus Dei will always be relevant, not because we're better people or the head of the class, but because we're in the midst of other men and women. Let's go in this direction, which is the right direction. We're not separated from the world. One can then always ask what one can do in a different circumstance."

What about structural change in Opus Dei itself?

"I don't see anything," Echevarría said. "For the moment, there's nothing to change. It's only at the personal level that people are asked to 'do' Opus Dei. We don't act as a group."

In itself, there is great spiritual wisdom in the response—don't dislodge responsibility to the organization, but take stock of yourself, looking into your own heart to see which weeds need to be pulled. Opus Dei issues an important reminder that organizations and systems can accomplish little if the people within them are not kind, decent, and generous. Yet such reasoning, if pushed to an extreme, can become a rationalization for never subjecting the organization to critical examination.

In reality, this is more a perceived problem than a real problem. If you get two or three numeraries together with the mini–disc recorder off, after a few beers, the challenge can sometimes be to get them to *stop* talking about the mistakes Opus Dei has made and what needs to change. All of this is born of a love for Opus Dei and a desire to see "the Work" prosper. Moreover, as this book has demonstrated, the history of Opus Dei is in many ways one of continual reform. In 1961 an Opus Dei official told *America* magazine that it was not in the nature of Opus Dei to have information offices; today Opus Dei has an information office in Rome and in virtually every country in which they've set up shop. In the 1950 "Constitutions" of Opus Dei, members were forbidden to disclose their membership without authorization from the director of their center; no such requirement appears in the 1982 "Statutes." In the 1940s, Escrivá encouraged members to practice "discretion" about what went on in Opus Dei; later he "canceled" the term from his vocabulary. In earlier eras the incoming and outgoing mail of numerary members was screened by the directors; today that practice has fallen into disuse.

One numerary of Opus Dei, to prove to me that members could be self-critical, offered his own personal list of the "seven sins of Opus Dei." In his version, they are: 1) poor communication, which has fueled the impression of secrecy; 2) an impetuousness of youth, a zeal, that historically gave rise to impressions of arrogance; 3) an emphasis on what makes Opus Dei different, so that what unites it with the rest of the Church got lost and Opus Dei could seem a "church within a church"; 4) a devotion to Escrivá's message about sanctifying work, or divine filiation, so powerful that members sometimes forget that the applications of these ideals aren't always clear, which creates impressions of rigidity and dogmatism; 5) a defensive and reactionary tendency in the postconciliar period, facing genuine crises in the Church, which created a profile of being traditionalists and refusing to change; 6) insisting so much on "fidelity" to Church teaching that members create the impression of formalism, an ethics of duty rather than of love; 7) finally, a passion for excellence in work so forceful that it can become an end in itself, creating impressions of a search for worldly wealth and power.

As organizational analysis goes, it's not bad.

So the problem is not so much that Opus Dei members can't be self-critical, but that for their own reasons they tend not to let the rest of the world in on this conversation. Part of this is the experience of having come under such ferocious attacks for so long that there's a natural tendency toward defensiveness with "outsiders" as well as a desire not to hand one's enemy additional weapons. Part of this is the fact that Opus Dei members tend to be passionately in love with their vocation and with Opus Dei for fostering it in them, and as with any pair of lovers, there's a reluctance to speak publicly about the faults of one's partner. Part of it, too, is the general bias of members against talking about Opus Dei, for fear of compromising their secularity, their sense of being just like everyone else, "contemplatives in the middle of the world."

All those instincts are natural, understandable, and in most ways spiritually commendable. Yet the cost is that many people, finding it impossible to get an Opus Dei member to say a critical word about the organization, conclude either that they're "brainwashed" or that there's a cover-up. The sneaking impression is, "Things in Opus Dei just can't be that perfect."

In truth, based on a year's worth of travel, more than three hundred hours of interviews and probably twice that in informal conversation, reading Opus Dei literature until my eyes threatened to pop out of my head, and littering my computer with notes and e-mails on the subject, my own sense is that things inside Opus Dei aren't so bad—or at least they're much better than is sometimes believed. Paradoxically, I suspect that the people of Opus Dei would be more successful in convincing the rest of the world of that if they took a breather from extolling the virtues of Saint Josemaría, or the great principle of sanctification of work, and showed us a bit more about where they're vulnerable, flawed, and in need of help—not just individually, but as "the Work." As Saint Paul wrote in Second Corinthians, "I am content with weaknesses. For when I am weak, then I am strong."

INDEX